Ancestral Journeys

JEAN MANCO

Ancestral Journeys

THE PEOPLING OF EUROPE FROM THE FIRST VENTURERS TO THE VIKINGS

with 124 illustrations, including 59 maps

Thames & Hudson

To my late father, for the gypsy in his soul

Frontispiece *Neolithic figurines from Cernavoda, Romania, late 4th millennium* BC.

First published in the United Kingdom in 2013 by
Thames & Hudson Ltd, 181A High Holborn, London WC1V 7QX

Ancestral Journeys © 2013 Thames & Hudson Ltd, London

British Library Cataloguing-in-Publication Data
A catalogue record for this book is available from the British Library

ISBN 978-0-500-05178-8

Printed and bound in China by Everbest Printing Co. Ltd

To find out about all our publications, please visit **www.thamesandhudson.com**.
There you can subscribe to our e-newsletter, browse or download our current catalogue,
and buy any titles that are in print.

Contents

Preface

This book is the unintended consequence of curiosity. I did not plan to write it. Such a work, I considered, should be written by a brains trust of experts from all over Europe, specialists in different periods, places and disciplines. How could one single head hold all the knowledge required? It is impossible. Yet questions persistently buzzed in my brain that could not be answered without pulling together the work of researchers in many fields. I began to throw text online where it could be criticized, with the disclaimer that the topic really needed a book. Readers began to urge me to 'keep writing the book'. Dismayed, I responded that I had no intention of writing a book. Worthier people would no doubt do so in the fullness of time. This went on until the day I awoke to the startled realization that I had, in effect, written a book.

The curiosity can be traced back many years. I entered the world of archaeology at one remove. As an historian my perspective was that of the outsider. That often encourages critique. I soon began to feel that the archaeological love affair with continuity had gone too far. An archaeological colleague to whom I confided my frustration surprised me. On a far distant shore, he told me, there was an archaeologist who agreed with me. That surprising person was David Anthony. The year was 1990. That gave me hope that one day I might be able to talk openly about migration without having my sanity called into question. David Anthony has continued to blaze a trail for those of us fascinated by the wanderings of our ancestors. My greatest debt therefore is to him.

Feeding my curiosity would have been impossible without the polyglot online communities following the progress of population genetics and participating in it. Their members alert each other to the publication of papers on genetics, comment on them, root out relevant material in many languages from other disciplines, create projects to investigate the origins of specific genetic lineages and support them financially. This work was written and rewritten in constantly evolving online draft while pelted with comments from far too many of them to thank individually here. During the transfer to print format, it was the turn of archaeologists Jim Mallory, Chris Scarre, James Graham-Campbell and David Miles, and geneticist Terry Brown, to point out

European Timeline

Dates rounded to the decade or century are approximate.

Palaeolithic (Old Stone Age)

46,000 years ago: humans arrived in Europe

Mesolithic (Middle Stone Age)

20,000–18,000 years ago: Last Glacial Maximum

10,000 years ago: people re-colonized northern Europe

Neolithic (New Stone Age)

6200 BC: farmers spread into mainland Europe

Copper Age

5000–4000 BC: copper-using Balkan cultures

3500 BC: wheeled vehicles; ploughs; wool sheep

Bronze Age

2300 BC: bronze made widely

Iron Age

800–500 BC: Hallstatt culture in Central Europe

450 BC: La Tène culture began

Roman Period

458 BC: Romans began to expand

AD 116: Roman empire reached its maximum extent

AD 395–476: decline and fall of the Western Empire

Migration Period

AD 395: Huns pushed into the Eastern Empire

AD 400: Angles, Saxons and Jutes enter Britain

AD 481–511: Franks expanded under Clovis

AD 500: Slavs settled around the Oder

AD 660: Slavs took the Elbe-Saale region

Viking Age

AD 800: Viking raids began

AD 880s: Rus took Kiev as their capital

AD 1090: fall of the last temple to the Norse gods

Abbreviations

aDNA	ancient DNA		NRY	Non-recombining portion of the Y chromosome
CRS	Cambridge Reference Sequence		PIE	Proto-Indo-European
DNA	deoxyribonucleic acid		SNP	Single Nucleotide Polymorphism
IBD	Identity by Descent		TMRCA	time to the most recent common ancestor
LBK	Linearbandkeramik			
MK	Michelsberg culture		TRB	Trichterbecher or Funnel Beaker culture
mtDNA	mitochondrial DNA			
			Y-DNA	Y chromosome DNA

problems. My thanks go to all those throughout this lengthy process for the kindness and care with which they responded to my request for critique. Their aid has been invaluable. Particular thanks are due to my editor Colin Ridler, who guided the project to fruition, and all the team at Thames & Hudson, and to Richard Rocca for supplying up-to-date maps of the distribution of three R1b haplogroups. Any remaining errors are my own.

CHAPTER ONE

Who Are the Europeans?

W here did the people of Europe come from? That question has sparked curiosity for millennia. Tribes and nations developed origin myths for lack of better knowledge. Much that we would like to know is lost in the mists of prehistory. Anthropologists and archaeologists have long been labouring to shine a light into that forgotten past. They have achieved much. Most scholars now accept that our distant forefathers emerged in Africa to people the globe.[1] Despite mighty barriers of desert, sea and mountain, anatomically modern humans had spread right across Asia and Europe before the last Ice Age forced them into habitable pockets amid the wastelands. [1] Only after that crisis had passed did our ancestors begin to take up farming, the first step on the way to civilization.

Yet trenchant disagreements remain over many of the particulars. Was farming spread into Europe by immigrants or by resident hunter-gatherers taking up agriculture? Why at the dawn of history were people from India to Ireland speaking languages of remarkable similarity? Did migrating Neolithic farmers bring with them the prototype of the Indo-European languages? Or did later Copper and Bronze Age herders do so? Or can we explain this pattern without migration?

These issues have been debated for decades. Others have more recently emerged. The spread of farming was traditionally pictured as one long wave inching its way across the continent of Europe from the Near East over thousands of years, whether by the movement of people or ideas. In the 1990s some archaeologists began to dissent. A new model appeared of farmers leapfrogging their way over previous settlements to create new colonies. Newer still is the idea of farmers arriving in Europe not in one wave, but a complex series of them. Could this be true?

The burgeoning field of population genetics offers hope of resolving such wrangles. Within us all we carry evidence of our ancestors. Now that we can read our own code, what stories of our past can it reveal? Ancient population movements can leave a trail in our DNA, pointing to distant relatives

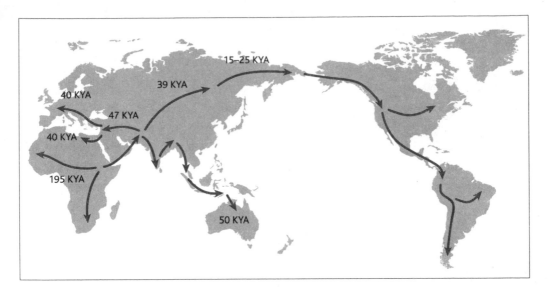

1 *The expansion of anatomically and behaviourally modern humans out of Africa.*
Times and routes are very uncertain. KYA = thousand years ago.

we didn't know we had. It was clues from the genes of living people that provided the conclusive evidence, not only that *Homo sapiens* spread out of Africa, but that the most likely route was across Arabia (see pp. 21–22, 52).[2]

When James Watson and Francis Crick described the spiral-staircase structure of DNA in 1953,[3] we were a long way from being able to read its code. Their breakthrough was the understanding of how the code worked. Previously, the mechanism of genetics had been a mystery. Gregor Mendel, working in his monastery garden in the 19th century, had worked out some of the basic rules of inheritance by cross-breeding peas. How were the instructions for inheritance passed on from generation to generation?

Inside the cells of all living organisms – in the nucleus of the cell – lives the code for making the organism. [2] Its building blocks are just four bases. That simplicity makes it so adaptable that it can code for anything from a virus to an elephant. Adenine (A) on one strand of the double spiral of DNA pairs with thymine (T) on the other. Guanine (G) pairs with cytosine (C). The sequence of these bases is the genetic instruction book. Before it could be decoded, it needed to be transcribed. Geneticists transcribe it into one long chain of letters such as AGGGTTACC and so on. The human genome has around three billion of these base pairs. So mapping the whole human

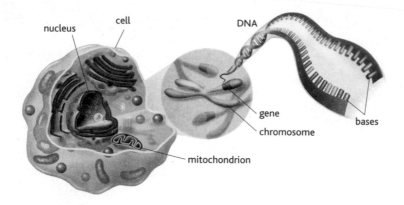

nucleus cell DNA

gene

chromosome

bases

mitochondrion

2 *Diagrammatic representation of the key structural features of the cell and DNA.*

genome was a mammoth task. Working drafts were published in 2001. It was not until 2012 that roughly 80 per cent of the code was cracked.[4]

Another part of our DNA had already been sequenced. Mitochondrial DNA (mtDNA) is found not in the cell nucleus, but in energy-generating mitochondria (sing. mitochondrion) throughout the rest of the cell. Since there are up to 1,000 mitochondria per cell, it is the most abundant human form of DNA. It is also different in another way. It is passed down exclusively from mother to child. Picture an unbroken chain of life from simple forms 1.5 billion years ago to the earliest humans and then through countless generations to your maternal grandmother and your mother and finally down to you.

How exactly is it passed down? The two strands of the double spiral can unzip themselves and then latch on to pairing molecules to create two identical spirals. So your mtDNA should be exactly the same as your mother's. Sometimes, though, there are faults in replication. You could see it as a typing error in those chains of letters. Such errors, often called mutations or variants, can tell us a lot. If a sequence variant is found in you, but not in your mother, then we can be certain that it occurred in you. If you are female, it will be passed down to your children and any grandchildren by your daughters, and become a way to identify your female line descendants.[5]

A mutation a thousand years ago could link you to people far away, providing a clue to the origins of an ancestor. So if your interest is in tracing your own ancestry or the travels of the whole of humankind, mtDNA is a prime player. By testing the human populations of the globe, geneticists have been able to work out the order in which many of these mtDNA changes occurred. A phylogenetic tree has been constructed which leads back to a genetic Eve – the maternal ancestor of all living humans.[6]

In 1984 a momentous discovery was unveiled. Researchers at the University of California had succeeded in extracting mtDNA from a fragment of dried quagga muscle. What made this headline news was that the quagga (a member of the horse family) was extinct.[7] Visions of resurrecting dinosaurs formed in the mind of science fiction author Michael Crichton. His novel *Jurassic Park* (1990) was adapted into the blockbuster film of the same name. Such terrifying experiments were a long way from the minds of geneticists. They were gripped by what ancient DNA (aDNA) could tell us about relationships between species, and indeed between people. Since there are so many more copies of mtDNA within the body than nuclear DNA, the chances of its survival after death are better. So early attempts to extract aDNA concentrated on mtDNA.

By the 1990s scientists were extracting DNA not just from preserved soft tissue, but also teeth and bones. Under favourable conditions, DNA can survive in remains for millennia. There was triumph when DNA was supposedly obtained from a 65-million-year-old dinosaur, until it was revealed to be human DNA. So much for *Jurassic Park*. The contamination of specimens by the DNA of those who have handled them turned out to be a major problem in this emerging field.[8] Today it is recommended that newly discovered human remains should be excavated and handled only by persons wearing sterile gloves, face masks and coveralls [see 15], and that everyone involved in the manipulation and study of the remains should have his or her DNA tested to compare with the ancient specimens.[9] Even so, contamination can creep in through the use of a standard biochemical technology.[10] Fortunately, an array of new techniques, known as 'next generation sequencing', avoids this problem and has vastly increased the amount of DNA that can be extracted from extinct organisms.[11] We now have the entire genome of the famous 5,300-year-old Alpine Iceman named Ötzi. We can work out that he had brown eyes, was lactose intolerant and at risk of heart disease. Infecting organisms can also be sequenced. Scientists found that Ötzi suffered from Lyme disease, transmitted to humans by the bite of infected ticks.[12]

Before results from ancient DNA could reach their present level of reliability, scientists were leaping joyfully to conclusions based on the DNA of living people. The eagerness with which some rushed to popularize and commercialize is understandable, but it is a prescription for confusion in this fast-moving field. Yesterday's ideas may reach television viewers just as they are being overturned. Commercial genetic testing is precariously balanced on the cutting edge of science. Firms promising a certificate of Viking ancestry or descent from Niall of the Nine Hostages were jumping the gun. The science shifted before the ink was dry on the publicity material.

Worst of all was a tendency to circular thinking. Genetic results were interpreted in the light of a convenient archaeological model; then the conclusion was taken as proof of the model. Other studies selected a migration familiar from the history books and set out to find its genetic traces. Any genetic marker along the trail of the known migration was then linked to it. The hitch here is that many migrations took similar routes to earlier ones. Furthermore, the mass of migration in modern times has frequently muddied the tracks. Simple answers are in short supply.

Yet despite teething troubles, the nascent science of human population genetics is full of promise. Over the last few years papers and books have poured out in a whirling stream. Some overturn long-held ideas. Others support them. For those trying to get a grip on the story of Europe's past, it has been the intellectual equivalent of white-water rafting: an exhilarating ride that leaves one breathless. Out of this seeming chaos a solid structure is emerging, piece by piece. Key publications have illuminated the great migrations in prehistory. Some are from archaeologists. Others are from population geneticists. Some of the most exciting work is yet to be published, but already different strands of evidence are being knitted into a complex answer to that simple question: where did Europeans come from?

The restless peoples of Europe have stirred the gene pool many a time, overlaying the signatures of more ancient population movements. The resulting palimpsest cannot be read in an instant. The aim here is to give a taste of the convergence of evidence that may ultimately give us a clearer answer to the question. What emerges is that visions of stability must give way to a more dynamic view of Europe's prehistory. The continent was not barred to incomers after the arrival of the earliest human beings. On the contrary, the tracks of Neolithic arrivals from the Near East can be seen in DNA. Nor were the Neolithic waves of migration the last ones of importance. Movements in the ages of metal had a massive impact, as did those after the fall of Rome.[13]

Europe is not a separate landmass. The idea that Europe and Asia are separate continents was perhaps the vision of early Mediterranean civilizations who had not penetrated far enough north to grasp the geography.

Yet the idea of separate continents stuck. So a notional boundary had to be hit upon, which in antiquity was the Don River. Today it is the Ural Mountains.[14] People have moved across that boundary, and across the Mediterranean, from time immemorial, so Europeans are closely related to their nearest neighbours.

Despite the high degree of genetic similarity among Europeans, there are still many places in the DNA code where one European might have a different sequence of bases from another European. By testing a huge array of these, it is possible to find national clusters.[15] These clusters overlap across neighbouring countries, as we should expect. Modern political boundaries have little time depth. A Briton today with a strong sense of national identity may be astonished to find herself grouped with the French or the Irish, while a Portuguese may be disconcerted to fall among Spanish samples. Yet that counts as a pretty good match. On average a pair of modern Europeans living in neighbouring populations share around 10–50 genetic common ancestors from the last 1,500 years, and upwards of 500 genetic ancestors from the 1,000 years before that. There are marked regional variations within these figures. Southeastern Europeans share large numbers of common ancestors dating to the Slavic expansions around 1,500 years ago. By contrast most common ancestors shared by Italians with other populations lived before 2,500 years ago.[16] Within modern national borders there may be regional genetic differences reflecting separate histories. A good example is Sardinia. The island joined the Kingdom of Italy in 1861, but still today the population of Sardinia is different genetically from that of mainland Italy.[17]

Much more remains to be learned about the migrations that created these patterns. Taking the plunge into explanation now risks being wrong in unforeseen ways, but that is ever the lot of an author. We can only make deductions from the evidence we do have, laying out the principles that we are following and the problems of interpretation. The next chapter covers these. The story of the peopling of Europe begins in Chapter 3.

CHAPTER TWO

Migration: Principles and Problems

The idea of migration in prehistory, so long out of favour, is now back on the agenda.[1] From the 1920s to the 1950s, V. Gordon Childe was a towering figure among anglophone archaeologists. In book after book he painted a picture of European prehistory in grand sweeps that drew together evidence from far and wide. For example, he visualized a 'Neolithic Revolution' spreading farming from the Near East.[2] It was Childe who introduced to English speakers the German concept of the archaeological culture:

> We find certain types of remains – pots, implements, ornaments, burial rites, house forms – constantly recurring together. Such a complex of regularly associated traits we shall term a 'cultural group' or just a 'culture'. We assume that such a complex is the material expression of what today would be called a people.[3]

Within this framework the movement of people was assumed to explain any significant cultural change. Then there was a paradigm shift in the 1960s, kick-started by Cambridge archaeologist Grahame Clark. He attacked the vision of Britain's past as one of wave after wave of invasion,[4] spreading his concept to the world stage in the 1970s.[5] The degree of enthusiasm with which his ideas were greeted varied from one country to another, but the New Archaeology took root widely.

'Pots are not people' became the guiding rule of Western archaeology. It was wise to make the distinction between cultural change and folk movement. The two do not always go hand in hand. Unfortunately, due caution excused migration-blindness.[6] As Barry Cunliffe wrote in *Europe Between the Oceans*:

> Some prehistorians went into a state of denial, implicitly refusing to accept that population movements had ever been a significant feature of European prehistory.[7]

The anti-migrationist stance reflected the zeitgeist of the post-imperial age. Invasion and colonization were no longer appealing concepts. Pride in indigenous culture rose. Continuity became the dominant theme. This revolution in thinking was useful in challenging assumptions. Yet history is a weave of continuity and change. Pull just one thread out of that tapestry, and we distort the picture. Gradually a weight of evidence accrued at odds with the prevailing orthodoxy. Eventually any intellectual cage will start to creak if facts won't fit into it. In this new millennium, the sound of bursting bars is upon us.

> Research on Mesolithic and Early Neolithic societies has continued to demonstrate that mobility and migrations have been the norm in European Stone Age societies ... not rare exceptions. Thus there is no reason to suppose that large-scale migration took place only once.... The interpretive climate in archaeology once again encourages the exploration of migration study perspectives.[8]

The new thinking is partly a consequence of the wealth of scientific techniques that have become available to archaeologists to supplement the trusty trowel and notebook.[9] The willingness to use these new tools bespeaks a shift towards more science-based archaeology. Prehistorian Kristian Kristiansen sets the movement into the historic context of a recurrent 'cycle of Rationalism and Romanticism' in Western thought. He predicts a change of focus towards larger, more global problems. 'Mobility and migration as well as ethnicity and warfare will dominate this research.'[10]

Along with scientific techniques come specialists to interpret their results: palaeoclimatologists, archaeogeneticists and dendrochronologists, to name just a few. Study of the distant past is becoming an increasingly multi-disciplinary affair. This is a strength. If evidence from independent, unrelated sources converges on a conclusion, then that answer will be more robust than any single line of enquiry could produce on its own. The greater the number of methods producing the same answer, the less likelihood that one is wrong.[11] For example, if a baby weighs 8 lb at birth, then 8 lb should be the result whatever type of scale is used to weigh it. If we get different results from different scales, we know that something is wrong somewhere, and it won't be the baby. Checking the weight with several scales adds to our certainty that we have the correct answer.

Archaeology can make its own contribution simply by intelligent deduction from material remains, if the typical patterns of mobility and migration are understood.[12] Burial rites are particularly interesting. The movement of just one or two traders should not affect burial customs. A foreign merchant dying far from home might be buried by the locals in the local manner. But if you have folk movement, you expect the newcomers to bring their own burial rites. Naturally this cannot be an absolute rule. Human beings are too complex and flexible for absolute rules about their behaviour. People may change their rituals when they adopt a different religion. Christianity is the classic example. Pagans who buried their dead with grave goods could turn into Christians who buried their dead without. A safer deduction is that the sudden appearance of a package of multiple material changes including burial type suggests migration.

The dictum that pots are not people remains valid. Ironically its lessons have yet to be fully learned. Pottery has been used to date archaeological sequences since Flinders Petrie established the method in the late 19th century.[13] So useful did pottery become to archaeologists that entire cultures were named for a pottery style, such as Bell Beaker [see 70] or Corded Ware. Pottery can then loom disproportionately large in thinking about that society. Fashions in pottery may change while more important features of a culture, such as its economic basis, remain constant, or vice versa. By creating the label Bell Beaker, archaeologists constructed a pot-is-person mind-set. This was understandable, since it was observed long ago that Bell Beaker pottery arrived in central and northern Europe with people who looked distinctly different from the previous inhabitants.[14] Migration in that case is a reasonable hypothesis (though one that needs to be tested with DNA). Yet that does not make their tableware more crucial than their technology.

With Bell Beaker pottery in Britain and Ireland came metallurgy. The move into the age of metal was far more significant than the curve of a pot, and carries profound implications. We need to look to a source of metalworking for our Bell Beaker people. One survey found the earliest examples of the pottery style in Iberia.[15] That led to the assumption that the entire culture and the people who carried it must therefore have sprung from Iberia. This is much like supposing that the Industrial Revolution began with Josiah Wedgwood. Metallurgy entered Europe from the east. It happens that those who brought metallurgy to Iberia chose later to make bell-shaped pots (see Chapter 10). In Norway, very little actual Bell Beaker pottery has been found, but the earliest metalworking arrived with people who can be identified by other artifacts as of the same culture.[16] At Sion in the Alps new people arrived not with the start of the Bell Beaker period, as had been long assumed, but in the middle of it, as power shifted between one group of Bell Beaker makers and another.[17] The simple equation of pottery and people can blind the observer to complex reality.

Another potentially deceptive legacy of traditional archaeological methods is the type-site approach to creating culture history. The first place where a particular type or style of artifact is discovered often gives its name to the culture. Sheer chance dictated the place that it was first found. Yet the fame of the site tends to shape thinking about how cultures develop, spread and relate to each other. La Tène, on the north side of Lake Neuchâtel in Switzerland, yielded an astonishing cache of artifacts in the 19th century, which were soon presented as the material culture of the Celts. Even at the time, similar richly decorated artifacts were being discovered in France. Archaeologists now consider that the power centres of the early La Tène culture lay in a band from the Marne and Moselle valleys to the Upper Elbe. That places the La Tène site itself towards the southern periphery of the culture.[18] Yet the allure of the La Tène name lingers on, conjuring up an Alpine wellspring of the best-known Celtic culture. Worse still, this early identification of La Tène with the Celts stiffened into the certainty that no other culture could be Celtic, making it a huge puzzle that Celtic speech elsewhere did not always seem connected to this Iron Age culture. The puzzle of the Celts is unravelled in Chapters 10 and 12.

The whole concept of an 'archaeological culture' came under attack along with the idea of migration. Indeed it is a concept that needs handling with care. Sites in one region may overlap in burial practice with those in a neighbouring region, while being distinctive in their pottery. How many features in common allow us to talk of a culture? Technologies and tastes evolve. At what point do we decide that a new label is appropriate?

> The cultures that ethnographers study are not pure, pristine entities developing in a vacuum. Rather, they are almost always hybrids, fissioning or coalescing, assimilating or modifying the customs of the neighbouring peoples with whom they constantly interact. Cultures are not primordial entities or essences once crystallized in time and then remaining forever the same; they are never made, but always in the making.[19]

Yet despite half a century of onslaught upon the notion, 'archaeological culture' remains firmly in place as the framework of prehistory. No better alternative presents itself. 'Culture' is far too useful to discard, but we need to be aware that usage of this term varies. What one person sees as a culture, another may want to divide into dizzying numbers of tiny cultures scarcely larger than a couple of villages. As with so much else in archaeology, culture is in the eye of the beholder.[20]

Scientific techniques

Radiocarbon databases and palaeobotany

Databases of radiocarbon dates have been eye opening.[21] [3] Archaeologists in the past tended to assume that once humans appeared in an area, then they stayed there. If evidence of human presence in a region was dotted between 10,000 BC and 500 BC, it was possible to imagine one uninterrupted lineage of parent begetting child, simply shifting their ways from knapping flint to working bronze and then iron. Once you have a chronological graph of numbers of radiocarbon dates of such evidence, things look different. You can see the peaks and troughs of human activity. You can see the revealing absence of evidence of human presence for certain periods. You can match the ups and downs with climate change, or show how changed technology went hand in hand with population growth.[22] So a more realistic view emerges of episodic regional extinction and re-colonization.[23]

There has also been a presumption of uninterrupted technological progress. For example it has been thought that once agriculture arrived in an area, it was a permanent fixture. So it was a surprise to find radiocarbon dates projecting a picture of boom and bust for Neolithic cultures in Europe.[24] Palaeobotany can reveal more. Pollen counts from different periods can show farmers deforesting a region, or the regrowth of forest as farmers retreat. If forest is cleared for grassland, we see pastoralists at work. Arable farming may disappear in a climate downturn, to be reintroduced later.[25]

Sophisticated analysis can wring yet more from the data. Exactly how fast changes happen can be a clue as to whether migration is involved. For example a sharp population growth coinciding with farming suggests incomers arriving with a lifestyle completely familiar to them. A slow growth suggests a lifestyle gradually adopted by locals.[26]

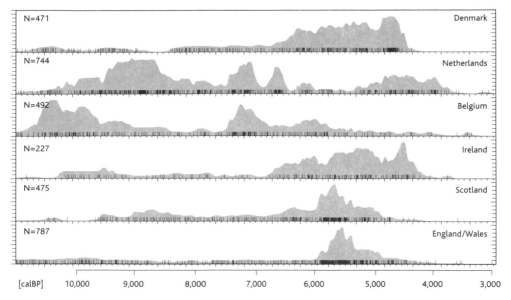

3 *Graph showing peaks and troughs in the numbers of radiocarbon-dated human sites in various European countries from 10,000 to 3,000 years ago. Belgium and the Netherlands show remarkably high concentrations of hunter-gatherer activity as the climate warmed after the last Ice Age. As the forests returned, hunting bands were fewer. They were followed by a population surge on the arrival of farming, then another fall. Farming arrived later in Scandinavia and the British Isles, boosting population levels there dramatically.*

Isotopes

Isotope studies can help us discover how far an ancient person moved in his or her lifetime. The geophysical character of the terrain in which a person grows up leaves a characteristic signal in the chemistry of bones and teeth. A man buried in some style in Roman Gloucester had silver buckles typical of those made by Goths and steppe peoples in the Crimea. Oxygen isotopes from his teeth confirmed the exotic origin. They suggested that he had spent his childhood in a cold region of eastern Europe.[27]

The origins of a young woman discovered in a Roman cemetery in York were pieced together by a combination of techniques. Her stone coffin alone displayed her high status. Her rich array of grave goods revealed a woman impressively adorned. They included jet and ivory bangles, a glass mirror and a blue glass jug which probably contained perfume or cosmetics. All can be dated to AD 350–400. The most famous object from this burial is an open-work mount of bone which reads: S[OR]OR AVE VIVAS IN DEO, or 'Hail, sister, may you live in God', presumably a gift from a Christian. The shape of her cranium indicated a mixture of western Eurasian and sub-Saharan ancestry suggestive of North Africa – then part of the Roman empire. Isotope results were inconclusive, but compatible with a childhood in the Mediterranean.[28]

DNA: the basics

Increasingly, hopes are pinned on the potential of DNA to reveal our origins. This is a complex subject, but we only need to grasp the basics to see what all the excitement is about. Geneticists have homed in on two types of DNA in tracing ancestry and human migrations: mtDNA and Y-DNA.

As described in Chapter 1, mtDNA is passed down from the mother to her child. Though bountiful in each cell of our bodies, it carries only a tiny proportion of our genetic code. The vast bulk of our DNA is carried on 23 pairs of chromosomes within the nucleus of each cell. Of those pairs, 22 are a mixture of DNA from both of our parents. The last pair depends on our gender. Normal females have two X chromosomes, while males have an X and a Y. The Y chromosome, which carries the instructions to create a male, is passed down from father to son. Since small parts of the Y chromosome from a man's father can recombine with the X from his mother at conception, it is strictly speaking the non-recombining portion of the Y (NRY) that is male-specific.[29]

For the sake of simplicity Y-DNA is used to mean NRY in what follows. The great value of mtDNA and Y-DNA is that they do not recombine during reproduction. They thus give us direct chains of descent respectively from mother to maternal grandmother and from father to paternal grandfather, all the way back to a genetic Eve and Adam shared by every human

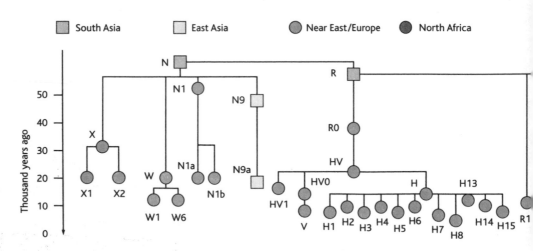

today. However, if mtDNA and Y-DNA had been passed down completely unchanged over millennia from our earliest human ancestors, it would give us no clue to lines of descent. It is the occasional faults in DNA replication that provide vital information.

Those readers who have had their DNA tested for ancestry-related markers will be familiar with the terminology. Each variant found in mtDNA is identified by its numerical position in the mtDNA sequence. For absolute clarity it is best to indicate the change of base. For example G8701A or 8701G>A shows that a G changed to an A at position 8701. That is one of the markers that defines haplogroup N – the parent of all the haplogroups common in Europe. What is a haplogroup? Think of it as a collection of markers shared by enough people to make it a significant branch or twig on the human family tree. [4]

G8701A appears not only in haplogroup N, but in all its descendants. That is how we know that they are descendants. Similarly, each of the daughters of N has its own defining markers, passed on to all of its descendants. It was by such discoveries that the phylogenetic tree of mtDNA was gradually deduced.[30] At the root of the tree is Mitochondrial Eve, whose earliest descendants fitted into haplogroup L. Those carrying L today are generally found in sub-Saharan Africa or among those with African ancestry. The most ancient mtDNA haplogroups, L0 and L1, are found among the Khoisan of South Africa. From L3 descend the large haplogroups M and N, which dominate South Asia. While some of the less common haplogroups in the Near East and Europe (X and W) descend directly from N, the commonest haplogroups in Europe descend from N via haplogroup R.[31] That chain of descent is a clue to human origins in Africa and the route into Europe. [5]

4 A section of the phylogeny of mitochondrial DNA, showing the mtDNA haplogroups common in western Eurasia and their ancestors in South Asia. The proliferation of subclades in H around 9,000–10,000 years ago suggests a burst of growth with the spread of farming.

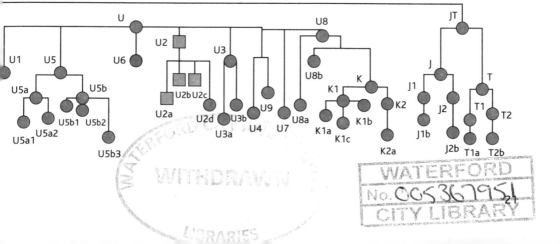

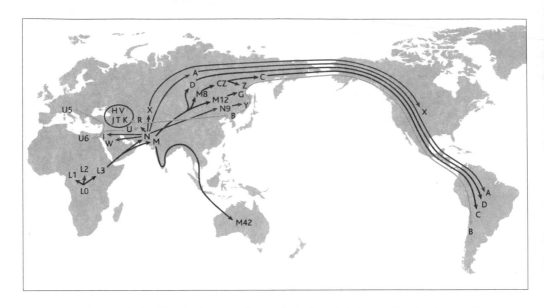

5 *The spread of mtDNA haplogroups. Those within the red circle arose from haplogroup R via intermediary haplogroups, most probably in the Near East. All arrived in Europe with early farmers.*

6 *A section of the phylogeny of Y-DNA showing the haplogroups common in Europe, which descend from the ancient CT, mainly via F. The root of the tree (not shown here) is even more ancient, going back to ancestral haplogroup A in Africa. Haplogroup H is found in India. Its subclade H1a-M82 is the most common haplogroup in European Romani, who descend from a group who left India about a thousand years ago.*

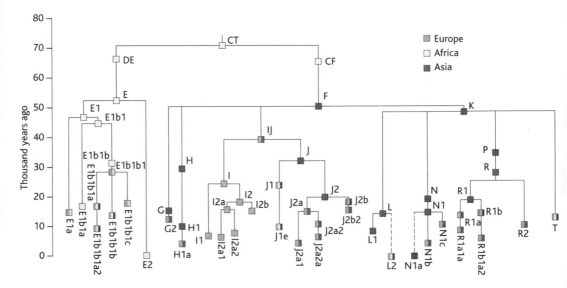

A DNA sequence variant can also be known as a Single Nucleotide Polymorphism, or SNP (pronounced 'snip'), a term frequently used in discussion of Y-DNA. SNPs in Y-DNA can be identified in much the same way as in mtDNA, for example rs17222279G>A shows a change of base from G to A at position rs17222279. Confusingly, they are also named in another way. Each laboratory researching SNPs in the Y chromosome finds it convenient to number them in sequence of discovery. So the very same SNP rs17222279G>A has been named M467, S29 and U198 by different laboratories. As with mtDNA, such markers are used to define haplogroups, which can be built into a phylogenetic tree for Y-DNA.[32] [6] Since the names of haplogroups change as new SNPs are discovered, it has become standard practice to use both the haplogroup name and its defining SNP(s), for instance R1b1a2a1a1a5b1 (M467/S29/U198) or some shortened form such as R1b-M467. An asterisk at the end of a haplogroup name, such as Y-DNA R1b* or mtDNA H1*, indicates a sample in which tests proved negative for markers which can be found downstream within that haplogroup. In other words the sample could not be resolved further to fit into a known subclade (subgroup) of that haplogroup.

At the root of the Y-DNA tree is the patrilineal ancestor of us all – Y-DNA Adam.[33] Unlike in the story in Genesis, the genetic Adam and Eve never met. They lived thousands of years apart. Each belonged to a human community, and some of the genes from those communities may exist in us still. If a man has daughters, but no sons, he could pass on his curly hair, but not his Y-DNA. Likewise, if a woman has sons, but no daughters, she will pass on much nuclear DNA, but not her mtDNA beyond her children. The genetic Adam and Eve are simply our most recent common ancestors (MRCA) of direct patrilineal and matrilineal descent.

DNA: making sense of the data
Phylogeography and its problems

Deductions can be made about human migratory routes in the distant past from these phylogenies in living people. In the broadest outline they are reliable. We can safely say that humanity began its journey in Africa and first crossed into the Americas via Asia. Subsequent migrations have smudged the details of the picture.

A common assumption has been that a modern population contains an ancient local gene pool. That would be convenient. It is a lot easier to obtain blood or saliva from the living than to retrieve DNA from the dead. One approach has been to take samples from people living close to known archaeological sites of a particular period in the hope that this will reflect the DNA of the relevant period. This presupposes continuity rather than testing for it. Just how mistaken such presumptions can be emerges when actual human remains of the period are tested. Over and over again ancient DNA (aDNA) has shown no relationship between ancient people and those who now occupy the same area.[34]

If we look at modern people alone, the greatest density and diversity of mtDNA H5* appears in the western Caucasus, which might suggest to the unwary that it spread from there. If we investigate human remains, H5 was present in Neolithic Syria.[35] So the Near East is the more likely point of origin. The Caucasus attracted Neolithic farmers from the Near East.

What is true for humans may also be true for their animal companions. Modern pigs in continental Europe all have mitochondrial haplotypes derived from European wild pigs. If we judged only by that, we would imagine that pigs were independently domesticated in Europe. Ancient DNA reveals a completely different story. The first domesticated pigs in Europe, from sites stretching from Romania through Germany to France, all displayed a Near Eastern signature. Once pig-farming arrived in Europe, stock was replenished from the wild, with the result that the early farming lineages have now been completely replaced, leaving no descendants in modern pig populations.[36]

There is no shortcut to ancient DNA in linking specific haplogroups to archaeological evidence and scientific dating. In the days before we had much aDNA, it was easy to assume that the distribution of mtDNA haplogroups we see in Europe today is largely a reflection of the earliest arrivals of *Homo sapiens*. After all, archaeologists had long been pressing the case for continuity. A decade ago, geneticists calculated from both mtDNA and Y-DNA that 80 per cent of native Europeans could trace their ancestry to European hunter-gatherers.[37] Now that we have hundreds of samples of aDNA from across the continent, that vision has been dramatically over-turned. It seems that most of the mtDNA haplogroups common in Europe today first appeared with farmers (Table 1, pp. 26–27).

Clines and waves

Geneticists developed the theory that the region where the greatest genetic variance of a haplogroup is found is likely to be its point of origin, since the longer a lineage has been in a place, the longer it has had to accumulate variations.

As with conclusions from phylogeny, tracking variance seems satisfactory in broad, continental outline, but later movements will have swirled the mix in ways that could mislead us if we expect variance today to match exactly that in prehistory. A present-day population could have acquired diversity from different waves of immigrants. We find a high variance within European haplogroups in the United States, but we know full well that these haplogroups do not have their origin there. So variance is most convincing when supported by phylogeny and other kinds of evidence. The commonest Y-DNA haplogroup of western Europe is R1b1a2 (M269). Debate has been intense over the variance within this haplogroup.[38] The variance within the whole R1b (M343) haplogroup is clearly highest in western Asia,[39] [7] and phylogeny tells the same story. The chain of SNP mutations within R1b runs westwards, with those that occurred earlier than M269 being most prevalent in Asia.

7 *Variance within Y-DNA haplogroup R1b (M343) – parent of the most common haplogroup family in western Europe. High variance towards the east suggests that it spread from east to west.*

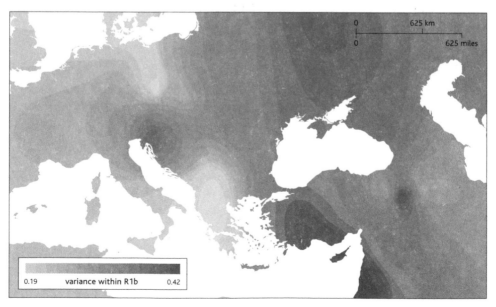

Table 1 *The first satisfactorily tested and dated appearance of each mtDNA haplogroup found in European ancient DNA down to c. 2600 BC.*

Period	Economy	Haplogroup	Location	Country	Source
30,000 years ago	Forager	U2	Kostënki	Russia	Krause 2010
18,000–15,000 BC	Forager	U	Nerja, Málaga	Spain	Fernández 2005
10,300 BC	Forager	U5	Erralla, Gipuzkoa	Spain	Hervella 2012
7800 BC	Forager	U5a	Chekalino	Russia	Bramanti 2009
8000–7000 BC	Forager	U5a1	Lebyazhinka	Russia	Bramanti 2009
7200 BC	Forager	U5b2	Falkensteiner Höhle	Germany	Bramanti 2009
6850 BC	Forager	U4	Bad Dürrenberg	Germany	Bramanti 2009
6700 BC	Forager	U5a2a	Hohlenstein-Stadel	Germany	Bramanti 2009
5500 BC	Forager	U2e	Uznyi Oleni Ostrov	Russia	Der Sarkissian 2013
5500 BC	Forager	C1	Uznyi Oleni Ostrov	Russia	Der Sarkissian 2013
5500 BC	Farmer	J*	Seehausen	Germany	Haak 2005
5500 BC	Farmer	T	Flomborn, Halberstadt & Schwetzingen	Germany	Haak 2005
5500 BC	Farmer	T2b23a	Unterweiderstedt	Germany	Adler 2012
5500 BC	Farmer	N1a1a	Unterweiderstedt	Germany	Haak 2005
5500 BC	Farmer	N1a1a1	Flomborn	Germany	Haak 2005
5500 BC	Farmer	N1a1a2	Halberstadt	Germany	Haak 2005
5500 BC	Farmer	N1a1a3	Unterweiderstedt	Germany	Adler 2012
5500 BC	Farmer	U3	Vaihingen an der Enz	Germany	Haak 2005
5500 BC	Farmer	V	Halberstadt	Germany	Haak 2005
5475–5305 BC	Farmer	K	Chaves	Spain	Gamba 2012
5475–5305 BC	Farmer	H	Chaves	Spain	Gamba 2012
5475–5305 BC	Farmer	X1	Can Sadurní	Spain	Gamba 2012
5471–5223 BC	Farmer	C	Yasinovataka	Ukraine	Nikitin 2012
5471–5223 BC	Farmer	C4a2	Yasinovataka	Ukraine	Nikitin 2012
5300 BC	Farmer	J1c	Vedrovice	Moravia	Bramanti 2008

Different kinds of genetic spread leave characteristic patterns. One has been christened the Surfing Effect. A genetic variant born in the wave front of an expanding population will have an advantage. It will have a better chance of becoming predominant within the breeding group, because that is where the migrating population is smallest. A successful mutation will surf the wave and end up at saturation level where the expanding

Period	Economy	Haplogroup	Location	Country	Source
5358–4993 BC	Herder	U5a1a	Nikolskoye	Ukraine	Nikitin 2012
5247 BC	Farmer	HV	Derenburg	Germany	Haak 2010
5117 BC	Farmer	T2b	Derenburg	Germany	Haak 2010
5000 BC	Forager	U5b2c1	La Braña-Arintero, León	Spain	Sánchez-Quinto 2012
5000 BC	Farmer	H3	Avellaner Cave, Catalonia	Spain	Lacan 2011b
5000 BC	Farmer	K1a	Avellaner Cave, Catalonia	Spain	Lacan 2011b
5000 BC	Farmer	W	Derenburg	Germany	Haak 2010
4600 +/- 65 BC	Forager	U5b1	Aizpea, Navarre	Spain	Hervella 2012
4625–4250 BC	Farmer	H5	Oberwiederstedt	Germany	Adler 2012
4625–4250 BC	Farmer	HV0	Oberwiederstedt	Germany	Adler 2012
4625–4250 BC	Farmer	T2e	Esperstedt	Germany	Adler 2012
4444–4326 BC	Farmer	T2b3a	Mezzocorona	Italy	Di Benedetto 2000
4250–3700 BC	Farmer	H20	Sant Pau del Camp	Spain	Gamba 2012
4200 BC	Farmer	X2	Prissé-la-Charrière	France	Deguilloux 2011
4090–3960 BC	Farmer	I	Paternanbidea, Navarre	Spain	Hervella 2012
3638–3370 BC	Farmer	T2a1b1	Verteba Cave	Ukraine	Nikitin 2010
3543–3488 BC	Farmer	X2b	Cova da Moura	Portugal	Afonso 2010
3500–3000 BC	Farmer	I1	Cami de Can Grau Granollers	Spain	Sampietro 2007
3500–3000 BC	Farmer	W1	Cami de Can Grau Granollers	Spain	Sampietro 2007
3350–3100 BC	Herder	K1f	Ötztal Alps	Italy	Keller 2012
3000 BC	Farmer	H1	Treilles, Aveyron	France	Lacan 2011
2700–2400 BC	Herder	W6	Esperstedt	Germany	Adler 2012
2600 BC	Herder	K1a2	Eulau	Germany	Adler 2012
2600 BC	Herder	K1ab	Eulau	Germany	Adler 2012
2600–2500 BC	Herder	W5a	Kromsdorf	Germany	Lee 2012
2600–2500 BC	Herder	T1a	Kromsdorf	Germany	Lee 2012

population meets a geographical barrier. R1b1a2 (M269) is a good example. It flooded over Europe from the east, spawning subclades as it went, until it was stopped by the Atlantic Ocean. On the Atlantic seaboard it pools into its highest densities.[40]

An historical example shows how this might work. Delving into genealogy, researchers found that the majority of the present population of

Saguenay Lac Saint-Jean in Quebec can be traced back to ancestors having lived directly on, or close to, the wave front of 17th-century European expansion in Canada.[41]

Refining by subclade

Early studies painted with a broad brush. Only a few mtDNA haplogroups had been discovered at that time; each was given a letter to identify it. Then researchers attempted to make sense of their distribution. The gradual process of breaking these parent groups down into subclades has created a more subtle picture. A close look at mtDNA H reveals its complexity. H itself was born in the Near East and spread into Europe.[42] H3 today is largely limited to Europe and North Africa. Both H1 and H3 have their densest distribution in Iberia. [8] It was initially thought that they were also most diverse there. From this it was argued that these two subclades spread from the Franco-Cantabrian glacial refuge as the climate warmed around 10,000 years ago.[43] This would be highly significant for the peopling of Europe. Not only is H itself the predominant haplogroup in Europe, carried by almost half of the population, but its commonest subclade is H1.

Yet breaking down H1 itself into subclades revealed that some are barely present in Iberia. H1a and H1b are densest in eastern Europe. Even more significantly, H1 and H3 have a low diversity in Cantabrian Spain and in particular among the Basques. The highest diversity and allelic richness of H1 and H3 in Europe are found in northeastern and north-central regions, while the Near East has the greatest overall diversity of H1, and North Africa that of H3, but what appears to be H3a has been found in Neolithic samples in Turkey. The once-popular idea of the Basques as the source population for most of modern-day Europe is not supported by this closer examination.[44] Instead, it suggests that H1 and H3 arrived in Europe with the first farmers.

Dating problems

MtDNA H1 is estimated to be nearly 10,000 years old and H3 nearly 9,000 years old.[45] Such dates would not quite rule out an expansion before farming, given the usual large margin of error, but they would make it less likely. How reliable is such dating? It rests on the idea that mutations occur at a regular rate, creating a molecular clock. How fast the clock ticks is the burning question. There are various ways to work it out. For example, we

8 *Distribution of mtDNA haplogroups H, H1 and H3. H is the most common haplogroup in Europe, carried by 40–50 per cent of most European populations, and also appears in North Africa and the Middle East. It is estimated to be around 12,800 years old. H1 is its most common subclade and H3 the next most common.*

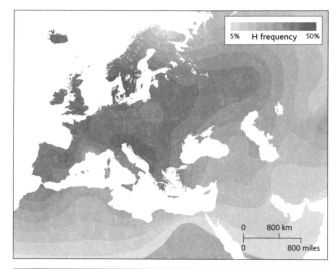

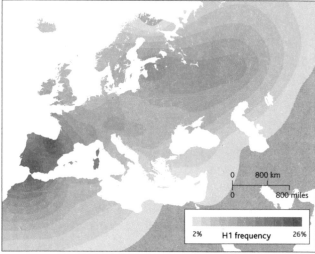

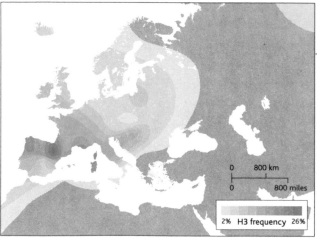

can roughly date the divergence between humans and chimpanzees from the fossil record. So the number of mtDNA sequence differences between modern humans and chimpanzees can be divided by the time since they diverged to provide a rate of mutation. Another method is counting mutations in pedigrees.[46]

It sounds so simple, but delve into details and you are sucked into quicksand. Dating estimates will vary according to which genetic loci are used, since some mutate faster than others.[47] The pedigree or genealogical rate will vary depending on the estimate of the number of years between generations. An average for recent centuries can be calculated from genealogical records, but how well does that fit the distant past when life expectancies were far shorter? Also, men may have a longer generation time than women, since women stop bearing children at the menopause. One study revealed an average female generation time of 29 years, while the average for men was 35.[48]

No wonder then that some calculations have gone awry. One mutation rate for Y-DNA produced unexpectedly late dates in some populations, which led to a revised 'evolutionary effective' rate,[49] and this has been widely adopted. This *ad hoc* adjustment might be appropriate for the specific loci used to calculate it, but not others.[50] Certainly, its indiscriminate use has produced incongruously early dates. For example in the Caucasus genealogical rates give a good fit with the linguistic and archaeological dates, while the 'evolutionary effective' rates fall far outside them.[51]

Dating disputes fuel the debate over Y-DNA R1b1a2 (M269). Once thought to have spread from Iberia as the bitter cold of the last Ice Age retreated, opinion has shifted in recent years to the view that it entered Europe with farming. This is partly based on the data from variance mentioned above, and partly on the striking evidence of a recent rapid expansion.[52] Yet a southeastern origin combined with recent rapid expansion better fits the Copper Age, in which the new technology spread faster than farming. Estimated dates are compatible with either, depending on the mutation rate chosen.[53]

Ancient DNA

Fortunately, direct evidence is beginning to appear from ancient DNA (aDNA). Early attempts to extract ancient DNA concentrated on mtDNA because of its better chance of survival. Y-DNA has begun to feature more in the last few years (Table 2).

Table 2 *Y-DNA haplogroups found in European ancient DNA from the Neolithic to the Bronze Age. No Y-DNA has so far been obtained from periods before the Neolithic.*

Period	Haplogroup
Neolithic	E1b1b1a1b (V13), F* (M89), G2a (P15), G2a1c (L30/S126), I2a1 (P37.2)
Copper Age	G2a1b2 (L91), R1b (M343), R1b1a2 (M269)
Bronze Age	R1a1 (SRY10831.2)

If Y-DNA can be obtained, why stop there? All sorts of other information can be gleaned from ancient nuclear DNA, such as the origin of genetic diseases or helpful traits. Scientists have recently been able to obtain complete genomes from the remains of humans, ancient hominins, plants and animals. Preservation of DNA is particularly good in cold conditions.[54] It is no accident that the most complete ancient human genomes so far have come from remains found in mountain caves, ice or permafrost. So today we can find not only the modern relatives of someone from prehistory, but also clues to his or her appearance. Reconstructions by artists from ancient skulls will be able to rely more on science and less on imagination.

The DNA of microscopic organisms can have a tale to tell of massive import. The deadly epidemic known as the Black Death ravaged Europe between 1348 and 1350, killing something like 30–60 per cent of the population. The disease was long suspected to be bubonic plague caused by the bacterium *Yersinia pestis*, which is carried by fleas living on black rats. Inevitably this was disputed, given the lack of direct evidence. The Black Death spread so fast in London – as many wills were being made in one week as in a normal year – that archaeologist Barney Sloane felt that the carriers had to be humans, not black rats. So was it really bubonic plague?[55] DNA from plague victims in stricken European towns and cities, including London, has now shown that *Yersinia pestis* was indeed the dealer in death.[56]

Yet we should still be cautious. When remains thought to be those of Luke the Evangelist were tested, the result aroused public interest, but scientific controversy. Though no mtDNA haplogroup was actually reported, H was ruled out by one marker, though another two markers had been previously found in H. The result seemed so odd it was suggested that the mtDNA of two people had been mixed.[57] That could have occurred in antiquity through handling of the relics. Some were emboldened to assume that Luke's haplogroup was H2.[58] In reality we do not know. As with so many early results, not enough of the mtDNA genome was sequenced to rule out contamination and securely identify the haplogroup. The problem of contamination bedevilled ancient DNA study in its early years. More recent studies generally report their methodology in reassuring detail. Ancient DNA is now seen as a reliable research tool.[59]

Even so, other problems persist. Until 2012 the standard method of assigning mtDNA sequences to haplogroups was by noting their differences from the Cambridge Reference Sequence (CRS). A group under Nobel Prize-winner Frederick Sanger at Cambridge University was the first to sequence a human mitochondrial genome in the late 1970s.[60] This became the Cambridge Reference Sequence. The donor remained anonymous, but it should come as no surprise that it was a person of European descent. It was later realized that this individual carried a variety of H, the most common haplogroup among Europeans today. When testing other mtDNA, if no differences from the Cambridge Reference Sequence were detected in the restricted strip of mtDNA most commonly tested, hyper-variable region one (HVS-I), the haplogroup of the testee was assumed to be H. This worked reasonably well with modern Europeans. The odds are good that if the whole mtDNA genome is investigated, the testee will be found to belong to this most common of modern European haplogroups. The same approach is unsafe for aDNA. An absence of differences from CRS over HVS-I alone can also appear in U, HV and R0, which are older haplogroups and so more likely to be found in ancient DNA.

The situation is worse still when only a fragmentary sequence of mtDNA has been retrieved. DNA starts to degrade as soon as death occurs. Where no differences from CRS are detected in such fragments, it is more realistic to count it as a non-result. Author after author has proclaimed genetic continuity in Europe from the Palaeolithic to the present on the basis of supposed mtDNA haplogroup H in ancient remains.[61] On the most recent estimate haplogroup H is less than 13,000 years old.[62] If so, it could not have entered Europe with the earliest hunter-gatherers. Dating estimates could be wrong, but publication of aDNA results would need to provide positive proof of that in the form of defining mutations for H. This should become normal practice. In April 2012 a new system for assigning mtDNA to haplogroups was published that replaces the CRS with the Reconstructed Sapiens Reference Sequence (RSRS).[63]

Another problem arises from sampling. Given the difficulty of extracting aDNA, samples from a single study tend to be too small for statistical significance. Conclusions about the entire population of Europe cannot be drawn from a handful of individuals from the same grave, very probably related. Far greater statistical weight can be placed on those studies which sample more widely and achieve a higher number of results, and on the collective results of multiple studies.

There is much more work to do. In the coming years we can expect projects now in the pipeline to bear fruit. The Anthropobiologie Moléculaire et d'Imagerie de Synthèse (AMIS) laboratory in France hopes to have sequenced the complete mitochondrial genome and Y chromosome of hundreds of ancient individuals by 2014. Bridging the European and Anatolian Neolithic (BEAN) aims to analyse ancient DNA from about 200 Mesolithic and Neolithic skeletal remains from Turkey, Serbia, Greece, Bulgaria, Romania and Hungary. These are just two of the larger projects under way.

Full genome versus uniparental markers

Mapping the first human genome was a huge project that took over a decade and cost over 3 billion US dollars. Today both the time and cost of sequencing have dropped so sharply that the 1000 Genomes Project has already exceeded its target to sequence that number of genomes from across the world, and the International HapMap Project has sequenced a similar number. Additional genomes are available from regional projects. So genome-wide population comparisons are increasingly popular. They give a broad picture of the genetic composition of a population and its affinities with others.

Yet these can only tell us if present-day population X has a similarity with present-day population Y. They cannot tell us how this arose. It is tempting to assume that the greatest concentration of a particular genetic component today must be its origin point, when it could equally well be the colony least disturbed by later migration.

The dating problems of the sex-specific markers in mtDNA and Y-DNA pale into insignificance beside those of attempting to date elements from the whole genome. One useful method is Identity by Descent (IBD). While all humans have a great deal of DNA in common, close relatives tend to share longer than average segments of DNA. These long segments are gradually broken down by recombination over the generations. So the longer the shared segment the closer the relationship is likely to be. At the personal level this technique can be used to track down your cousins to the ninth degree. At the population level interesting results emerge. The more recent common ancestors there are between a random sample of two populations, the more closely related they are.[64]

A method known as rolloff estimates the date of a population mixture event any time up to 500 generations in the past.[65] One study using this method investigated the history of sub-Saharan African gene flow into western Eurasia after the initial human dispersal out of Africa. It found that almost all southern Europeans have inherited 1–3 per cent African ancestry, with an average mixture date of around 55 generations ago.[66] That would fit the period of the conquest of much of Iberia by the Umayyad Caliphate. The Arabs began the slave trade that took so many sub-Saharan Africans into servitude far from home.

Sex-specific markers remain the clearest guide to migration, since mtDNA and Y-DNA are each passed down from parent to child without recombination. The accumulation of spontaneous mutations along these lineages provides evidence of direction of flow. They also make it possible to detect sex-biased migration, for example soldiers taking local wives. One potential problem needs to be taken into account. There may have been losses or gains in the prominence of certain haplogroups over the millennia due to genetic drift or natural selection. Mitochondrial function being critical to the human body in energy production, mutations to it may have physiological effects.[67] MtDNA haplogroup H confers an advantage in recovery after sepsis.[68] Y-DNA haplogroup I is correlated with HIV progression in Europeans, though the reason is unknown.[69]

Correlations with language or archaeological culture

Matching the genetic data to the spread of cultures and languages is the quest of this book and many of the studies cited here. It is exciting to find a correlation between a particular haplogroup and a linguistic community. Such relationships arise because people mainly learn their mother tongue from their parents, from whom they inherit their DNA. Similarly, we may hope to find haplogroups linked to the spread of farming or other major cultural changes. The concentration upon such correlations may, however, mislead the unwary reader into supposing the kind of ironclad connections that cannot exist in reality.

A statistically significant correlation simply shows that two things are linked more often than would be expected by chance. That is an interesting clue, but it is not the same as a one-to-one relationship. Though most children are descended from the persons from whom they learn their first language, some are adopted. Intermarriage goes on today between people of different languages and cultures. There is no reason to expect that adoption and cross-cultural marriage never happened in prehistory. It is unlikely that any group larger than an extended family of a few generations will contain only men of one Y-DNA haplogroup. Even in a patrilocal system, where women move to the home of their husbands, a few male outsiders may join the band or tribe, perhaps bringing haplogroups from a different lineage altogether. Groups may merge. Over time an ethnicity accumulates a diverse pool of Y-DNA and mtDNA haplogroups.

Haplogroups that form only a tiny proportion of a population are far more difficult to assign to any particular migration than predominant ones, because they could result from the movement of just one person, perhaps a trader, which could happen at any time. A scattering along a trade route of a haplogroup found mainly at the chief export hub of that trade is a hint worth investigating.

Yet some uncommon wanderers may have formed part of larger migrations. Take a hypothetical example. If imaginary haplogroups Green and Yellow are found both at Home and at Newhome, and Green and Yellow appear to be the same age at Newhome, we may reasonably surmise that they travelled together. If Green forms so big a proportion of the population of Newhome that this has to be the result of a significant event, we may be able to guess that event from history or archaeology. Then even if Yellow is much less common, we may be able to tie it to the same migration.

Over time new SNPs will arise within a lineage, creating new subclades. Such a mutation might happen at any time: during a period of cultural change, or before it, or after it. We cannot rely on convenient coincidence with any archaeologically visible or historically datable event. Biology has its own pace. Most importantly the date that a haplogroup arose does not tell us when it appeared in a particular place. Remember that a mutation first occurs in just one person. That person cannot live all over the world at the same time. Admittedly in these days of international airways, an amorous man could leave children on every continent. Even in the days of steam, sailors were notorious for having a girl in every port. We cannot push this picture back into prehistory though. A haplogroup could be confined for millennia to one comfortable niche until some impetus arose to travel.

More significant for migration is the dating of starbursts of mutations. In periods of population increase, more offspring survive, giving greater opportunity for new SNPs to survive and multiply. So a rapid population growth can be seen genetically as a burst of haplogroups appearing at around the same time from a single founder. Migration does not always go hand in hand with population expansion, but the opportunity to expand into new territory is one of the prime causes of sudden bursts of population growth. We can hope to link starbursts to major periods of colonization in Europe.

One final warning is needed. Even if we can show from ancient DNA that a particular haplogroup had arrived in a particular place by a particular date, there is generally nothing to prevent people of the same lineage moving there later as well.

The popular media enjoys stories of genetic connections between ancient remains and local people, but these are not always quite what they seem. The idea first struck British television producer Philip Priestley, who was filming the series 'Time Traveller' with archaeologist Mick Aston. One site chosen was Gough's Cave in Cheddar Gorge, England, famed for the discovery there of 'Cheddar Man' who lived around 7000 BC. Priestley approached geneticist Bryan Sykes, who explains: 'It occurred to Philip that it would make good television if he could relate, through DNA, some of the present-day residents of the town with Cheddar Man himself.' Sykes obliged by successful testing of the living and the dead. Cheddar Man carried mtDNA U5. Samples were taken from a local school. 'Knowing how often we had found Cheddar Man's sequence in modern Britain, I reckoned that there was a fifty-fifty chance of getting a close match in the twenty samples that we had taken.' In fact there were two exact matches and one with a single mutation difference. Since the two exact matches were children, whom Sykes was reluctant to expose to the media, he identified the close match, who happened to be a teacher, Adrian Targett. Targett became the centre of a media storm as the supposed descendant of Cheddar Man.[70]

No one knows better than Bryan Sykes that Cheddar Man could not have passed his mtDNA to any of his offspring; it descends from mother to child. He explained that Cheddar Man and Adrian Targett shared a common maternal ancestry, but inevitably the media tended to simplify. Far worse was the conviction that 'Adrian Targett and his family have lived in the same area of

Britain for 9,000 years', despite demurrals by Sykes that this was not necessarily so.[71] U5 is found all over Europe. Given the power of attraction that Britain has had for continental Europeans, mtDNA U5 would not rule out a Saxon or a Viking or a Norman matrilineal ancestor for a modern-day Briton carrying it. Indeed it seems likely that most U5 in Britain today descends from Copper Age arrivals at the earliest.[72]

Language

Today one language family dominates Europe, much of India and a stretch of territory between the two. [9] The similarity between the ancient Indian language Sanskrit and ancient Greek and Latin was recognized by scholars as long ago as the 16th century. These languages had to be related. It was gradually realized that many other languages also belonged to the same family. Their similarities could not be explained in any other way. Before

9 *Indo-European languages in* AD *1500. From a Copper Age homeland on the European steppe, Indo-European languages spread far and wide. This is now the dominant language family in Europe.*

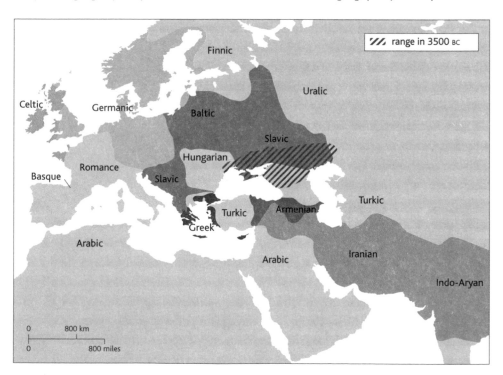

the days of modern transport and communications technology, a person in Ireland would have had no way to speak to someone in India. So similar words in their distant tongues must spring from a parent language. The term Indo-European was coined to describe the family, so the parent is Proto-Indo-European (PIE).[73]

Thanks to both its broad geographical spread in prehistory and European colonialism in more modern times, the Indo-European language family dominates the world today. Naturally, it has been intensively studied. Yet the world has numerous other language families, one of which has a significant presence in Europe – Uralic (see Chapter 4). All language families spring from a parent spoken in a linguistic community – people who regularly talk to each other. Language is always changing. Just in one person's lifetime, new words will be coined and pronunciation may change. So if a group of people move so far away from their parent linguistic community that they can no longer communicate with them, the languages of parent and child communities will diverge. Both will go on changing, but separately. Think of British and American English. When European settlers first moved to America, the season before winter was commonly known to English speakers as 'the fall of the leaf'. That became Fall in American English, while the British settled on the more formal alternative, Autumn, with its roots in Latin.

English has ringed the globe within a few centuries, which is proof enough that a language can explode from a small homeland. What happens next? English speakers today can still understand each other whatever country they live in. Would that still be true after thousands of years without the ability to communicate? That was the situation for the very first people to enter the Americas. Having made the difficult crossing from Asia, they were then cut off from their linguistic parent. Their language would become so different that they would not be able to understand a distant relative in Asia. Thus new languages are born. Those new languages in turn can give birth to a whole family of languages.

In the absence of mass education and government policy, the area that one language can cover is limited to the regularly communicating group. Such groups were small in the days before farming. The diversity of Native American languages provides a good example. Many language families and isolated languages developed in a continent spread thinly with hunter-gatherers.[74] We can expect a similar linguistic patchwork in Palaeolithic Europe.

Cambridge archaeologist Colin Renfrew argued that the Indo-European languages were brought to Europe by farmers.[75] This was a bold and attractive hypothesis. There is little doubt that many of the language families spoken today spread with agriculture. An exceptionally clear case is provided by the Bantu. Genetics, linguistics and archaeology unite to show how the Bantu changed the face of Africa. From a tropical homeland in eastern Nigeria and western Cameroon, Bantu-speaking farmers expanded east and then south from around 2000 BC. Hunter-gatherers related to modern Khoisan people were swallowed up by the advance or trapped in zones uncongenial to agriculture. Language itself provides evidence when it includes agricultural terms.[76]

Indo-European certainly includes farming terms, but it reflects later innovations as well. The first farmers used digging sticks rather than ploughs. They had no wheels or wagons, no gold or silver. They kept cattle for beef, not milk and cheese. They did not make wine. They did not spin wool. Yet PIE had words for all these things.[77] In an impressive display of cross-disciplinary scholarship, J. P. Mallory championed the alternative hypothesis that PIE spread later, along with metallurgy, from the Pontic-Caspian steppes.[78] PIE is not recorded in writing. It had broken into separate, far-flung languages by the time written records appear. So scholars have painstakingly reconstructed as much as possible of its vocabulary by comparison of words in its daughter languages. There are about 1,500 reconstructed PIE roots and words. This must fall far short of the full language. Yet the PIE lexicon reveals a great deal about the lifestyle of its speakers. They were familiar with agriculture and metallurgy. They coined words for wheels and wagons. They had a concept of social ranking, but few words for specific occupations or other clues to urban life. The lexicon reveals a Copper Age society, but not an urbanized state.[79]

No doubt the early farmers entering Europe did bring languages from the Near East. Submerged under the tide of Indo-European, most vanished before they could be written down. So linguists seek traces in place-names or words that might have been borrowed from older languages. The Afro-Asiatic family of languages seems to have originated in the Near East and spread into Africa with farming.[80] Did it enter Europe as well? Some linguists detect clues, but others dispute them.[81] Place-names on Mediterranean islands were certainly not planted there by hunter-gatherers, who made only fleeting visits at most. So they must have arrived with farming settlers or later. At least one ancient language can be detected in Sardinia. A pre-Hellenic language dotted place-names from Anatolia to Greece across the Cyclades, but even that may be Indo-European (see Chapter 11). Where we can be reasonably certain of the origins of non-Indo-European languages in Europe (Etruscan, Finnish and Hungarian), these arrived millennia after the first farmers, as we shall see.

Dating languages

It would be enormously helpful to be able to put a precise date on the development of a particular language in prehistory. We know that language evolves. For example the first type of English written down was Old English, the language of the epic poem *Beowulf*. Old English developed into the Middle English of Chaucer and then Modern English. Today most English speakers need to read even Chaucer in translation, while the original *Beowulf* seems like a foreign language. It starts '*Hwæt! Wé Gárdena in géardagum.*'

In the 1950s Morris Swadesh developed the idea of a linguistic clock.[82] Two languages can be identified as related if they share 'cognates', which are strictly defined. Any two languages in the world will share words that sound similar. There are only so many syllables available. By sheer chance a few of those similar-sounding words might have a similar meaning, arrived at independently. To be identified as cognates, two words in different languages should have clear similarities in form and meaning, and sound correspondences that are systematic between the languages, for example a 'p' in one language corresponding to an 'f' in the other. Glottochronology counts the number of surviving cognates from a list of vocabulary for universal concepts such as 'ear' and 'water'[83] to calculate the age of the common ancestor, assuming that words will be replaced at a regular rate. As with genetic dating, the rate must be calibrated externally.

The problem is that language does not conveniently change at a regular rate. Swadesh calculated that 86 per cent of the core vocabulary remains after 1,000 years. Yet English shows a retention rate of 68 per cent, while Icelandic is more conservative, with a 97 per cent retention rate over the same period.[84] There could be a burst of change as two languages come in contact.[85] Literacy may slow the process of change, as people then gain vocabulary partly from accumulated literature. Latin for example was conservative, at least in its written form.[86] The size of the linguistic community may also make a difference.[87]

Recognizing that the complexity of language change is not readily susceptible to number-crunching, few linguists embraced glottochronology.[88] That has not stopped the eager search for the perfect formula, especially in these days of huge computer power. The lure of a press-button answer has drawn into the debate a number of non-linguists familiar with complex mathematical algorithms. They may be less aware of the constraints on linguistic dating.[89] Naturally, if the computer throws up a date of 1000 BC for a language that includes the word 'television', then anyone would realize that there is something wrong with the programming. 'Television' is an example of lexico-cultural dating. We know that television was invented in 1926. So any text that includes the word must post-date 1926. Taking the method back into prehistory, many inventions can be at least roughly dated from archaeological evidence.[90] That provides fixed points to which any model should give preference. Mathematical models are enticing, particularly when they can produce attractive maps and diagrams, but they are only as good as the data fed into them.

Language shift

Today languages can be spread by education and modern communications. In prehistory the only way was by personal contact. So a complete language replacement in a region signifies a population change. It has become fashionable to argue that the change could simply be the arrival of a foreign elite. Certainly, large areas of Europe adopted Latin after they were absorbed into the Roman empire. However, that process was reinforced by the state, and even so took many centuries. The mechanism should not be projected back unthinkingly into illiterate societies.

Two factors loom large in language replacement: time and numbers. The longer two languages are in contact, the more time there is for the speakers of one or both groups to become bilingual. If one of the two groups is much larger than the other, the members of the smaller group are more likely to become bilingual, which is the most common route to the death of the minor language. One reason that the major language predominates is that its speakers are likely to belong to the dominant culture, socially and economically, making a third factor in language replacement.[91] More complex societies tend to engulf less complex groups. Political complexity is a good predictor of the size of the territory of a language.[92] Europe abounds in fascinating case studies.

The Romans created a legal system, a network of government and a bureaucracy, all of which rested upon literacy and education in Latin. This they exported throughout their empire. Once Christianity was adopted as the official religion, with worship in Latin, the dominance of their language was complete, at least in the Western Empire. Greek was the second language of Roman literacy and predominated in the Eastern Empire. Within western Europe, Latin became the key to achievement, power and position, both lay and religious. There was every incentive among Roman subjects to learn Latin as a second language. Over the centuries that the Roman empire held sway, Latin even replaced some native languages as the mother tongue. Romance languages such as French and Spanish, descended from Latin, are still spoken over a large part of the former empire.

The familiar case of the dominance of Latin has encouraged the notion that the language of any incoming elite will invariably be adopted by the majority. Yet other foreign elites have made little or no linguistic mark. The Goths and Vandals spread from the Baltic as a folk movement, bringing their Germanic tongue with them. Yet their rule left the languages of Iberia and Italy untouched (see Chapter 14). Both to this day are dominated by the speakers of Romance languages. What was the crucial factor? Where an incoming elite takes over an already established apparatus of government and bureaucracy, conducted in the majority language, there is little need for the ruled to learn the language of the rulers. Nor did the ruled of Iberia and Italy need to learn a new language in order to worship. Latin remained the language of the Church of Rome. In stark contrast, the Angles and Saxons entering Britain ignored the previous economic, religious and legal system. They settled as families, creating their own social structure and laws. Naturally, they retained their own language.[93]

The sheer numbers involved in migration have an impact. Mass migration ensures that there is a community able to maintain a language by constant interaction. It also facilitates marriage within the language community, providing mothers who can teach the language to their children. Male-dominated immigration tends not to lead to a change of language in the host population. Genetic studies indicate that Vikings settling close to Scandinavia were mainly families, while more distant forays were usually by single males, who could take a local wife. Norse families took their language with them to Orkney, where the variant of Old Norse known as Norrœna, or Norn, was spoken until the early 15th century. The Irish by contrast did no more than borrow useful Scandinavian words from their Viking visitors. As for the Normans, Gearóid Mac Eoin puts it succinctly:

> The Norsemen who ... invaded Normandy in the tenth century turned into the French-speaking Normans of the eleventh. These French-speaking Normans invaded Ireland in the twelfth century and became the Irish-speaking Gaill of the fourteenth.[94]

A useful approach is cost-benefit analysis. How difficult is it to abandon a mother tongue completely? What would provide sufficient incentive? It is certainly far more difficult to switch languages than costume. We use language to think. Bilingualism profoundly affects the brain, which has to become super-efficient in processing sound.[95] Some communication goals can be achieved with much less mental effort. To participate in religious rites one might memorize responses in a long-dead language. To do business abroad one might become fairly fluent in a second language. A common choice for a second language is one that is widely spoken already. This can become a lingua franca used by speakers of a variety of minority languages to communicate with each other. Yet most people never lose their mother tongue. If they can continue contact with other speakers of it, it remains the language that leaps to their lips. The strongest possible incentive to switch languages is finding it impossible to communicate with the people around you in any other way.

Place-names

People may move and take their languages with them, but place-names are fixed to the territory. Thus they can provide clues to the sequence of languages spoken in a region. The names we see on signposts today have typically gone through a long process of evolution. For example, modern French 'Amiens' is derived from the name given to the town by the Romans: *Samarobriva Ambianorum*. The first word is a Latinized version of the Celtic name meaning 'bridge on the river *Samara*' (now the Somme).[96] The second word reflects the Roman habit of affixing the name of the local tribe to place-names. In an empire as large as theirs there might be a number of similar place-names, so to clarify matters, this was Samarobriva 'of the Ambiani'. The Romans seldom completely changed place-names that they encountered in their campaigns of conquest. Roman geographers recorded

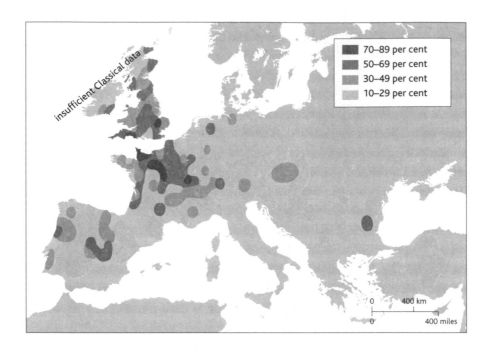

10 *The density of Celtic place-names in Classical sources. Such sources are more plentiful within the former Roman empire.*

many a settlement with a recognizably Celtic name.[97] The distribution of these names shows that Celtic languages were once spoken over a much wider area than today. [10]

While people come and go, great rivers run on. Incomers to a territory may adopt the existing name for a river even as they build new settlements and give them names in their own language. So the hydronyms (river-names) of Europe have attracted close attention. Though many European river-names are derived from specific Indo-European languages, the most ancient layer of hydronyms seems more generally Indo-European. This 'Old European Hydronymy' can be found scattered across the range of territory that Indo-Europeans are known to have settled: in Iberia north of the Tagus River, central Europe, Baltic and Slavic regions, Italy, Britain and Scandinavia, and also in Anatolia and India. For example, attempts to find a Celtic etymology for the Shin River in Scotland having failed, it has been suggested that the name derives from a supposed PIE root *sindhu* ('river'), in turn deduced from the Sanskrit name for the Indus River. That might also explain the *Sinn* (Germany), *Sinnius* (Latin, Italy) and *Senne* (Brabant).[98]

Alternatively, German linguist Theo Vennemann argues that the Old European Hydronymy is actually non-Indo-European.[99] His own preferred interpretation of these ancient river-names as allied to Basque has met with little support. Larry Trask, an expert in the Basque language, protested that 'None of the roots or suffixes listed by Vennemann for Old European looks anything like Basque, save for the root *iz- "water".'[100] Most linguists find an Indo-European origin more plausible.[101] Yet the debate is proof enough that an Indo-European etymology is not unshakable. Without evidence of a PIE origin independent of river-names themselves, 'One linguist's Indo-European names become another's proto-Basque, or Caucasian or anything else', as Mallory remarks.[102]

So what is left of the Old European Hydronymy as Indo-European if we demand solid proof of PIE roots? The Danube and the Don are derived from a PIE root that appears in early Iranian as *danu*, meaning 'river'. That is not surprising since they run through the deduced PIE homeland. Even the sceptical Mallory also allows a PIE root *drewentih*, seen in river-names as widely separated as Gaul (*Druentia*) and India (*Dravanti*).[103] It would be a leap of inference from so little to argue that the initial spread of PIE left traces in river-names before the full development of daughter languages, though there is nothing implausible about that.

We can expect field-names to be more recent than hydronyms, and yet they may be old enough to reveal linguistic layers beneath the modern. The Austrian region of East Tyrol has a complex linguistic history. After the fall of the Western Roman Empire, incoming Slavs were halted in AD 610 by a battle within the present territory of East Tyrol, creating a division between the Romance-speaking southwest and the Slavs in the rest of the region. Later Bavarian expansion converted East Tyrol into a completely Germanic-speaking region by the 15th century. Study of pasture-names can detect the former linguistic divide. There remain corresponding genetic differences.[104]

Ethnonyms

Before entering the realms of history, it is as well to brace yourself for the confusion caused by the ability to write things down. The modern name for a past people may not be the name that they used for themselves, or the one that turns up in the records of other people encountering them. One and the same people could be called by different names in different languages or at different times. People could identify themselves in different ways for different purposes, just as we do today. For example, someone today might see himself as a resident of Warsaw, a Pole, a Slav and a European, or even a New Yorker, a Pole, a Slav and an American. These modern multiple identities are no mystery. We are accustomed to the concept of nations, which may be viewed as the same as, or different from, ethnicity. We understand that language or religion may count more than birthplace in a person's self-identification. But the past, as so famously said, is a foreign country. So it is necessary here and there in what follows to explain the path that is being picked through the fog.

One principle is followed throughout. Historic peoples are here defined by their language. So the definition of a Celtic people is that they spoke a language that we can currently classify as Celtic. Peoples who spoke a language belonging to the Slavic group are classed as Slavs, and so on. This is regardless of whether we can find an ancient reference to a specific people or tribe as falling into such a category. Whole theories of ethnicity have been based on what a people were called in antiquity, when this is largely irrelevant to the classifications by language that best help us to understand the relationships between ancient peoples.

The modern names for language families were generally selected because at least some of their historic speakers identified themselves in that way, or were commonly identified by others under that name. It would be naïve to expect consistency in such ancient identifications. What happens when a colony moves away? The English speak English. So do the people of New Zealand and Australia. It would be confusing in the extreme if they all called themselves English. They do not.

The great migrations that spread a language over wide stretches of territory would inevitably (in the days before modern transport) cause the break-up of that language into separate languages of the same family. The sense of belonging to the same mother-group would weaken and eventually dissolve. People would need some means of self-identification that was more specific, such as a local tribal or geographical name.

Much has been made by some authors of the fact that there is no ancient reference to the peoples of the British Isles as Celtic,[105] or that specific definitions of the Croats as Slavs are few.[106] That may be a clue to how the people concerned regarded themselves. Neighbouring and related peoples could be rivals rather than allies and more likely to emphasize their differences than their similarities. Language gives us the broader picture.

Types of migration

Does the reviving interest in migration mean a return to an old-fashioned view of the past? Should we picture waves of invasion by conquering armies? Undoubtedly there were invasions. Many have been recorded. Yet we are also familiar with the massive migrations to the New World and Australasia in the 19th century, long after those territories had been claimed by European nations. Such migrants did not see themselves as invaders. Many were fleeing from oppression or poverty in their homelands.

If we look at the driving forces behind historic colonizations, we see an array of motives. We see restless curiosity and a desire to explore. We see the gleam of gold, which can lure the adventurer to camp in a wilderness for years in the hope of finding it. We see people seeking to escape hard times. When drought strikes, the prospect of rain could be the greatest lure of all. Yet there are other motives, religious and political, which we would scarcely guess from the material remains left behind. Projecting the present into the past is not without its dangers. Yet if we consider the great variety of reasons for mobility today, it may help us to keep an open mind about the reasons for movement in the past. Instead of waves of invasion, let us think more neutrally of waves of wanderers.

There are many kinds of mobility. Refugees may move in one desperate rush. Those with the luxury of time to plan may trickle, generation after generation, in a promising direction. A common pattern is for pioneers to find new prospects and then return home to collect family, or barter precious goods. News then spreads of routes that others may be tempted to follow. One school of thought assumes that migration only arises from population density. Certainly, overpopulation can lead to people searching out new territory, but there are methods of population control. So migration can be a choice. We can see factors which pull people in a certain direction, such as a better climate, sources of raw materials or social opportunities, and factors which push people out of their current home, such as disaster, climate change and social strife. An interplay between pull and push factors can govern migration choices, as long as transportation is within reach, together with information on attractive destinations.[107]

Movement is not always voluntary though. Millions of people were taken as slaves from Africa to the Americas. Some 50,000 British criminals were transported to America prior to the Declaration of Independence in 1776, and then about 160,000 to Australia. Orphaned and destitute British and Irish children were as little able to resist their fate when taken to the colonies in the 17th century as indentured servants, and when sent to Canada and Australia under the Empire Settlement Act of 1922 and 1937, or the Children's Act 1948.[108] Looking back to the earliest empires, we find the forced movement of millions. Entire communities were moved from one corner of the vast Assyrian empire to another. It is estimated that 4.2 million people were forcibly displaced in the three centuries of that empire.[109]

Human movement can have a massive impact, or a barely detectable one, on the cultural and genetic landscape of its destination. Much will depend on how heavily populated the destination region was beforehand. Farmers could overwhelm regions where a few hunter-gatherers roamed, since farming can support so many more people to the acre. The price is being tied to the territory, at the mercy of drought, disaster and pestilence. If farming fails, then the stark choice may be migration or starvation. Land may be deserted and open to new colonists long after farming first appeared there.

How does migration affect self-identification? Some of those fleeing hardship may see themselves as temporary refugees, but others may never return to the land of their birth. The new land becomes the homeland for their descendants. Sometimes a movement that began as an expansion of territory ends up creating separate tribes or nations, who may even become enemies in the course of time. The idea of a permanent ethnic or national identity that can be tracked through time from the Palaeolithic to the present is a chimera.

CHAPTER THREE

The First Europeans

T he Earth's climatic cycle of freeze to fry tugged humans hither and thither. Warm spells enticed early hominins out of Africa, while cold spells every 125,000 years or so drove them to extinction or withdrawal from northerly climes.[1]

Anatomically modern humans (*Homo sapiens*) crossed into Europe some 46,000 years ago.[2] At the time the Black Sea was a lake, with a land bridge to the west of it linking Europe and Asia. This was the most likely first entry point. People could also wander into Europe by a more easterly route. The Caucasus Mountains were a forbidding barrier east of the Black Sea, but a few braved it.

When forensic facial reconstruction artist Richard Neave was asked to create a reconstruction from the earliest *Homo sapiens* skull found in Europe, he commented that it looked like a mixture of modern western Eurasian, East Asian and sub-Saharan African. The continental differences we see today had yet to evolve. The 35,000-year-old skull was discovered in the Peştera cu Oase (The Cave with Bones) in Romania.[3] So how do we know that *Homo sapiens* arrived in Europe some 10,000 years before the man from Peştera cu Oase? Teeth from Grotta del Cavallo, southern Italy, have been recently reclassified as belonging to *Homo sapiens* some 45,000–43,000 years ago,[4] while an anatomically modern human jaw from Kent's Cavern, southern England, has now been redated to between 44,200 and 41,500 years old.[5] Without DNA evidence, niggling doubts may remain over whether these anatomical fragments are truly those of *Homo sapiens*. So let us look at another kind of evidence: the things our forefathers left behind.

These early arrivals were hunter-gatherers using stone tools. (Our name for the period, Palaeolithic, comes from the Greek for old and stone.) Tool use is high on the list of features that we recognize as human. Yet earlier hominins such as Neanderthals also used stone tools. *Homo sapiens* improved the tool-kit, with complex projectile weapons such as the bow and arrow and spear-thrower and dart.[6] The ancestors of the early Europeans had evolved into resourceful hunters who changed the balance of power between themselves and far larger, stronger mammals. Around 100,000 years ago in Blombos Cave in South Africa, *Homo sapiens* were also grinding and mixing ochres to make red and yellow paint.[7] Pea-sized Nassarius shells found at Blombos Cave and at the equally ancient sites of Oued Djebbana in Algeria and Skhul, Mount Carmel, Israel, were perforated as though they had been strung together into necklaces or bracelets. There were signs of wear from a leather string. If the aim was personal adornment, then these are the earliest known pieces of jewelry.[8] Art and craft are among the defining signs of human behaviour. Long before *Homo sapiens* left Africa, they were burying their dead, engaging in exchange networks and generally acting in ways that require knowledge passed on within a community, and so imply language.[9]

From another cave in South Africa comes evidence that as early as 44,000 years ago a foraging culture emerged that was ancestral to that of the San.[10] The San are among the few peoples on Earth today who still follow the way of life of our distant ancestors, hunting and foraging for food. So the San can teach us much about the first Europeans. Among them communities are small and mobile. Foragers need extensive hunting grounds to support each band, and may move with the seasons to take advantage of different food sources. A limited number of mouths can be fed this way, so fertility levels are low among nomadic hunters; late weaning spaces out births.[11] To avoid inbreeding among each small group, the habit is to take marriage partners from other bands, who may be encountered periodically.[12]

Homo sapiens had spread right across Asia and into Australia before a burst of warm weather made it possible to move north from Central Asia into the Levant and from there to Europe. [see 1] We can track the tools they left along the way. [11] Flint tools cannot be radiocarbon dated, but ancient people also used bone and antler, which can. A characteristic tool made by those spreading across Europe is the Aurignacian split-base antler point. These split-based points appear earliest in the Levant. In fact they occur there as part of the Ahmarian tool-set, prior to the development of Aurignacian types. Crucially, remains of a fully modern human were found in the Ahmarian layer at Ksar Akil, Lebanon. Split-based points occur next in southeast Europe.[13]

While the Kent's Cavern humans fit into the Aurignacian culture, the discovery at Grotta del Cavallo belongs to a distinctive form of stone-tool

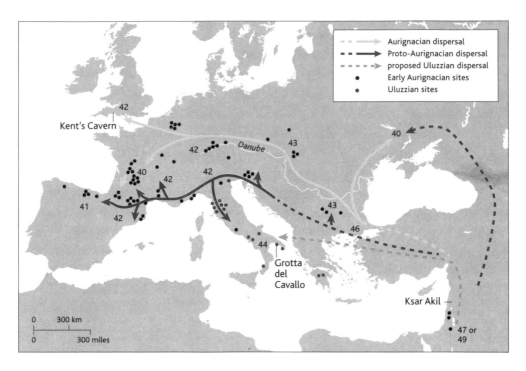

11 *The inferred dispersal routes of anatomically modern humans across Europe. The numbers are the earliest radiocarbon dates for human tools in thousands of years ago. The map shows the modern coastline, but at the time the Black Sea was a lake. There were land routes into Europe both west and east of it.*

culture known as the Uluzzian, previously thought to be Neanderthal. Claiming it for *Homo sapiens* is a challenge to those who argue that European Neanderthals had independently achieved many aspects of 'modern' behaviour. Lively debate is likely to ensue. Yet one can trace stone forms similar to the Uluzzian back to Ksar Akil in archaeological levels associated with some of the earliest modern human occupations.[14] Also, Neanderthal DNA is starting to reveal that there are significant differences between the modern human brain and that of Neanderthals, which throws into doubt their capacity for 'modern' behaviour.[15]

A third entry into Europe has been termed Proto-Aurignacian, since it shares some features with Aurignacian, such as split-based points. Its tool-set is similar to that of the Levantine Ahmarian, and included bone needles, useful for making clothing.[16]

Early DNA evidence

A trail through the Caucasus of material similar to Aurignacian shows that some people had headed for Europe by a separate route. They can be linked to sites in the Don River valley, Russia, dating from 40,000 years ago, including Kostënki 14.[17] The earliest DNA retrieved from an anatomically modern human comes from a 30,000-year-old man unearthed at Kostënki 14. Scientists were able to study his mitochondrial DNA (mtDNA). His haplogroup was U2.[18] [12]

All the satisfactorily tested mtDNA from Palaeolithic Europeans falls into haplogroup U. One sample from Nerja, Spain, and two from Hohle Fels, Germany, are classified as U*.[19] Haplogroup U descends from the African L3 via N and its daughter R. Haplogroup N and its sister M, as well as R, are all ancient in South Asia. This suggests that anatomically modern humans crossed from East Africa to Arabia and then across the Persian Gulf into Central Asia. There wide spaces opened up before them, with tempting prospects all around. Groups scattered, some to move westwards to the Levant and Europe, others to populate Asia and move on to Australasia and the Americas [see 5].

Haplogroup U* probably reached the Levant at the head of the wave of incomers from the Asian crossroads. Then came another parting of the ways. Some U carriers moved into North Africa, where U6 arose.[20] Others moved into Europe and gave birth to U4 and U5.[21] Yet more branches of U were probably born in the Levant. U3 for example does not appear in ancient DNA from Europe before the arrival of farmers from the Near East (see Table 1, pp. 26–27). U2 has its own, separate story. It sprang from its mother U in the Asian crossroads before some U2 carriers drifted off into South Asia and Europe. Today its oldest branches (U2a-c) are centred on South Asia, while U2e seems to have arisen in Europe.[22]

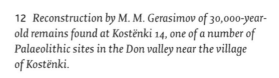

12 *Reconstruction by M. M. Gerasimov of 30,000-year-old remains found at Kostënki 14, one of a number of Palaeolithic sites in the Don valley near the village of Kostënki.*

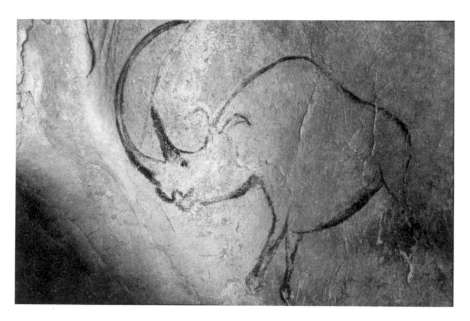

13 *This vigorous depiction of a rhinoceros is among the earliest known cave paintings. Preserved for thousands of years by a rockfall, Chauvet Cave in southern France records in lively art the species that roamed Europe in the Aurignacian era, including lions, bison and mammoths.*

Hardy hunters

The first Europeans did not only live to hunt. They were creative. Aurignacian people carved simple flutes from mammoth and bird bone.[23] Their figurines of animals include the now extinct mammoth, carved from the animal's ivory.[24] They left lively cave paintings of species that have long deserted Europe, such as lion, bison and rhinoceros.[25] [13]

The culture that followed the Aurignacian is known as the Gravettian, after La Gravette in France, where small, pointed blades used for big-game hunting were found; these became recognized as characteristic of the period from about 28,000 to 23,000 years ago in western and central Europe. Though named for a site in France, the Gravettian tool-set appears earliest in eastern Europe.[26]

Some people roamed far to the north. At Sunghir, on the East European Plain outside Vladimir, a group of reindeer hunters camped about 25,000 years ago. No doubt they had followed the herds as they moved north in the summer. These hunters were tall and massively broad-shouldered. We can picture them clad in skins and furs. Along with reindeer they hunted

---

Prehistoric transport 1: People power

People spread across the world long before the days of modern transport. As clues are found by archaeologists, sometimes in unexpected places, we are beginning to see more clearly how our distant ancestors managed to move so far. The first of our species moved on foot, so they needed to travel light. Infants would be carried. It might occur to people to use animal skin or interwoven lianas to make a sling to carry a baby. The baby-sling could be seen as a key invention. To grow larger brains after birth, our ancestors needed to sacrifice the advantage of newborns who can already run with the pack. Our young continue to develop and learn for many years – a huge investment in the future of the species. While other apes carry their young, clever *Homo sapiens* could contrive baby-slings. This freed up their arms for other activities, while protecting the helpless infant, whose brain can then continue to grow.[28]

Hunters would generally butcher large game where it was killed, rather than try to carry a whole beast miles back to camp.[29] Even so it might be convenient to tie or sling game or fish from a stick or a spear, to be carried over the shoulder of one man, or between two men. A sling on a thick pole could also carry an injured comrade. Two poles with skins strung between them would make a stretcher.

Yet why heft what could be dragged? Pulling firewood back to camp with smaller sticks piled on top of a large, forked branch might suggest the basic A-frame of the travois, used by Plains Indians of North America to drag loads.

---

mammoth and arctic fox, whose pelts would make warm clothing and bedding. The astonishing thing about their dress was the degree of ornamentation. It must have taken many patient hours to create the thousands of mammoth ivory beads that were sewn on to every item of clothing, to judge by the finds in graves. Such tailored clothing was made possible by the invention of the needle, crafted in these early days from bone. The most spectacular burial at Sunghir is that of two children. A boy aged about 13 years old and a girl about 10 years old were laid in the same grave. Each child had an outfit decorated with around 5,000 tiny ivory beads, and was accompanied by ivory pins, pendants and animal carvings, among them a simple image of a horse. The wild herds of horses on the plains added variety to the hunting.[27]

One example has been found from prehistoric Europe.[30] The same A-frame laid flat and pushed downhill over grass or snow could have sparked the idea of the sledge (also called a sled or sleigh) – a platform on runners. Both ideas probably date far back into prehistory. Sledge runners have been found in Finland from the days before farming.[31] The first sledges would have been pulled by people. The idea of harnessing animals to pull any kind of vehicle was far in the future.

Skis in the Old World and snowshoes in North America were a useful aid to getting about over snow. Rock carvings showing men on skis have been found in Norway, Sweden and Russian Karelia. [14] Remarkably, some ancient skis have survived. The oldest skis and sledge runners ever discovered were preserved in peat bogs near Lake Sindor in Russia. They date to around 6000 BC.[32]

14 *Two rock carvings depicting people on skis: (left) hunters on skis in Late Stone Age Karelia; (right) a skier in Norway in the Iron Age.*

Neanderthals

We assume these first adventurers must have encountered Neanderthals, their distant genetic cousins who had been in Europe from about 400,000 years ago.[33] Yet the arrival of *Homo sapiens* in a particular area seems generally to signal the departure of Neanderthals, who never formed a large population. It has even been suggested that *Homo sapiens* never crossed the path of a Neanderthal in Europe. In the Caucasus there is little or no overlap between the Neanderthals and the *Homo sapiens* who replaced them. There and elsewhere there are few reliably dated Neanderthal fossils younger than about 40,000 years old.[34] It was thought that Neanderthals survived longest in southwestern Iberia, though this is now in doubt.[35] It was a surprise to discover a typical Neanderthal tool-kit dated between 31,000 and 34,000 years ago at Byzovaya, in sub-arctic Russia. This site in the polar Urals may be one of the last refuges of the Neanderthals.[36]

Are we descended from Neanderthals? The simple answer is no. Neanderthals belong to a different branch of the hominin tree. Neanderthal mtDNA is different from that of modern humans. There is no sign of it in those few Palaeolithic Europeans whose mtDNA has been retrieved, or in people living today.[37] That does not rule out all genetic connection. We have many genes in common with Neanderthals, since we share a common ancestor with them. Indeed we share DNA sequences with all life on Earth. The question is whether our ancestors mated with Neanderthals and so acquired genes specific to Neanderthals, who had developed outside Africa.

Debate over archaic admixture

Did our ancestors interbreed with archaic hominins such as Neanderthals? One genetic model from modern DNA predicts two such events in human history which left a record in our code, one about 60,000 years ago in the Near East and one about 45,000 years ago in eastern Asia.[38] Similar studies suspect archaic admixture in Africa.[39] Yet an alternative model dispenses with any such events.[40]

Now that the Neanderthal genome has been sequenced from ancient DNA, it is possible to make direct comparisons. [15] A preliminary survey found that Neanderthals shared more genetic variants with the present-day people of both Europe and East Asia than with sub-Saharan Africans. That suggested

15 *A researcher collecting samples for DNA analysis from Neanderthal remains in El Sidrón Cave, Spain.*

The Ice Age

Climate change almost evicted the first Europeans. As the last glacial gripped Europe, glaciers advanced, while plants and animals retreated. At its height, around 18,000 to 20,000 years ago, ice sheets miles thick covered much of northern Europe. [16] Even before this, the population of Europe was tiny by comparison with today. It has been estimated at 4,400–5,900 inhabitants.[49] The climatic clampdown reduced Europeans to the status of an endangered species.

It was not just areas of the globe close to the poles that suffered. Levels of rainfall dropped, expanding deserts and reducing forests everywhere.

---

that Neanderthals mixed with the ancestors of non-Africans in the Middle East before the future Europeans went one way and Asians another.[41] A subsequent comparison reduced the estimate of Neanderthal input overall and found Europeans less similar to Neanderthals than populations to the east.[42] Were there two separate interbreeding events? Or could there be another explanation? The greater similarity to Europeans and Asians might simply spring from insufficient sampling of the more diverse African population.[43] The people who populated the globe beyond sub-Saharan Africa descended from a comparatively small group. That means that they would not carry the full range of human genetic diversity.[44] It might simply be chance that they were slightly more similar to Neanderthals. Coupled with genetic drift over millennia, one result could be an artificially biased genetic similarity to Neanderthals with increasing distance from Africa.[45] In other words, ancient population structure in Africa could be the key. A model taking this into account concluded that common ancestry, without any hybridization, could explain the genetic similarities between Neanderthals and modern humans.[46]

Another archaic hominin entered the picture in 2008 with the startling discovery of a strange finger bone and teeth in a remote cave in the Altai Mountains of southern Siberia. A complete mtDNA genome was extracted, which proved to be neither human nor Neanderthal.[47] The newly discovered member of the hominin family was named Denisova, after the cave in which she was found. The cold cave preserved the ancient DNA so well that scientists were also able to obtain a full nuclear genome. It revealed a girl with brown eyes, hair and skin. There is a small but significant affinity between the Denisovan DNA and that of Aboriginal Australians and New Guineans, but not mainland East Asians. So although Denisova happened to be found in the cold Altai, interbreeding with humans probably took place much further to the south, on the route to Australia.[48] This debate continues in full spate. We can expect more discoveries to keep it lively for years to come.

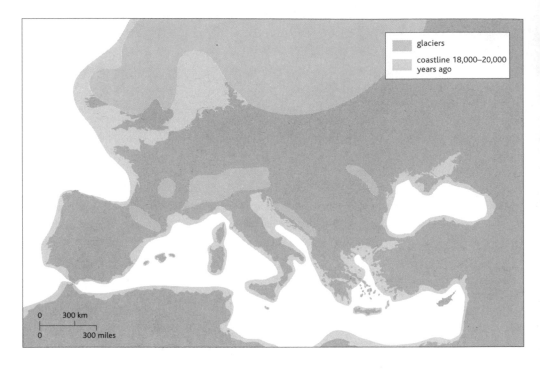

16 *Europe at the maximum of the last glaciation around 18,000–20,000 years ago. The sea level was lower than at present, creating a land bridge between Italy and Sicily and linking the British Isles to the Continent.*

On every continent humanity was squeezed into shrunken zones that could support human life. During the iciest period, the expanded Sahara cut off any escape route from Asia to the tropical refuge in western Africa. Meanwhile, the Himalayan mountains and swathes of desert and semi-desert surrounded a reduced rainforest in the northeast of the Indian subcontinent.

Europeans could take refuge in southern Europe or Asia Minor. As they disappeared in northern Europe, they increased three-fold in Cantabrian Spain. This area was clearly a major refuge. Italy and the Balkans also remained partly forested. In a belt to the north of the forested areas, steppe offered rich summer grazing for animal herds. Some hunter-gatherer bands developed a pattern of wintering in the sheltered valleys of Lower Austria and Moravia, then moving 170 km (105 miles) or more into the steppe in summer, to follow the herds. A similar pattern of summer hunting on the steppe and tundra is seen right across Siberia. Forested areas around the Black and Caspian seas may have provided winter refuges for some of these hunters.[50] Others found cover further to the east in coniferous forest refuges around Lake Baikal and also the upper reaches of the Yenisei River valley, sheltered between the Altai and Sayan mountains.[51] We shall meet some of their descendants later in the story.

Though the climate gradually improved after the ice sheets reached their maximum extent around 20,000 years ago, the ice warrior made one more attack. The big freeze came with devastating speed. The first warning was a period in which the climate oscillated from warm to cold. Then in a single year, around 12,700 years ago, northern Europe went from a temperate climate to glacial conditions.[52] Once more Europeans were threatened with extinction, but managed to survive.

CHAPTER FOUR
Mesolithic Hunters and Fishermen

The people who ranged northwards as the ice sheets melted around 10,000 years ago were still using stone tools, but their style had changed. Tiny bladelets were set into composite weapons such as harpoons. This characteristic tool-kit enables archaeologists to recognize what are called Mesolithic (Middle Stone Age) sites. These were seldom permanent. Europeans were still highly mobile. Boats would have provided the easiest way to travel, and these bold colonizers knew how to build and use them. The seas, and the big rivers that drained into them, formed a transport system through Europe. Rich with fish and shellfish, they also provided a large part of the Mesolithic diet. So it is not surprising that many Mesolithic sites hugged the coast or riverside.

The fisher-folk of Lepenski Vir, on the banks of the Danube in the Iron Gates gorge, took advantage of the plentiful fish supply to build a permanent village. Their enigmatic sculptures seem to combine man and fish. [17] Yet Mesolithic people also adapted to the advancing forest, while some climbed the greening slopes of the Alps, where they could use caves as dwellings or camp beside lakes.[1]

With so much water still locked into glaciers, the sea level was low enough at the start of this period for people to be able to walk to Britain from continental Europe across the now submerged Doggerland. From there they crossed the sea to Ireland – the first humans to do so.[2] Mesolithic hunters entered Fenno-Scandia by the land route around the Baltic.[3] Even so, the British Isles and Scandinavia were initially less appealing than more southerly regions of Europe; signs of human activity are sparse so far north until after 7,000–6,000 years ago.

17 Is it a fish or a man or a river deity? The fisher-folk of Lepenski Vir, Serbia created the first monumental sculpture in Europe.

Comparison with modern hunter-gatherers suggests that once Mesolithic people had fanned out to re-colonize the north, their population would be maintained at replacement level. Our modern overcrowded planet makes it hard to imagine how few people there were in Europe then. Population density would vary according to the terrain and climate, but has been estimated as between 0.04 and 0.1 persons per square kilometre.[4]

Pottery and climate

As the glaciers melted, water was released and rainfall increased, encouraging the spread of grassland across former deserts. Grasses with edible seeds offered themselves as a plentiful human food source. Rivers and lakes formed, providing not only drinking water but also aquatic foods. Foragers needed efficient ways to collect, store and serve this bounty, and to cook it too, as heating cereals increases their digestibility.

Clay pots were a versatile and practical solution. Though plastered baskets, wooden bowls, gourds or ostrich eggs could be used to gather and store cereals, they were not fireproof. An ancient method of cooking was to heat stones in a fire and then drop them into a clay-lined pit filled with liquid, which could be brought to the boil and left to simmer. Another method was to wrap food such as fish in clay to protect it as it cooked within a fire. Either of these two uses of clay could have suggested a more portable and permanent clay container. Pottery led to a revolution in cooking. Though there is no hard evidence that pottery-making was a female preserve, it would spring more naturally from the needs of foragers than hunters, and among surviving hunter-gatherers, men tend to hunt while women gather.

Pottery was independently invented at different times in several parts of the globe, from Amazonia to China, in response to the same needs.[5] Yet foragers were collecting wild grains long before the idea came to sow the seed. Evidence is building that pottery moved from east to west across Eurasia and south to north in Africa, independently of farmers.[6]

The first pottery was made in the Far East, thousands of years before farming. The earliest sherds so far discovered are from the Xianrendong Cave in China, radiocarbon dated to between 20,000 and 19,000 years old.[7] Early Asian pots had thick walls and a pointed base, ideal for heating foods within an open fire. The heat would be evenly distributed through the pot, helping to prevent cracks and breakages. The craft entered Japan from south

Prehistoric transport 2: Floating along

Those early peoples with a diet heavy in fish, including open-water species, must have mastered the art of boat-building.[8] A floating tree-trunk probably suggested to many an early traveller a way to cross water. A single log makes a precarious craft though. It can roll the rider off. But several roped together make a raft.

A simple canoe could be made from a hollowed-out log. Using a fallen tree would avoid the need for laborious felling with limited tools. Controlled burning could be used to reduce the labour of hollowing out. Wood decays unless preserved by anaerobic conditions such as bogs or deep water, yet hundreds of these dugout canoes have been found. Most are comparatively recent – such boats continued to be built well into the historic period. A notable exception is the logboat found at Pesse in the Netherlands, radiocarbon-dated to about 8000 BC – the oldest boat so far found in the world.[9]

Great lakes encouraged boat-building. The oldest dugout canoe in Africa was found at Dufuna, in northeast Nigeria, far from the sea but close to the once much larger Lake Chad. It has been dated to *c.* 6000 BC. It is more elegant in form than the Pesse boat. The sides are thin and the bow and stern worked to points, which would make the boat lighter to carry and speedier across water. Boat-building was increasing in sophistication.[10]

The earliest images of boats, dating from 12,000–8000 BC, are found among Mesolithic petroglyphs (rock drawings) at Gobustan, Azerbaijan, on the coast of the Caspian, classed either as a sea or the world's largest lake.[11] [18] The curved shapes of these boats suggest that they could be made of reeds. Reed stems will float. Ingenious thinkers would see the potential for bundling them together to make a raft, from which more complex reed boats evolved. In ancient Egypt, papyrus grew thickly in the Nile Delta and up to 2–3 m (5–9 ft) tall, and river boats were made from it. They are depicted in paintings and models found in the tombs of the wealthy. But the earliest depiction yet found of a Nile boat is painted on a pebble dating to the early 7th millennium BC.[12]

18 *Petroglyphs showing a boat above hunters with bows from 12,000–8000 BC. Stone 29 at Beyukdash Mountain, Gobustan, Azerbaijan.*

19 *The first pottery in Europe. A vessel from Staraya Elshanka on the Samara River, Russia. It was designed for cooking. The pointed base distributed the heat of the fire evenly.*

Siberia with the Jomon people, ancestors of the Ainu. By around 15,000 years ago ceramics had also appeared in the Russian Far East.[13]

The idea was then carried westwards across Siberia by hunter-gatherers. Around Lake Baikal in Siberia the favoured form of pot combined the pointed-base shape with an everted rim. The pots were mainly built up from clay coils, pinched together, and often left undecorated. This type of pottery reached the Samara region in the middle Volga River valley by 7000 BC; it was the first pottery in Europe. [19] From there pottery of the same type had spread to the Baltic and Scandinavia by about 5500 BC, before any sign of contact with farming (see p. 66).[14]

Mesolithic DNA

U5 is one of the oldest European mtDNA haplogroups.[15] Cheddar Man lived about 7000 BC near Cheddar, England. As mentioned in Chapter 2, mtDNA was extracted from one of his teeth by Bryan Sykes in 1997 and found to be haplogroup U5.[16] At the time, Sykes had no idea that this pioneering discovery was a portent. U5 would turn out to be the signature of the European Mesolithic. It seems to have evolved in Europe and spread northwards in the Mesolithic as the climate warmed. U5b1 probably radiated from Iberia, while U5b3 seems to have expanded along the Mediterranean coasts from a refuge in the Italian peninsula. U5a is more strongly eastern European and may have evolved in a refuge in the Balkans or elsewhere in southeastern Europe.[17] Mesolithic remains tested in central and northern Europe belong almost exclusively to the mtDNA U family. The oldest was found in someone living about 13,400 BC at Hohle Fels, in Germany, who carried mtDNA U*. These represent early adventurers north, before the last cold attack. U4, U5a, U5a1, U5b1 and U5b2 were found among later hunter-gatherers in Germany, Lithuania, Poland, Russia and Sweden, some of whom made pointed-base pottery.[18] Further to the west, Mesolithic U5 was found in Reuland-Loschbour in Luxembourg,[19] and U5b1 in Aizpea in Navarre, Spain.[20] Two remarkably well-preserved 7,000-year-old male skeletons from a mountain cave in La Braña-Arintero, in northern Spain, yielded full mitochondrial genomes. Both turned out to be U5b2c1. Taking advantage of the high DNA preservation, researchers also retrieved a significant part of their nuclear genomes. When they compared these ancient hunters to modern people, they found no resemblance to current populations from either the Iberian peninsula or other parts of southern Europe. Indeed, there was no close match to any modern population, but the ancient hunters were more like modern northern than southern Europeans.[21]

The Urals were no barrier to mobile foragers. U5a1 and U4 appear in Siberia in the 4th millennium BC, mixed with such East Asian haplogroups as C. No haplogroups linked to farming were found. So East had met West on the Siberian plain while hunting was still the way of life.[22] MtDNA haplogroup C probably expanded in the Mesolithic from the Ice Age refugia around Lake Baikal and the Yenisei valley in the Altai-Sayan mountains.[23] This haplogroup was among those carried by the pottery-makers near Lake Baikal by about 5500 BC.[24] Today 39 per cent of the Tubalar in this region carry mtDNA C4a2. They seem to be the descendants of hunter-gatherer bands who found refuge in the Altai-Sayan Mountains.[25] C4a2 was found on the European steppe among those making the distinctive pottery that passed into Europe from Lake Baikal.[26] As for mtDNA haplogroup U5, today it is widely spread over Europe, though comparatively thinly (7 per cent) outside the far northeast, which was relatively untouched by the farmers who brought new mtDNA haplogroups to Europe from the Near East. The highest level today (56.8 per cent) is among Norwegian Saami.[27]

Since it is far more difficult to extract Y-DNA from ancient remains than mtDNA, we still have no Y-DNA from so early a period. No clear picture has therefore emerged of which Y lineages dominated the European Mesolithic. Probably the direct lines of many Mesolithic men died out long ago, leaving for geneticists a jigsaw puzzle with most of the pieces missing. Ancient haplogroups such as F* (M89) or IJ* (M429/P125) may have been more common then than now. We have a few living examples of F* and IJ* in Iran.[28] Two men of F* lived at what is now Derenburg Meerenstieg in Germany in 5247 BC.[29] Farming had arrived by then, but they may have been descended from earlier hunter-gatherers.

Among the more common Y-DNA haplogroups today, a hesitant finger points towards I, which represents nearly one-fifth of the present European population. It rarely appears outside the boundaries of Europe and former

20 *Distribution of Y-DNA haplogroup I-M170. This is the only major Y-DNA haplogroup found almost exclusively among Europeans and their descendants.*

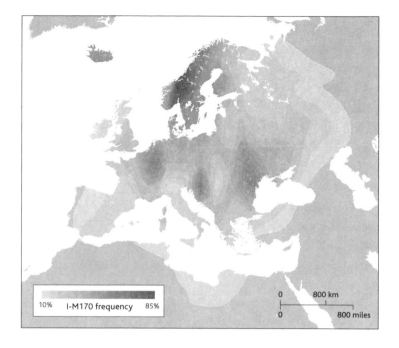

10%   I-M170 frequency   85%

0   800 km

0   800 miles

European colonies. [20] This means it is not a good candidate for arrival with farmers from the Near East. Nor does it seem the prime candidate for spread with the Indo-Europeans, since they travelled both west into Europe and east into the Indian subcontinent. The natural conclusion is that haplogroup I has been stalking around Europe since the Stone Age. Even so, we should not imagine that each of its subclades sprang up in the deep past wherever it is now found. Some of the most common seem to have travelled widely in the great wanderings after the breakdown of the Western Roman Empire. The slender clues to the original source of haplogroup I are its diversity in southeastern Europe and its correlation with known or suspected migrations from that region, mostly long after farming had taken over from fishing and hunting.

An expanding population can leave its genetic mark in a burst of new branch-lines within a haplogoup. We see such a radiation in haplogroup I2 (M438) around 6000 BC, as farming reached the Balkans, suggesting that some men carrying I2 adopted agriculture.[30] So did the fisher-folk of Lepenski Vir have I-men among them? They were already a settled and successful people when farmers arrived in their district, and were thus able to adapt to farming on equal terms, making it more likely that whatever Y-DNA they carried would survive. [31]

The subclade I1 (M253) is most diverse in Denmark, suggesting that it arose from I* there. Unlike I2, it shows no indication of expansion with farming. It has its densest distribution in Fenno-Scandia.[32] Here we find another notably successful culture of hunter-gatherers: the Ertebølle of southern Scandinavia. They had southeastern links. As we have seen (p. 63), a distinctive type of pottery spread up the Volga to the Baltic. It appears in the Ertebølle and as far west as the Low Countries around 5000 BC.[33] So did men of haplogroup I arrive with this pottery? It is possible, but by no means certain. The lineage that led to I1 separated from its brother I2 so long ago that there is no guarantee that it shared the same Ice Age refuge. Instead, the ancestor of I1 could have been the masculine partner of the U5b1 that trekked northeast from Iberia as the glaciers retreated. However it arrived, the rich fishing and hunting of this northern niche would help preserve hunter-gatherer Y-DNA.

Saami

The ancestors of the modern Saami of Fenno-Scandia probably followed herds of reindeer and other thick-coated, cold-adapted animals as they moved northwards on the retreating steppe and tundra, ending up in the Nordic lands. [21] The dominant Saami mtDNA haplogroup is U5b1b1a, surprisingly closely related to the U5b1b found among Berbers in North

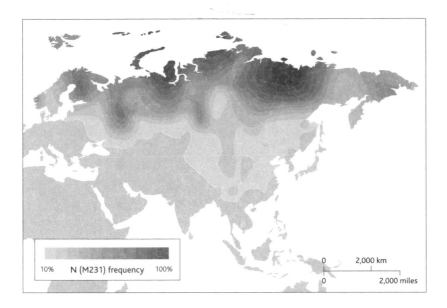

Africa. We can envisage their joint matrilineal ancestors sheltering in Iberia before going their separate ways, the ancestors of the Saami to trek northeast across Europe. Yet the paternally inherited Y-DNA tells a different story. Though haplogroup I1 is the second most common among the Saami, the most common is N1c, which spread north from Southeast Asia. So the modern Saami are a mixture of peoples who met long ago.[34]

The Y-DNA haplogroup N is densest across the whole north of Eurasia from Siberia to Norway. [22] It is estimated to have arisen about 20,000 years ago.[35] It cannot have arisen in the far north, which was uninhabitable at the time. N presumably spread northwards from Southeast Asia as the climate warmed. Interestingly, its distribution falls into the Surfing pattern (see p. 26), in which a mutation at the head of a wave of migration multiplies, reaching saturation level where it hits a geographical barrier. The absence of haplogroup N in the Americas indicates that it spread across Asia after the submergence of the Bering land bridge.[36] The haplogroup is common today among widely separated peoples who turned from hunting

21 (opposite) A tent-dwelling Saami family in Norway between 1890 and 1900, warmly wrapped against the Nordic cold. Even today some Saami remain semi-nomadic reindeer herders.

22 (above) The distribution of Y-DNA haplogroup N (M231) tells a story. This haplogroup sprang from ancestors in Southeast Asia. It was carried northwards by hunters following herds of cold-adapted animals as the climate warmed after the Last Glacial Maximum.

to herding reindeer in historic times, such as the Saami at the western end of its range, and the Yakuts towards the eastern end.[37]

Within Europe, subclade N1c1 (M178) is strong among peoples speaking Uralic languages, reaching 70 per cent in the eastern Finns.[38] The western branch of the Uralic family probably arrived in Finland with the Comb Ware culture between 4000 and 3000 BC. Saami seems to have developed as a distinct language there in the Iron Age.[39] A genome-wide study of Finnish Saami showed an average 6 per cent East Asian ancestry today.[40]

The Saami spread into Scandinavia about 650 BC. They may have been reinforced at around that time by a new influx from the Volga-Ural region. Some Saami carry the Asian mtDNA haplogroup Z1a. This could have arrived in Finland earlier, except for one factor. The common ancestor of Z1a in Finns, Saami and folk of the Volga-Ural area has been calculated at just 700 BC.[41]

The Saami are famed for their constancy to the reindeer. Until well into the historic period they continued to hunt these animals. The Viking Ottar told King Alfred that he loaned six tame deer to the Saami as decoys, enabling them to catch wild deer.[42] By the 11th century AD, the Saami were beginning to turn from hunting to herding.[43] It was a slow process, and incomplete to this day, for wild herds still exist in Norway and Finland.[44]

Uralic languages

The hardy speakers of Uralic languages long ago braved the icy forests of the far north, and many still live there today. [23] An exception to this picture is Hungarian, which arrived in Europe in the Middle Ages with the Magyars, sweeping up the Danube from the steppe (Chapter 16). In terms of numbers of native speakers, Hungarian is also the major language of the family, with some 14 million speakers, including expatriates, followed by Finnish with about 5 million. By contrast, the speakers of some of the more northerly languages have dwindled to a few hundred. While Saami is not so endangered, its speakers number no more than about 35,000.[45] The family takes its name from the deduction that the parent language – Proto-Uralic – developed near the Ural Mountains.[46] An ancestral language was probably spoken somewhere in the Sayan region of south-central Siberia.[47]

This language family is usually divided into two branches: the Samoyedic languages, spoken east of the Urals, and the Finno-Ugric languages to the

23 *Map of the present distribution of the Uralic languages. Hungarian dominates today in the number of its speakers, but geographically it is an outlier. It arrived in what is now Hungary in the Middle Ages, having travelled far from its northeastern relatives Khanty and Mansi.*

west. [24] Proto-Uralic was a language of hunter-gatherers: it had no words for farming. This is as we would expect if it was spoken in the north, where the Mesolithic lifestyle continued for so long unchanged. It is plausibly argued that Proto-Uralic was spoken among the people of the Ljalovo or Pit-Comb Ware culture (5000–3650 BC) around the Volga-Oka region. From there the related Comb Ware culture penetrated the forests of northeastern Europe from eastern Fenno-Scandia to the Urals.[48] That would fit the linguistic picture of a group splitting away westwards to develop Proto-Finnic, the ancestor of the Finnic branch.

The Fenni make their first appearance in the written record as a people on the furthermost edge of the world known to the Romans, beyond Germania and the Balts. From the Roman point of view, they were 'astonishingly wild'

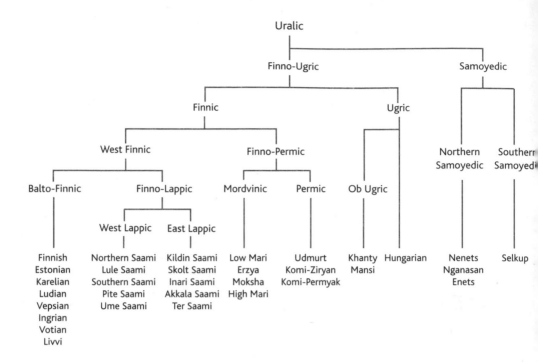

24 *The Uralic language family is usually divided into two branches: the Samoyedic languages, spoken east of the Urals, and the Finno-Ugric languages mainly spoken to the west. Hungarian is linked to two languages spoken in the Asian part of Russia.*

and dependent on hunting. 'Yet they count their lot happier than that of those who groan over field labour, sweat over house building and venture in hope and fear of their own and other men's fortunes', as Tacitus wrote.[49] The Comb Ware culture extended south as far as the Vistula, suggesting that Finnic speakers once roamed over a larger territory than today. Even in historic times Finnic speakers occupied the northern half of what is now Latvia, leaving place-names of Finno-Ugrian origin.[50]

DNA from Pitted Ware sites

Scandinavian archaeologists were intrigued by the appearance of foragers in the region as late as 2800–2000 BC, long after farming had arrived. These people hunted seal and wild boar, and fished the teeming Baltic waters.[51] They probably traded seal oil and furs to farmers inland or further south. Their sites, mainly along the coast or islands between Sweden and Finland, are marked by masses of a kind of pottery named Pitted Ware after its decoration. Culturally, Pitted Ware represents the westernmost extension of the Comb Ware and Pit-Comb Ware tradition.[52] One school of thought contended that the Pitted Ware culture was the result of local people returning to hunting and fishing after an initial experiment with farming.[53] Others have argued for the Pitted Ware makers as an ethnically distinct group.[54]

Here were hypotheses that could be put to the test of genetics. MtDNA samples were taken from human remains from three Pitted Ware sites on the island of Gotland, which were compared to samples from early farming sites elsewhere in Sweden. There was no relationship. Almost all of the hunter-gatherers carried mtDNA U4 or U5. The farmers had a different collection of haplogroups, which will be discussed in the section on Neolithic DNA (Chapter 5).[55] A second study managed to extract 249 million base pairs of genomic DNA from three of the hunter-gatherers from Gotland and a Neolithic farmer from Sweden. This enabled them to make comparisons with modern-day genomes. They found the farmer was genetically most similar to present-day people living in southern Europe and Anatolia, in sharp contrast to the hunter-gatherers, whose distinct genetic signature is closest to that of people living around the Baltic.[56] So we can conclusively say that the Pitted Ware people were not local farmers returning to the hunting way of life.

What language did they speak? That we do not know for sure. They left no writing or obvious cultural descendants. The Pitted Ware culture faded away eventually, dispersed or absorbed by Bronze Age arrivals. The genetic runes are hard to read. Finno-Ugric speakers today carry a pattern of mtDNA haplogroups similar to other Europeans, apart from higher levels of U4 and U5, and a light scattering of the more exotic Z1a.[57] U4d may turn out to be a clue. It was identified in one of the hunter-gatherers from Gotland.[58] This haplogroup was only recognized in 2008 from complete mitochondrial genome sequencing. Since present databases generally contain results from much more limited mtDNA testing, the modern distribution of U4d is unknown. It certainly includes some Tatars from the Volga-Ural region of Russia. They are descendants of the Bulgar and Kipchak Turkic tribes who in the 8th century AD settled on the Volga, where they mingled with Ugric-speaking peoples.[59] So perhaps the Pitted Ware people spoke a now lost branch of Uralic.

CHAPTER FIVE
The First Farmers

The change from foraging to farming was one of the great human revolutions. Control of food sources has an obvious appeal. Farming supports many more people per acre than foraging.[1] It was the beginning of a population explosion, which would lead to further innovations and ultimately the first civilizations. It was a profound change in human lifestyle.

The Near East is one of the handful of heartlands from which farming spread. That has long been accepted. Yet our picture of the process has gradually changed. The civilizations of Mesopotamia and ancient Egypt captured the attention of archaeologists from the earliest days of antiquity-hunting. Their temples and pyramids could scarcely be missed. Their wealth of art and craft seduced the eye. [26] Their writings made their societies comprehensible. An arc from the Nile to the Tigris and Euphrates, christened the 'Fertile Crescent', was seen as the homeland of farming. By the 1960s attention had shifted to its 'hilly flanks'.[2] [25]

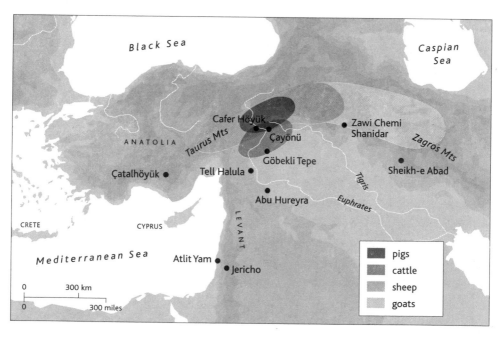

25 (opposite) The heartland of the Near Eastern Neolithic, showing the regions where sheep, goats, pigs and cattle were first domesticated, and major sites mentioned in the text.

26 (right) Wheat and flax harvests, depicted in the tomb of Sennedjem, Deir el-Medina, Egypt, c. 1300 BC.

Plenty of rain and river water made for lush vegetation in the hills where the Levant meets Anatolia. Here grew the wild cereals and pulses that became the cultivated staples of European diet. Here were wild herds of sheep, goats, cattle and pigs that could be domesticated. It has taken the techniques of modern archaeology to uncover in seeds and bones the clues to the development of farming. Now we have evidence of plant cultivation and stock-breeding over five millennia before the first civilizations. There was a leap in understanding in the 21st century. By the mid-1990s a consensus had formed that animal domestication began around 10,000 years ago. Then scientists gained new tools: genetic analysis and improved radiocarbon dating. Fascinating new findings have pushed that date back to 11,000 years ago. The native sheep and goats of the Taurus and Zagros mountains were the earliest domesticates, with pigs and cattle following.

While in the 1990s the southern Levant was seen as the core area of crop and animal domestication, new techniques shifted the spotlight northwards. Studies of animal bones show that domestication in the hills around the heads of the Tigris and Euphrates was earlier than in the Levant. The first crop cultivation also flourished on higher ground, where fields could be rain-fed, rather than needing irrigation.[3]

The first farmers were cautious. They did not abandon hunting immediately the idea occurred of rearing animals for meat. At first, domesticated animals contributed only a small proportion of the total meat in their diet. By 6500 BC that had risen to 40–45 per cent within the heartland of the Neolithic. It was this increasingly confident new way of life that was exported south into the Levant.[4] Wild einkorn wheat is found today all over the Taurus and Zagros mountain region, but the domesticated forms are

The pace of change

The pace of technological change has speeded up dramatically over the millennia. Our ancestors spent many thousands of years as hunter-gatherers, during which time the pace of change was glacially slow. It is not that there was no innovation. Humans have always innovated. It just took a lot longer. The pace of change shifted up a gear with the transition to farming and again with industrialization. A key factor seems to be the number of people within a communicating group.

A larger community gives greater scope for invention. The greater the number within a group, the more likely it is that among them will be an inventive type who thinks up something new. Inventors are a tiny percentage of any society. Among the small hunting bands before farming, it might be generations before an exceptionally creative individual cropped up in any given band. Also, the larger the communicating group, the greater the exchange of ideas, and the less chance of innovations being lost.

Farming could support larger communities, and industrialization created huge cities. Both can produce a surplus beyond immediate subsistence needs. They can support the occasional inventive soul through the trial-and-error process of innovation. Just as importantly, the economic basis of a society dictates the communication range of any individual within it. Innovation can increase that range. Agriculture generated writing. Industry generated communication devices such as the telephone.[5]

Inventors these days can not only build upon a vast knowledge base established by generations before them, but also test their ideas among like-minded people around the globe. Are we seeing another step-change in the pace of innovation as a result of the Internet? It could be. Will today's inventors find answers to the problems we have created through our ability to increase the world's population? We shall have to wait and see.

genetically linked to the wild variety of southeastern Turkey. It is in this region too that emmer wheat was probably domesticated.[6]

Before cultivation even began, abundant resources in the region where the Levant meets Anatolia, and down the Mediterranean edge of the Levant, encouraged hunting and foraging groups into a more settled life-style. The best-known of these sedentary foraging cultures is the Natufian (12,500–9500 BC). The Natufian people built villages of round pit-houses on stone foundations. Similar villages grew up at the junction of the Taurus and Zagros foothills from about 10,000 BC.[7] Such structures could be built from materials ready to hand: loose stones and fallen tree branches.

The density of population in the hilly flanks of the Fertile Crescent must have been far higher than average for hunter-gatherers.[8] Population density seems to be one of the crucial triggers of technological change. Then technological change can itself increase productivity from the land, making possible a yet higher population density.

Early experiments

Foragers made use of the stands of wild wheat, barley and rye that had sprung up along the edge of the upland zone roamed by wild sheep and goats. Peas and lentils are native to the same region. The earliest tentative experiments in plant management can be discerned 12,000 years ago, though crop domestication was not well established until 8000 BC, when the climate was improving. The first clear evidence of domesticated wheat comes from Cafer Höyük and Çayönü, in the hills near the headwaters of the Tigris and Euphrates. Meanwhile both sheep and goats were domesticated in the mountain and piedmont band stretching from the northern Zagros to southeastern Anatolia. These closely related species are suited to hill country.[9] [27]

Farming began before the first Near Eastern pottery was made, so the earliest farming period there is known as Pre-Pottery Neolithic A (PPNA). Populations grew rapidly at this time.[10] Yet once humans were in close contact with animals, diseases could spread from one to the other.[11] Brucellosis can pass to humans from goats, cows, dogs and pigs. Even today it remains a major cause of death and disruption in endemic areas. Tuberculosis can be caught from cows and leishmaniasis from dogs. DNA of the tubercle bacillus has been discovered in human remains from Atlit Yam, a now submerged Pre-Pottery Neolithic village in the Levant.[12]

27 Wild sheep. The first domesticated sheep lacked the fleece of modern breeds, which was the result of selective breeding for wool c. 4000 BC.

In the Zagros Mountains people had begun abandoning their cave dwellings to create villages while still hunter-gatherers. Some of those villages, such as Zawi Chemi Shanidar in northern Iraq, bridge the change from foraging to farming.[13] In western Iran the Pre-Pottery Neolithic site at Sheikh-e-Abad in Kermanshah province includes the remains of a house and a ritual space decorated with horns of sheep and goats. It was founded by farmers c. 9810 BC, making it one of the earliest Neolithic villages in Southwest Asia.[14]

Spectacular discoveries in recent years have illuminated the very start of our love of monuments and ritual spaces. At Göbekli Tepe in Turkey the world's earliest megalithic monument has been uncovered. Remarkably, its first phase dates to around 9000 BC, a period when foragers were turning into farmers. Circles of standing stones are adorned with elaborate animal reliefs. [28] The T-shaped pillars look like stylized human bodies; some are carved with arms and hands.[15]

28 A T-shaped standing stone at Göbekli Tepe, Turkey, carved with animals in relief.

From the majestic stone temples of Malta to the massive mound of Newgrange, in Ireland, megalithic monuments have captured the imagination of millions. How were such huge stones moved? Who built these structures? What was their purpose? They are the grandest monuments from the times before history. The people who made them left no written records. Naturally, speculation has run wild. Over the centuries they have been attributed to giants, magicians or aliens. What a lack of faith in our own species! Gradually, answers to the puzzles have appeared. A picture emerges at Göbekli Tepe of Neolithic farmers banding together to honour their dead. Human flesh is mortal, but stone may stand eternal as a symbol of the departed. Thus communities could create a sense of continuity.[16]

It is a much smaller and later monument that provides the clue to purpose. An 8th-century BC stele from Zincirli in southeastern Turkey depicts a royal official named Kuttamuwa at his funerary banquet. Kuttamuwa himself tells us so. The text on the stele states that Kuttamuwa commissioned the stele during his lifetime, and that at its inauguration in the mortuary chapel offerings were made to various gods. The most enlightening line explains that one of the offerings was 'a ram for my soul that will be in this stele'. It is the first inscription to make clear that ancient people of the Near East could visualize their soul being transferred to a memorial stone after death.[17]

Farming starts to spread

Farming reached Cyprus by about 9000 BC.[18] This is a case study in colonization. Though hunter-gatherers might make occasional visits to islands in the Mediterranean, they did not take to permanent island life. These islands were settled by farmers. They had to bring stock and seed with them; the islands were not home to wild goats, sheep, pigs or cattle. So here we have a clear-cut example of the spread of farming by migration. We can compare events on Cyprus with continental Europe to see whether the pattern there too resembles colonization. Farming arrived on the island in the PPNA, but sheep did not appear until the following period.[19]

The next stage of development in the Near East (c. 8550–6600 BC) is conventionally labelled the Pre-Pottery Neolithic B (PPNB). By about 7500–7000 BC diverging economies had crystallized. There were farmer-herders living on domesticated crops and livestock; there were herders supplementing their

Prehistoric transport 3: Out to sea

Coastal trips might be managed in a light craft. Venturing out into the open seas is a bolder enterprise. It requires not only a seaworthy craft, but also some means of navigation beyond sight of land. The colonization of Cyprus *c*. 9000 BC shows that early farmers could move themselves and their stock across the sea. But until recently it was thought that before the Neolithic period our ancestors hugged the coastline and were not capable of long-distance seafaring. Great was the surprise therefore when two camp-sites of an earlier period were discovered on the coast of Cyprus. Flints thought to be a millennium older than the first permanent settlements in the island were found. Now we can picture people in small boats paying seasonal visits to the island before settlers arrived. These were daring voyages of at least 80 km (50 miles) across open water.[20]

It was also a puzzle to find that some Mesolithic hunter-gatherers on the Greek mainland used tools made of obsidian from the island of Melos. The possibility that these were actually Neolithic artifacts that had intruded into lower layers has now been ruled out by direct dating. The sea route to obtain this volcanic glass would have included crossings of about 15–20 km (9–12 miles) between islands.[21]

Early farmers ventured even further than Cyprus by sea. They colonized Crete. It is now thought that most of the early farming colonies along the Mediterranean coast were also planted by seafarers. On the island of Andros, in the Cyclades, depictions of seagoing craft were scratched into rock. They have been dated by luminescence to *c*. 3520 BC.[22] These graffiti seem to show high-prowed rowing boats, like those in a Minoan fresco on Santorini (Thera), also in the Cyclades. [29] Though the discovery of the graffiti is exciting, these images are millennia later than the boats that the early farmers must have used. The construction of the earliest seagoing vessels is unknown.

29. Detail from the Minoan flotilla fresco in the West House at Akrotiri, on the Greek island of Santorini (Thera).

diet by hunting, and coastal farmers who were also fishermen; and there were nomadic foragers. With these divisions come the first hints of tribal life.[23]

Farmers took Near Eastern wheat, barley, sheep and goats from eastern Iran to the Indus Valley region, where they settled at Mehrgarh, in Pakistan, around 7000 BC. In this region local species were also domesticated. They were to become staples of the economy that supported the Indus Valley civilization: zebu cattle, river buffalo, cotton and sesame.[24] Farmers had also by now set sail from Cyprus to Crete.[25] It made sense to move east and west, following the latitudes where farming had begun, for the climate would be suitable for the crops and animals domesticated in the Near East. Not everywhere within those latitudes was suitable though. High altitudes make for a cooler climate and were avoided.[26] Water sources were essential.

In the Near Eastern farming belt, a new kind of settlement appeared. In striking contrast to the round houses of the Natufian period, these villages evolved into complexes of rectangles. For the first time, people were fashioning their own building materials. Walls were built of sun-dried mud brick, plastered over. Roofs were formed from felled timbers. Examples include Çatalhöyük, begun around 7400 BC, and Çayönü, occupied between 7400 and 6800 BC, both in Turkey, and Abu Hureyra in Syria. They were conglomerates of buildings without streets. People moved around on the flat roofs, entering their houses by ladders leading down from them through hatches. [30] Such a huddle would give protection from predators but lacked the characteristics of truly urban living such as public buildings.[27]

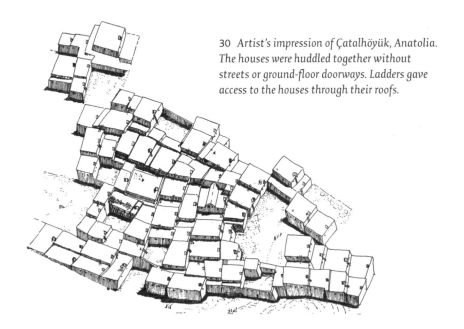

30 Artist's impression of Çatalhöyük, Anatolia. The houses were huddled together without streets or ground-floor doorways. Ladders gave access to the houses through their roofs.

It has been tentatively proposed that pottery entered the Near East from Central Asia.[28] This appealing idea faces a major problem. The earliest pottery in the Near East is different from the V-shaped ware of East Asia (see Chapter 4). A simple type found widely across the Upper Mesopotamian plains was flat-bottomed and not designed for use in cooking. Placed over an open fire, the base would heat up faster than the sides and cracks would appear. The clay was heavily tempered with chaff or other plant material, making it too porous to store liquids. The type is known as coarsely made, plant-tempered (CMPT) ware. Well-fired CMPT pots were made from around 6550 BC, such as examples from Tell Sabi Abyad, Syria.[29] [31]

Why the different approach to pottery? Food was not boiled over a fire in the early days of pottery-making in the Near East. Boiling was achieved by updating the ancient method of heating stones. At Çatalhöyük balls of clay were heated up and placed into containers with food and liquid.[30] Grain was not boiled; it was ground into flour, then made into bread, baked in an oven.[31] The pots were even made differently. Early Near Eastern pottery was of sequential slab construction, not coil. Furthermore, there was a phase of experimentation with sun-baked ceramics from about 7000 BC, leaving behind a trail of crumbling sherds in northern Mesopotamia. That is a clear indication of local invention. The same slab technique has been found as far east as Mehrgarh in Pakistan, and as far west as Merimda in the Nile Delta.[32]

Around 6800 BC at Çatalhöyük cooking methods changed. Clay cooking balls went out of use and cooking pots appeared. Their function is clear. Not only do they show the surface sooty smudging that we expect from a pot put over a fire, but they are adapted to the purpose. The new pots were large, thin-walled and mineral-tempered. Experiments have shown that

31 Pottery of 6600–6500 BC from Tell Sabi Abyad, Syria. These flat-bottomed pots were not used for cooking over a fire. Made in various shapes and sizes, they would be useful for storage.

heat transfer is more efficient in mineral-tempered pots than in organic-tempered ones. The rounded base protected them from cracking in the fire, just like the earliest pots from the Far East and Africa.[33] With cooking pots, food would be free from the wood ash transferred on cooking balls.

The surprise in recent years has been the discovery of fine pottery at sites in Syria and southeastern Turkey in levels earlier than the coarse ware. This pottery has thinner walls, is made of a finer, mineral-tempered clay and is thus suited to burnishing and painting. Burnishing is a time-consuming technique that makes pottery harder and more waterproof. The pot was rubbed inside and out with a smooth object, such as leather, a pebble or bone, until it became glossy. When fired this gave a lustrous finish. The pots were mainly dark grey, but could be painted in stripes. Such loving attention to pot-creation would make an expensive product; not surprisingly the results are thin on the ground, compared to CMPT. These sophisticated wares appear around 7000–6700 BC, immediately above deposits entirely devoid of ceramics. That suggests they were not made locally, but came initially from elsewhere.[34] The source is so far unknown, but this fine ware springs from the sequential slab construction tradition of the Near East.[35]

The technique was used in central Anatolia before 6400 BC and exported westwards to the southeast of the Sea of Marmara, even reaching a few sites near the southern Danube. The people using it around Marmara lived in rectangular houses of mud brick or wood, clearly modelled on central Anatolian sites such as Çatalhöyük.[36] Farming was filtering into Europe.

Crisis forces movement

The burgeoning farming communities may have over-exploited the land. Constant cultivation, over-grazing and tree-felling would lead to erosion and loss of fertility. The first woodworking tools were made in the PPNA period: heavy-duty axes for tree felling and smaller tools for carpentry. Sedentary societies would need to clear land for planting. They might also need to manage the remaining forest to provide a constant source of timber for building and fuel. The rectangular structures of PPNB made use of massive beams and posts.[37]

The farmers could scarcely be blamed though for the crisis that struck the region around 6200 BC. A far-distant event – a huge North American post-glacial lake bursting into the Atlantic – shook the climate across the

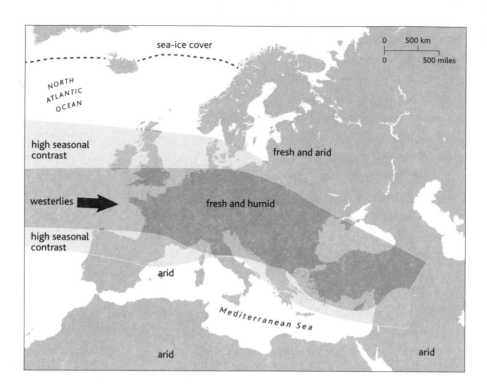

32 *An outpouring of glacial water from North America into the Atlantic c. 6200 BC created hyper-arid conditions around parts of the Mediterranean, and cooler and wetter conditions in western and central Europe.*

northern hemisphere. The result was hyper-arid conditions in southern Iberia and Italy, North Africa and the southern Near East. North of that belt were bands of marked seasonal swings, sandwiching between them a cool and wet belt from the Atlantic to Anatolia. [32] This event had far-reaching consequences. It hit foragers as well as farmers. Across the northern Mediterranean and along the Danube, many forager sites were abandoned. Farmers abandoned Cyprus and a number of sites in the Near Eastern cradle of farming, while new farming sites suddenly appeared in northwest Anatolia, Thrace, Macedonia, Thessaly and Bulgaria, areas which offered better conditions for rain-fed cereal farming.[38] The earliest farmers on Cyprus, Crete and the Greek mainland had made no pottery. Their culture was derived from the Pre-Pottery Neolithic of the Near East. The new wave of farmers after 6200 BC carried pottery with them.[39]

Çatalhöyük was one of a number of sites abandoned around this time. Further south, Jericho was deserted along with other PPNB settlements of the Levant.[40] As groups of farmers looked for new areas to settle, there was piecemeal migration on to the plains of the Tigris and Euphrates, the Mediterranean coast, and the banks of the Karkeh River in what is now southwest Iran.[41]

Social upheaval on this scale is seldom stress-free. We can imagine starvation, fighting over scarce resources and the breakdown of the familiar social order. In the Lake District of Anatolia, within the central western Taurus Mountains, four sites show fortifications being built and large-scale destruction by fire coinciding with the crisis. Unburied victims of the fires are the best evidence that these settlements were razed by enemies. In all four cases there is a break in occupation after the signs of strife. It is a similar, though less clear-cut, picture in eastern Anatolia at Mersin-Yumuktepe and at Tell Sabi Abyad in northern Syria.[42] A young man was shot in the back by an arrow at Aktopraklık in northwest Anatolia at around this time, but buried normally, so that may be an unrelated incident.[43]

Languages and Y-DNA

One language family is clearly linked to the spread of farming from the Near East. The Afro-Asiatic family includes ancient Egyptian and other languages that appear in early written records, such as Akkadian in Mesopotamia. There has been much debate over the birthplace of Proto-Afro-Asiatic. Some linguists have argued that it dates back long before the Neolithic and arose along the African coast of the Red Sea or in the Ethiopian Highlands. Yet Proto-Afro-Asiatic incorporated farming terms.[44] That does not rule out a predecessor language arising in east or northeast Africa and being carried into the Levant. Languages change along with their speakers. As people adopted farming, so they would need words to describe what they were doing.

There is a genetic hint of arrivals from Africa. The African mtDNA L2a1 has been found at the farming settlement of Tell Halula in Syria at the pre-pottery level.[45] So far no ancient Y-DNA has been extracted from any remains in the Near East, but the present distribution of subclades of Y-DNA E1b1b1 (M35.1) across both the northern and southern coasts of the Mediterranean is a clue that it was the male partner of L2a1. The paucity of any branch of E1b1b1 (M35.1) today in the Caucasus and the Indus Valley suggests that this haplogroup was not involved in Neolithic movements eastwards and northwards from the Zagros Mountains. It may have arrived in the Levant from North Africa once the desert had receded enough to allow passage. Thus it would not have taken part in the very earliest stages of the Neolithic in the hilly flanks of the Fertile Crescent, but moved north gradually to join the farmers. Then the subclades of E1b1b1 helped to spread farming around the Mediterranean.

In North Africa there is an east–west cline in the subclade E1b1b1b1a (M81), with genetic diversity increasing towards the Near East. The estimates of the time to the most recent common ancestor (TMRCA) suggest a largely Neolithic origin. So it seems that Afro-Asiatic-speaking pastoralists from the Near East dispersed across North Africa, generating the Berber languages and ancient Egyptian.[46]

The Chadic languages of Africa, spoken around Lake Chad, are related to the Berber group. Yet there is a marked correlation between Chadic and a completely different haplogroup, R1b1c (V88). How could that come about? R1b1c appears in the Levant. Picture an R1b1c (V88) man deciding to marry into a distant village. He would need to learn the language of the villagers, which in our hypothetical case was Proto-Afro-Asiatic. His descendants might make quite a tribe of their own within a few generations, but closely allied to other Afro-Asiatic speakers who happened to be dominated by E-M81. So groups of farmers leaving for North Africa from that source population would carry at least those two haplogroups. Clannishness might ensure that the tribe of R1b1c (V88) then mainly wandered its own way. The distribution of the haplogroup suggests that it moved south across the Sahara to Lake Chad, leaving a pocket of V88 in what is now the Siwa Oasis near the western border of Egypt. This is consistent with a deduction from linguistics that Proto-Chadic emerged about 5000 BC among a people who had migrated to Lake Chad across the Sahara.[47] Among the Libyan Tuareg, some R1b1c (V88) can be found among groups mainly carrying E-M81 and E1b1a1a1g (U175).[48]

Another haplogroup found in North Africa is J1 (M267). Today there is a strong correlation between Y-DNA J1 and speakers of Arabic, which belongs to the Semitic branch of the Afro-Asiatic family. Akkadian is an early representative of this branch. Among its modern relatives are Amharic, Hebrew and Maltese. Arabic-speaking Egyptians, Kuwaitis and Jordanians have far more J1 than J2 (M172), whereas the opposite is true for Persian-speaking Iranians.[49] This makes it difficult to disentangle the earlier movements of

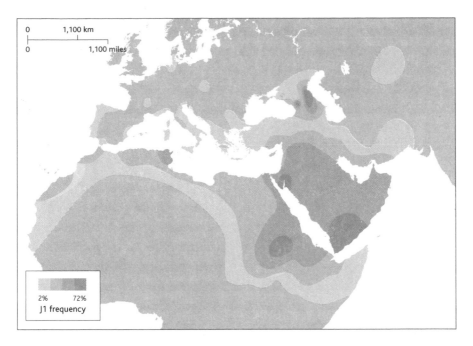

33 *The distribution of Y-DNA haplogoup J1 (M267) can be linked both to the spread of farming and the Arab conquests in the early Middle Ages.*

J1 from its later spread with the Arab expansion. When Arabs burst across North Africa in AD 709, they encountered peoples speaking Berber and Coptic (the descendant of ancient Egyptian). The Arabs went on to conquer much of Iberia by AD 718, as well as Crete, Cyprus, Malta, Sicily and parts of southern Italy – all areas in which J1 might have arrived earlier with farming. Prior to the discovery of markers distinguishing subclades of J1, attempts to calculate the various J1 dispersals were complex.[50]

The long and convoluted story of J1 is gradually becoming clearer. Today the greatest density of J1 centres on the southern Levant, if all its subclades are included. [33] Without subclades the parent J1* clusters most strongly in the Zagros/Taurus mountain region, the cradle of the Neolithic.[51] J1 no doubt spread from there with farming. It is found at a low level in Europe and appears in the Caucasus with non-Afro-Asiatic languages.[52] The association with the Semitic languages seems to begin within the large subclade J1b2 (P58). J1b2 is found in nearly half the men who report themselves members of the hereditary Jewish priesthood (Cohanim).[53] It also has a strong presence in Palestine and Jordan. The highest diversity of J1b2

(P58) is found in the Zagros/Taurus region. High diversity provides a clue to origin. So men carrying haplogroup J1b2 (P58) may have helped to take pastoralism into the Levant.[54] Proto-Semitic probably arose in the Copper Age.[55] So it may turn out that J1b2 (P58) pre-dates Proto-Semitic by millennia. A rare form of J1b2 with the marker M368 has been reported among the Avars in Dagestan in the northeast Caucasus, where a completely different language is spoken.[56] The subclade J1b2b (L147) appears much larger and promises to contain many men whose ancestors spoke a Semitic language in the Copper Age.

It has been argued that J2 is connected to a very old Middle Eastern language, nicknamed the 'banana language' from the syllabic duplication which appears in some words in Sumerian texts, such as Inanna, goddess of love.[57] Enthusiasts see it as the tongue of Mesopotamia before the Sumerians, which left clues in words absorbed by Sumerian. It is a notion to fire the imagination. Critics detect more imagination than substance. Sadly for this interesting idea, the existence of any such language is doubted. Under the intense linguistic lens, the vision evaporates like morning dew. Borrowing from multiple sources can be detected in Sumerian. Words from different languages were travelling with the inventions they named. As for the syllable duplication, it seems to be a naming practice.[58] The same pattern is found in the neighbouring Elamite language of southwest Iran.[59] Who knows where it first appeared?

Although Iran has some of the highest levels of J2 in the world, the greatest genetic diversity within the haplogroup is found today in southeastern Anatolia, northwestern Iraq and among Palestinians living in coastal Israel.[60] As with J1, the pattern hints at a spread from the heartland of the Neolithic. [34]

The Caucasus and Armenian plateau are particularly interesting, as they show only spasmodic signs of human occupation before farmers settled there. Genetics testifies to the predominantly Near Eastern descent of the varied Caucasian populations.[61] Languages have survived in the Caucasus from language families other than the Afro-Asiatic that dominates the Near East today, giving us some idea of how complex the linguistic landscape once was. Proto-Afro-Asiatic may originally have been spoken in the Levant, while other languages sprang from the Zagros/Taurus region.

The Caucasus is a patchwork of many languages in various language families, isolated from each other by the mountainous terrain. We can picture a

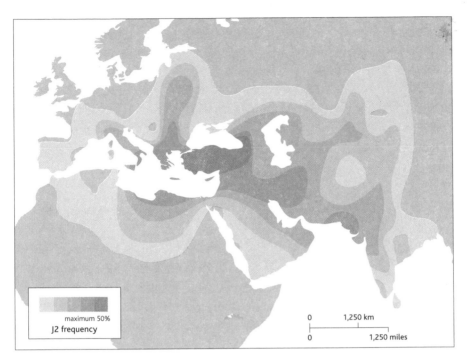

34 *The distribution of Y-DNA haplogoup J2 (M172) mimics the spread of farming from the Near East more widely than J1, since it reaches India. J2 was probably involved in many later migrations too.*

small group of individuals arriving in each pocket of habitable land. Contact with even a neighbouring valley might be rare. Over the millennia, some of the founding Y-DNA haplogroups in a particular valley would gradually die out by chance as men of those lineages had only daughters. Other haplogroups would increase as men of those lineages happened to have more sons. Geneticists call the process genetic drift. The end result is a striking correspondence between genes and language trees in the north Caucasus.

Within each of four language groups a particular haplogroup is predominant. In the small isolated population of the Kubachi, haplogroup J1* (M267) has become virtually fixed. Their language forms part of the Dagestan family, in which J1* predominates. Although J1 also occurs in the neighbouring Nahk language group, the dominant haplogroup there is J2a1b* (M67). Among the Shapsugs of the northwest Caucasus G2a1c2a (P303) strongly dominates, and it also appears among the other members of their language group. G2a1a1a (P18) seems to have a long history in the Caucasus, being spread across the region and forming many branches.[62]

As we shall see, G2a also appears in ancient DNA from the European Neolithic. The homeland of haplogroup G was probably somewhere in or near the heartland of the Neolithic – eastern Anatolia to western Iran – as this is the only region today where one can find its deep basal branches together with high sub-haplogroup diversity.[63]

Routes into Europe

Following the trail of domesticated plant dispersal and DNA from cattle, we can trace two main routes into Europe beyond the Balkans: one making use of seaways, the other travelling overland. These two roving cultures are labelled by their pottery: Impressed and Linear. We can add a third route – via North Africa to Iberia, which is just as well supported by cattle DNA as a route direct from the Near East.[64] [35]

35 *Early farming cultures in Europe. Mountainous zones were skirted by the earliest farmers. River valleys could be followed. Impressed Wares spread by sea and river. The exact route of the North African Neolithic is unclear.*

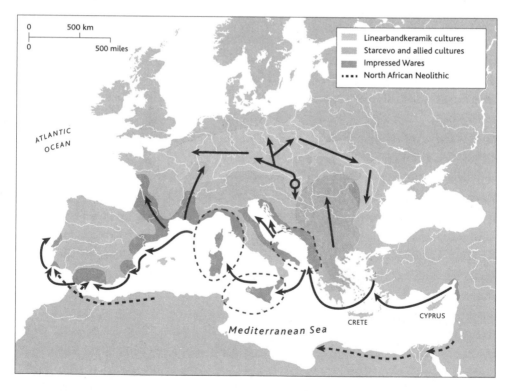

36 *Cardial Ware is named for its distinctive decoration. Potters pressed the serrated edge of the cockleshell (cardium in Latin) into the soft clay to create wavy lines.*

After the climate crisis of 6200 BC (pp. 81–82), farming was carried across the Mediterranean in a staggered series of seaborne hops from one colony to the next.[65] This route is marked by Impressed Ware, which, as the name suggests, has patterns pressed into it. It seems to have spread from the Near East following mainly coastal routes. Some has been found on the western coast of Anatolia.[66] It reached Corfu in western Greece and from there flowed along the coasts of the Adriatic.[67] Farming followed island-hopping and coastal routes west along the Mediterranean and through the Strait of Gibraltar to the Atlantic coast. It moved so swiftly from central Italy to Portugal that radiocarbon dates for the earliest sites on this route all cluster around 5400 BC.[68] In places this culture is known as Cardial after the tool used to decorate its pottery. [36] Cardial Ware is found in Sardinia, Corsica and on the Ligurian and Tuscan coast of Italy, and spread from there into the south of France and along the coasts of Spain and Portugal.[69]

Farming entered North Africa from the southern Levant.[70] Interesting new evidence is emerging that farmers then crossed from northwestern Africa to the southern coast of Iberia. In fact they seem to have arrived in the Algarve and Andalusia before the makers of Cardial Ware. There are distinct similarities between the way of life of the earliest farmers of southern Iberia and those across the Mediterranean.[71] This may explain why cattle of the most common mtDNA haplogroup in North Africa (T1) are also found in Iberia today, though they are absent from most of the rest of Europe.[72]

The Neolithic had already been introduced to Crete and Thessaly c. 7000 BC by pre-pottery farmers. Mesolithic sites were so few and far between in Greece that the farmers cannot have been in serious competition with hunters for land. A new wave of pottery-makers from the Near East around 6200 BC spread farming deeper into eastern Greece and the Balkans.[73] Another Neolithic culture known from its pottery as Linearbandkeramik (LBK) spread from the Hungarian Plain from 5500 BC west into what is now France. A late branch moved southeast down the Dniester and then south as far as the Danube.[74] This culture too was spread by colonists. Isotope studies of early LBK cemeteries show that many of those buried in them were immigrants.[75] Physically they were distinctly different from their Mesolithic predecessors.[76] Their earliest settlements were in areas of Central Europe largely abandoned by hunter-gatherers. The LBK incomers kept a distance between their settlements and forager zones, perhaps hoping to avoid clashes.[77]

Spread by ideas or people?

Between 9,000 and 6,000 years ago farming transformed the way of life of most Europeans. How did it spread across Europe? The simple explanation would be that farming folk migrated west together with their stock of seeds and animals in search of new land. Certainly, sheep and goats were introduced into Europe, which had previously lacked them, together with Near Eastern domesticated pigs, cattle and the cultivated strains of cereals.[78] Could these have been acquired by European hunter-gatherers through barter? Theories have swung from one extreme to another as fashions in archaeological explanation have changed. In the first half of the 20th century migration was assumed. From the 1960s a vision of cultural diffusion developed: farming was thought to have spread by the passage of ideas. Anti-migrationism is on the wane in the 21st century, and not simply because the genetic evidence is compelling that farming was brought by farmers to most of Europe. Archaeological evidence too has amassed in favour of the same conclusion.[79]

The demic diffusion of agriculture (its spread by migration) was first proposed on genetic grounds in 1971 in a seminal study by Albert Ammerman and Luca Cavalli-Sforza, which they expanded in 1984. Using the distribution of what are now known as classical markers, such as alleles for blood groups and antigens, they showed a genetic cline across Europe from southeast to northwest. This was strikingly similar to the advance of farming judged by radiocarbon dates from 53 early Neolithic sites. They deduced a steady wave of the advance of farmers from Anatolia at an average 1 km per year.[80] The assumption of a largely land-based spread into Europe via Anatolia went unchallenged until recent years, when so much more data has accumulated. Ammerman revised his own model using radiocarbon dates from 735 early Neolithic sites. This changed the likely point of origin to the northern Levantine/Mesopotamian area.[81] Analysis of early Neolithic cultivars also shows an island-hopping trail from the Levant.[82]

The idea of a steady wave of advance has also collapsed under the weight of accumulated evidence. Analyses reveal a punctuated progress, with long halts in places and periodic leaps across geographical or climatic barriers.[83] The most sophisticated recent model of the process grapples with complex reality. It reveals a slow start, a burst coinciding with the climate event c. 6200 BC mentioned above, and the most rapid expansion of all as farming entered the British Isles and Scandinavia around 4000 BC.[84]

These analyses make use of databases of radiocarbon dates from Neolithic sites to map the transition to agriculture in Europe. Where the appearance of an early Neolithic population was abrupt, it is likely to reflect new arrivals. In such areas hunter-gatherer sites tend either to disappear well ahead of the arrival of farming, or to continue well after it at a fairly constant level, showing the two lifestyles continuing in parallel. The pattern expected if hunter-gatherers adopt agriculture would be for the foraging sites to tail off gradually and overlap considerably with those of early farming. An analysis in 2003 cautiously supported the idea of migration of farmers into Greece, former Yugoslavia, Italy, Germany and Belgium, while leaning towards adoption of agriculture by local people in France and the British Isles.[85] This now looks over-generous to the concept of cultural diffusion. Subsequent analyses of the radiocarbon dates for Britain have come down strongly in favour of an introduction of farming by migrants.[86]

Yet we do not need to reject altogether the mosaic model of the spread of farming – a mixture of the movement of both ideas and people. Anthropology supports it for certain outlying regions of Europe. Comparing the crania of early European farmers with those of Mesolithic Europeans points to a new people arriving in southeastern and central Europe from the Near East.[87] Similar comparisons on the eastern fringes of Europe – the European steppe and the Baltic – show that some hunter-gatherers there adopted the new ideas.[88] In places where hunter-gatherers occupied an exceptionally productive niche for hunting and/or fishing, particularly one that was less suited to arable farming, they had a better chance of survival. The number of Mesolithic hunters who adapted to the new way of life may have been low, but in a twist of fate, their descendants were to have a huge impact on Europe's population millennia later (see Chapter 8).

Genetic evidence

The most convincing evidence that farming was spread by farmers comes from those farmers themselves. Their remains have been enlightening. Ancient mtDNA from the LBK showed without doubt that the first farmers of Central Europe were not descended from local foragers. The foragers overwhelmingly carried haplogroups mtDNA U4 and U5. The first farmers brought a completely new range of mtDNA haplogroups (see Table 1, pp. 26–27). T and K have been found in the DNA of early farmers in both the Levant and Europe. Haplogroup J also appeared in LBK farmers,[89] which comes as no surprise. Both the frequency and variance of mtDNA J are highest in the Near East.[90] More specifically T1, T2, J1a and K2a all show greater genetic diversity in the Near East.[91] Other arrivals among LBK farmers were haplogroups U3 (which has a frequency peak in the Near East) [37], W (most common today in Pakistan) and, unexpectedly, N1a1a, which is not common in Europe today.[92] H has also been found in the LBK, though mainly varieties of it which seem to have subsequently died out. [93]

Similar results have come from the Neolithic Mediterranean route. At two Cardial Ware sites in Spain we find K, H and two haplogroups very rare in Europe today: N* and X1.[94] A few hundred years later H3, K1a and T2b were buried alongside the more ancient U5 at Avellaner Cave in Catalonia.[95] K and N* appear again in the last phase of the early Neolithic in Spain at Sant Pau del Camp, this time with H20.[96]

Only three LBK individuals have yielded Y-DNA. Two were ascribed to haplogroup F* (M89), now extremely rare. This is so ancient a haplogroup that it probably arrived in Europe long before farming. But the third Y-DNA sample was G2a1c (L30/S126).[97] G2a (L31/S149, P15) is found at highest density in the Caucasus, which was populated overwhelmingly from the Near East in the Neolithic, and so G2a is a likely Neolithic marker in Europe. Support for this comes from more examples of G2a from the southern strand of the European Neolithic – the farmers of the Impressed Ware tradition. From

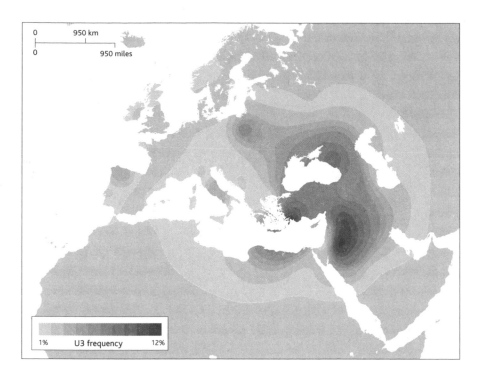

37 *MtDNA haplogroup U3 is relatively rare in most of Europe, but more frequent in the Near East and Anatolia.*

the remains of *c.* 5000 BC in Avellaner Cave, six males were identified. Five carried G2a (P15), and the other E1b1b1a1b (V13).[98] E-V13 represents about 85 per cent of European haplogroup E (M78). Its cline of frequency from the southern Balkan peninsula (19.6 per cent) to western Europe (2.5 per cent) suggests an entry point into Europe from Anatolia, where E-V13 is found at a low level. It also appears at low levels in the Near East and the Caucasus.[99]

Another 20 examples of G2a (P15) were found in 22 males among the burials in the Cave of Treilles in Aveyron, in the south of France. The Treilles culture of *c.* 3000 BC is the very last phase of the Neolithic in the region before the arrival of copper-workers. The concentration of G2a among the cave burials suggests that they were a closely related group. Their haplotypes place them on a Mediterranean branch of G2a, different from the G2a in the Caucasus. The two lines presumably had a common ancestor in the Near East. The other two males in the Treilles cave burials carried I2a1 (P37.2).[100] It was suggested in Chapter 4 that I2 may have been assimilated by farmers in southeast Europe. The I2a1 branch seems to have moved westwards with

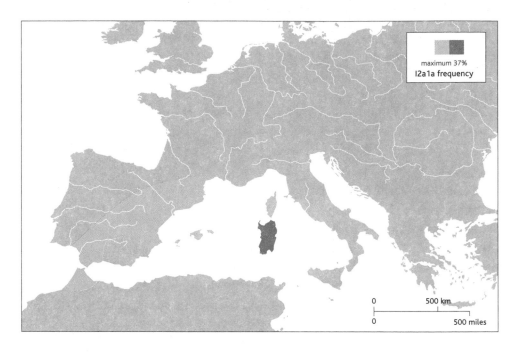

38 *The distribution of Y-DNA haplogroup I2a1a (M26) suggests that it arrived with Impressed Ware farmers [see 35]. These farmers found Sardinia unoccupied, so I2a1a cannot have arrived with hunter-gatherers.*

Impressed Ware, though in a more patchy way than G2a. Its descendant I2a1a (M26) represents about 37 per cent of the Y-DNA in Sardinia and is found at lower levels along the Mediterranean coasts of Italy and Iberia, and among the Basques.[101] [38] The high level in Sardinia suggests a founder effect. Although hunter-gatherers had visited Sardinia, it had been empty for a thousand years before farmers arrived.[102] So just one man carrying I2a1 could become one of the founding fathers of a new community.

Other haplogroups that may have entered Europe in the Neolithic are Y-DNA J2 and additional subclades of E.[103] The Near East is strong today in haplogroups E1b1b1 (M35.1), J1 and J2. The present-day distribution of haplogroup J2 (M172) mirrors the spread of the Neolithic from the Near East [see 34]. Yet J2 was almost certainly involved in a slew of later migrations. Phoenicians, Minoans, Greeks, Romans and Jews all no doubt played their part in its spread. For any European male carrying J2, there is a dizzying range of potential origins, which should gradually be whittled down to greater and lesser possibilities as subclades of J2 are more closely investigated.

CHAPTER SIX
Dairy Farming

The first herders kept animals for slaughter. The idea of milking them came later. How can we tell when milking started? Archaeologists first deduced this from the study of animal bones. We would expect animals kept for meat alone to be killed young. That is indeed the picture gained from early Neolithic sites in the Near East. If the average age at slaughter rises, that is a clue that domesticated animals have another use for their keepers. If the sex ratio shifts to a predominance of females, that is indicative of intensive dairy farming.

More recently, scientific analysis of fat residues on pottery has allowed us to pinpoint the place and time that milking became important. A study of more than 2,200 pottery vessels from sites in the Near East and southeastern Europe found low levels of milk fat at two sites in the heartland of the Neolithic, but the hot-spot was the lowland coastal region around the Sea of Marmara. Pottery from these sites dating from 6500–5000 BC showed a significant amount of processed milk. Processing into cheese and other products would enhance milk's keeping qualities. It would also break down the lactose for a people that had not yet developed the ability to digest milk as adults.[1] [39]

39 *Milking (right) and milk-processing (left) depicted on a temple frieze, c. 2500 BC, from Tell al-'Ubaid, Iraq.*

Dairy farming was an easy way to ensure a constant input of protein into the diet. Pastoralists adapted to it. Natural selection favoured those whose ability to digest milk was not switched off after weaning. Several different genes for lactose tolerance have been discovered. As we shall see in Chapter 9, their spread across Europe is a key piece of evidence for the important role of migrations later than those of the early farmers.

Farming had gradually spread west across Anatolia. After a sparse sprinkling of pre-ceramic sites, Fikir Tepe and similar settlements were established by the Sea of Marmara between 7000 BC and 6400 BC.[2] Cattle were not predominant in the early stages. Domestic sheep and goats seem to have spread across Anatolia first, followed by cattle in about 6500 BC.[3] The high rainfall and greener grazing of the coastal lowland favoured cattle-keeping.

Sites on both the European and Anatolian coasts of the Sea of Marmara have revealed evidence of frequent milking and a preference for cattle over other domesticated animals, though not all were keeping animals primarily for milking, as many cattle were killed young. Yet the addition of cow's milk to the menu on a regular basis seems to have started here. Then the rich pastures beside the Danube attracted cattle farmers. Milk residues, though not at levels as high as around the Sea of Marmara, were found on pottery from a site of c. 5500 BC on the Romanian bank.[4] At Hamangia and Boian sites around the Danube in southern Romania there was also a preference for domesticated cattle over sheep and goats.[5] [40]

Continuing up the Danube, dairy products played a part in the Lengyel culture (c. 5000–3400 BC), to judge by the preference for cattle and their late age at slaughter.[6] Lengyel has much in common with the Rössen culture (c. 4500–4000 BC) of Central Europe. In addition to dairy farming they shared trapezoid houses, like a cross between the longhouses built by the LBK farmers and the shorter trapezoid shape of the houses at Lepenski Vir in the Iron Gates gorge of the Danube. The shape seems to be echoed in the long barrows (houses of the dead?) that appeared in the Lengyel culture. The concept was then transmitted to Britain.[7] Further north, at Mälardalen in eastern central Sweden, milk residues have been found on Funnel Beaker (TRB) pots.[8]

At the southern edge of Rössen influence a lake village on the Bavarian side of Lake Constance shows every sign of specialized dairy farming. Almost all potsherds from the lakeshore settlement of Hornstaad-Hörnle (3922–3902 BC) produced fat residues from calves or lambs and ruminant

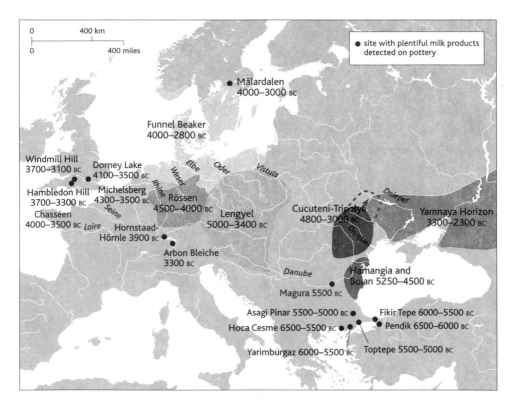

40 *The spread of dairy farming. The cultures marked in colour show evidence of dairy farming.*

milk. This is typical of sustained dairy farming.[9] From there, dairy farming could move down the Rhine Valley. Half a millennium later, evidence of milking appears on the Swiss shore of Lake Constance at Arbon Bleiche.[10]

Pastoralism was adopted from their Balkan neighbours by foragers north of the Black and Caspian seas in two stages. The first did not involve dairy farming. In the forest-steppe zone the Dnieper-Donets I foragers transformed themselves into Dnieper-Donets II cattle farmers around 5000 BC.[11] Craniometric studies link Dnieper-Donets people to other hunter-gatherers across Europe.[12] Ancient mtDNA reveals a more complex picture. Along with the U5a1a which we expect in European foragers were the H and U3 found at European Neolithic sites, as well as haplogroups normally found in East or Central Asia (C and C4a2).[13] We should not be too surprised. Mixing with the neighbours is a human habit. Intermarriage with Balkan farmers would explain the Neolithic haplogroups, while some human agency would be required to bring pottery from Lake Baikal (see Chapter 4). This type of pottery was made by the Dnieper-Donets I foragers before they took up cattle farming.[14]

The first cattle on the steppe were apparently acquired from the adjacent Cris Culture, derived from early farmers in Greece. Low levels of dairy residues have been reported at two Cris-Körös sites in the Danube basin, but cattle dominated at neither site, so this fits the early Neolithic pattern of occasional milking.[15]

Dairy farming arrived later. The Hamangia and neighbouring Boian cultures of the lower Danube seem to represent new ideas from Anatolia.[16] At one Hamangia site (Cheia) cattle show the most signs of dairy use, though at another (Techirghiol) slaughter ages reveal that cattle were bred for both meat and milk.[17]

In the thickly forested valleys of the east Carpathians, late LBK farmers met incoming Boian cattle farmers to form the Cucuteni-Tripolye culture c. 4800 BC.[18] So Cucuteni-Tripolye, developing in the zone between Hamangia and the steppe, is the most likely channel of intensive dairy practice to the steppe. The great Cucuteni herds of cattle were kept for meat, milk and as draught animals too.[19] [41] Linguists deduce that their steppe neighbours had developed the Proto-Indo-European language by about 4000 BC. Thanks to its scholarly reconstruction, we know that its speakers were familiar with milk, curds and whey.[20]

One clue to the importance of the Danube route for dairy farming lies in the genes of modern European breeds of dairy cattle. All have their origins in cattle first domesticated in the Near East. The parent haplogroup has been found in ancient DNA there. Yet there is a genetic distinction between northern and southern European cattle. The present breeds are the result of considerable movement in historic times, yet even with that in mind, a more ancient pattern can be detected. Two Y-DNA signatures predominate. Y2 seems to be the earlier haplogroup to arrive in Europe, with the first farmers from the Levant. It is found in cattle bred for mixed use and

41 *Cucuteni toy ox on wheels. Cattle were important in this culture for meat, milk and traction. Oxen pulled ploughs, sledges and, later, wheeled wagons.*

dominates the European Mediterranean region. Y1 appears to be a later arrival, found in the pied and red dairy breeds of the North Sea and Baltic coasts. We can picture Y1 among cattle bred for milk along the Danube and moving northwards in the late Neolithic, reinforced by later waves from the same direction. Interestingly, both Y1 and Y2 are found in Britain and in Iberia, but Y1 overwhelmingly dominates in Britain and is the only haplogroup so far found in Irish Dexter cattle.[21]

Northern Europe

Farming arrived late in northern Europe – so late that it was spread by dairy farmers. Earlier farmers may have been daunted by the northerly climate. Furthermore, the North Sea coastline was a productive niche for hunter-gatherers, who could compete effectively for space with incoming farmers.[22] In the coastal strip of the Low Countries some foragers took gradually to the farming life.[23] Another problem was the heavy clay soil of the North European Plain. Farmers equipped only with hoes could not work it effectively. For over a millennium they halted on the southern rim of the plain, south of the heaviest alluvial soil.

Climate change made farming feasible further north around 4000 BC. This was during a cold era on the European continent.[24] At such times the prevailing winds shift from latitudinal (east and west) to meridional (north and south). Southerly winds brought drier winters and warmer summers to the British Isles and southwestern Scandinavia, areas temperate for their latitude due to the North Atlantic Drift.[25]

The Funnel Beaker culture, named for the shape of its characteristic pottery vessel, appeared on the North European Plain around 4100 BC and reached Scandinavia around 4000 BC. [42] It is often known as

42 *The Funnel Beaker culture was named for the funnel shape of its typical pottery. This example is from Skåne, Sweden.*

TRB – the abbreviation of its German name, Trichterbecher.[26] At its greatest extent, it stretched from the Carpathians to southern Norway and from the Netherlands to eastern Poland. While the southern part of this region had taken to agriculture earlier, the northern part moved gradually from fishing and hunting to a productive type of farming that made it worthwhile to till and herd so far north. Unlike the first farmers to arrive in Europe, the farmers of the TRB were already familiar with dairy farming.[27] By about 3400 BC they had acquired wheeled vehicles and the ox-pulled plough.[28] So by the time it ended c. 2800 BC this culture had wrought a remarkable transformation. The plough made it possible to work the heavy clay soils of the North European Plain, though not effectively. The wooden plough of the time (the ard) could only scratch the surface. It would take the four-wheeled, iron-shod plough of the Middle Ages, drawn by up to eight oxen, to turn over this soil, gaining at last its full productivity.

Origins of the TRB culture

The TRB was once seen as the result of local foragers adopting animal husbandry and new technology from their neighbours. Yet studies of ancient DNA have shown no similarity between north European hunter-gatherers (mtDNA U, U4 and U5) and the TRB peoples, who carried mtDNA J, H and T2b.[29] Evidently migration brought this new way of life. The TRB farmer who carried H was further tested for 249 million base pairs of nucleic DNA. When compared to modern-day peoples, hers proved to be most similar to inhabitants of southern Europe and Anatolia.[30] Interestingly, at Ostorf in northern Germany a Mesolithic enclave was surrounded by TRB farmers. There, mtDNA U5 survived, though mixed with such typically Neolithic haplogroups as J, K and T2e.[31] It seems that these late farming arrivals were not averse to contact with local foragers. Those foragers who inhabited highly productive fishing or hunting niches need not be at an economic disadvantage beside the incomers, and indeed could set up exchange networks with them.[32]

Craniometric analysis links the people of the TRB to the Neolithic people of Hungary and Romania.[33] Copper axes and luxury wares from the Hungary-Serbia region travelled over 1,000 km (620 miles) to the Baltic shore in the early 4th millennium BC to end up in TRB graves.[34] Another link is revealed by the Funnel Beaker pottery itself. Its decorative patterns were picked out with a paste made of bone. This technique originated in the Carpathian

Basin.[35] So the TRB may have been the result of farmers fleeing settlements stricken by the climatic downturn in the Balkans and Carpathian Basin for the milder climate of northern Europe. Later innovations such as wheeled vehicles, the plough and wool spinning seem to have fed into Funnel Beaker from its advanced southern neighbour, the Late Cucuteni-Tripolye culture (see Chapter 7).[36]

In Scandinavia the TRB only penetrated the south. To the north and east, the foraging life continued over huge areas.[37] Even in the TRB, the rich marine resources of the Baltic continued to play a notable part in the diet of coastal people.[38] Indeed, fishing and foraging were never completely abandoned and form part of people's diet today.

The arrival of farming in Britain

Farmers spread swiftly across the British Isles.[39] They brought dairy farming with them. Residues on pottery reveal processed milk use among the earliest farmers in the British Isles. An early farming settlement was discovered during the excavation to create Eton Dorney Rowing Lake, Buckinghamshire. It produced an abundance of sherds with predominantly dairy fats. Of the domesticated animals analysed, 70 per cent were cattle. This was a settled herd. By contrast, cattle may have been brought from some distance for slaughter at special events on Windmill Hill in Wiltshire and Hambledon Hill in Dorset. At both sites the cattle age and sex structure suggest dairy herds.[40]

How had dairy farmers reached Britain? [43] Across the Channel, the northern Chasséen culture spread over northern France. There have been tentative suggestions of Chasséen dairy farming. The slaughter age for cattle at the Chasséen site of Catenoy (Oise) was mainly around 2–3 years, typical of beef production, but some were so much older that another use suggests itself, whether traction or dairy.[41] An ingenious isotope study of bovine teeth from the Chasséen site at Bercy (Paris), c. 4000 BC, showed that calves were weaned early, perhaps to reserve more milk for human consumption.[42] Bovine mtDNA from this site falls into three different haplogroups, strengthening the suspicion that the late Neolithic in this region combines influences from the Mediterranean and Central Europe. These haplogroups include T3, which dominates modern European breeds of cattle.[43] However, the T3 from Bercy is not an exact match for a T3 Neolithic sample from Kilgreany, Ireland.[44] No grand conclusions should be drawn from single

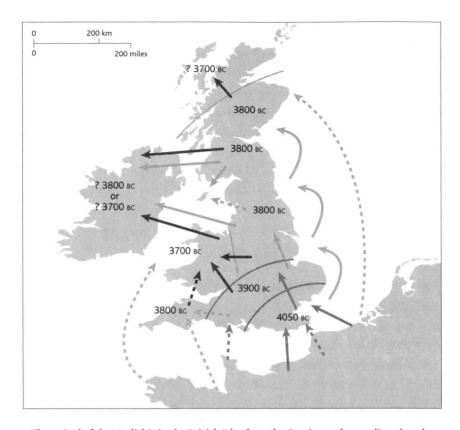

43 *The arrival of the Neolithic in the British Isles from the Continent, from radiocarbon dates.*

samples, but (as mentioned above, p. 99) present-day Irish Dexter cattle carry the Y1 Y-DNA haplogroup that seems to have spread up the Danube with cattle bred for milk.

The Michelsberg culture (MK) appeared c. 4300 BC beside the Rhine. MK is thought to have its roots in the Bischheim group of sites, in the Bas-Rhin department of Alsace, France. Some see this group as a form of Late Rössen. Certainly it springs from Rössen territory.[45] So dairy farming seems likely. MK had a dramatic impact on the landscape. The density of its population is estimated to be ten times that of the LBK.[46] It could muster the numbers to create communal centres, dotting causewayed enclosures down the Rhine valley from 4200 to 4000 BC. These enigmatic circular bank and ditch structures may have functioned as meeting places for an expanding community. Archaeologists sometimes place the Paris Basin in the MK zone. Whether Chasséen or MK, causewayed enclosures appear in the Paris Basin too in the same period. In the TRB zone and the British Isles they were erected centuries later, when farming was well established.[47] Windmill Hill is a causewayed enclosure. The farmers of the MK took over empty territory in places; the first wave of farming had failed in the loess area of the Low Countries that had been favoured by the early farmers because of the easily worked light soils. MK farmers were also willing to make use of uplands in the Alpine zone and Black Forest, probably for summer pasture.[48]

So did farmers enter Britain from the Chasséen or MK? Radiocarbon dates suggest that the first point of entry into the British Isles was southeastern Britain. The dominant motif is the carinated bowl (i.e. a bowl with a sharply angled profile). Carinated bowls form at least part of the pottery at all the earliest farming sites of the British Isles, except perhaps for Cornwall.[49] They are among the early Neolithic pottery at Dorney that revealed dairy fats.[50] In Scotland too milk fat has been found in carinated bowls.[51] So dairy farming presumably arrived with the makers of this pottery, but that does not resolve the issue of exactly whence they came. Most of the British carinated ware is undecorated, similar to plain pottery found at Spiere-Helkijn in Flanders with a carinated profile.[52] Carinated bowls comparable to the earliest English type also appear rather later in the Hazendonk group of sites in the Dutch coastal area.[53] On the other hand a decorated pot from Achnacreebeag in Argyll, Scotland, is a close match to one from Vierville in Normandy, France.[54] [44] Many boatloads of farmers probably arrived in Britain, not all from the same point of departure on the Continent.

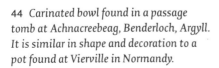

44 *Carinated bowl found in a passage tomb at Achnacreebeag, Benderloch, Argyll. It is similar in shape and decoration to a pot found at Vierville in Normandy.*

Short- and long-term impact of the first waves of farmers on Europe's population

How many immigrants did it take to spread farming? Hunter-gatherers were always thin on the ground because of their need to range widely for food. It seems that their population fell to particularly low levels in Europe before the first farmers arrived, probably because developing forest cover decreased animal population densities. Then certain areas were badly hit by the climate crisis of 6200 BC (see pp. 81–83). The remaining hunter-gatherers could have been easily outnumbered by a modest, but rapidly growing, influx. Farming boosted growth in the population, which can be detected as a youth bulge in human remains.[55]

Relative population growth can be depicted graphically through DNA. It is a simple process. From studies of ancient DNA (see Table 1, pp. 26–27), take mtDNA U to represent European hunter-gatherers and H to indicate farmers. Then count the number of mutations in mtDNA sequences of Europeans. H-type mtDNAs have on average six differences in their coding region, while U-type mtDNAs have on average 18 differences. That suggests a much older population expansion in U than in H.[56] The line for mtDNA H shows a dramatic growth spurt around 9,000 years ago (7000 BC) with the spread of farming into Europe, but it then begins to level out around 4000 BC while the line for mtDNA U slowly gains. Why is that? [45]

The farming pioneers in Europe, initially reaping the benefits of a virgin land, were to suffer severely in later centuries. It is not clear exactly what caused the population crashes or desertion of territories. It need not be the same problem in every case. In Germany and Poland signs of human activity fall dramatically around 4700 BC, remaining low for over a millennium. The LBK agriculturalists, who had settled so successfully there, failed to thrive in the long term.[57] In northern Greece there is a gap in the archaeological record from c. 4000 BC to c. 3370 BC.[58] In Britain evidence of cereals declines so sharply after 3350 BC as to virtually disappear. The agrarian collapse was probably accompanied by population decline.[59] In Ireland bog built up over abandoned Neolithic field systems from 3000 BC, preserving them for archaeologists to find in the modern era.[60]

Then, after the Neolithic, Europe saw two great bursts of migration, both from fringe regions where farming had been adopted by foragers. One came from the European steppe in the Copper and Bronze Ages (see Chapter 9). The other was the spread of their Germanic and Slavic descendants in the

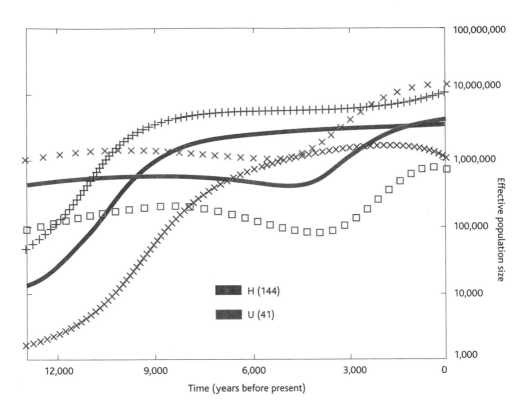

45 *Graph of the Neolithic growth spurt in Europe estimated from mtDNA. Solid lines represent the estimated mean for each haplogroup; upper and lower lines the range.*

medieval Migration Period (see Chapter 14). This explains why the ancient European forager mtDNA U5 continues to expand long after foraging had been replaced by farming. Both U5 and U4 appear among steppe nomads, along with Neolithic T1 and K2b, and haplogroups H, H5 and H6.[61] So some haplogroups that first appeared in a given region of Europe in the Mesolithic or Neolithic could well have arrived again in the Copper Age, and again in the Migration Period. It is a tangled web that our ancestors have woven.

CHAPTER SEVEN

The Copper Age

Even before smelting was invented, people were attracted by the colour and shine of natural copper. From about 10,000 BC copper was worked cold into beads and ornaments for display in the heartland of the Neolithic where Anatolia meets the Levant. By 8000 BC some within that core area had discovered that heat (annealing) made copper-working easier. Then around 5000 BC smelting and cast-copper objects appeared both east and west of the heartland: at Tal-i Iblis in Iran and Belovode in Serbia. This simultaneous surge of the same technology makes a single locus of invention likely, probably in eastern Anatolia, the centre of the range of early smelting.[1]

This new technology could speed up the production process of a whole varity of objects, both practical and decorative. Once a mould was created, it could be filled with molten copper over and over again. Given the difficulty of acquiring the technology, it is likely that knowledge of copper-working was passed from master to apprentice. Apprentices could be found readily to hand in the younger members of the master's family. Thus knowledge could reside within a family or clan, who might travel widely if there was not work enough for them in one place. Gordon Childe first envisaged the travelling metallurgist.[2] The idea fell out of favour during the anti-migrationist decades. It became orthodox to assume that metallurgy sprang up independently in various parts of Europe. That particular prop to immobilism has been vigorously kicked away in recent years by Benjamin Roberts of the British Museum. He and other experts in ancient metallurgy have come down firmly in favour of a single invention, for the same reasons articulated by Childe. The craft is too complex to have sprung up spontaneously, fully formed, in multiple locations. The most likely locus of invention is that in which we can see a process of early experimentation.[3]

The urban Near East

The first cities in the world appeared in Mesopotamia. Where there are cities we can speak of civilization. Whether civilization is a good thing is best left to philosophers to decide. We can only observe that the whirligig of time has crushed many a civilization while humankind managed to survive by retreating to a simpler life. As with technology, so with society: the more complex it is, the more ways there are for things to go wrong.

Cities are not just large conglomerations of people. The hallmarks of a city are trade and industry, public buildings, bureaucratic records and legal codes. Towns grew up in the Copper Age. In northern Mesopotamia the beginnings of urban life can be seen at Nagar (now Tell Brak in northern Syria), which controlled one of the major roads leading from the Tigris Valley north to the metal sources in Anatolia and west to the River Euphrates and the Mediterranean. By 3800 BC it had large buildings, extensive workshops and an estimated population of 20,000 people, not counting its suburbs.[4] Some of the largest early towns emerged close to the limits of rain-fed agriculture.[5]

The first substantial settlement in southern Mesopotamia was Eridu, around 3700 BC. The powerful city of Uruk flourished beside the Euphrates around 3500 BC. In Egypt, Hierakonpolis achieved city status about the same time.[6] Similar cities developed in Elam. The Elamite culture flourished to the east of Mesopotamia, on the Khuzestan Plain in what is now Iran.[7]

Agriculture on the alluvial plain created by the Tigris and Euphrates rivers required community effort. Rainfall was very limited and here crops needed irrigation. The reward was a food surplus from the rich soils, which could be used to support temples, leaders and the bureaucrats required to run a complex administration. So the Uruk period saw the development of a more stratified society. Full-time specialist artisans emerged, such as potters, weavers and metalworkers. The fast potter's wheel aided the process of converting a part-time domestic craft into a trade. As with metallurgy, the technique would be passed from master to apprentice, and specialist potters could be itinerant.[8] However, the plains lacked timber, building stone and metal deposits. Surplus grain could be traded for copper and timber from Elam and further afield. Trade routes developed.

Up the Euphrates from the expanding city of Uruk were the copper-producing strongholds of Hacinebi and Arslantepe, in modern Turkey, which began to trade with Uruk around 3700 BC. From Arslantepe it seems that scouts discovered the gold, silver and copper in the Caucasus Mountains. The trade route thus created brought wealth and metallurgy to what had been a quiet corner of the northwest Caucasus. The result was the Maikop (or Maykop) culture (c. 3700–3100 BC). Physically the Maikop appear different from their steppe neighbours to the north – they seem more Near Eastern. The astonishingly rich tombs of Maikop chiefs seem to be one end of a cultural corridor to the palace and tombs at Arslantepe and on to the cities of Sumer (in Mesopotamia). By this time smiths had discovered that arsenic mixed with copper made a harder alloy – the first type of bronze. Some kind of upheaval in Sumer brought an end to the trade with the Maikop people, and thus their culture.[9] The cultural trail suggests that some moved northeast to blend with the people of the European steppe.[10]

Goods were also imported to Mesopotamia by sea up the Persian Gulf, such as copper from the vast deposits in Oman.[11] We know this partly because trade and administration generated records. Writing was invented once people developed the kind of centralized organization that requires records to be kept. Egyptian hieroglyphics have been dated as early as about 3300 BC,[12] about the same period as Sumerian proto-cuneiform writing. [46] So we have evidence of the languages of the farmers of the Near East, albeit millennia after farming began. By that time probably a number of local languages had perished as groups amalgamated. As communities expanded and consolidated into kingdoms and empires, we would expect few languages to survive long enough to be written down, and even fewer to be still spoken today.

46 *The beginning of writing. This clay tablet dating to about 3000 BC notes the use of a large quantity of barley grain. It employs pictorial symbols, which were later to develop into the more abstract cuneiform (wedge-shaped script) (see also* [64]*).*

Since writing began in the cities of Mesopotamia and art was also advanced there, the first indisputable written record or image of an innovation often appears there. Many innovations were therefore credited to Mesopotamia which now seem to belong rather to the hilly flanks of the Fertile Crescent, the Eurasian steppe or even further afield. Pottery appeared in the Far East and Africa long before it was made in the Near East (see Chapter 4). Agriculture began along the great curve of the Taurus and Zagros mountains. Metalworking too began in the hills that provided the ore.[13] Horses were domesticated on the steppe (see Prehistoric transport 5, pp. 126–27) and donkeys in North Africa.[14] Wheeled vehicles were probably first made in the European forest-steppe zone (see Prehistoric transport 4, pp. 124–25). Wine was first produced on the southern slopes of the Caucasus, where grapes grew wild.[15] Dairy farming first appeared around the Sea of Marmara (see Chapter 6). Wool sheep may have been first bred in the Caucasus, where the earliest surviving woollen textile has been discovered, dating from the 4th millennium BC.[16]

There is a similar problem with languages. The first record of a language provides such solid proof of its existence that it may be a struggle not to assume that it was first spoken on that spot. Yet by the chance of literacy and preservation the first record of a language may appear far from its original home. The first written evidence of an Indic language appears in northern Mesopotamia. Do we imagine that the Indo-European languages of India emerged there? This is not at all likely. Its speakers in Mesopotamia were a foreign elite (see Chapter 8). Sumerian was spoken in southern Mesopotamia at the time writing began, but probably had an ancestor in the heart of the Neolithic. The earliest Sumerian records give us names both Sumerian and Semitic. A Semitic dynasty ruled that part of Mesopotamia known as Akkad, speaking the ancient Semitic language Akkadian. Sargon of Akkad (2334–2279 BC) brought all of Mesopotamia under his control. Within three or four centuries Sumerian was a dead language, though it continued to be written by bureaucrats, in a curious linguistic half-life.[17]

The Secondary Products Revolution

Metalworking went hand in hand with wider social and economic changes. Europe was transformed in the 3rd millennium BC. New ways of living spread across the continent. Overland travel was speeded up with horse-riding and wheeled vehicles; cultivation was made easier with the ox-drawn plough. The influential archaeologist Andrew Sherratt labelled this great change the 'Secondary Products Revolution'. Instead of just killing animals for meat, farmers began to keep them for renewable secondary products, such as milk, cheese and wool, and for transport and traction. Horses and donkeys could be ridden or carry a pack; horses or oxen could pull a plough or a wagon. Thus more could be gained from stock and soil with no increase in human effort. Any society adopting this new way of life had a marked advantage in wealth and mobility, and could expand rapidly. These innovations did not all crop up at the same time and place. Sherratt, like Gordon Childe before him, tended to assume that innovations had spread from the Near East. The picture is now more complex. Milking appeared earliest, spreading before the Copper Age as we have seen (Chapter 6), followed by ploughs, carts and woolly sheep. The revolution envisaged by Sherratt came with the bundling of them all into a new lifestyle, with secondary products used on a far larger scale.[18]

Wool sheds rainwater and takes dyes better than any plant-fibre textile, but it was a comparatively late addition to the options available. Wild sheep did not have a woollen fleece, but rather a coat of long, coarse hair, similar to that of a goat. [see 27] Beneath it was an insulating undercoat of tiny, curly fibres, which moulted each spring. Once sheep were domesticated, this shed wild wool could have formed a crude felt mat in their pens as they slept on it. Perhaps that gave people the idea of plucking the wool before it shed, to create the first man-made felt. The next step would be selective breeding for longer wool fibres that could be spun into thread. It was a lengthy process. The first woollen fibre was comparatively coarse. Really fine wool fleeces did not appear before the 1st century AD. Yet woolly sheep are depicted on the Uruk Trough of c. 3000 BC, now in the British Museum, and are mentioned in texts from Uruk of around the same date. It seems from earlier animal figurines that they were unknown before 5000 BC. So the first spinnable wool probably appeared in the Copper Age.[19] Wool has to be twisted much more tightly than flax, so the spindle had to rotate faster. A new type of light, fast-rotating spindle-whorl appeared in the Copper Age.[20] As mentioned above, the earliest remains of woollen textile so far discovered date from the 4th millennium BC and are from the north Caucasus.[21] Genetic studies suggest that the breeding of long-wool sheep began somewhere in Southwest Asia. Earlier types of domesticated sheep had moved into Europe with the first farmers. Relicts of those first migrations include the Mouflon. Long-wool sheep spread widely into Europe in a second wave.[22]

The earliest farmers used sticks as simple dibbers and hoes. Once the idea occurred to use animals for traction, the ox-pulled plough appeared. With fewer hands required to tend the fields, settlements could be smaller and more scattered. The earliest type of plough, known as an ard or scratch plough, was made of wood. It could do no more than scratch the surface of the soil, creating a shallow furrow for planting seed. There is no sign of the ard in use by early farmers in Europe. It has been argued that parallel furrows found under certain Neolithic long barrows in northern Europe were made by ploughing, but they are more likely to be the result of site preparation for burials. The first unequivocal evidence of the plough comes in Mesopotamian pictographs from around 3500 BC, but its use somewhat earlier in the Copper Age is suggested by the increase in mature cattle.[23] Though simple, the ard functioned adequately enough that little change was made to the design for millennia. Indeed the ard is still in use in places on light soils. The plough share could be reinforced with metal for greater durability, but this did not become common until the Iron Age.

Copper Age Europe

The first metal to be worked anywhere in Europe was copper. The earliest appearance of the new technology was in the Balkans. Farmers had prospered on the rich, silt soils of the lower Danube Basin. Hamlets in what is now Bulgaria, Romania and Serbia grew into solidly built villages of multi-roomed houses. Rebuilt again and again on the same site, the remains of such villages form a mound or 'tell'. Pottery kilns fired at high temperatures paved the way for metallurgy. Smelted copper tools and ornaments began to circulate around 5000 BC.[24] Gumelniţa is one such site in Romania, which has lent its name to a wider culture stretching from the Danube estuary to Thrace. To the north of the Gumelniţa culture was the impressive Cucuteni-Tripolye culture, within present-day Romania, Moldova and Ukraine (see also p. 98). It emerged between the Carpathian Mountains and the Middle Dniester around 4800 BC and spread gradually northeast.[25] To the west, in present-day Serbia, the long-lived Vinča settlement stood on the banks of the Danube from around 5500 to 4000 BC. It too gave its name to a wider Balkan culture. [47]

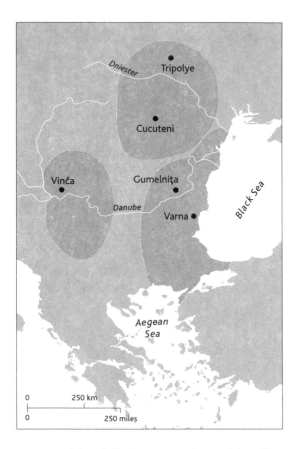

47 *(above left) Copper Age cultures of the Balkans, named for the notable sites at Gumelniţa, Vinča, Cucuteni and Tripolye. The last two belong to the same culture, known as Cucuteni-Tripolye.*

48 *(above right) A wealth of gold objects accompanied this man to his grave at Varna, demonstrating his status. His bracelets are among the world's oldest gold jewelry.*

The Balkans had deposits of copper, which would be an attraction to metalworkers. They also had gold. Gold is too soft to use for tools, but it is the king of metals for personal adornment. It is easily worked, does not tarnish and gleams like the sun. The earliest gold objects in the world have been found in the Balkans. The wealth of the Varna necropolis (4600–4200 BC) in Bulgaria is astonishing. [48] The bulk of the gold there was found in just three of the hundreds of graves. These three were also distinctive in having staffs or sceptres among the grave goods: symbols of royal or spiritual power. Social stratification had entered Europe.[26] Today we take rank for granted. Leaders have been a part of European life for the whole of recorded history. Yet European prehistory shows little sign of marked distinctions between individuals until the Copper Age. Gold in burials becomes one of the strongest clues to high status. The golden crown was to become the emblem of royalty.

Before these Balkan cultures could evolve into civilizations, the sun went down upon them. A cold period afflicted Europe from 4200 to 3800 BC.[27] Tell settlements in southeastern Europe were abandoned. Balkan metallurgy collapsed. The focus of metalworking in southeast Europe gradually shifted to the north of the Black Sea. The Maikop culture (see p. 108) introduced to the steppe the arsenic-copper alloy which did duty as bronze before the invention of true bronze (copper alloyed with tin).[28]

The only survivor among the rich Balkan cultures was Cucuteni-Tripolye, which adapted its economy, dropping arable farming in some regions. The Cucuteni farmers were already keeping cattle for milk (see Chapter 6). Following the climate crisis, they gradually adopted the entire Secondary Products package. The late Cucuteni farmers recognized that if oxen could be harnessed to pull a plough, they could also pull a sledge, which, if wheels were added, became a cart (see Prehistoric transport 4, pp. 124–25). The gain in productivity seems to have fed an increased population, who lived in giant enclosures of intriguing layout: a ring of houses (sometimes concentric rings) surrounding an open space, probably to protect their herds from rustlers.[29] Light spindle whorls reveal that they were spinning wool.[30]

A new culture appeared in Sardinia c. 4000 BC, which takes its name from the type-site at Ozieri. A rash of new settlements has been explained in terms of population growth.[31] Yet some degree of immigration is likely, since among the innovations appearing was the complex craft of metallurgy. The island is rich in metals, which may have drawn craftsmen from afar. The Ozieri copper and silver smelting was the earliest in the central Mediterranean.[32] The Ozieri culture was also capable of fine ceramics, the product of high-temperature kiln firing. These include the first tripod vessels on Sardinia, and pots decorated with spiral forms, both familiar from Cucuteni.[33] [49, 50] Alongside such pottery are stylized female statuettes, similar to those characteristic of the Cyclades, but earlier.[34] The date at which this culture springs up is suggestive. It was around this time that many tell settlements in the Balkans were abandoned. Their craftsmen would need another home. Yet if climate was driving movements, refugees from Anatolia might also have been seeking the more temperate conditions to be found on islands.

The ancient language(s) of Sardinia might provide clues to the origin of its Copper Age people, if linguists can agree on its affinities. Today Sardinians speak a Romance language derived from Latin, which arrived on the island in the 3rd century BC. The older language(s) left traces in place-names and the modern Sardinian language. It is argued that Paleo-Sardinian is related to Basque.[35] This does not necessarily imply that the language travelled from the Pyrenees to Sardinia or vice versa, since both might have a common origin elsewhere. One thing is clear: Sardinians have a low level of ability to digest milk (*c.* 15 per cent),[36] in contrast to the high level (*c.* 91 per cent) among the Basques.[37] Y-DNA haplogroups in Sardinia include some found also in Basques, but not the high level of R1b that characterizes the Basques today. So the two populations are by no means an exact match, but both may have something to tell us about Europe before the spread of the Indo-Europeans.

The Alps were also rich in copper, which was discovered by metalworkers *c.* 4500–4000 BC. Experiments were made in smelting the local ore at Brixlegg above the Middle Inn Valley in the Austrian Tyrol. The smelters may have been Balkan prospectors. Those early attempts do not seem to have prospered, for it is not until the Bronze Age that the people of the Alps became notable copper-producers.[38] Initially copper would have been taken from

49 *(left) This complex ceramic vessel from the Cucuteni-Tripolye culture is decorated with sinuous lines.*

50 *(below) A similar fondness for curving lines can be seen in this bowl of the Ozieri culture in Sardinia.*

surface outcrops, but when those gave out, mining began. The search for copper had spread to northern Italy by c. 3500 BC, where the earliest known copper mines in western Europe were found at Monte Loreto (Castiglione Chiavarese, Liguria).[39] Copper Age cultures sprang up in Italy: Remedello and Rinaldone in the north, and Gaudo in the south.[40]

Around 3200 BC Ötzi, the famous Alpine Iceman, was above the Inn Valley when he was struck by an arrow and died of his wound. His naturally mummified body caused a sensation when it was discovered in 1991 emerging from the ice of a glacier. As well as a bow and arrows, he carried a copper axe of the Remedello type, made in the Po Valley of northern Italy, using the ores of Tuscany. Isotope analyses of his teeth and bones show that he spent his entire life in the Alps, while his clothes suggest that he was a herder. Ötzi's mtDNA is of a K1 subclade first found in him, and so named K1ö for Ötzi, but now officially denoted K1f.[41] His Y-DNA is G2a1b2 (L91), which is rare in most of Europe today – running at less than 1 per cent across the European mainland. Only on two relatively isolated islands do we find his haplogroup at higher density today: 25 per cent in southern Corsica and 9 per cent in northern Sardinia. Comparing his whole genome with modern-day people, Ötzi clusters closest to Sardinians. Like most modern Sardinians, he could not digest milk.[42] This does not necessarily mean that Ötzi's ancestors came from Sardinia. Rather it suggests that Sardinia is a reservoir of a DNA signature more common in Europe 5,000 years ago. Ötzi also clusters close to a TRB farmer in Sweden.[43]

The search for copper had spread westwards along the Mediterranean by the end of the 4th millennium BC. The earliest known copper mine and metallurgical complex in France is in the mountains of Languedoc at Cabrières and Péret.[44]

At around the same time a rich Copper Age culture appeared in Iberia, accompanied by social changes. The earliest dates of copper-working there (c. 3100 BC) are for specialized, large-scale mining-metallurgical factories in southwestern Iberia, such as Cabezo Juré and Mocissos.[45] Yet the two foci for Copper Age Iberia became the lofty, fortified settlements of Zambujal (Torres Vedras, Portugal) and Los Millares (Almería, Spain). Both were distant from the main sources of copper. Both were set on promontories commanding approaches by river or sea. Zambujal and its satellites had the more easily defended position on a peninsula carved out by the great River Tagus where it met the sea. Ease of defence was combined with ease

51 *Model recreating the prehistoric town of Los Millares, Spain, in the visitor centre there. It was more of a defended settlement than a town. New walls were built as it expanded.*

of access from the ocean. The Tagus estuary formed a natural harbour, and Zambujal itself once had a channel to the sea close by. The position speaks of a seaborne people, anxious to defend itself. Both Zambujal and Los Millares began as small strongholds, and expanded with the creation of new walls enclosing larger areas: four walls have been discovered at Zambujal.[46] There is ample evidence of warfare in weaponry and death by violence.[47]

There are also clues to clannishness in enigmatic plaques found in burials, whose markings may record the lineage of the dead.[48] When copper-working appears around the Tagus, so do artificial cave-tombs. Around Los Millares we see the emergence of the beehive tomb or tholos, with a circular chamber and corbelled vaulted roof. Gold and ivory, statues and jewelry found in such tombs suggest wealth. We can build a picture of heavily defended centres of regional power.[49] Yet even the two largest Iberian settlements are more like defended villages than truly urban. There is no sign of public buildings in Los Millares. [51] Essentially it was a collection of dwellings for farming folk. Craftwork was mainly carried out on a small scale in the home.[50]

Where had the copper technology come from? Claims have been made for an independent discovery of metallurgy in Iberia, but there is no evidence of a long period of experimentation. Metal objects from Zambujal were made of copper and an arsenic-copper alloy. Higher levels of arsenic, which produces a harder metal, were found in objects such as daggers, which require a hard edge.[51] So the incorporation of arsenic was no accident. Metalworking had arrived in Iberia in a sophisticated form.[52] As we shall see (Chapter 10), the evidence points to people whose origins lay on the European steppe.

The Basques

The Basque region straddles the French-Spanish border between the curve of the Bay of Biscay and the lofty Pyrenees. [52] The mountains capture the sea winds laden with moisture, which falls as rain all year round, keeping the Basque country green. To English and French speakers its people are the Basques, and to the Spanish they are Vascos. The Basques identify themselves as speakers of Euskara, one of the few non-Indo-European languages spoken today in Europe. Isolated in a sea of Indo-European, Euskara has proved a magnet for bizarre linguistic theories. There have been numerous attempts to link it to an astounding array of other languages, none of which has survived sceptical scrutiny. Euskara has no close relationship with any other language currently spoken anywhere in the world.[53]

Today ten times as many Basque speakers live in Spain as live in France. Yet this does not reflect the pre-Roman pattern. The Basques first appear under that name as one people among many that the Romans fought in their conquest of Iberia. In the early 1st century AD the Greek geographer Strabo describes the Ouaskonous living about the town of Pompelo and the coastal town of Oiasona.[54] About a century later another Greek geographer also allocated the coastal Oeasso and a promontory of the same name beside the Pyrenees to the Vascones, together with 15 inland towns, including Pompelon.[55] Pompelo/Pompelon is easily identified as Pamplona in Navarre. Oiasona/Oeasso is a little more complicated. While the name itself is preserved in Oyarzun in the Spanish Basque Country, 10 km (6 miles) to the east lies the border port of Irún, where a Roman harbour and other remains have been uncovered. Irún has become the accepted identification of the Roman town.[56]

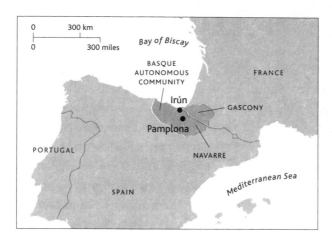

52 *The Basque country bestrides the border of France and Spain. In Spain, Basque speakers cluster in Navarre and the Basque Autonomous Community. In France they traditionally live in Gascony, derived from Vasconia, meaning 'land of the Basques'.*

Across the border in Roman Gaul the Basques appear under another name. The Aquitani of southwestern Gaul spoke a language different from the Celtic-speaking Gauls.[57] No complete texts in Aquitanian have survived, but personal names in inscriptions show it to be an ancestral form of Euskara. The Roman province of Aquitania Gallia did not strictly demarcate the region of the Aquitani. To judge by tribal names, the northern part of the province was inhabited by Celtic-speaking Gauls, while the Aquitani proper clustered closer to the Pyrenees. Even so, the Aquitani held far more territory in Gaul than in Roman Iberia over the border. South of the Pyrenees the only evidence for Aquitanian/Euskara in Roman times consists of three inscriptions found in eastern Navarre, an area associated by Strabo with the Vascones. There is no sign of Basque place-names at that time in what is now the Spanish Basque Country (which excludes Navarre). Instead the region was Celtic-speaking. So it appears that the Basque language spread west from Navarre into Bizkaia, Gipuzkoa and Araba after the collapse of Roman power.[58] The migration has been dated to the 6th and 7th centuries AD.[59]

One theory is that the ancestor of Basque arrived in Aquitaine along with the Neolithic Cardial culture. Basque vocabulary includes words for domestic animals and plants, and implements used in food production, which it is argued have cognates in northwest Caucasian languages, suggesting a common ancestor.[60] Scorn has been poured upon this idea by several linguists.[61] Also there is no genetic resemblance between the present-day speakers of northwestern Caucasian and Basque.[62] The characteristic Y-DNA haplogroup among speakers of the northwestern group of Caucasian languages is G2a1c2a (P303),[63] absent from the Basques.[64]

Yet one important point raised by this theory cannot be dismissed: the farming vocabulary. The idea that the ancestors of the Basques arrived with farmers will come as a shock to many. It has been taken for granted that they are a Palaeolithic relic population. This was an attractive theory in the days when population geneticists had only blood groups to consider. Their high percentage of blood type O Rh-negative together with their non-Indo-European language made the Basques a precious resource in efforts to understand the prehistory of Europe. They have been a much-studied people. Researchers have tended to find what they expected – something unusual about the Basques.[65]

After geneticists gained the sharper tools of mtDNA and Y-DNA they gradually realized that the Basques are not markedly different from any other European population in their ancestral markers. The most common western European Y-DNA haplogroup, R1b1a2 (M269), is as strongly represented in Basques as it is in their neighbours.[66] The subclade R1b1a2a1a1b3 (L21) – characteristic of France and the British Isles [see 75] – is found in approximately 20 per cent of Basque-speaking men. A rarer subclade, R1b-M153, is found in nearly 17 per cent of Basque men, though only lightly sprinkled across the rest of Iberia and southern France.[67] Elsewhere, R1b-M153 seems restricted to those of Basque, Gascon or Iberian descent. That is the kind of distribution we would expect of a post-Roman mutation, which has not had the opportunity to travel widely except in the colonization of the New World. Tracking back in time, the ancestral line from which M153 sprang is R1b1a2a1a1b1 (DF27). This brother clade of R1b-L21 is common in Iberia.[68] So although M153 most probably arose in the Basque population, it emerged from an Iberian background shared with peoples speaking other languages.

Otherwise, the Basques are distinguished by remarkably low frequencies of Y-DNA haplogroups E, G and J, associated with Neolithic farmers. By contrast, they have a significant level (7 per cent) of a rarer Neolithic marker, I2a1a (M26),[69] found in coastal regions of Spain and Italy settled by Cardial Ware makers, but otherwise rare except in Sardinia [see 38]. Another remarkable feature is the 6.25 per cent of Y-DNA E-V12* among French Basques. This haplogroup is found at its highest concentrations today in southern Egyptians. It occurs in few places in Europe; apart from the Basques, it is mainly confined to the Mediterranean coast and islands such as Sardinia, and even there does not reach 1 per cent of the population.[70]

Much was made in early studies of the supposed absence in the Basque population of mtDNA J (a Neolithic marker). More recent research found haplogroup J in both French and Spanish Basques.[71] Another popular theory was that the density of mtDNA haplogroups H1 and H3 in Iberia, and particularly among the Basques, reflects the Mesolithic re-colonization of Europe from the Franco-Cantabrian glacial refuge. Yet the greatest diversity of H3 is in North Africa, and that of H1 in the Near East.[72] This suggests that both arrived with early farmers. H1 and H3 show a low diversity among the Basques.[73] Most significantly, 91.7 per cent of Basques have the ability to digest milk as adults, which we can connect to dairy farming (see pp. 154–57). They have the 13910T mutation common in modern Europeans.[74] In short, there is no evidence that the Basques are a living fossil of the original European gene pool.

One genome-wide study of Spanish Basques did not find them particularly differentiated from other Iberian populations.[75] A similar study redressed the balance. The French and Spanish Basques do form a homogeneous group, which can be distinguished from non-Spanish European populations (such as French and Sardinian) to roughly the same degree that those populations can be distinguished from each other.[76] The Basques are a people with their own genetic footprint.

Still, they are a modern people, not an ancient one miraculously preserved. So we should expect them to be a genetic mixture, as all Europeans are, rather than 100 per cent pure descendants of the artists of Lascaux Cave. They could be the product of layer upon layer of peoples sheltering in the shadow of the northern Pyrenees. Their high level of mtDNA U5b hints at Mesolithic hunters.[77] Their Y-DNA I2a1a (M26) and perhaps E-V12* appear to link them to the strand of early farmers noted for Cardial Ware. Certainly, Cardial Ware moved up the Garonne from the Mediterranean to what is now Gascony. [see 35] Copper Age arrivals could have added another ingredient to the mix – the predominant Y-DNA R1b1a2. One study of a set of Basque R1b1a2 carriers calculated an expansion in the Basque population around 5500 BC coupled with a very high population growth rate.[78] Given the uncertainties of the dating process, that might indicate either a Neolithic or a Copper Age expansion from a tiny founding group.

Curiously, an mtDNA haplogroup that appears in only a small proportion of Basques is the most revealing clue to the Copper Age component. The rarity of HV4a1 makes its history easier to trace. HV4a1 has a sister in the Near East, HV4a2, which makes it likely that HV4a arose there. One branch of HV4a appears to have entered eastern Europe, where HV4a1 arose. Tracking its movements through modern populations we reach Italy and then southwestern France, where HV4a1a appeared at an estimated 3400 BC. HV4a1a is certainly most diverse in the Franco-Cantabrian region. It generated at least three subclades in this area. Its highest density today is in the Spanish Basque Country.[79] So it looks distinctively Basque. If the dating is correct, it suggests a movement from somewhere in eastern Europe to southwestern France in the Copper Age.

Euskara does appear to be a language from the age of metal. It includes indigenous Basque words relating to agriculture, wheeled vehicles and metallurgy, such as shepherd (*artzain*), millet (*artatxiki* – formerly *arto*), wine (*ardo*), cart (*gurdi*), wheel (*gurpil* from **gurdi-bil*, meaning cart-round), smith (*[h]arotz*), iron (*burdina*), lead (*berun*), gold (*urre*) and silver (*zillar* or *urre-zuri* – literally white gold).[80] Oddly, the most common Basque words for tin (*eztainu*), copper (*kobre*) and bronze (*brontze*) are all borrowed from Romance. However, Euskara originally had its own words for these metals.[81]

The collapse of the Copper Age cultures of the Balkans, apparently due to climate change around 4000 BC (see p. 113), could provide the context for the spread westwards of refugees looking for literally greener pastures. A common origin in the Balkans might explain the perceived similarity of Paleo-Sardinian and Basque.[82] Also there is one curious similarity between Euskara and Proto-Indo-European. The suffix -*ko* in Basque is so similar in its behaviour to the same suffix reconstructed for PIE that they must have a common origin. Since most scholars took it for granted that Euskara had developed in western Europe, while PIE developed far from there, they could make no sense of this.[83] Yet if Paleo-Basque came from somewhere near the PIE homeland, it may make a great deal of sense.

One possible clue comes from ancient DNA. A site of 2500 BC in Navarre has yielded evidence that some of its inhabitants could drink milk as adults, thanks to the 13910T mutation.[84] Pastoralists of some sort had arrived.

It seems most likely that the ancestor of Euskara was spoken by a Copper Age group drawn to the Pyrenees by its copper resources and its moist climate, though the evidence for any particular place of origin is too slight to build upon. The Basques remain something of a mystery. Only further study of ancient DNA seems likely to resolve it.

CHAPTER EIGHT

The Indo-European Family

James Mallory argued the case for the Pontic-Caspian steppe as the Proto-Indo-European (PIE) homeland.[1] [see 9] This was one of many competing theories. Mallory's expertise in both linguistics and archaeology gave weight to it. We can locate PIE in time by lexico-cultural dating and in space by its linguistic neighbours. Crucially, Proto-Uralic must have evolved in contact with PIE. Farming vocabulary was absorbed from PIE and its offspring by Proto-Uralic. So we can deduce that PIE was spoken somewhat to the south of Proto-Uralic, closer to the sources of farming.[2] PIE in turn borrowed words from more southerly languages. There are linguistic clues that such words trickled through the Caucasus from Mesopotamia to PIE on the steppe.[3] Culturally that is feasible. The Maikop culture provided a direct link between Mesopotamia and the steppe. In one example a word probably moved both north and south from the Caucasus. The word for 'wine' is similar in PIE, Proto-Semitic and the southern Caucasian language Kartvelian. Since wine was first made in the southern Caucasus,[4] we may guess that the word arose there.

The steppe homeland thesis for PIE has a long history. Marija Gimbutas developed the idea in the 1950s. Although her core concept of the place and time of PIE has stood the test of time, other aspects of her case have since been drastically revised. She pictured the spread of PIE by force. How else could Indo-European languages have overcome those spoken by established Neolithic communities? As we have seen, the staying power of European Neolithic communities has been overestimated. In places Indo-European languages entered empty territory. In others, though, the question remains. Andrew Sherratt's concept of the Secondary Products Revolution (see p. 109) provides a more satisfactory answer. The new economy had advantages for its users. The Indo-Europeans had their own words for this whole package of inventions and appear to have carried them east and west. However, there is not always a clear archaeological trail from homeland to destination.[5] Recent work has bridged major gaps. The fall of the Iron

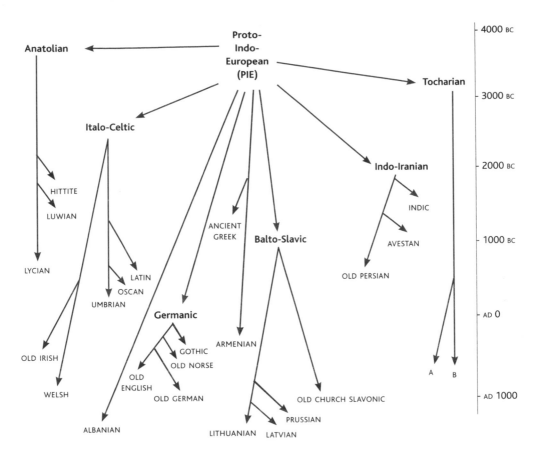

53 A tree of Indo-European languages, adapted from Nakhleh, Ringe and Warnow 2005, showing the estimated time period that a group broke away from the Proto-Indo-European parent, so that its speech developed independently and became a daughter language, and then the estimated time of any splits in that daughter language. The first appearance of a language in writing is indicated by the names in small capitals, such as HITTITE. The names in **bold**, such as **Balto-Slavic**, are the creation of linguists; these languages were not recorded in writing.

From Latin descend the Romance languages such as French, Italian, Portuguese, Românian and Spanish. Old Church Slavonic is the oldest written form of Slavic, close to the common ancestor of modern Slavic languages such as Bosnian, Bulgarian, Polish and Russian. From Indic sprang languages such as Bengali, Gujarati, Hindi, Punjabi and Urdu, spoken in India, and the language of the Romani. Old Persian gave rise to modern Farsi and Kurdish. Afrikaans, Danish, Dutch, English, Flemish, German, Icelandic, Norwegian and Swedish are modern languages of the Germanic family.

54 *Reconstruction of a man from a Sredni Stog culture site at Aleksandriya, Ukraine, 4750–3900 BC.*

Curtain opened up the archaeology of the steppe to Western archaeologists.[6] A prominent example is David Anthony. Like Mallory, Anthony links the early Indo-European speakers to the Sredni Stog culture [54] along the rivers Dnieper and Don, and its more mobile successor the Yamnaya (Pit-Grave) culture of the European steppe. [see 57] He knits together the archaeological and linguistic

Prehistoric transport 4: Rolling along

The invention of the wheel increased human mobility immensely. Images from Sumeria led to the supposition that it took the lead. The war wagons on the Standard of Ur, *c.* 2600 BC, have wheels of the earliest type, solid rather than spoked. [55] Yet these are by no means the earliest images of wheeled vehicles. Pictographs of wagons appear around 3500 BC on clay tablets from Uruk in Mesopotamia and on a Funnel Beaker pot from Bronocice in Poland. Wagons were still rare then. Pictographs of sledges are far more common from Uruk.[9]

The earliest evidence of the wheel comes from the late Cucuteni-Tripolye culture in the form of wheeled toys. [see 41] Around 3600 BC this culture produced models of sledges harnessed with oxen.[10] By the inventive stroke of adding wheels, it seems that the sledge became the cart. The forest-steppe zone had both the big trees needed for solid wheels and also access to plains traversable by wheeled traffic, and so was ideal for the development of vehicles.[11] Just as oxen had pulled sledges and the first ploughs, they were the early choice for wheeled vehicles, as shown in cart models of *c.* 3000 BC from Altyn-depe, in western Central Asia.[12] At Bronocice, where the Funnel Beaker pot with a wagon pictograph was found, some 20 per cent of the cattle bones came from castrated males.[13]

The remains of about 250 wagons or carts, dated around 3000–2000 BC, have been found in kurgans (burial mounds) on the Russian and Ukrainian steppes. Such burials were often rich in grave goods, and the possession of a vehicle itself indicates an important individual. The inventors of a technology are the first to name it. Others who adopt the technology often adopt the name for it as well.

evidence for the breakaway of various language branches from the parent Proto-Indo-European (PIE).[7] [53] Today we have genetic evidence too (see Chapter 9).

The Dnieper-Donets II people were the first to take up cattle farming in the region (see Chapter 6). Sredni Stog people lived at or near Dnieper-Donets II sites, but the winds of change had blown through the area. From the west the influence of the advanced Cucuteni-Tripolye culture had been felt as far as the Volga. Copper-working had arrived at Khvalynsk on the Volga, along with herding. The wind was not blowing all one way though. Influences from Khvalynsk contributed to a new cultural blend in Sredni Stog.[8]

Swings of climate seem to play a large part in triggering movement from the steppe. The colder climate of 4200–3800 BC probably weakened

Proto-Indo-European had words for wheels and wagons that were clearly derived from PIE roots, rather than being borrowed from another language.[14]

The new technology soon spread. Working on a pile-dwelling settlement in the Ljubljana marshes in April 2002, Slovenian archaeologists discovered an ancient wooden wheel in amazingly good condition and, nearby, a wooden axle, both preserved by the oxygen-free bog. Radiocarbon-dated to between 3160 and 3100 BC, the wooden wheel is among the oldest so far found in the world.[15] The square-cut axle would have rotated with the wheel. It was probably part of a single-axle ox-cart. Early wheels found in the Alps are of the same revolving-axle design. This created more drag and was less efficient than the revolving-wheel design found in northern Europe and on the steppes, but it was easier to make.[16]

55 War-wagon depicted on the Standard of Ur, 2600 BC, now in the British Museum. It had solid wheels, unlike chariots, which were a later development. Oxen were the usual choice to pull wagons, but this was drawn by four equids that look most like onagers (wild asses).

the agricultural economies of Europe at the same time that steppe herders pushed into the marshes and plains around the mouth of the Danube, where they found winter fodder and cover.[17] With farmers facing crop failures, the pastoral tribes from the steppe, rich in animal resources, had the advantage. Mounted on horseback they could move large herds long distances to find pasture.

Perhaps such a search eventually introduced the ancestor of Hittite, Luwian and related languages into Anatolia. This now extinct language branch had a PIE-derived word for a thill or harness-pole, but seems not to have had a PIE-derived word for wagon or wheel, so it is logical to suppose that it left the parent language community after animal traction was in use for some purpose (drawing sledges or ploughs), but before wheeled vehicles appeared. Anthony sees this early split from the linguistic parent expressed archaeologically by herder settlements of the Suvorovo group appearing

---

Prehistoric transport 5: Horse power

When pedestrians turned into riders, people could speed across land as well as water. Across the world humans have managed to coax many convenient species into acting as beasts of burden. The big breakthrough in mobility came with the harnessing of the horse. Strong and fleet of foot, the horse made an ideal mount.

Horses ran wild on the wide grasslands of the Eurasian steppes. Once plentiful across Europe, horses had become vanishingly rare outside the steppe by the time they were tamed.[20] In the western Eurasian steppes, roughly between the Dnieper and Ural rivers, horses were constantly hunted for food around 5000–4500 BC. [56] Domestication might start with an orphaned foal or two reared as pets, or used as breeding stock for a herd kept initially for meat.[21]

Bones of large horses, probably from the steppes, begin to appear in the archaeological record in the Danube Valley, central and western Europe, the North Caucasus, Transcaucasia and eastern Anatolia by about 3500 BC. At the same time the Botai culture appeared in the steppes of northern Kazakhstan. The people of this culture had a close relationship with the horse – it provided them with meat, milk and transport. They were probably horse-hunters until taking up horse-herding. Horse domestication at Botai is indicated by traces of mare's milk and phosphorus-enriched soils, suggestive of dung deposits, inside what could be the remains of horse corrals.[22]

Domestication of the horse need not involve riding. It could simply be kept as a meat animal or as beast of burden.[23] Yet riding would make it possible to control much larger herds of animals, and to venture further with them. Traces of bit wear

in the Danube Valley about 4200 BC. Anthony suggests that groups from this culture entered Anatolia around 3000 BC, founding Troy. The earliest level of the citadel that Homer called Troy or Ilios (Wilios) and the Hittites called Wilusa had in front of its south gate an anthropomorphic stele akin to those found in Ukraine and the Crimea of the same period.[18] This level also held pottery closely linked to Balkan cultures such as Ezero. The only example of Bronze Age writing from Troy is a 12th-century BC bronze seal. The text is in Luwian.[19]

Tocharians

The first Indo-European move east had all the boldness that would come to characterize the steppe nomads. A group set out from the Volga-Ural region to trek some 2,000 km (1,250 miles) to the high steppe of the Altai

on horse jaw bones from Botai provide the convincing clue that some of their horses were ridden.[24] The evidence from Botai clinches the argument that horse domestication went hand in hand with riding.

Naturally, these discoveries led to claims that the horse was first domesticated by the Botai. However, the spread of horses c. 3500 BC east, west and south of the European steppe suggests a trade in tame horses radiating out from somewhere within that region.[25]

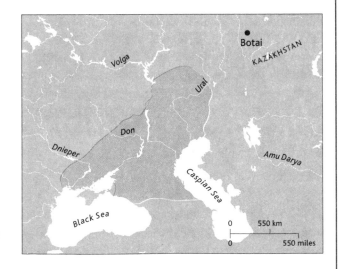

56 *The area in which horses were constantly hunted for food – shown coloured here – is the most likely place of horse domestication.*

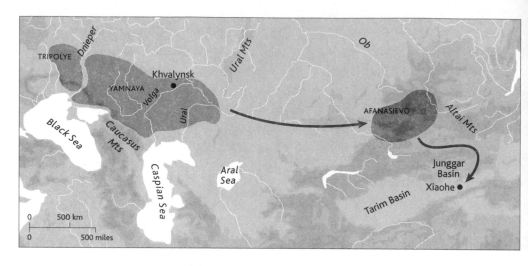

57 *A group of people travelled from the Volga-Ural region of the Yamnaya homeland to create the Afanasievo culture in the Minusinsk Depression, a bowl between the mountain ranges of the Altai. Later there was a migration south from the Afanasievo culture into the Tarim Basin, where the desert preserved their burials as natural mummies.*

Mountains c. 3300–3000 BC. [57] There they created the first mobile pastoralist culture east of the Ural Mountains – the Afanasievo (or Afanasevo) culture. They brought domesticated cattle, sheep and horses into the Altai. This new way of life sprang from a horse-loving culture known as Repin at the east end of the European steppe.[26] One Indo-European language with archaic features crops up millennia later along the Silk Road. When writings in this language were discovered, it was named Tocharian after the people known to the Greeks as Tokharoi.[27] So we can deduce that Repin folk spoke the parent of Indo-European languages.

What enticed these pastoralists eastwards? The Afanasievo culture colonized the Minusinsk Depression, a bowl between mountain ranges. It was empty of human life before they arrived. The local climate explains why. Higher up on the mountain slopes were foragers whose ancestors probably came from around Lake Baikal, but until about 5600 BC the lowland basin was too arid to be inhabited. Gradually the climate shifted to wetter conditions. Forest crept down the mountains to meet grassland. The pastoralists arrived as the humidity level was rising towards a maximum.[28]

Despite having travelled so far to their virgin land, the Afanasievo people were not entirely cut off from their origins. People continued to trek back and forth between the colony and its motherland, bringing new influences east, such as copper metallurgy. Foragers to the northeast of the Minusinsk Depression began to acquire metal objects and other Afanasievo influences. East had met West once more.[29] This contact may be the origin of bronze-making in East Asia. The technology may have begun as early as 2135 BC in what is now northwest China.[30] Eventually China also gained domesticated sheep, horses and wheeled vehicles via this trail across the steppe.[31] Sheep are a late addition to Chinese farming, appearing around 2500 BC.[32] How did they arrive in China? A team investigated sheep DNA from four Bronze Age archaeological sites in northern China. All but one of their samples carried mtDNA A, the most common today in all Chinese sheep and most Mongolian sheep.[33] This haplogroup is found in the Near East and seems to have undergone an expansion at around the time of domestication there.[34] It is common in the North Caucasus and middle Volga region.[35] So it would seem that long-wool sheep arrived in the Far East in the Bronze Age via the nomads of the Eurasian steppe. Wool was to become a staple of nomadic life. Mongol nomads still live in yurts made of felt.

The Afanasievo culture thrived in its sheltered niche until around 2400 BC. Then its people seem to have moved south. A related culture appears in the Altai foothills on the north side of the Junggar Basin from about 2000 BC. At around the same time, yet further south, the first settlers appear in the Tarim Basin, now in the Xinjiang Province of China. Within this basin the arid Taklamakan Desert has conserved bodies to a remarkable degree. A mass of them were found at Xiaohe, wrapped in woollen garments; these burials are very similar to those of the Afanasievo culture, and of the intervening site in the Altai foothills.[36] This ties in neatly with the linguistic evidence that the Tocharian languages, spoken around AD 500 in the caravan cities of the Silk Road through the Tarim Basin, derived from an ancestor which broke away from PIE before the Bronze Age.[37] These natural mummies astounded archaeologists, since they appeared to be westerners.[38] DNA analysis of the earliest mummies has confirmed a western origin. All seven of the males from the oldest burials at Xiaohe proved to carry Y-DNA R1a1a – an Indo-European signature, as we shall see. The mtDNA of both males and females was mainly the Siberian C4, though the western Eurasian H and K were also present. So these early arrivals were already a genetic mixture of East and West. The first contact had taken place in the Altai.[39]

Yamnaya Horizon

Around *c.* 3300 BC Yamnaya archaeology appears on the steppe. The Repin culture had contributed to its development, but Yamnaya was different in crucial ways. This was a mobile, wagon- and tent-based herding economy which could use more of the steppe grassland. These people are deduced to be the late Proto-Indo-European speakers whose language included words for wheel and wagon. Other significant words are those for sheep and wool. It seems that wool sheep were bred from around 4000 BC in the North Caucasus and perhaps the steppe.[40] As noted in Chapter 7, the earliest example of a woven woollen textile comes from a Maikop site (3700–3200 BC).[41]

The Yamnaya cultural package is distinctive. Its influence was to spread far and wide. The most visible element of this culture today is the round tumulus or barrow (kurgan). It shows a new emphasis on the individual by being a single grave, or at least a joint grave used once, rather than a collective grave often reused. From the Early Bronze Age, burial mounds with one-time burials are found across Europe not only on the landscape but also in literature. In Homer's *Iliad*, Achilles built a great mound for Patroclus, and the Trojans did likewise for Hector.[42] The idea may have been introduced by the Maikop chieftains.[43] The grave could be further personalized with an anthropomorphic stele. Kurgans were not created for all. They marked the death of significant adults, both male and female. Rich grave goods in certain burials suggest that the Yamnaya people were led by chiefs. Burial with tool-kits shows the special status of metalworkers.[44]

The collapse of the rich metalworking cultures of the Balkans had led to a decline in metallurgy. It was revived within the Yamnaya Horizon. New weapon designs included the tanged dagger and the shaft-hole axe, which had been introduced by the Maikop metallurgists. The Yamnaya people wore woven clothes, gold or silver spiral hair rings (*lockenringe*), distinctive bone toggles and decorated bone discs.[45] The hair binders are found in pairs with both men and women, and would have been worn on the ends of braids to keep them from unwinding. Turning again to the *Iliad*, we find the Trojan hero Euphorbus with tresses bound with gold and silver.[46] Cord decoration was common on pottery. The technical innovations of horse-riding, wheeled transport and metalworking were gradually adopted across Europe and Asia, often accompanied by other Yamnaya characteristics that consolidate the link to the cultural progenitor.[47]

What was the impetus driving this massive cultural spread? A shift in the climate after 3200 BC may have encouraged an exodus from the European steppe. Conditions became colder and drier. In the forest-steppe belt the forest was reduced and the steppe expanded. The region was at its most arid between 2700 and 2000 BC.[48]

The new lifestyle travelled along multiple routes. [58] The next movement visible in the archaeology flowed to the western end of the steppe, integrating the lowland steppe and upland farming communities of Late Cucuteni-Tripolye origin into the Usatovo culture around the mouth of the River Dniester. David Anthony has argued the case for this culture as the first link in a long chain leading to the Pre-Proto-Germanic dialect splitting away, the next link being migration up the Dniester through Late Cucuteni-Tripolye territory into the widespread Corded Ware culture (2750–2400 BC).[49] Yet Proto-Germanic did not develop until about 500 BC.[50] So it might be more helpful to visualize migration up the Dniester as part of the spread of a dialect that would have been intelligible to Indo-Europeans across a broad expanse of Bronze Age Europe.[51]

The orthodox view of the Corded Ware culture as native to the North European Plain once seemed supported by a local pottery sequence. The first pottery was the pointed-bottom and everted lip type of the hunter-gatherers. Then we have the Funnel Beaker or TRB type with everted lip (Chapter 6), followed by Corded Ware with everted lip. This vision of continuity has been overturned. Ancient DNA shows clearly that the TRB people did not descend from the hunter-gatherers who made the previous type of pottery.[52]

Nor is the Corded Ware culture, with its influences from Yamnaya, a straightforward cultural descendant of the TRB. Archaeologically it seems to be the result of people moving up the rivers Prut, Dnieper and Dniester from the steppe and blending with previous peoples of the North European Plain. What does that mean in human terms? The TRB had already adopted much of the technology of the Secondary Products Revolution and appeared to be thriving on it c. 3400 BC. There was a diversity of burial rites, but the creation of large causewayed enclosures speaks of a society well able to co-operate. Then there are signs of a population decrease from about 3350 BC. New types of burial customs appear at TRB sites after about 3000 BC. The dead are mainly buried collectively, but individual burials with weapons appear. These typical warrior burials suggest conflict appearing within

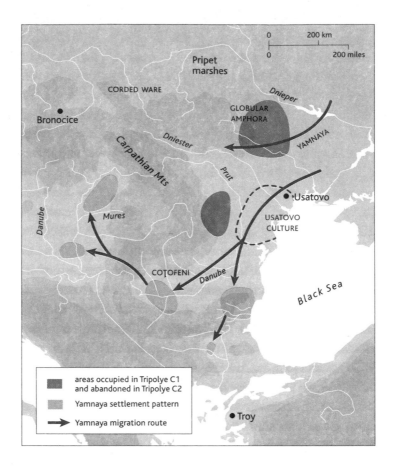

58 Yamnaya migrations 3100–2600 BC absorbed the remnants of the Cucuteni-Tripolye culture. Movement up the Prut, Dniester and Dnieper rivers created the Corded Ware culture. Mass migration up the Danube fed Yamnaya influences into the Balkans and beyond. Three thousand years later, a family of languages was recorded within the European part of the Roman empire which can be traced back to this dispersal of peoples.

this society, possibly the result of internal pressure over scarce resources, given the climate change mentioned earlier. Then the population rose again after about 2900 BC, which probably indicates the arrival of the people later identified by their characteristic Corded Ware pottery and with their own warrior burials.[53]

This complex picture presents an interesting challenge for genetics. So far we have mtDNA from one TRB site in Sweden (H, J and T2b).[54] We have Y-DNA R1a from one Corded Ware site in Germany, together with a wider mixture of mtDNA haplogroups (H, I, K1a2, K1b, U5b and X2).[55] These mtDNA samples are too small for meaningful comparison. So what is needed is more aDNA from a range of sites of these cultures, including Y-DNA. One scrap of evidence though is perhaps significant. As mentioned in Chapter 6, scientists managed to extract a large part of the nuclear genome of the TRB farmer carrying mtDNA H. It was more similar to modern-day southern Europeans and Anatolians than Scandinavians.[56] If this pattern holds good for other samples, modern Scandinavians are not the undiluted descendants of TRB farmers.

One feature of the Corded Ware culture is the 'battle-axe'. There is enough of a connection between cranial injuries and possession of a battle-axe to suggest that this axe was indeed a warrior's weapon, as long suspected.[57] Corded Ware is one of several related cultures in which it appears; collectively they are known as the Battle Axe cultures. Their domain stretched over northeastern Europe from Finland and the Baltic south to the Upper Volga, and across the North European Plain as far west as the Netherlands. These cultures include the Fatyanovo culture, which we shall see has been linked with Proto-Baltic. A range of dialects of Indo-European may have been spoken within this massive segment of Europe, only some of which survived to develop into modern languages.

A more archaeologically visible flow westwards between about 3100 and 2800 BC suggests the ancestor of the Italic, Celtic and Illyrian families splitting away. Yamnaya herders moved through and past the Usatovo culture into the Danube Valley, ending up in what is now eastern Hungary. The evidence lies in their kurgan cemeteries. This was a true folk movement, leaving thousands of burials.[58] It introduced the Bronze Age into what is now Albania and Bosnia.[59] The Vučedol culture in Croatia also begins at the right time to be Indo-European, c. 3000 BC. Its people appear different from the preceding farmers of the region.[60] Vučedol is followed by the Cetina culture, the elite of which were buried with archers' wrist-guards, as in the Bell Beaker culture (Chapter 10). From then on a continuous culture appears in the archaeology of this region until the appearance in history of the Illyrian tribes, who spoke a branch of the Indo-European language family.[61]

The departure of people whose descendants would eventually speak Greek and Armenian is not at all obvious archaeologically, but linguistically can be placed around the same period as the flow up the Danube.[62] If we can trust 'the father of history', the Greek Herodotus (d. c. 425 BC), the split between the two languages took place in the region that is now Greek Macedonia. Describing the Persian army of Xerxes, Herodotus says:

> According to the Macedonians, the Phrygians were called Briges[63] for as long as they lived in Europe next to the Macedonians, but when they moved to Asia, they changed their name along with their country and were called Phrygians. The Armenians were fitted out just like the Phrygians – but then they were originally emigrants from Phrygia.[64]

The Phrygians entered Anatolia after the fall of the Hittite empire and had carved out a kingdom for themselves by the 9th century BC. Their language is well enough known to confirm its similarities to Greek. Armenian arrived south of the Caucasus in the 6th century BC. Its speakers entered a territory previously known as Urartu. The language of Urartu was recorded in inscriptions, so we know that it was related to the Hurrian of northern Mesopotamia rather than belonging to the Indo-European family.[65] A homeland for what is often called the Balkan group of languages can be dimly perceived in Thrace and Greek Macedonia. So the parent of Greek and Armenian could have arrived in Thrace as part of the same southern movement that created the Coțofeni culture [see 58], sometimes seen as generating the ancestor of the now lost Thracian language.

Steppe groups penetrated Late Cucuteni-Tripolye towns on the Middle Dnieper, together with elements of Globular Amphora and Corded Ware, creating a hybrid that gradually became its own distinct culture. This seems to represent the dialect that became Proto-Balto-Slavic. Linguists calculate that it split into Baltic and Slavic branches around 1400 BC. The community certainly remained together long enough to leave Baltic river-names in the area, before a group moved north to the Upper Volga and Oka rivers, creating the Fatyanovo culture (3200 BC–2300 BC), eventually to settle on the Baltic and develop Lithuanian and Latvian, as well as the now dead Prussian language. [59]

Baltic river- and lake-names show that the Proto-Baltic people were spread over a wider area than that in which Latvian and Lithuanian are spoken today. This was a thickly forested region, mainly unsuited to agriculture, and only thinly settled. The Slavic peoples by contrast, as the ones who stayed behind as riverine farmers, seem to have had a relatively small

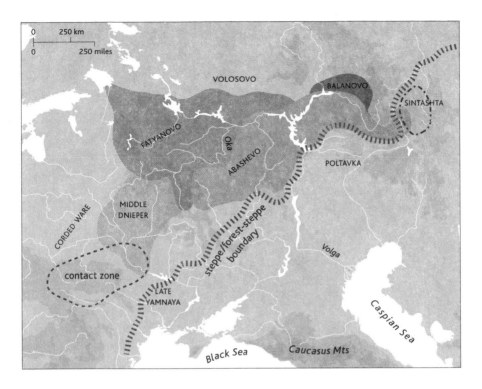

59 *Cultures of the Middle Bronze Age in southeast Europe. The Middle Dnieper culture is thought to be the home of Proto-Balto-Slavic, and the Fatyanovo culture the breakaway from it which developed Proto-Baltic. Sintashta seems to be the start of the split which created the Indo-Iranian branch.*

homeland where Proto-Slavic developed.[66] From there, the Slavs burst out in all directions early in the Middle Ages (Chapter 15). As they pressed towards the Baltic, both Balts and Slavs moved into areas where previous waves of Indo-Europeans had gone before them. The forests of northeastern Europe were penetrated time after time by small groups whose descendants were then absorbed linguistically by the succeeding wave.[67]

The Indo-Iranians

A final expansion east to Sintashta apparently set the Indo-Iranian languages on their way. Major attractions were the copper deposits in the Ural Mountains, and the marshlands vital for over-wintering cattle in a drying climate. Here the first fortified settlements appeared on the steppe.

Prehistoric transport 6: Speeding along

The invention of spoked wheels around 2000 BC made possible a lighter vehicle – the horse-drawn, two-wheel chariot, which could be used to devastating effect in warfare. Early images of the technology appear in the Near East, but its origin lies in the Eurasian steppes. In the Sintashta culture, Russia, a man could be buried with his chariot. As the wood rotted, it left stains in the ground that preserved the shape of the two-wheeled vehicle, including the spokes of the wheels. So far at least 16 such graves have been found. They are dated 2100–1700 BC, older than any chariots elsewhere. From the steppes, chariots were introduced into the Near East together with steppe horses and studded disc cheek-pieces.[68]

In northern Mesopotamia the Mitanni were famed charioteers. The names of their kings appear in the record from about 1500 BC. These names were Indic. One meant 'having an attacking chariot'. The mass of their people spoke the non-Indo-European Hurrian language. Their aristocracy had its origin in military charioteers. So we may guess that an Indo-European band had used the chariot to seize power.[69]

The swift-moving chariot became the favoured transport of the elite. From the Levant it was taken to Egypt, probably by the Hyksos, a Semitic people who invaded Lower Egypt. Once the Egyptians adopted chariot warfare themselves, they were able to expel the Hyksos. It was an early example of the arms race.

Meanwhile the chariot also moved westwards via the steppe into Europe. Its progress up the Danube can be tracked by chariot burials and cheek-pieces from horse harness.[70] From the Carpathian Basin it seems that the chariot reached Mycenaean Greece by about 1600 BC. The characteristic Mycenaean type had four spokes per wheel. [60] The concept had spread right across Europe by about 1300 BC, when chariots are depicted on engraved slabs in a noble's tomb in Sweden and on warrior stelae in southwest Iberia.[71]

60 *Wall painting from the Mycenaean palace at Tiryns, Greece, c. 1300 BC, showing two ladies in a chariot.*

Sintashta and Arkaim (2100–1800 BC) were curious structures, reminiscent of the Cucuteni-Tripolye giant settlements, but on a smaller scale. Two concentric rings of combined dwellings and metal workshops were protected by a timber-reinforced bank and ditch. They were not towns, but more like industrial outposts in hostile country. There are more than 20 such metalworking colonies between the Ural and Tobol rivers. These sites are the earliest phase of the more widespread Andronovo culture. The local demand for metal probably came from the Bactro-Margiana Archaeological Complex (BMAC). The people of the BMAC were irrigation farmers, living in brick-walled villages and towns beside rivers and oases, both east and west of the upper reaches of the Amu Darya River (known as the Oxus in antiquity). The origin of their culture lay in the Near East and had arrived by way of what is now Iran. The earliest evidence of chariots has been unearthed at Sintashta (see opposite). These light vehicles with spoked wheels were in demand by the princes of the BMAC, Iran and the Near East by 2000–1900 BC.[72]

Thus contacts were made between the steppe and the urban world of the BMAC, which seems to have introduced a new vocabulary into Proto-Indo-Iranian, and even more words into its daughter language Indic. The language of the BMAC is lost; it was never recorded. So it can only be deduction that the borrowed words came from the BMAC, but they certainly fit its culture. Terms borrowed include those relating to cereal-growing and bread-making (bread, plough share, seed, sheaf, yeast), water-works (canal, well), architecture (brick, house, pillar, wooden peg), tools or weapons (axe, club), textiles and garments (cloak, cloth, coarse garment, hem, needle) and plants (hemp, cannabis, mustard, Soma plant).[73]

The Andronovo culture borrowed more than just the vocabulary for water-works. People of Andronovo origin channelled the waters of the Amu Darya River where it forms its delta in the Aral Sea to create irrigation agriculture after the BMAC pattern. The culture they created is known as Tazabag'yab. Around 1800 BC the BMAC fell upon hard times. Indeed this date is considered by some scholars to mark the end of the culture, though life continued within the crumbling walls of its strongholds. Pottery of the Andronovo-Tazabag'yab type occurs widely within and around the BMAC centres. In the highlands above the Bactrian oases in Tajikistan, kurgan cemeteries appeared with pottery that mixed elements of the late BMAC and Andronovo-Tazabag'yab traditions. Here we can picture the Indic language and culture developing.

Over the next two centuries this blended culture grew rich on control over the trade in minerals and pastoral products, and gained a military advantage from chariot warfare, before abandoning the BMAC territory for pastures new in the Indian subcontinent and further afield. About 1500 BC a band of chariot warriors took control of a Hurrian-speaking kingdom in northern Syria, which became known to the Egyptians as Mitanni. The names of the Mitanni aristocracy are of Indic origin (see also p. 136). Their oaths referred to deities and concepts central to the *Rig Veda*, compiled in the Punjab at around the same date.[74] (In the Middle Ages an Indic language would enter Europe with the Romani.[75])

Pastoralists who presumably spoke Proto-Iranian had moved into Iran and Baluchistan around 1700 BC. From the northeast, two groups moved deeper into Iran. Around 1000 BC some took the route that became known as the Khorasan Highway into the Zagros Mountains of western Iran. Their arrival is marked by the spread of horse burials. In the Zagros valleys they bred horses and long-horned cattle; there they became known as the Medes. They were not a united people, but separate tribes, each with

61 *This 5th-century BC bas-relief shows soldiers of the Medes and Persians. The Apadana Palace, Persepolis, Iran, northern stairway detail.*

62 *Chariots in rock art from the Koksu Valley, Dzhungar Mountains, Kazakhstan.*

its own chieftain. The Assyrians, who took over the region in the late 8th century BC, marvelled at the stud farms of the Medes, with their numberless steeds. Horses made pleasing tribute. Unfortunately for the Assyrians, the Medes grew dissatisfied with the demands of their overlords. United under Cyaxares in 615 BC, the Medes swooped upon Assyria. Victorious, the Medes unexpectedly found themselves in charge of an empire. [61]

The Assyrians had also encountered a tribe in northeastern Iran in 843 BC called the Parsua. Later, the Parsua established themselves in the ruins of the southern kingdom of Anshan, between the southern Zagros and the Gulf, where they became known as the Persians. Under Cyrus (ruled 576–530 BC), the Persians defeated the Medes and created a united Persia.[76] By the time Darius the Great (who ruled Persia 521–486 BC) had his auto-biography carved on a cliff-face at Behistun, the Persians had acquired an enormous empire covering the entire Near East and beyond, from the Indus Valley to northern Greece, and from Central Asia to southern Egypt.[77] His inscription is in three languages, including Old Persian, ancestor of modern Persian (Farsi) [see 53].[78]

Iranian languages were spoken not just in Iran, but also by pastoralists who spread far across the Asian steppe. Andronovo people had reached the Tian Shan Mountains of southeastern Kazakhstan by 1610 BC. One of their settlements has been found in the Asi Valley, on the north side of the Zailiysky Alatau range. Just 2 or 3 km (1–2 miles) to the north of the settlement are rock art carvings, including an image of a two-wheeled chariot.[79] Somewhat further to the north, still within southeastern Kazakhstan, the Dzhungarian Alatau range, which forms the border with China, harbours remarkable concentrations of petroglyphs, including many Bronze Age scenes of horse-drawn chariots.[80] [62] Descendants of the Andronovo culture entered the Minusinsk Depression, once home to an earlier wave of Indo-Europeans. They also followed the Ili (or Yili) River valley from the steppe, and traversed the Chawuhu Pass to enter the Tarim Basin about three centuries after the Tocharians.[81]

In the Ili Valley the Iranian speakers encountered a species of tree unknown it seems to their PIE-speaking ancestors. The wild apple of this region (*Malus sieversii*) produces a large and edible fruit. DNA analysis has shown it to be the progenitor of the cultivated apples we eat today.[82] The English word 'apple' has cognates in various western Indo-European languages, such as Old Irish, Lithuanian and Russian, and possibly in Pashto, but cannot be extended back with certainty to PIE.[83] Apple seeds could have been transported westwards from Central Asia into Europe along two trade routes: the steppe corridor or via Iran and Anatolia. DNA studies suggest that the apple was domesticated early in Iran, as there is a high level of genetic diversity in the cultivated apple stock there.[84] Comparisons place Iranian apples in an intermediate position between the domesticated varieties and wild species.[85] The apple was certainly cultivated in Europe by the time of the ancient Greeks and today is one of the most widespread and popular fruit trees in the world.

Scythians, Sarmatians and Amazons

Those Iranian speakers who retained a nomadic life on the Asian steppe first appear in history as the Scythians or Saka. These roaming tribes spread

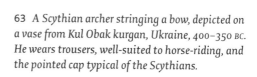

deep into Central Asia. [see 111] Scythians cultivated trade, controlling sections of the Silk Road from China to the West. This was the probable source of their wealth, expressed in spectacular royal kurgans containing objects of silk and gold, exquisitely worked.[86]

63 A Scythian archer stringing a bow, depicted on a vase from Kul Obak kurgan, Ukraine, 400–350 BC. He wears trousers, well-suited to horse-riding, and the pointed cap typical of the Scythians.

As East Asian nomads grew in strength and pushed westwards, the Scythians could either join them or flee west before them. Studies of ancient mtDNA indicate the point at which East Asian peoples came to predominate over Western Eurasian in Central Asia. In Kazakhstan only Western Eurasian lineages have been found from the 14th to the 7th century BC. After that a mixture of eastern and western haplogroups has been detected, with almost half coming from the east.[87]

The impact on the West of this turn of the tide was an explosion of East Iranian-speaking tribes on to and through the European steppe. The beginnings of the movement were but dimly recalled when Herodotus encountered Scythians in the 5th century BC. Those he knew had long been settled on the European steppe. Delving into their origins, he shrewdly preferred the least glorious story – that they had entered Europe in flight from the Massagetae of the Asian steppe. He was uncertain whether the Massagetae were also a Scythian people (they were), though he did know that there were Scythians remaining on the Asian steppe, called Saka by the Persians.[88] In fact the Scythians were a considerable threat to the Persian empire. [63] The Persian Achaemenid dynasty waged war after war against them. Cyrus the Great was killed by the Massagetae, led by their queen Tomyris, according to Herodotus.[89]

On the steppe east of the Don River early Greek travellers located the Sauromatians, later known as Sarmatians.[90] These were yet more Iranian speakers – related in language and culture to the Scythians settled on the European steppe. The Sarmatians crossed the Don at the end of the 4th century BC and surged westwards, subjugating the Scythians and giving the new name of Sarmatia to the European steppe.[91]

Herodotus had a wondrous tale to tell of the Sauromatians. He had heard that they were the descendants of a band of young Scythian men who had taken as wives a group of Amazons who insisted on retaining their way of life: hunting, riding and going to war. Perceiving the potential for conflict if the combined group settled with the other Scythians between the Danube and the Don, they found a territory for themselves east of the Don.[92]

The fighting female Amazons, living without men, appear in Greek literature from the 8th century BC in so confusing a variety of locations and stories that they are often regarded as pure invention, the symbolic enemy of Greek patriarchy. Yet the graves of warrior women are found on the European steppe, one of the two places most strongly associated with the Amazons by ancient Greek authors. The other location was beside the Thermodon River, which is modern Terme in Turkey. According to one account the Amazons lived originally beside the Don River, but moved to Themiscyra on the Thermodon on the opposite shore of the Black Sea.[93] Herodotus reverses the flow. In his story, Amazons taken prisoner by Greeks at the battle of Thermodon had drifted by ship on to the Scythian shore of the Black Sea after overpowering their captors. To stress their foreign origin, he tells us that the Sarmatians spoke Scythian, but ungrammatically, because the Amazons had never learnt it properly.[94] This may be the earliest account of language contact as a cause of language change.[95]

It is a pity that it can't be true. Certain Sarmatian women were buried with armour and weapons. Yet, contrary to the story told by Herodotus, such burials do not appear only in the Volga-Ural region inhabited by the early Sarmatians, but also in the Scythian region between the Danube and the Don. A kurgan near Akkerman, southern Ukraine, contains an impressive example. The woman buried there owned bronze and silver bracelets, a bronze mirror, a necklace of glass beads and a lead spindle-whorl; so far so feminine. Yet she also had a quiver with 20 bronze arrowheads, as well as two spearheads and a massive battle-belt of leather covered with iron plaques. This weaponry was not just for show. The redoubtable woman had suffered several head wounds from cutting blows, and a bronze arrowhead was lodged in her knee joint.[96] More damaging still for the credibility of Herodotus are the warrior women of the Asian steppe. The Iron Age grave of a 16-year-old girl at Ak-Alakha in the Altai Mountains contained an iron battle-axe and other weapons. Furthermore, she was dressed in male attire.[97] The Scythians had brought a heritage of fighting females with them from the Asian steppe.

Some 20 per cent of Scythian-Sarmatian graves containing weapons and harness are those of women. To put it another way, 80 per cent of warrior burials were of men.[98] This was no gender role reversal. The pattern suggests a female home guard. Greeks coming across Scythian women minding the home fires while their mobile males were away herding or raiding might have thought them a tribe without men. Imagine their surprise when apparently defenceless females whipped out weaponry in a business-like fashion. Thus are myths born.

A more modern myth needs to be tackled here. The ethnonym Aryan was hijacked by the Nazis to fit a vision of Nordic supermen. It rightly belongs to those who so described themselves in ancient times – the Iranians. The country name Iran comes from Aryan. The word 'aryan' seems to derive from Proto-Indo-European *haeros* or *haeryos*, meaning 'member of one's own group'. It appears in Hittite as *ara* – 'member of one's own group, peer, friend' – and in another Anatolian language as *arus*, meaning 'citizen'. It is quite common for an ethnonym to arise as a means of denoting an insider as opposed to an outsider. The transformation of this particular PIE word into an ethnonym seems to have taken place only in the Iranian branch of the tree. There is no evidence that the Proto-Indo-Europeans had an ethnonym. Certainly, as Indo-European speakers spread, they adopted various ethnonyms to distinguish themselves. That includes the speakers of Iranian outside Iran. The exception is the Iranian-speaking Alans, who appear to have taken their ethnonym from the same source as Aryan. One subdivision of their descendants in the North Caucasus, the Ossets, is known as Iron.[99]

Herders to Hellenes

Why were Indo-European speakers so successful? Some point to their warlike culture and mastery of the chariot. Others have been keen to stress the signs of peaceful integration with Neolithic people. Some see the key as the collapse of Neolithic cultures. Others envisage a diaspora led by trade, driven partly by the need for metals, especially tin – the rare, vital component of true bronze. No doubt all such factors played a part in places. For example, the chariot seems to have been an element in the creation of the kingdom of Mitanni, but it was too late a development to influence the spread of Indo-European languages in Europe.

The fundamental advantage of Indo-European speakers was their economy. If we return to the concept of the Secondary Products Revolution (see p. 109), we see that using animals for traction and transport meant higher yields from the same man-hours.[100] That would generate a greater food surplus, which not only permitted population growth, but also supported specialists, such as metalworkers and a warrior aristocracy. The late Copper to Bronze Age cultures of Europe were more mobile, more socially stratified, more dispersed in the landscape than the cultures they supplanted. There was a new stress on the individual, visible in single graves. Their elite members were buried with pomp.[101] This new way of

64 *The clay tablet of doctor Zarpija of Kizzuwadna written in Hittite and Luwian. These are two languages of the Anatolian branch of the Indo-European family, the earliest to be recorded in complete written texts.*

living fits the picture we get from the reconstructed PIE vocabulary. They had chiefs and warriors. They spread new technology across Europe: horse-riding, wheeled vehicles and metallurgy in gold, copper and bronze.[102]

Yet these wanderers were neither urban nor literate. So as they advanced there was a fascinating collision of cultures in key zones, out of which sprang the great civilizations of the Classical world. The Indo-European speakers absorbed a great deal from the cultures they eventually overtook. We first see this pattern in Anatolia, where incoming pastoralists arrived perhaps around 3000 BC, to coexist with an established and successful agricultural society. Their speech gradually evolved into Hittite and other Anatolian languages. It was over a thousand years later that Hittite war-lords took over Hattic kingdoms, borrowing the vocabulary to go with them, such as words for 'king' and 'queen'. They also acquired the literacy that is so useful to state rulers, writing in the cuneiform script that had first emerged in Sumer.[103] [64] As we shall see in Chapter 9, the genetic evidence suggests that the Indo-Europeans generally filtered into such thriving urban societies, melding with their inhabitants over time, whereas areas where farming had not prospered to the same degree offered greater possibilities for expansion.

CHAPTER NINE

Indo-Europeans and Genetics

I t is commonly argued that the shift to Indo-European languages could have been triggered by Indo-European speakers establishing themselves as elites among other peoples. While that cannot be ruled out in every case, there are genetic clues to a much larger impact on the population. One genome-wide study of South Asians estimates that there was a major genetic mixture 1,200–4,000 years ago, overlapping the time when Indo-European languages arrived in the Indian subcontinent.[1] The dramatic genetic heritage of the Indo-Europeans in both Asia and Europe is revealed most clearly in Y-DNA.

Y-DNA R1

The subclades of Y-DNA R1 are pre-eminent in both Europe and India. R1a1a (M17) dominates northern India and is also found strongly in eastern Europe [65], particularly in Slavic and Baltic populations, while R1b1a2 (M269) dominates the rest of Europe. [66] That is a geographical match to the distribution of Indo-European languages.[2] The idea that such an over-whelming genetic signature could date from as late as the Copper Age is startling. Yet that is the picture emerging. It is not a black and white picture, however. R1b1a2 and R1a1a only had to be present among, not exclusive to, the group speaking PIE for these correlations to appear. Nor are they the only haplogroups that seem to have spread with the Indo-Europeans. Nonetheless, R1 is the part of the picture that leaps to the eye.

The geographical correlation between R1a1a and Indo-European languages was spotted in the late 1990s. From this, geneticist Spencer Wells deduced that R1a1a (M17) arose in the Pontic-Caspian steppe.[3] Studies of ancient DNA have followed the archaeological trail eastwards along the steppe, testing remains of a succession of related cultures in the Minusinsk Depression, from Andronovo to the Iranian-speaking Scythians. Their DNA indicated mainly blue- or green-eyed, fair-skinned and light-haired people. Y-DNA R1a1a predominated in the males tested.[4] Bronze Age mummies in

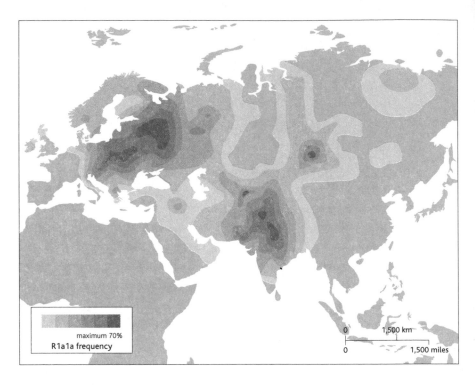

65 *The distribution of Y-DNA haplogroup R1a1a is strongly correlated with certain branches of the Indo-European tree.*

the Tarim Basin also proved to carry R1a1a and are presumed ancestors of Tocharian speakers.[5] In Europe the earliest R1a1 (SRY10831.2) so far found was in a Corded Ware context,[6] while R1b1a2 first appears on a Bell Beaker site.[7] This too would fit an Indo-European arrival.

Now that the massive R1a1a block has been broken into subclades, a geographical pattern is emerging. There was a great expansion in R1a1a1 (M417) in the Copper Age, with a starburst of new lineages. Early results show a break-up into an Asian lineage (Z93) and a European line (Z283).[8]

R1b1a2 (M269) provides the other half of the story. [66] It seems to be around 5,000–10,000 years old and the first R1b to enter Europe.[9] Predecessor and brother haplogroups appear in Western Asia. Its earliest subclade is thinly spread in Western Asia and eastern Europe, with no sign of a major population impact at that stage. [see 67] It was R1b1a2a1a1 (L11) that suddenly produced two huge subclades (U106 and P312) with fast-appearing clusters of offspring mutations – the sign of a population in rapid, massive growth.[10] These saturated western Europe.

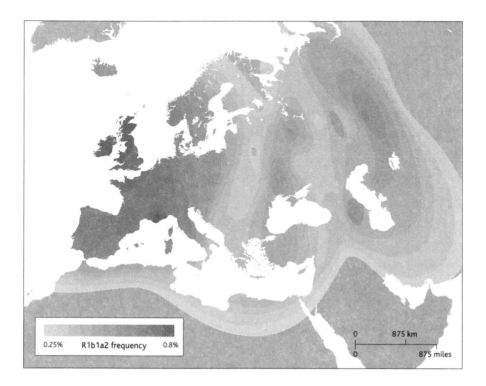

66 Y-DNA haplogroup R1b1a2 (M269) overlaps with R1a1a. Together the two cover the historic range of Indo-European languages.

Several recent authors have suggested that R1b1a2 spread into Europe with the first farmers.[11] That would not explain how carriers of R1b1a2 share with carriers of R1a1a a high percentage of lactose tolerance, connected to dairy farming. Ultimately the matter will be settled by ancient DNA. In the meantime we can only proceed by deduction.

The Basques speak a non-Indo-European language which might have its origins in the Copper Age Balkans, in contact with PIE (see Chapter 7). If there was a pool of R1b1a2 somewhere in that contact zone, that could explain why the Basques have as much R1b1a2 as their Indo-European-speaking neighbours. Judging by the end results of Indo-European migrations, the Volga-Ural region of the steppe, whence sprang the Afanasievo and Andronovo cultures, was strong in R1a1a, while the region around the Sea of Azov was strong in R1b1a2.

As we have seen (Chapter 5), R1b1c (V88) appears in the Levant and seems linked to the spread of farming into Africa. If R1b1 men were living close enough to the Neolithic heartland to be swept up in one farming exodus, then it is possible that some joined another. We may hazard a guess that R1b1a2 fed into the steppe with dairy farmers. As noted (see Chapter 6), dairy farming developed around the Sea of Marmara, and contributed to the Cucuteni-Tripolye culture adjacent to the steppe. The Late Cucuteni-Tripolye and Yamnaya influences cross-fertilized each other and then merged in the pressure cooker of climate change. That would fit the genetic picture. Some R1b1a2 could have drifted up the Danube with dairy farming, but its major impact came later. From R1b1a2, one lineage progressed through a chain of mutations over perhaps 2,000 or 3,000 years, suggesting a period of stability. The subsequent burst of population growth can be calculated to around 3000 BC using the pedigree mutation rate (see p. 30).[12] Southeastern Europe has been too churned up by subsequent movements to rely on present populations as a guide to ancient ones, but it is perhaps worth mentioning the results of a sample of men of the Lviv region of Ukraine tested for Y-DNA. The dominant pattern today is typically Slavic (see Chapter 15), but there is a low level of R1b1a2 as well as other types of R1b1-P25, and E1b1b1 (M35.1), which may be another relic of Neolithic farmers.[13]

A brother lineage to R1b1a2 is R1b1a1 (M73, M478). It is extremely rare in Europe, but appears at low frequencies along the central Eurasian corridor linked by the steppe, most markedly among the Iranian-speaking Hazaras in Pakistan and Turkic-speaking Bashkirs.[14] That distribution suggests that it spread east with Indo-European steppe nomads and was then absorbed by East Asian steppe nomads as they spread west. It does not appear to be part of the movement into India and Iran, and so probably spread along the Silk Road sometime after the collapse of Andronovo. That places at least one R1b1a progenitor in the vicinity of the steppe.

Looking back in time to the origins of R1, Iran may hold the key. Rare basal types of the haplogroup appear there, both R1* (M173) itself and its offspring R1a1* (SRY1532.2) and R1b* (M343).[15] So the split between R1a and R1b may have happened hereabouts. There is a link between the southern Urals and the southern Caspian Basin. The Yangelskaya culture which appears in the former area around 9000 BC is virtually identical with finds in the latter area. Contacts between the two continued into the Neolithic.[16] Here we have a clue that Mesolithic people carrying R1 may have moved between summer hunting on the steppe and winter quarters in the sheltered forest refuge fringing the southern Caspian.[17] Transport by boat would avoid the snow-capped Caucasus Mountains. Images of boats, which from their stratigraphic location must be over 10,000 years old, appear among the famed petroglyphs of Gobustan beside the Caspian in southeast Azerbaijan.[18] [see 18] Perhaps R1a arose among those of their descendants who settled on the steppe, while R1b appeared among those descendants who favoured the southern homeland, and so became involved earlier than R1a in agriculture. A niche on the northern side of the Zagros would be on the fringe of the Neolithic, out of the mainstream of movements, which might explain the seemingly limited involvement of R1b in the initial spread of the Neolithic. It should be stressed that this scenario can only be speculative in the absence of ancient DNA.

Genetic fellow-travellers

We should not assume that the Indo-Europeans were all descended from the R1 founder. Nor is the R1a1a/R1b1a2 division so neat that there is no overlap. The two could travel together. Certain other haplogroups also appear to travel with subclades of R1 in the migrations of Indo-European speakers. A group of Bronze Age skeletons found in Lichtenstein Cave, Lower Saxony, provide a concrete example of Y-DNA haplogroups mixed within one band. The men included two possibly of Y-DNA R1a1 and one of R1b, but no fewer than 12 of I2a2b (L38/S154).[19] The last two haplogroups continue to reflect the connection shown in the cave. The present-day distributions of I2a2b and R1b-L21 both flow along the Rhine and into the British Isles.[20]

As we have seen, I2a1 appears among some early farmers of western Europe (Chapter 5, p. 93). It probably reflects hunter-gatherers assimilated by farmers in southeast Europe. So Cucuteni-Tripolye farmers may have contributed I2a into the Yamnaya-with-Cucuteni-Tripolye cultural amalgam. If I2a was associated with Usatovo and the villages along the Dniester, that would explain why I2a2b (L38/S154) appears alongside R1a1a after apparently migrating up the river and around the Carpathians into present-day Germany (Lichtenstein Cave).

Some I2a1b3a (L147) carriers could have been living in the Late Cucuteni-Tripolye towns of the Middle Dnieper. If their descendants chose to remain in what became the Proto-Slavic heartland, together with R1a1a men, in one of whom the M458 mutation arose, until population growth pushed them outwards in all directions in the early Middle Ages, that would explain the pattern we see today. These two haplogroups are strongly correlated with the distribution of Slavic languages (see Chapter 15). A splinter group of the parent haplogroup I2a1b3* (L621) split off about 4000 BC and appears today in Scotland and Ireland, so its ancestor probably moved up the Danube with an Indo-European band, leaving descendants who arrived in Britain with the Celts.[21]

So far we have been viewing R1 and R1b as the predominant Y-DNA haplogroups among Indo-European speakers. It is not always so. R1b and R1a appear as minority haplogroups in several Indo-European-speaking populations today.

The Ossets of the North Caucasus speak an eastern Iranian language, related to those spoken in Central Asia until the Turkish conquest of the region.[22] Ossetian can be traced to the settlement in the North Caucasus of elite families of Alans in the 7th century AD.[23] Rich tombs near the village of Brut probably contained Alan rulers.[24] On the evidence of their language, the Alans descend from the Scythians. Ancient historians agreed. Josephus declared the Alans to be Scythian.[25] Both Ammianus and Cassius Dio regarded them as Massagetae, a Scythian tribe.[26] DNA from Scythian graves is predominantly R1a1a.[27] Although the language of the Alans survived, their Y-DNA genetic signature appears relatively weak, suggesting that they blended with local people of Neolithic origin. The strongest signal of their arrival is 15.7 per cent R1b1a2 (M269) among Ossetian men of the Digorian branch. The date of R1b1a2 (M269) among the Ossets generally, calculated using the pedigree mutation rate, corresponds to the incoming Alans. The incoming language was associated here with an elite. The puzzle lies in the apparent genetic composition of that elite. There is only a tiny trace of R1a1a in the Ossets (0.4 and 0.8 per cent in the two branches).[28] An explanation occurs. The Alans were fighting men. Their story is one of battles against, and together with, Goths and Huns. By the time they retreated to the North Caucasus, the remnant of the Alans may have been overwhelmingly female.

Rare early lineages of Y-DNA R1b – R1b1a2* (M269) and R1b1a2a (L23) – are found among Armenians, both in Armenia itself and in Iran. In Europe these early lineages appear at the highest frequency in the Balkans. This is consistent with the ancestor of the Armenian language coming from the southeastern Balkans. The R1b lineages make up about a third of the total in Armenia, and the rest are largely haplogroups that we can guess arrived in the Neolithic, notably J (M304), but also G2a (P15) and J1 (M267). The

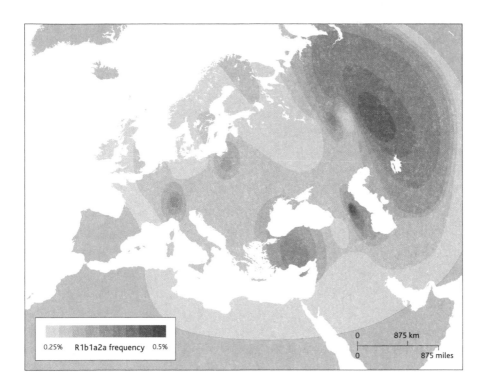

67 *The distribution of Y-DNA haplogroup R1b1a2a (L23) is thin if its most prolific offspring are excluded – the descendants of R1b1a2a1a. Most of what is considered L23* on this map may turn out to belong to R1b1a2a1b (L584) or other subclades.*

sprinkling of I2* (M438), I2a2a (M223), J2b1, J2b2 and E-V13 could have travelled with the R1b carriers, since all appear in the Balkans. It is impossible to be certain without aDNA, since low levels of any haplogroup in a population need not be linked to major migrations, and could have arrived with trade or imperial administrators. Armenia formed part of the Macedonian and Roman empires.[29] Still, treated with caution, evidence from present-day Armenians provides us with a clue to the genetic composition of the Indo-European speakers who branched off to the Aegean. They have none of the R1b mutations most common in Europeans. The R1b1a2a (L23) lineage gave birth to these mutations eventually, but clearly not on the route that led to Greece and Armenia. [67]

Greece too is not dominated by R1b1a2 (M269) and has more R1b1a2a (L23) than western Europe. R1a1a appeared at 21 per cent in a sample from Macedonia and at lower levels elsewhere in Greece, but this appears to fall mainly within the Slavic subclade defined by M458 and reflects Slavic incursions into that area in the Byzantine period. No Y-DNA haplogroup can be considered predominant in Greece. J2 is strongest on Crete, but does not reach 50 per cent of males even there. E-V13 is in the same position in the southern mainland.[30] It is a complex genetic picture. What else should we expect of a seagoing people at the crossroads of civilizations? Disentangling the genetic threads in Greece will take time (see Chapter 11).

In Iran also no Y-DNA haplogroup reaches 50 per cent of the male population, but J2a (M410) makes the strongest showing, followed by R1a1a (M198), with substantial contributions from G (M201) and R1b1a2 (M269). The Medes and Persians had entered a region long settled by farmers. At their entry point in Khorasan, R1a1a outnumbers J2a, as it does in the southwest, where Persians settled, but the pattern overall is as complex as we would expect in a country composed now of multiple ethnicities and languages, many of which arrived long after the Medes and Persians. The Iranian R1b is mainly composed of R1b1a2* (M269) and R1b1a2a (L23), some of which is found in Armenians, whose ancestors arrived in Iran in 1600 as captives, and yet more (29.2 per cent) in modern Assyrians within Iran, who speak the Semitic language Aramaic. The low level of R1b1a2a (L23) in Khorasan is similar to that in Pakistan and suggests that little of this haplogroup actually arrived in Iran with Medes and Persians.[31]

The Y-DNA J2a (M410) in Iran provides insights also into the complex population structure of South Asia. Since farming of the Near Eastern type seems to have entered South Asia via Iran, we would expect to find J2a among the people of the Indus Valley civilization (late 4th to 2nd millennium BC). That is not the end of the story though. The Bactro-Margiana Archaeological Complex (BMAC) also seems to have arisen among farmers whose ancestors arrived from Iran, and Proto-Indic appears to have entered the Indian subcontinent with an amalgamation of Andronovo and the BMAC. So we would expect J2a among them too. J2a seems to have spread widely across the subcontinent from a highest density in the northwest.[32] Since both the Indus Valley Neolithic and the Indo-Europeans entered the subcontinent from the same direction, that is not surprising. In India J2a appears to be a fellow-traveller with R1a1a (M17), insofar as that the two reach their highest levels in the upper castes.[33] Study of subclades may disentangle the story-lines.

Mitochondrial DNA

The mtDNA haplogroups that travelled with Indo-European languages were varied, to judge from those found in ancient DNA. We would expect haplogroups U4 and U5, which are found among Mesolithic peoples of the North European Plain, to be as common among the hunters of the steppe who formed one strand of the Indo-European mixture. From the farming strand of the Indo-European mixture we would expect Neolithic haplogroups H, K and T, found in remains from the Cucuteni-Tripolye culture in Ukraine. Indeed, U4, U5, H, K and T all appear in aDNA from Andronovo. The comparatively rare T2a1b1 appears in remains from both Cucuteni-Tripolye and Andronovo.[34]

The discovery of four family graves in Eulau, Saxony-Anhalt, Germany, of the Corded Ware culture provided an opportunity to use an array of research techniques. They were all victims of a violent attack, which killed men, women and children. Family relationships were traced through DNA. One Y-DNA haplogroup R1a1a father was buried with his mtDNA K1b wife and their two sons. Strontium isotope results showed that the men and children had grown up in the local area, whereas the women had spent their early lives some distance away, suggesting a patrilocal society.[35]

The levels of mtDNA H in early Neolithic aDNA so far discovered in Europe are distinctly lower than in modern Europeans, where H represents about 45 per cent of the population. Levels of H appear closer to modern in late Neolithic to Early Bronze Age Europeans.[36] The cause of the rise of H is unclear. MtDNA H5a seems to have dispersed partly with the Indo-Europeans.[37] Yet that would not wholly account for the dominance of H today. One possibility is that natural selection has been at work, since persons carrying mtDNA H recover better after sepsis.[38]

The rare haplogroup U2e seems Indo-European in its distribution [68], but appearances can deceive. It is far older than PIE. A recent estimate of its date was over 17,000 BC.[39] It probably occurred among U2 hunter-gatherers roaming the steppe and forest-steppe around the Urals. (Remember the U2 found in a 30,000-year-old man at Kostënki in Russia, p. 52.) It was present in northwest Russia by the 6th millennium BC (Table 1, pp. 26–27) and western Siberia by the 4th millennium BC.[40] We can deduce a presence on the European steppe at the time of PIE, as U2e appears in remains from archaeological cultures of west and east linked to the Indo-Europeans: Bell Beaker and Andronovo.[41] It was also found in two Iron Age cemeteries,

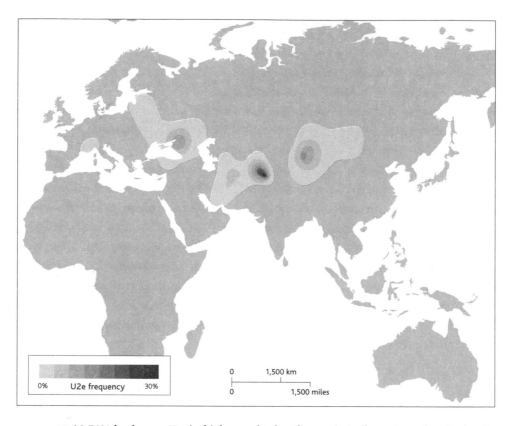

68 *MtDNA haplogroup U2e is thinly spread today; there are just a few regions where its density is high enough to register on this map. It is interesting as a rare hunter-gatherer haplogroup that seems to have entered the Indo-European family mixture.*

one near Qiemo, Xinjiang on the old southern Silk Road,[42] and the other at Bøgebjerggård in Denmark.[43] In modern populations U2e reaches a peak of nearly 16 per cent among the Kalash of northern Pakistan, a polytheistic people who speak an Indo-European language. East of that hot-spot there are lesser hot-spots along the former Silk Road, and to the west around the Black Sea.[44] [68] U2e seems to be scattered at lower levels right across the distribution of Indo-European languages.

Lactase persistence

Another clue to the impact of pastoralists from the steppe is the fact that most European adults can drink milk. This is the result of a helpful genetic mutation that confers lactase persistence. Lactase is the enzyme in the intestinal system that can metabolize lactose, a sugar found in milk and other dairy products. Mammals produce this enzyme as infants so they can digest their mother's milk. The production of lactase shuts down automatically after infancy in all mammals except some human beings. East Asians and many Africans are lactose intolerant as adults, while the reverse is true of most Europeans, Pakistanis and those African and Middle Eastern populations historically associated with pastoralism.

There have been at least six separate mutations that cause the lactase switch-off to fail. Lactase persistence genes of East African origin are 13907G and 14010C. A compound allele (13915G and 3712C) found in Saudis and East Africans probably originated in the Middle East.[45] A rarer lactase persistence allele (13913C) was discovered in two cases in Italy, and subsequently reported in Cameroon, Sudan and Ethiopia, and in the Bedouin population in Saudi Arabia.[46]

The dominant mutation in Western Eurasia and South Asia is 13910T or rs4988235(A). In South Asia it decreases southwards and eastwards from a peak in the northwest. This allele is found within different haplotype backgrounds, i.e. the stretches of DNA code either side of it. One of these predominates in both Europe and South Asia, indicating a common origin.[47] The 13910T mutation also appears in Central Asia, though at lower levels: 30 per cent for Kazakhs and 19 per cent for Tajiko-Uzbeks.[48] [69]

Another mutation, 22018A or rs182549(T), was first recognized in Finns. While it is generally found with 13910T in Europeans, it can appear as an independent cause of lactase persistence, for example in Pakistanis and in the Kazakhs of northern China.[49] The haplotype containing these two alleles (13910T and 22018A) is common in northern-European-derived populations (77 per cent in European Americans). It is largely identical over a long chain of DNA. Such lengthy stretches of identical DNA indicate recent origin; older DNA has had more time to be broken up by recombination in each generation. The haplotype could not have risen quickly to such high frequency without the aid of natural selection. Strong selection has occurred within the past 5,000–10,000 years, a time frame we would expect in the setting of dairy farming. Even more recent estimates were obtained for a Scandinavian population, suggesting stronger and more recent selection there.[50] On the other hand, the exceptionally high lactose tolerance levels in Sweden (74 per cent) and Finland (82 per cent) can hardly be explained by selection in situ, since fresh cow's milk has not been part of the traditional

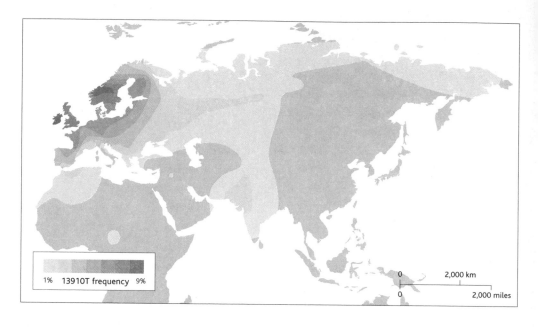

69 *The distribution of the lactase persistence allele 13910T shows a correlation with Indo-European and Uralic languages, though it also appears in parts of Africa.*

diet of Swedes or Finns until recent times. So this high level could be the result of a burst of immigration by lactose-tolerant people into a previously sparsely populated region.[51]

As we have seen, evidence of milking on a significant scale first appears around the Sea of Marmara c. 6500–5000 BC, but initially the milk was processed into yoghurt or cheese, which would make it more digestible for those without lactase.[52] The lack of 13910T in Anatolia except for that part beside the Sea of Marmara suggests that the mutation did not occur in the early Neolithic, but among dairy farmers spreading into southeast Europe in the late Neolithic. Analysis of ancient DNA has so far confirmed that deduction. 13910T has not been found in early European Neolithic (LBK and Epicardial) human remains,[53] or late Neolithic remains from the south of France,[54] but appears in Final Neolithic and Copper Age remains in northeast Spain[55] and in the TRB.[56]

13910T could have moved up the Danube with dairy farmers, but also into the Cucuteni herders adjacent to the steppe and thence into the steppe peoples adopting pastoralism. The distribution of 13910T and 22018A suggests that they were spread by Indo-European speakers both east and west. If these alleles arrived on the steppe with dairy farming, there must have been interbreeding between the Cucuteni and steppe peoples to disseminate these genes thoroughly before the migrations. There was much contact between the two.[57] As mentioned, the comparatively rare mtDNA haplogroup T2a1b1 appears in remains from a Cucuteni site in Ukraine and a later Andronovo site, suggesting gene flow from the former into the latter.[58] In a patrilocal system, in which wives moved into their husband's home, intermarriage would have no impact on which Y-DNA haplogroup was predominant within a family. Patrilocality has been deduced on linguistic evidence for PIE speakers.[59]

The mutation 13910T [69] is found among nations in which R1a1a is dominant and also those in which R1b1a2 is dominant, and indeed among the Finns, who carry little of either haplogroup. It crops up across the far north of Europe and Asia, where Uralic languages are spoken. Intermarriage between Indo-European speakers and Uralic speakers over millennia could explain the spread of 13910T to the latter. A low level of 13910T (1 in 20) was found in a sample of remains from the Pitted Ware culture in Gotland (Chapter 4), who were probably Uralic speakers.[60]

Adults who could digest raw milk had an excellent source of food on the hoof. Cattle could go on turning grass into milk for years before they were slaughtered for beef. It has been proposed that lactase persistence was the genetic edge that allowed the dairy pastoralist Indo-Europeans to spread. Dairy farming produces five times as many calories per acre as raising cattle for slaughter.[61] The protein and calcium of milk certainly build bones. Prehistoric dairy farmers tended to be taller than other farmers.[62]

CHAPTER TEN
Beaker Folk to Celts and Italics

T he movement of a people presumed to have spoken Proto-Italo-Celtic can be traced up the Danube as far as the Carpathian Basin by their kurgans.[1] We then start to see the Bell Beaker culture (2700–2000 BC) spreading over a swathe of Europe. This culture is recognized by its characteristic pottery, shaped like an inverted bell. [70] Bell Beaker ware is found as far east as Poland,[2] as far south as northern Morocco, as far north as Scotland,[3] northern Denmark,[4] and even the southern tip of Norway.[5] [71] Archaeologists have found the distinctive beaker so useful in identifying the culture that rather too much emphasis has been placed upon it. There are far more important aspects to this culture than its pottery. With Bell Beaker we find the plough, wheeled vehicles, woolly sheep and horse power.[6]

The Beaker culture arrived in much of Europe with immigrants. Recognition of this represents a return to ideas once commonplace. An anti-migrationist perspective was introduced in the 1970s.[7] Migration was generally downplayed in subsequent explanations of Bell Beaker until at least the end of

70 Bell Beaker from Hungary, with the characteristic shape like an inverted bell. Such beakers were often decorated with bands of incised patterns, which could be picked out in white paste made of crushed bone.

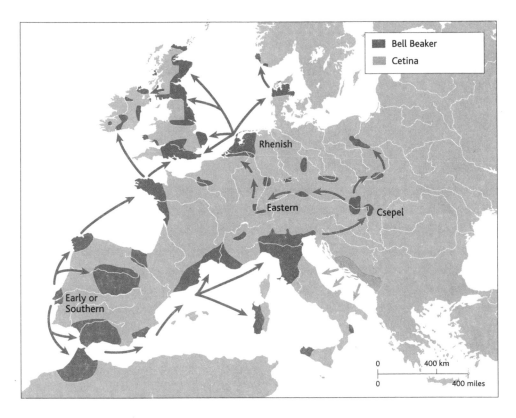

71 *Bell Beaker pottery spread by sea and river routes. If it was made by women, its dispersal may be partly linked to a search for marital partners among the scattered kin of a mobile Copper Age people.*

the 20th century. Now clues to the astonishing mobility of Beaker folk are building up from isotope, craniometric and inherited dental trait studies.[8] What little aDNA we have from Bell Beaker sites confirms this picture. The earliest comes from Kromsdorf in Germany (2600–2500 BC). One small burial ground yielded results from six people. Only two Y-DNA results could be extracted. In contrast to the haplogroups so far found in Neolithic men, both were R1b (M343). Among the mtDNA haplogroups at Kromsdorf, T1a and W5a have not been found earlier in Europe (Table 1). The rare U2e also appears.[9] As discussed in Chapter 9, U2e may have an Indo-European link.

By the time that Classical authors began to note the Celts, over 2,000 years later, they could be found over much of Europe west of the Rhine and in pockets east of it. Some lived in the Alps and northern Italy, while Italic speakers were in central Italy. This geographical distribution coincides

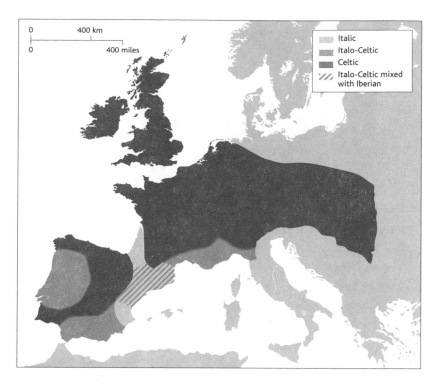

72 *By c. 500 BC Italic and Celtic languages were spoken over a large swathe of Europe. Languages which probably descended from a common ancestor of Italic and Celtic fringed Celtic from Iberia to Italy. The Etruscans created the gap between Italo-Celtic and Italic languages.*

fairly well with that of Bell Beaker. [72] Between the period when archaeologists can see the new, intrusive Beaker culture arrive and the point at which historians find written evidence of the Celts and Italics, a long continuity is apparent in the archaeology in many places from Bronze to Iron Age cultures. So the finger points at the Bell Beaker people as the carriers of the dialect that developed into this branch of Indo-European. Both their mobility and the comparative uniformity of their widespread culture make the idea plausible.[10] The notion that the Celts first arrived in the British Isles and Iberia in the Iron Age was once popular, and one can see why. There are clear indications of Celtic arrivals in that era (see Chapter 12). The problem is that they cover too limited an area of Ireland and Iberia to explain the full distribution of Celtic languages there.[11]

In Portugal, Zambujal (already a Copper Age nexus) became an important Beaker centre. One type of Bell Beaker, known as Maritime, appears from an early date and seems to have spread by sea from a Bell Beaker colony beside the Tagus. Zambujal and its satellites, known as the Vila Nova de São Pedro culture, was the hub of a complex web of contacts along the Atlantic and northern Mediterranean coasts, and sometimes far inland. The Beaker people seem to have arrived swiftly in Iberia. Some of their earliest sites are found in Portugal. Or to be more exact, they appear to be the same people who had brought copper-working earlier.[12] There is no change in the metal-working technology when Bell Beaker pottery began to be made.[13]

It has been optimistically argued that the famed bell shape of Bell Beakers developed from earlier Vila Nova de São Pedro wares of slightly concave outline.[14] Yet all the ingredients of the Bell Beaker design have precise predecessors on the Pontic steppe or in the Carpathian Basin. Pots of the same shape have been found from before 4000 BC among Cucuteni and Svobodnoe types.[15] Bell Beaker ware from 3rd-millennium BC Spain was decorated with white paste made of crushed bone. This technique was used earlier in the Carpathian Basin and on Funnel Beaker ware (see pp. 100–01).[16] One of the most widespread early types of Bell Beaker pottery, known as All Over Corded (AOC), is decorated with impressions made with cord. That similarity to Corded Ware, together with the other features that the two cultures share, and the fact that they overlap geographically, led to the assumption that Bell Beaker developed from Corded Ware. It is now recognized that the two are contemporary.[17] Their similarities, including cord impressions in pottery, reflect a shared cultural parent in Yamnaya (see p. 130). In short, the influences that culminated in this pottery could have travelled over time along the same route that brought copper-working to Iberia.

The Stelae People

A study of inherited dental traits found that the Bell Beaker people were newcomers in Hungary and the Czech Republic, but a different picture emerged in southern France, northern Spain and western Switzerland. Here Bell Beaker folk not only shared the graves and settlements of their Final Neolithic and Copper Age predecessors, but were actually related to them. One crucial site showing this relationship is Petit-Chasseur, at Sion in Switzerland. It is famed for its anthropomorphic stelae, which continue from the Final Neolithic to Bell Beaker.[18] They play a part in explaining the genesis of Bell Beaker.

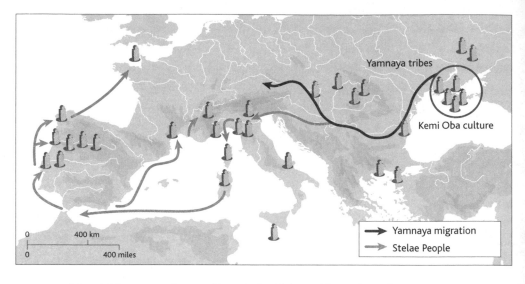

73 (above) *The suggested route of Proto-Italo-Celtic-speaking stelae makers.*

74 (below) *The Kernosovka stele from Ukraine depicts a moustached man with a club, dagger and three axes.*

The earliest anthropomorphic stelae of this type have been found in Yamnaya burial mounds in Ukraine. [74] They are particularly associated with one subculture, the Kemi Oba, centred on Crimea. Similar stelae are found at Bell Beaker sites in the Swiss and Italian Alps, and in the Italian regions of Lunigiana and Trento-Alto-Adige, southern France and Iberia. Other examples are scattered as far afield as Malta and the Channel Islands. These figures are curiously stylized and slab-like, quite different from earlier and later depictions of the human form. Males are generally given tools or weapons. Females often have necklaces. The stelae probably recorded honoured ancestors.[19] We can trace the concept back to the early Neolithic and the astonishing site of Göbekli Tepe (see p. 76).

Copper-workers may have arrived in Iberia initially with a small company of migrants, to be gradually reinforced over time by others seeking pastures new. Carved stone anthropomorphic stelae mark the trail of these copper-workers, so let us call them the Stelae People.[20] [73] A splinter group from the Proto-Italo-Celtic parent would explain why the ancient Lusitanian language of what is now Portugal appears to be Italo-Celtic.[21] A similarly mixed language was spoken by the Ligures in what is now northwestern Italy and southeastern France. There is tantalizingly little evidence for Ligurian, but it appears to meld Celtic and Italic.[22]

Is it a coincidence that the earliest copper mine has been found in the territory of the Ligures?[23] Or was there a clan-run industrial network stretching across the Mediterranean? Copper-working had already arrived in Italy and Sardinia, perhaps from the Balkans, before Stelae People started to appear. So knowledge of the resources of Italy could have filtered back to the Balkans, enticing another wave westwards. It seems possible that a group of Proto-Italo-Celtic speakers left the Danube corridor to travel through the Vučedol culture (Croatia), which would give them a relatively easy route to the Adriatic Sea and from there to northern Italy, along the River Po to Liguria and on to Iberia by sea.

Early Beaker elements are found within the Vučedol culture, but only later do the two fuse to form the Cetina culture [71], as might happen if the route was used back and forth over centuries, combining settlement and trade. The Cetina culture spread across the Adriatic to the eastern coast of Italy.[24] Contacts continued across the Adriatic as the descendants of the Cetina coastal people developed into the Liburni, noted shipbuilders and seafarers, who controlled the Adriatic down to Corfu and were accused of piracy by the Romans.

Another return route from Iberia for the Stelae People might be up the Rhone. The Rhone Valley is rich in Bell Beaker sites, while eastern tributaries lead to the Alpine stelae and Beaker sites at Sion and Aosta. The early phases of Bell Beaker in this area have strong affinities with those of Iberia.[25] Bell Beaker sites in southern France and Tuscany share the early dates found in Portugal.[26]

We can also picture the mother group of Proto-Italo-Celtic speakers gradually moving further up the Danube from the Carpathian Basin and developing Proto-Celtic. If the Stelae People had created trade routes across Europe from the Carpathian Basin as far as Portugal, we can see how Bell Beaker ware could have been developed in Portugal and yet crop up in

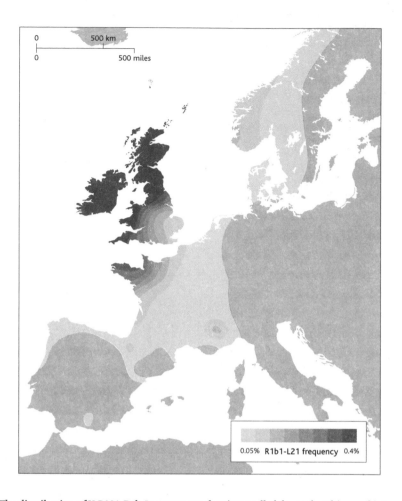

75 The distribution of Y-DNA R1b-L21 suggests that it travelled down the Rhine and into the British Isles, where it is now densest in the regions least affected by post-Roman arrivals. The high level in Brittany may reflect the post-Roman migration of Britons, after whom it was named.

Hungary. A Bell Beaker site on Csepel Island in the Danube proved to be remarkably early for Eastern Bell Beaker. It has given its name to about 60 sites of the Bell Beaker Csepel group, clustered around Budapest. Hungary has no other Bell Beaker. Anthropologically and culturally, the isolated Csepel group appears an intrusion, so its origin was something of a mystery. Now a study of inherited forms of teeth links the Bell Beaker folk of Csepel to those of western Switzerland, while the latter in their turn cluster with the Southern Bell Beaker group in Iberia and southern France.[27]

From Hungary the Bell Beaker style of pottery travelled up the Danube and down the Rhine.[28] The people who carried it may have been recognized by the Southern Bell Beaker group as distant cousins – part of the clan. If the pottery was made by women, it may have been spread partly through marriage. The search for marriage partners outside the home group would have created a constant mobility between the scattered Bell Beaker settlements.[29] Yet the split into two streams proposed here would give the Southern and Eastern Bell Beaker groups centuries to drift apart, linguistically and genetically, before Bell Beaker pottery appeared in Central Europe, c. 2500 BC. That would explain why comparatively few Iberians (under 8 per cent) or Italians (under 3 per cent) carry the L21 mutation within Y-DNA R1b, common in the rest of the former Celtic world, particularly in Ireland.[30] [75] Instead, its brother clade, R1b-DF27, is frequent in Iberia.[31]

Artifacts found with Bell Beaker pottery have their own tales to tell. A characteristic item in high-status male Bell Beaker graves is the wrist-guard. It takes the form of a thin rectangle of stone with holes at both ends that could have been used to tie it on to the wrist. A natural assumption was that the stone guard was fixed to the inside of the wrist, like a modern archer's wrist-guard, to protect human flesh from the whip of the bowstring. It was a surprise, then, to find the guard on the outside of the wrist in those burials where the position is clear. That recognition set off a wave of specu-

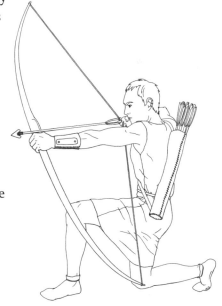

lation on alternative functions. Probably the answer is that the stone bracer was fixed to a leather wrist-guard. [76] More significantly for those trying to trace migration, there were two main styles of bracer. The only type found among the Early or Southern Bell Beaker group is narrow with two holes, one at each end. Broader, four-holed types predominate in Central Europe. England and Scotland lean heavily towards elaborate four-hole

76 *Archer with stone bracer fixed to a leather wrist-guard.*

types, while Ireland has almost exclusively two-holed types.[32] Here again is evidence of two routes.

North of the Alps, people of the Eastern Bell Beaker group established themselves in what was to become a powerful trading nexus. On the east the Rhine linked the Carpathians and the North Sea; on the west the Saone-Rhone corridor linked the Mediterranean and Central Europe. The Alpine passes could also be controlled from north of the Alps. To judge by an abrupt change of orientation and new arrivals at the Alpine sites of Sion and Aosta, that control was exerted as early as *c.* 2425 BC, at the expense of their distant cousins the Stelae People. Objects distinctive of the Eastern Bell Beaker group appear, such as bow-shaped pendants.[33] Isotopes reveal a distant origin for one man, who had the type of cranium typical of the Eastern Bell Beaker group.[34] The evidence adds up to a power shift in the middle of the Bell Beaker period from the mouth of the Tagus to the head of the Rhine. The Bell Beaker communities of the Rhone corridor who had looked to Iberia shifted their gaze eastwards and northwards. As at Sion, bow-shaped pendants appear, along with pottery designs from the Eastern Bell Beaker group.[35] If traders and settlers were spreading down the Rhone from the Alps, then the trail would lead to Iberia. Around 2200 BC a new style of Bell Beaker appeared in central Spain.[36] An ancient language of northeastern Iberia may reflect an influx at this time of speakers of the developing Proto-Celtic. Celtiberian is the most archaic form of Celtic.[37] It has even been argued that it was not quite Celtic.[38] Yet it does seem to represent a later linguistic stage than Lusitanian.

When the Stelae People first emerge into history, all but the Italic speakers among them seem to have been labelled *Ligyes* or *Ligures* (Ligurians). This conclusion rests rather insecurely on the few references by ancient Greek geographers to *Ligures* outside present-day Liguria (northwestern Italy). There is a vague passage in the 4th-century AD *Ora Maritima*, which draws on a now lost 6th-century BC description of the sea coasts. The author talks of Ligurians on the Atlantic coast of Europe having been driven away by Celts.[39] The huge geographical range of speculation about where exactly these Ligurians were is proof enough that the *Ora Maritima* is too garbled for certain identification. Fortunately, Stephanus of Byzantium records from a lost early source a more precise reference to Ligystine, 'a Ligurian city of the west', close to Tartessos. Presumably this was near the *Ligustinus Lacus*, the marshes at the mouth of the Guadalquivir.[40] The Greek geographer

Eratosthenes (c. 276–195 BC) evidently linked Ligurians to Iberia, for he called the Iberian peninsula the Ligurian.[41]

The Periplous of Pseudo-Skylax (338–337 BC) describes the *Ligyes* along the coast of the Mediterranean Sea from Emporion (in present-day Catalonia, Spain) to Antion (Antibes in southeast France). The Greek colony of Massalia (Marseilles) was in the territory of the Ligurians.[42] Here we are on safer ground, for other Greek sources also mention the Ligurians around Massalia.[43] Later writers call them Celtoligures, confining the name Ligures to the people of present-day Liguria in northwest Italy.[44]

Who were the Celts?

Our modern definition of a Celt is a person speaking a Celtic language, but we should not expect every Celtic speaker in the past to be consistently labelled as such by his contemporaries or even by himself. The Celtic world was one of tribal affiliation, though tribes could be lumped together by geography. Thus the different tribes of the British Isles were collectively known as Britons.[45]

The earliest surviving mention of the Celts comes in the works of Herodotus. As a Greek writing in the 5th century BC, he was well informed about the Mediterranean world, dominated in his day by Greeks. His grasp of the geography of Europe further north was naturally more limited. He seems to have added together two different sources on the Celts to draw a curious conclusion. On the one hand he knew that Celts lived beyond the Pillars of Hercules (the Strait of Gibraltar). On the other he also knew that the River Ister (Danube) rose in the land of the Celts. So he concluded that the Danube rose in the Pyrenees.[46] Ephorus, a Greek historian of the 4th century BC, saw *Celtica* as including most of Iberia. Strabo, writing in the early 1st century AD, marvelled at so large a vision of the Celtic realm. By his day *Celtica* had become just another name for Gaul (present-day France).[47] Julius Caesar famously declared Gaul to be divided into three parts, only one of which was inhabited by Gauls, 'who call themselves Celts'.[48] This Roman attitude was seen as ignorance by the Greek historian Diodorus Siculus, for whom the coastal tribes of Gaul (known to earlier Greeks as *Ligures*) were Celts, while those north of the Alps were Gauls.[49]

What are we to make of all this? From the earliest days of linguistics, authors have taken Caesar's word for it and identified Gaulish as Celtic. Thus similar languages, such as those once spoken in the British Isles, could be placed in the Celtic family. North of the Alps powerful Bronze Age chiefdoms were succeeded by Iron Age cultures, which spread over Gaul, the Rhineland and northern Alps, and spawned inscriptions in Celtic languages once in contact with literacy (see Chapter 12). The distribution of Celtic place-names in ancient times is another helpful clue to their whereabouts [see 10].

Contemporaries varied in whether or not to label the Ligurians as Celts. Modern linguists have the same difficulty. Strabo weighed up the matter as well as anyone, saying that while the Ligurians of the Alps belong to a different people from the neighbouring Celts, they were similar in their mode of life.[50] Whatever label we put on them, we may see the Ligures as the descendants of the Southern Bell Beaker creators. In Italy there was no hard-edged division between Ligures and the tribes to the south who would become Italic speakers, until the Etruscans drove a wedge between them (see Chapter 13).

Celts arrive in the British Isles

The Bell Beaker culture brought the Bronze Age to the British Isles. To be more exact, Beaker folk initially brought the Copper Age around 2450 BC, homing in on the copper belts of Ireland and Wales. They left their characteristic beakers at a copper mine on Ross Island, in Lough Leane, Co. Kerry.[51] Judging from chemical composition, copper from Ireland was traded into Britain,[52] along with gold from the Mourne Mountains.[53] The incomers boosted what had been a dwindling population of farmers and created a thriving society.[54] From around 2200 BC Bell Beaker interest in Britain intensified as Cornwall was discovered to be a prime source for tin, the rare and precious component of true bronze. This resource gave the British Isles a head start in Europe in making bronze.[55]

For decades a vision of prehistoric population continuity shaped a view of Bell Beaker in the British Isles as a purely cultural phenomenon. Though in the 1960s several authors saw the origins of the Celts in the Beaker people,[56] the idea of Celts arriving at any time ran counter to the growing anti-migrationist mood. In the 1990s there was increasing Celto-scepticism among archaeologists, undermining the whole concept of Celts in the British Isles.[57] With or without the Celtic connection, the idea of 'Bell Beaker Folk' seemed a thing of the past.

The discovery of the Amesbury Archer near Stonehenge reignited the debate. This man lived around 2350 BC and was buried with Beaker pots and wrist-guards. His gold hair binders are the earliest gold artifacts found in Britain. Isotope tests were carried out on the Archer's teeth and bones. They indicate that he probably came from central Europe, near the Alps. The copper of his knives was also from the Continent (northern Spain and western France). Significantly, he was also buried with a rare cushion stone, thought to be used by metalworkers. His grave was so crowded with tokens of his life that he must have been held in high esteem.[58] Such high-status Bell Beaker burials are rare: only 12 have been found so far in the whole of Europe.[59]

Other discoveries followed. The Boscombe Bowmen, a group of somewhat earlier Beaker burials near Stonehenge, came from a region with a more ancient geology than Wessex, where they were found, according to their isotope signatures. That covers a wide range of possibilities, including places within the British Isles, but the date of the burials pushes them towards the head of a wave of Beaker arrivals from the Continent. Theirs was a collective burial, more common among Beaker groups on the Atlantic fringe of Europe than the centre. Brittany and Portugal have a geology to match the isotope traces of the Boscombe Bowmen.[60] The Ross Island miners could also have originated in Atlantic Europe. They arrived with a fully fledged technology of clearly continental origin, particularly similar to that of Atlantic France.[61] By contrast, a Dutch-style Beaker grave in Upper Largie, Argyll and Bute, western Scotland, hints at immigration from the Lower Rhine area. A young adult buried on the Hebridean island of Coll c. 3880 BC had an isotope signature that could include the Netherlands.[62] Genetically, the predominance of R1b-L21 over R1b-DF27-derived subclades of R1b-P312 in the British Isles suggests that British and Irish Bell Beaker people mostly arrived via the Rhine route.

So what language did the Bell Beaker folk bring to the British Isles? Why were two types of Celtic spoken there by the time we have any records? Gaelic seems the more conservative form.[63] We can picture an archaic form of Celtic spoken by the Late Bell Beaker period that evolved over the millennia into Gaelic. By contrast the Brittonic (or Brythonic) language of Britain was closely related to Gaulish, spoken across the Channel by the Roman period. That suggests that Britain received more or heavier waves of Celtic migration than did Ireland, continuing into the Iron Age. This fits the archaeological picture (see Chapter 12). One complication is that Gaelic and Brittonic did not evolve in isolation from each other. Constant communication within the islands created similarities between all the insular forms of Celtic. So even the earliest written form of Gaelic, recorded in inscriptions from around AD 400 using the ogham alphabet, should not be seen as an unalloyed, direct descendant of the first Celtic spoken in the British Isles.[64]

The Bell Beaker networks created an inter-connected era, which intensified in the Late Bronze Age. From approximately 1300 to 700 BC prestigious items were exchanged over long distances. The major centres were southern England and Ireland, northwestern France and northwestern Iberia.[65] One site is particularly intriguing. The Isle of Thanet on the southeastern tip of England was probably an early landing site for Copper Age arrivals. Separated from the bulk of the North Downs by the Wantsum Channel, Thanet was a true island at the time. (Silting up between the island and the coast of Kent has since joined it to the mainland.) Offshore islands make convenient trading posts. Positioned at the mouth of the Thames estuary and close to the Continent, it has been a traditional landing/departure point for visitors. Thanet has an outstandingly dense distribution of Bronze Age burials.[66] Overlooking Pegwell Bay, a number of round barrows stand on the highest point of the coastline where they could be seen from out at sea. The location was probably chosen to ensure that key figures among Copper Age arrivals would not be forgotten. As often found elsewhere, later burials cluster close to one of these barrows. This later cemetery was used from the Late Bronze Age through to the Middle Iron Age. Isotopic analysis revealed where these people came from. Of the 22 skeletons tested, eight were local, seven were from Scandinavia and five were from southwest Iberia. Interestingly, the earliest phase was the most mixed: local, Norse and Iberian.[67] Norway has rich copper resources. Were Bell Beaker people prospecting in Norway? That might explain Bell Beaker finds there.[68] We can picture the Isle of Thanet as a hub for long-distance travellers first created in the Bell Beaker period.

CHAPTER ELEVEN
Minoans and Mycenaeans

The cultured Minoans of Crete were more sophisticated than the ancestors of the Hellenes in the Early Bronze Age, but eventually found themselves under new management – the warrior elite of Mycenae from the Greek mainland. There is more than one twist to this tale. The Minoans seem to have arrived in the Aegean at around the same period as the Mycenaeans. This is by no means an established fact. Argument has been fierce on the origins of both the Minoans and Mycenaeans.

The Minoans had so appealing a culture that one cannot wonder at the rival claims to it.[1] Were they descendants of the earliest farmers on Crete? That would make the Minoan the first civilization with European roots. Or did new arrivals from older civilizations foster the new lifestyle? The definition of civilization used here is a complex and organized society, with specialist crafts and mass-produced goods, public buildings, literacy and record-keeping. The Minoans left writing dating from 2100 to 1600 BC.[2] They built great structures which their first excavators called palaces and archaeologists today more cautiously describe as communal buildings.[3] These were decorated with frescoes of an island people, alive to the beauty of the world around them. Dolphins frolic in their decor. An octopus writhes on one much-photographed Minoan flask. [77] Hand-made pottery was overtaken by wheel-thrown, a sign of mass-production by a specialist potter.[4]

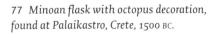

77 *Minoan flask with octopus decoration, found at Palaikastro, Crete, 1500 BC.*

When British archaeologist Colin Renfrew proposed in 1972 that the Minoans were native to Crete,[5] this was bound to meet with a good deal of European satisfaction. Doubts continue to surface. The Minoans would have had no concept of themselves as European. Indeed they would have had no concept of Europe.[6] The vista of this seafaring people ranged itself around the eastern Mediterranean and the Aegean. For the Bronze Age peoples of Egypt and the Near East, Crete was the western edge of civilization. The interconnections between the powers of the civilized world were close. The cultural flow between them is reflected in Minoan art and artifacts in Egypt and Near Eastern concepts in Crete.[7]

None of this necessarily implies that the flowering of Minoan civilization depended on immigrants in significant numbers. So are there linguistic clues? The Minoan script has never been satisfactorily deciphered, but there is agreement that it is not Greek.[8] There can be no doubt that Proto-Greek speakers encountered non-Hellenic languages in Greece. One in particular was widespread. From western Anatolia across the Aegean islands to mainland Greece, the map is dotted with place-names ending in -(s)sos and -nthos, such as Telmessos, Knossos, Korinthos and Zakynthos, which are foreign to Greek. Greek borrowed a number of words with the same two endings. Argument continues among linguists over whether this lost language has a Neolithic origin or could actually be Anatolian, specifically Luwian.[9]

Even in the times of Homer (c. 750 BC) and Herodotus (d. c. 425 BC) the Greeks were aware of a pre-Hellenic people in Greece, whom they called Pelasgians. Herodotus admitted that he was not in a position to say for certain what language the Pelasgians formerly spoke, but judging by those still existing in his day, it was a non-Greek language. In that case, he wrote, 'the Attic people (which used to be Pelasgian) must also have learned a new language at the time they became Hellenized'. This is a fascinating insight into language switch along with cultural change. He goes on to say that although the Hellenes were weak initially, they expanded until they encompassed a great many peoples, in particular the Pelasgians, along with quite a few other non-Greek peoples.[10] This leaves open the possibility that Minoan was a different language from Pelasgian.

Homer describes multicultural Crete after the arrival of Greek speakers:

Out in the dark blue sea there lies a land called Crete, a rich and lovely land, washed by the waves on every side, densely peopled and boasting ninety cities. Each of the several races of the isle has its own language. First there are the Achaeans; then the genuine Cretans, proud of their native stock; next the Cydonians; the Dorians with their three tribes; and finally the noble Pelasgians.[11]

The Greek speakers alone came with multiple ethnic labels, two of which Homer names on Crete: Achaeans and Dorians. That still leaves us with three non-Greek languages spoken on Crete. With the aid of the now lost work of an ancient Greek historian, Strabo interpreted this passage in Homer. He tells us that the native Cretans lived in the south of the island and the Cydonians in the west. He thought the Cydonians too were native, but that simply means pre-Greek.[12] The modern port of Chania in north-western Crete has a settlement history going back to the Minoan period and is generally equated with Cydonia.

Strabo's analysis fits the picture from archaeology. A sharp cultural change can be seen on Crete around 3000 BC, dividing the Neolithic and the Early Bronze Age. There was an influx not only of new styles and technology, but also of new social structures. The pattern suggests immigrants arriving in a large number from the east, part of an island-hopping movement from Anatolia.[13] Along the whole northern coast of Crete burial customs appear that are previously seen in the Cyclades. By contrast, continuity from the Neolithic is evident in parts of the interior. This was not a complete population replacement.[14] It was a time of vigorous change, which ultimately gave rise to the Minoan civilization.

One thing is certain. The Minoans were wine-drinkers. One of the few items that can be deciphered from Minoan texts is the sign for wine.[15] This is not a frivolous remark. With agriculture came alcohol, but farmers took some time to work up to wine. The earliest alcoholic drink in the Near East was probably a beer made from fermented barley.[16] This partly explains why beer-drinking spread so widely in the West. The habit would have travelled across Europe with the first farmers. The other reason why wine-drinking was more circumscribed than beer-swilling in the ancient world is that grapes flourish in sunny climates. Grapes grew wild on the southern shores of the Black and Caspian seas, climbing trees like lianas. They seem to have been first cultivated on the sunny southern slopes of the Caucasus.[17] The earliest complete winery was found in a cave in southern Armenia, close to Iran, complete with press, fermentation vats and storage jars. The species of grape was confirmed to be the domesticated variety. The complex has been radiocarbon-dated to 4100–4000 BC.[18] A genetic study of varieties of grape vine supports an origin of grape domestication in the Near East.[19] Clearly Crete was not cut off from contact with the outside world after the arrival of farming.

We can expect modern Greeks to be a genetic mixture from waves of settlement from the Neolithic onwards, but someone must have brought an Indo-European language to Greece, which developed into Greek. Unfortunately no consensus exists about either the time that Proto-Greeks arrived or the direction whence they came.[20]

Can genetics provide clues? Crete and Anatolia are higher today in Y-DNA haplogroup J2a (M410) than J2b (M12), in contrast to Thessaly and Greek Macedonia, where the positions are reversed. Haplogroup E-V13 is markedly higher on the mainland than in Crete. This pattern has been interpreted as the product of different waves of early farmers, in a study that took samples from men living close to Early Neolithic sites.[21] The problem with this approach is that a hiatus of centuries appears in some of these locations between the end of the Neolithic and the start of the Bronze Age. Current populations cannot safely be taken to represent Neolithic ones. So could this pattern owe more to Bronze Age movements? One study did calculate that the expansion time of E-V13 and J2b in Europe was much younger than expected for haplogroups linked to the Neolithic, and proposed a Bronze Age expansion from the Balkans.[22] Can that be reconciled with the discovery of E-V13 in Spain around 5000 BC? (See Chapter 5.) It can if we accept that living Europeans may descend rather more from Bronze Age expansions than from Neolithic ones.

Attempts to extract DNA from Neolithic and Bronze Age samples from Greece and Crete have been largely unsuccessful to date.[23] MtDNA was obtained from the elite of the Bronze Age citadel at Mycenae, with the aim of testing rival theories about the relationships between the individuals buried in Grave Circle B. The study generated mtDNA K and U5a1.[24] These haplogroups are familiar from Bell Beaker and Andronovo, but since both were present in Europe long before, mtDNA is not the most useful of tools for detecting new arrivals in the Bronze Age.

Archaeologists have eyed keenly any evidence of breaks and changes in the cultural record. The layer of destruction around 1900 BC at Lerna on the Argive coast excited interest from the time of its excavation. Warlike invaders were imagined. That vision dimmed as other key sites were uncovered.

The expected wide disruption at this period failed to materialize.[25] So attention has shifted to an earlier period. Did the elusive ancestors of the Mycenaean Greeks trickle into Greece from Thrace in the Early Bronze Age? That would make for a quieter beginning. Bronze Age arrivals from the northeast entered a landscape that had been largely depopulated for centuries.[26] There is a gap in the archaeological record from c. 4000 BC to c. 3370 BC, with no evidence of human occupation in northern Greece from western Macedonia to Thrace.[27]

This is around the time the Cyclades were being settled. These islands form stepping stones across the Aegean between Anatolia and the Greek mainland. The Cyclades had been by-passed by early farmers, but climate change in the Late Neolithic would have made the more temperate climate of islands more attractive. The islands closest to Greece seem to have appealed to farmers on the Greek mainland, while those closest to Anatolia drew settlers from that landmass.[28] The first tin-bronze anywhere in what is now Greece was brought by Trojans to Kastri on Syros.[29] The Aegean region had no source of tin, so the techniques of true bronze-making had to be imported. The need for metal helped to create a far-reaching trade network along which other commodities could flow.[30] This in turn fostered urban living from Anatolia across the Aegean during the 3rd millennium BC. Citadels appear, such as that at Troy, and administrative buildings. Wheel-made pottery and tin-bronzes are evidence of specialist crafts.[31] Strong connections were being forged between Greece and Anatolia, which were to continue into recorded history.

It is against this background that we can set developments on Crete. The Minoans had developed a sophisticated culture around 1900 BC. Although it shares features with older civilizations, it has its own distinctive character. Monumental architectural ensembles were the hubs of small states ruled by governing elites. Aided by sailing ships,[32] Minoan power spread through the Cyclades. Then came catastrophe. A volcanic eruption c. 1600 BC on the island of Santorini (Thera) buried the Minoan town of Akrotiri.[33] Twice, island-wide shocks devastated the 'palaces' on Crete. By 1550 BC all but Knossos were out of use. In this time of Minoan weakness the Mycenaeans seized hegemony of Crete, perhaps by dynastic marriage.[34] [78] As we saw with the Hittites (Chapter 8), the new ruling class adapted the script of the old one for their language, in this case an early form of Greek. Close links between the Mycenaeans and Anatolia are clear from Hittite records and archaeological remains. As early as the 14th century BC, Mycenaean trade is evident along the coastline of Asia Minor.[35]

Then came the Dark Age of Greece. Between the late 13th and early 12th centuries BC, Greek palatial centres were destroyed and abandoned. There was a sharp drop in population. Writing ceased. There was a return to village life. Monumental architecture was left to crumble. This sudden change also afflicted the rest of the eastern Mediterranean and Aegean. The Hittite empire dissolved. What caused this devastation? Climate change has long been suspected. Evidence has been amassing of a long arid period, lasting until the Roman Warm Period. The high population density in urban centres could not be sustained if agricultural returns were poor. That could trigger the dissolution of polities, as central authority and economic systems collapsed.[36]

The revival of the Greek population and agriculture began c. 900–800 BC, along with the adoption of iron. The Greeks learned once more to capture their thoughts in writing, this time using an adapted Phoenician alphabet. Urban life returned. Trading contacts sprang up towards the end of this period. A trading post was founded c. 775 BC on Ischia in the Bay of Naples. When the Greeks began to plant such colonies outside the Aegean, it was not a national endeavour. There was no Greek nation. City-states developed from about 750 BC. Colonies were then founded from the mother city. [79] No doubt an element of the impetus was Mediterranean trade, in competition with the Phoenicians, but rising population probably also played a

78 (left) *The Mycenaean elite were sent to their graves with lavish displays of wealth. This funerary mask was made of exceptionally thick gold sheet. The warrior who wore it in death also bore a gold breastplate. It comes from Shaft Grave IV of Grave Circle A at Mycenae.*

79 (opposite) *The seafaring Greeks colonized coasts and islands. A mother city-state would establish one or more daughter colonies.*

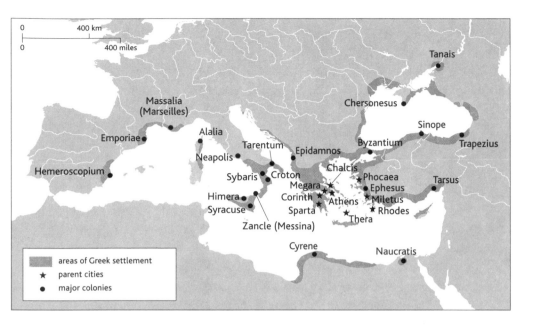

part.[37] The expansion of the Greek world to southern Italy, Sicily, Corsica, Provence, Asia Minor and the European coast of the Black Sea seems to have left genetic traces in the spread of Y-DNA E-V13 and J2a3b1 (M92).[38] Southern Italy became so heavily settled by Greeks that one name for it was *Magna Graecia* (Great Greece). The other name used by the Greeks was *Italia*, and this was adopted eventually for the whole peninsula.[39] The considerable Greek presence in Asia Minor was only ended by the 1923 population exchange between Greece and Turkey.

The Minoans and Mycenaeans are generally viewed as the forerunners of Classical Greece. Yet there is little cultural continuity between Bronze Age and Iron Age Greece. The long Dark Age destroyed a way of life, which could not be resumed. When the Greeks burst back into history, their outlook was different. Their architecture was different. Their monuments were temples. The Classical Greeks developed a civilization all their own, which has influenced every succeeding one in Europe. Furthermore, they came to think of themselves as Europeans.[40] The turning point was their astonishing defeat of the Persians at Marathon (490 BC) and Thermopylae (480 BC), which kept Greece out of the Persian empire. This not only encouraged the concept of a division between Europe and Asia. It was a huge boost to the confidence and prestige of the Athenians. They began to tread an independent path intellectually as well as politically.[41]

CHAPTER TWELVE

Iron Age Traders and Warriors

S ocial changes that began in eastern Europe and Western Asia around 2300 BC were consolidated across Europe during the Bronze and Iron Ages. Warrior aristocracies developed. Travelling on horseback, warriors could cover long distances. The invention of the spoked wheel made the war chariot possible (see p. 136). There was a marked increase in the manufacture of weapons. In the Stone Age, axes and daggers were made which could be used in a fight between humans, among other purposes, but there was no tool specifically for fighting. The long sword by contrast was the work of bronze-smiths and clearly a weapon of war. It had no other function. Sheet-metalworking developed in the Urnfield culture of the Late Bronze Age, making possible shields and armour. With this focus on conflict came the development of fortifications.[1] From the Tollense Valley of northern Germany the debris of violent death has been dredged up: weapons and smashed human and horse bones. It speaks of a battle around 1200 BC.[2] Warfare itself was not new. What we see in the Bronze Age is the development of a society in which the warrior had a special place, indeed a leading role.

Power centres north of the Alps could control trade from the Mediterranean coming up the Rhone, and from the Adriatic through Alpine passes from the Po Valley. From the Alps sprang the headwaters of the Rhine, a major trading artery leading north. Nearby were the mineral riches of the Alps, the wherewithal to make bronze goods to trade. Wealth could accrue in the hands of chieftains commanding such a trading nexus. Innovations within it could spread along trade routes. [80]

Urnfield culture

One such innovation was a shift in burials to cremation rather than interment around 1300 BC, which gave archaeologists a name for this burgeoning culture – Urnfield. The typical Urnfield burial used an urn to contain the

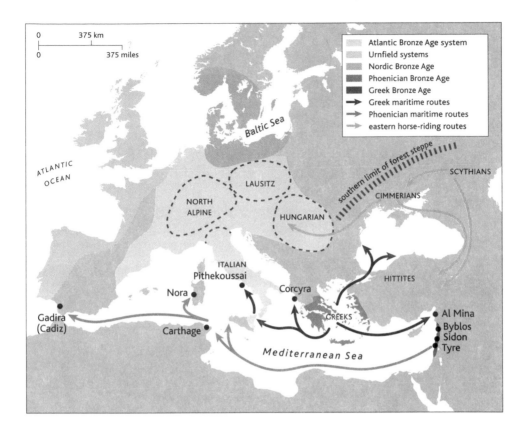

ashes of the deceased, capped by an upturned bowl, set into a pit. [81] The usage had spread over much of Europe by 1000 BC. Within this widespread complex, regional types occur, such as the Lusatian, or Lausitz, culture, which is found over much of Poland and eastern Germany.[3]

Any type of cremation was uncommon earlier over most of Europe except the Carpathian Basin, where it appears among Bell Beaker and other groups as early as c. 2700 to 2400 BC. So this region has often been considered the

80 (above) Late Bronze Age cultures of Europe.

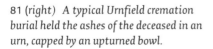

81 (right) A typical Urnfield cremation burial held the ashes of the deceased in an urn, capped by an upturned bowl.

starting point for the Urnfield tradition. Two of the Middle Bronze Age cultures of Hungary favoured cremation, but only one of them placed a capped burial urn in a pit. That was the Vatya culture of sheep-breeders living in tell settlements along the Danube. These settlements were well placed for trading, as well as having good grazing land nearby.[4] So the idea could easily have travelled up the Danube to the trading nexus at its head. From there cremation spread west and north into Germany and Poland, and south into Italy. Finally it moved into France and part of Spain. There was also a transition to cremation burial in Scandinavia and the British Isles in the Late Bronze Age, but without the vast cemeteries of continental Europe.[5]

The distribution of Y-DNA haplogroup R1b-U152 is similar to that of the Urnfield culture, though it also has features suggestive of the Iron Age movements of the Celts. [82] The density of R1b-U152 is greatest in northern Italy and Corsica and radiates out from there.[6] This pattern is informative. A radiation in all directions from a high-density centre is what we would expect if a mutation occurs within a comparatively static population. With no mass movement going on in any particular direction, the mutation will

82 Y-DNA R1b-U152 radiates from a high-density core in northern Italy and Corsica.

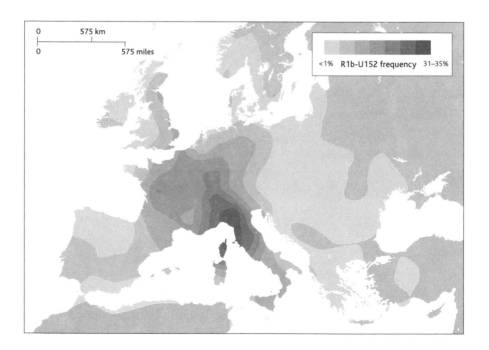

percolate gradually outwards from its origin point.[7] Picture individuals travelling and trading, mainly over short distances, over a long period of time. With such a pattern the mutation would not become predominant anywhere. Indeed R1b-U152 nowhere reaches 50 per cent of males. Though R1b-U152 may have fanned out initially within Urnfield, it looks as though later movements by Gaulish Celts contributed to the distribution we see today. Some R1b-U152 appears in central Anatolia, which was colonized by Gaulish Celts, known there as Galatians. R1b-U152 is far more widespread over Iberia today than Urnfield ever was. The sweep of slightly higher levels from northeast to southwest Iberia may echo the arrival of Gauls.

Phoenicians and Iberes

One enterprising people had sailed the length of the Mediterranean by the 8th century BC. Like so many trading nations that came after them, they established colonies beside good harbours. Eventually their western colonies coalesced into the Punic empire, headed by the city of Carthage in North Africa. Where had they come from? The language we call Phoenician was first written down in the coastal strip of the Levant between the mountains of Lebanon and the Mediterranean Sea. Ancient authors saw this strip as the northern part of the land of Canaan. Today it mainly falls into Lebanon. Phoenician is a Semitic language of the Canaanite branch; its closest living relative is Hebrew. The Phoenicians had no name for themselves as a whole. Each of their prosperous trading cities, such as Byblos, Sidon and Tyre, was independent to the point of mutual competitiveness. It was the Greeks who labelled Semitic sea-traders Phoinix (Phoenix), from which we get our name Phoenician. What the Greeks meant by it is a mystery. The word had several meanings. Rather than the mythological firebird, they may have had in mind the colour purple-red, since the purple dye obtained from the murex marine snail was among the most prized of Phoenician trade goods.[8]

The present genetic pattern in the population of Lebanon will not be an exact mirror of that in the days of the Phoenicians. Yet it is notable that Lebanese have more J2 (M172) (29.4 per cent) than J1 (18.9 per cent), whereas the opposite is true for most other Semitic speakers.[9] J2 appears at an elevated level at some of the places where Phoenicians settled.[10] However, J2 is far from exclusive to the Lebanese. Indeed it seems to have been spread also by the Greeks, trade rivals of the Phoenicians.

Phoenician trading posts in western and southern Iberia have long been recognized. The attraction was metals: tin and silver in particular, though Iberia could also offer copper, iron and gold. Gadira (modern Cadiz) was founded by Tyre in the 8th century BC.[11] In the region between Gibraltar and the Algarve the kingdom of Tartessos thrived on trade before vanishing as a polity before 500 BC. A leader there named Arganthonios (Celtic, meaning 'pertaining to the god of silver') was encountered by Greeks around 640 BC and 550 BC. Later authors concluded that this 'king' had lived 120 years! Though the name could have been passed down from father to son in a chiefly lineage, another possibility is that it designated the office of silver controller. Using Phoenician script, the people of Tartessos left the earliest inscriptions in Iberia, which appear to be in Celtic.[12]

The eastern coast of Spain was an area of Greek influence by 550 BC, but the earlier story is just as interesting. The Phoenicians took the dominant trading role in northeastern Iberia between 630 and 575 BC. A recent survey mapped 73 sites of Phoenician finds along the eastern coast, with a particularly dense cluster around the mouth and lower reaches of the River Ebro.[13]

The Iberes rose on the tide of trade. In the territory known to the ancients as Contestania, between the Júcar and Segura rivers, local leaders grew rich through control of contacts with Phoenicians and, later, Greeks. Wealth elevated an elite, who created fortified power centres which could control the countryside around. Within the walls of such towns merchants and craftsmen could safely trade. Among the crafts was wheel-thrown pottery.[14] The much-travelled Hecataeus of Miletus encountered the Iberes c. 500 BC in Contestania. To the south of the River Segura he found another community, the Mastienoí, named after their town of Mastia (now Cartagena). To the north of the Júcar were the Eídetes, and then the Ilérgès between the Ebro and the Pyrenees. These polities had been established c. 550 BC, after a period of local conflict, as rural life began to give way to a more hierarchical society. By 420 BC the Iberes were reported along the whole Mediterranean coast of what is now Spain and had spread into southern France, mingling with Ligurians as far as the Rhone. The Iberes became so prominent in contacts with the Greeks that by the 2nd century BC Greek geographers were calling the whole peninsula Iberia.[15] So inscriptions which have been found along the broad coastal strip from Almería in southeast Spain to the Hérault River in southern France are attributed to the Iberes.[16] There has been much debate about their long-dead language, which remains largely undeciphered. It appears to be non-Indo-European. It might be a distant relative of Basque, but it is not close enough for Basque to assist in translating it. Alternatively, the resemblances might have resulted from contact.[17]

Since the eastern part of the territory where Iberian inscriptions are found (the Languedoc and Catalonia) falls within the Urnfield culture, it has been argued that some of the people on the move at that time might have brought the mysterious Iberian language with them, rather than a Celtic dialect.[18] The homogeneity of Iberian *c.* 400 BC, when the first inscriptions occur, speaks against this idea. A language that had arrived with the Urnfield culture would have had many centuries in which to diverge into dialects. An alternative is that Iberian had spread by population movement from Contestania not very much earlier than the first inscriptions.[19]

Place-names provide clues that an Indo-European language was spoken in Contestania before Iberian.[20] So the Iberian language seems to be an intruder into Iberia sometime after the Copper Age. It may have arrived with the Argaric culture. The sudden creation *c.* 2200 BC of the fearsomely fortified town of La Bastida in southeast Iberia in a style reminiscent of the second phase of Troy and the urban world of the Levant suggests arrivals from the Near East.[21] The Argaric culture collapsed around 1600 BC, but we may picture a remnant of its people living on, to rise in importance in the Iron Age.

The fusion of East and West generated a rich and complex society. Aristocrats could commission astonishingly lifelike sculptures, such as the Lady of Elche, which owe much to Greek artistic traditions.[22] [83] The wine-loving Greeks who encountered the Iberes remarked on their abstemious water-drinking. Their amazing wealth was lavished on expensive clothing.[23] The intricate headdress and jewels of the Lady of Elche bear out at least one Greek

83 *The majestic Lady of Elche wears a striking headdress and three necklaces. This bust was originally brightly painted.*

impression. The Iberes did not hold out long against wine though. The Phoenicians seem to have introduced viticulture, as well as new olive cultivars.[24] Both wine and olive oil were staple Hispanic exports in Roman times.

Close to the mouth of the Ebro, El Puig de la Nau, Benicarlo (Castellon), transformed itself in spectacular fashion from a country village into a walled town in the late 5th century BC. Ancient DNA from El Puig de la Nau and other such Iberian sites in Valencia, Castellon and Catalonia produced a range of mtDNA haplogroups that would be at home almost anywhere in Europe after the Neolithic, but equally at home in the Near East. Since the Iberes preferred cremation, the remains tested were atypical burials.[25] So these individuals could have been foreign to the Iberes. This illustrates a wider issue in ancient DNA testing: we need to be aware that burial was not granted to all.[26]

Cimmerians and steel

Early metallurgists on the Pontic steppe had experimented with forged iron as early as the Yamnaya Horizon. Seams of copper ore are interbedded with iron-bearing sandstone in the Volga-Ural region.[27] Iron was too soft to take an edge suitable for cutting tools and weaponry. However, when alloyed with a little carbon to make steel, it is harder, stronger and holds a sharper edge than bronze. This early form of steel was difficult to make and therefore expensive. Iron objects were rare for many centuries. Perhaps a shortage of tin for bronze tipped the balance in favour of carbonized iron. This technology was practised by later metalworkers of the Pontic steppe. Archaeologists refer to them as the Chernogorovka (c. 900 BC) and Novocherkask (c. 800 BC) cultures. Historians have another name for them – the Cimmerians.[28]

These people lived on the very edge of history, glimpsed in early sources as the Gimmirai (Akkadian) or Gimmerai (Assyrian). For Homer, the distant land of the Cimmerians was wrapped in mist and cloud.[29] This was so vague that some commentators have dismissed the Cimmerians as mythical. Yet they were all too real for those on the wrong end of Cimmerian swords and arrows. They swept into Anatolia around 700 BC and terrorized it for a century. [84] They seized the Greek colony of Sinope on the Black Sea shore of Anatolia and went on to break the power of Phrygia.[30] Herodotus, writing in the 5th century BC, explains that the Cimmerians were driven in a body

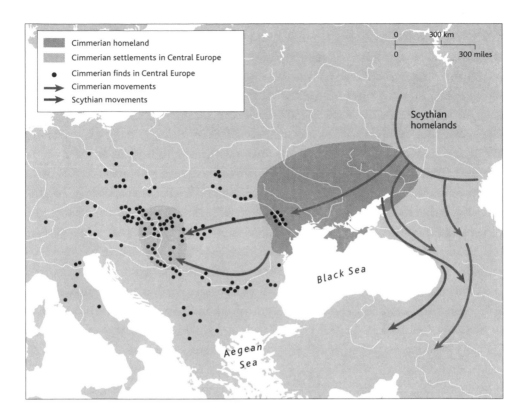

84 *The Cimmerians fled west and south under the pressure of Scythian advances.*

from the Pontic-Caspian steppe by fierce Scythians from further east.[31] This happened so long before his time that his dramatic account has been doubted. Certainly he told only half a tale. He had sources for the incursion into Asia Minor, but archaeology shows that the Cimmerians fled west as well. Moving up the Danube into the Carpathian Basin in the 9th and 8th centuries BC, they brought horses bred for speed and strength, and iron swords and daggers.[32]

Hallstatt and La Tène cultures

So iron-working and chariot horses filtered through from the steppe to Central Europe, where the Hallstatt C culture formed around 750 BC. The elite of this culture adopted wagon burials similar to those on the steppe, leaving a wealth of grave goods. By this time the scattered children of

Proto-Indo-European had developed into separate languages. The people of Hallstatt C are presumed to be Celtic speakers. It is impossible to say whether the Cimmerians could understand the Celts. Yet the effort to communicate seems to have had a linguistic result. Celtic shares one abstruse linguistic feature with Iranian that is not shared with either Proto-Indo-Iranian or Proto-Italo-Celtic.[33] This points to a meeting between Celtic and Iranian speakers sometime after c. 2000 BC. The feature is also shared by Baltic, Slavic and Albanian, which can similarly be explained by the Cimmerian contacts on the steppe and up the Danube.[34] Other evidence of the language spoken by the Cimmerians is limited to those few names of their leaders mentioned in Assyrian records. Yet it is logical to expect it to be a member of the Iranian family.

Another linguistic curiosity is the special word for 'saddle horse' in both Celtic and Germanic that is not attested in other Indo-European languages. From a root reconstructed as *mark-os* we get for example the English word 'mare' and Old Irish 'marc' (horse). Similar words appear in Welsh, Breton and Gaulish. This word has parallels in Altaic languages such as Mongolian. So it has been suggested that the word travelled into Central Europe with Scythians, who had close contact in Asia with Altaic speakers.[35] It is perhaps less likely, but still possible, that the word arrived earlier, with the Cimmerians.

Long-distance trade routes across the Hallstatt zone linked the Mediterranean with Jutland and the Baltic, whence came the prized amber. [85] Thus Etruscan influences could reach as far as the North European Plain, where a funerary urn with personality developed. [86] At the very end of the Hallstatt period (c. 480–440 BC), Etruscan luxury goods were traded through the Alps to emerging elites on the northern fringe of the old Hallstatt core, particularly the Middle Rhine. There the spectacular La Tène culture emerged, with its swirling, naturalistic art forms. The Etruscan link may be the key to understanding the sound shift ('kw' or 'q' becomes 'p') that created the Gaulish form of Celtic (see Chapters 10 and 13).

Greek authors give us the first references to the Celts (Keltoi), which can be linked to this Iron Age culture. The influence of La Tène styles spread quite widely across Gaul, Britain and further afield. Trade, gifts and

85 *(opposite above) The Hallstatt culture and its trade connections.*

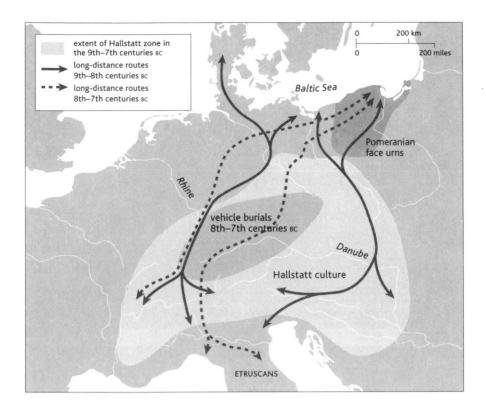

emulation can account for some of this spread. But history records a series of Celtic migrations between 400 and 200 BC. Gauls moved into northeastern Italy around 400 BC. Others spread southeast even as far as Greece and Anatolia. The Gauls are remembered in the name Galatia for a region in central Turkey.[36]

Galicia in northwestern Spain is presumably also named for the Gauls. It was certainly Celtic-speaking by the time Roman geographers began to note the place-names of the region.[37] Significantly, Pliny the Elder referred

86 *Pomeranian face urns were a development from Urnfield burials. These would originally have been capped with hat-like lids. The historical region of Pomerania is now divided between Germany and Poland.*

to the people of Galicia as Celts.[38] This was at a time when Celt meant Gaul to Roman geographers (see Chapter 10). So Roman references to Celts elsewhere in Iberia may hint at other incursions of Gauls. Indeed Strabo claims that the Celts of Galicia were kinsmen to those living around the River Guadiana, now forming part of the Portuguese-Spanish border.[39] Between these two groups linked by Strabo lived the Lusitanians, who spoke a language derived from an intermediate stage between Proto-Indo-European and Celtic.[40] We may see them as the descendants of the Stelae People. Further towards the northeast of the Iberian peninsula a Celtic language retaining 'q' where Gaulish had 'p' left its mark in inscriptions from the 3rd century BC. Linguistically it is clearly distinct from Gaulish, so it is confusing that Roman geographers refer to its speakers as Celtici or Celtiberi. Some blend of immigrant Gaul and Iberes has been surmised by authors ancient and modern.[41] Yet there is little sign from place-names that Iberes ever lived in that region,[42] and archaeologically there is scant evidence of La Tène influences on Celtiberia.[43] So the name Celtiberi may simply have arisen to distinguish long-established Celts in Iberia from those across the border in Gaul (see p. 166).

Since Iron Age Celts must have been genetically similar to their ancestors, it may prove difficult to distinguish these later waves from earlier ones by modern DNA, but where R1b-U152 appears in Britain, Greece and Iberia [see 82], it may reflect Hallstatt and La Tène movements, in addition to the earlier Urnfield. Some Gauls might also have carried R1b-L21 [see 75]. In Britain they would be entering an island already saturated with L21, but that is not the case in Iberia, where L21 is therefore likely to be a signature of the Gauls or British. (There were settlers from Britain in Galicia in the post-Roman period.[44]) The relative rarity of L21 in Iberia is one clue that the incoming Gauls did not completely replace the existing population, but simply added another contribution to the already complex mix.

Britain has more La Tène material than Ireland. The Iron Age Irish were struggling to survive. Ireland's rich metal resources had supported a cultural flowering in the final Bronze Age, but demand for copper and tin fell as iron became the favoured metal. The dramatic drop in signs of human activity from c. 800 to 400 BC must reflect a disastrous population crash. Pottery was no longer made. The Irish became almost invisible. Climate change may have played a part in this. In the last centuries BC, La Tène material spread across the northern half of Ireland from the northeast, probably

87 *The end of a bronze trumpet found at Lough Shade, Co. Armagh, decorated in the La Tène style.*

from northern Britain.[45] [87] The earliest Irish records mention British people (Cruithin or Cruithni in Gaelic) in northeastern Ireland.[46] Could the La Tène style have arrived with them? Or do the people known as Cruithin represent a later wave of British incomers in the early post-Roman period, when there was renewed contact between Ireland and north Britain?[47]

Y-DNA haplogroup I2a2a1 (M284) is almost exclusively British and seems to have arisen there among the Celts. It is rare in Ireland, but there is a concentration of it in northeastern Ireland. This haplogroup is shared by men of several surnames which are Gaelic in origin, and so cannot reflect gene flow from Britain in modern times. Its most recent common ancestor in Ireland has been dated to about 300 BC. The haplogroup appears in McGuinness and McCartan men, who descend from the Cruithin King Eochaidh (d. *c.* AD 552).[48] This all looks a neat fit to La Tène. The only query is whether the descendants of men who arrived in Ireland in 300 BC would still be seen as foreign *c.* AD 550. It seems doubtful, despite the estimated dating.

A more likely genetic signature of La Tène in Ireland is Y-DNA R1b-M222, carried by up to 44 per cent of men in parts of Northern Ireland today.[49] Given the earlier population fall in Ireland, it would not have taken many incomers to have such a strong genetic impact. A study restricted to the counties forming the Republic of Ireland found 20 per cent of men in Donegal in the northwest were R1b-M222, much higher than in other parts of the Republic. Northwestern Ireland was supposed to be the territory of the Northern Uí Néill, descendants of the fabled 5th-century warlord, Niall of the Nine Hostages. R1b-M222 seemed particularly common among those with some surnames traditionally linked to Uí Néill, such as Gallagher, Boyle, Doherty and O'Donnell. It also appears among the Connachta, supposed descendants of the brothers of Niall. So R1b-M222 was initially labelled as the lineage of Niall.[50] Alas, this attractive idea rested on genealogies which

189

were tampered with around AD 730 to make the famous Niall the ancestor of unrelated kings based in Donegal, who then claimed to be the Northern Uí Néill.[51]

Wider sampling subsequently showed the highest concentrations of R1b-M222 in northeastern Ireland (Belfast 44 per cent) and western Ireland (Mayo 43 per cent). Outside Ireland there are roughly 10 per cent of men carrying M222 in northern England (Yorkshire), western Scotland (Skye) and northeastern Scotland (Moray).[52] This is not the pattern we would expect from Irish migrants into Britain. So R1b-M222 hints at La Tène movements into Ireland.

In Britain, La Tène finds come mainly from the southeast, such as the bronze shield boss found in the Thames at Wandsworth, London. [88] Yet La Tène influence burst upon East Yorkshire in the 1st century BC. The Arras culture, notable for its chariot burials, appeared there. Chariot burials are more common on the Continent. Those in the Marne area of France characteristically lie within a square mound and surrounding ditch. Their distribution can be linked to that of a tribe known as the Parisii, from whom Paris takes its name.[53] In Roman times East Yorkshire was the territory of a tribe known as the Parisi.[54] This seems more than a coincidence of name. The Arras culture burials are within square barrows, similar to those of the Marne Valley. Unlike chariot burials on the Continent, however, those of the Arras culture contain dismantled vehicles. It has been argued that this difference from continental practice rules out a migration to Britain.[55]

Recent discoveries suggest otherwise. A chariot buried intact *c.* 300 BC was found in a square barrow at Ferry Fryston in West Yorkshire. This seems connected to the Arras culture

88 *Bronze shield boss decorated in La Tène style, found in the River Thames at Wandsworth, London.*

– perhaps the earliest manifestation of it. The occupant of the chariot came from further afield, possibly Scandinavia, the Highlands of Scotland or Brittany.[56] Another intact chariot found at Newbridge near Edinburgh is also early and more like continental types.[57]

The continental Parisii may have been pushed westwards out of the Marne area into the Seine Valley by the Belgae pressing in from the east. Belgic tribes also settled in southeastern England in the 1st century BC. They brought new ideas from the Continent – minting coins and creating defended settlements that might function as tribal centres and market towns.

The voices of the Celts speak to us in their own language long after their glory days. Early Irish literature is proof of a love of language, but the Celts came slowly to writing. So the first records to mention the Celts are all from foreign hands. For the ancient Greeks the world north of the Mediterranean civilizations was largely unexplored. The ethnic labels used for the peoples of these mysterious lands varied by period and source.

Taking a simple definition of a Celt as someone speaking a Celtic language, the Celtic world once covered a vast swathe of western Europe. Yet it was better recorded in its decline, as one Celtic tribe after another was absorbed into the expanding Roman empire.

Even before the Roman conquests, the Late Iron Age migrations of the Gauls impinged on the busily literate civilizations of the south, whose historians bewailed the incursions of fierce savages. Admittedly, the accounts that have survived were written centuries after the events they record, but echoes can be found in the archaeological record. Livy explains that overpopulation drove the Celts of Gaul into Italy, where they first defeated the Etruscans and established Milan. Then in July 390 BC they fell upon Rome and had to be bought off by 1,000 pounds of gold. The appearance of La Tène material in the Po Valley around this time bears out his story.[58] Perhaps these movements were partly driven by pressure from the Germanic tribes expanding out of Jutland. They in turn seem to have been driven by climate change. The Belgae were ousted from their lands east of the Rhine and settled in northeastern Gaul, Britain and probably Ireland. And still the Germanic tribes advanced. The Boii were pushed out of Bohemia in the time of Julius Caesar. Caesar argued that Gaul would have to be taken over by the Romans if it were not to become Germanic.[59] Perhaps he was right. When the Western Empire collapsed, Germanic tribes poured into it (see Chapter 14).

CHAPTER THIRTEEN

Etruscans and Romans

The Etruscans had a literate and urban culture in the 8th century BC, while the ancestors of the Romans were shepherds on the Seven Hills. [89] The Etruscan language is not Indo-European. In fact it does not belong to any living language family, though it resembles two other extinct languages: Raetic, testified by inscriptions in the Alps, and a language spoken on the island of Lemnos in the Aegean Sea.[1]

Studies of mtDNA from ancient Etruscans may indicate an origin in Anatolia,[2] but at what time? Could that resemblance date back to the Neolithic? Archaeology and DNA studies of Tuscan cattle breeds suggest not. The ancestors of the Etruscans seem to have arrived in Italy around 1200 BC.[3] Herodotus reported that the Etruscans were from Lydia (in Anatolia). He treats them as Lydians[4] – an Indo-European-speaking people. Yet what little survives of the Etruscan language shows no such character.[5] On the contrary, the Etruscans were probably thrust out of northwestern Anatolia by the expanding Lydians.[6]

Spreading into what is now Tuscany, the Etruscans formed a solid wedge between blocks of Indo-Europeans to north and south, particularly after their expansion northeast into the Po Valley in the 6th century BC. [90] The people they supplanted were Umbrians, as Herodotus tells us.[7] Place-name evidence supports him. The Umbrians

89 *Etruscan bronze mirrors were often decorated on the reverse with scenes taken from Greek myth, the characters labelled in Etruscan script. Here Paris is wooing Helen with the aid of the goddess Aphrodite.*

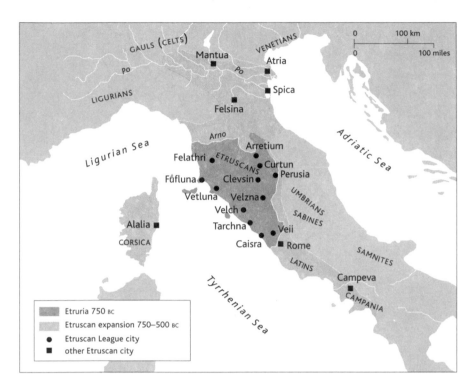

90 *Tuscany is named after the Etruscans who settled there. Their later expansion into the Po Valley made them a power from coast to coast.*

(*Umbri*) were presumably so named from the River Ombrone (*Umbro* in Latin), which flows through Tuscany to the Tyrrhenian Sea. Place-names incorporating 'Ambra' or 'Umbra' are dotted through Tuscany and into the Po Valley.[8] That would make the Umbrians neighbours to the Ligurians of northwestern Italy. Indeed Plutarch tells a tale that indicates a tribal link. He recounts that these Ligurians, fighting for the Romans against a Germanic confederation who had descended on Italy in 113 BC, found themselves shouting the same war-cry as the enemy: 'Ambrones!' How disconcerting that must have been! The Ligurians explained their cry as an old ethnonym.[9] The Germanic Ambrones, who were marching with the Teutones and Cimbri, probably derived their coincidentally similar ethnonym from the River Emmer, a tributary of the Weser in Lower Saxony. This story has confused readers of Plutarch ever since. Some connection between the Ligurians and the Germanic Ambrones has been imagined, while a far more plausible connection with the Umbrians has been overlooked.

Thus the Etruscans made a breach between local peoples who once saw themselves as one. This created a linguistic barrier, which no doubt encouraged the separation of the Celtic and Italic families of languages. More surprisingly, it may have contributed to a linguistic development that spread as far as Britain. Etruscan influence may have been responsible for the sound shift from Proto-Indo-European 'kw' ('q') to 'p' in two Italic languages (Oscan and Umbrian) and in Gaulish, from which it spread to Brittonic, the precursor of Welsh, Breton and Cornish.[10] The sound shift appears in inscriptions around Lugano, on the Swiss-Italian border, using an Etruscan-derived script and dating from the 6th to 1st century BC. The language is Lepontic, a form of Celtic later replaced in the region by Gaulish.[11]

As Italy edges into history we can dimly see the Latin speakers in central Italy among other Italic tribes, sandwiched between two urban civilizations: the Hellenized south and the Etruscans to the north. Yet the Romans ultimately prevailed over the Etruscans, conquered the Greeks and Carthaginians, took over a large part of Celtic territory and created an empire that spread their language far and wide. [91] From Latin sprang

91 *The extent of the Roman empire in* AD 117.

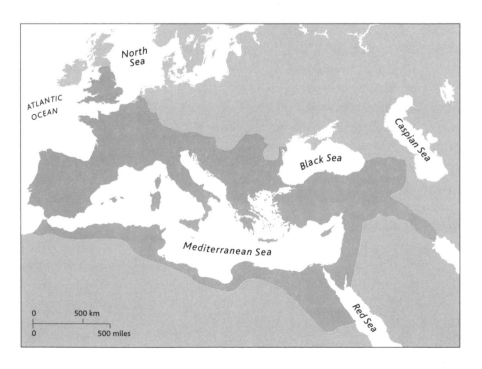

the Romance languages such as French, Italian, Portuguese, Romanian and Spanish.

Civilization was not an unmixed blessing. The technology that brought fresh water into Roman towns also poisoned people slowly through the use of lead pipes.[12] Crowded urban environments help disease to spread. Between 600 and 300 BC cattle as a share of livestock fell sharply in Mediterranean Europe and remained very low until the end of the Western Roman Empire. Rome lived on grain and vegetables, with meat mainly for the rich. So native Romans were smaller than their uncivilized forefathers.[13] As the empire expanded, Roman soldiers found themselves fighting milk-fed Celts and Germans who towered over them. Diodorus Siculus described the Gauls as tall of body, with rippling muscles.[14] Strabo marvels that mere lads from milk-drinking Britain were half a foot taller than the tallest people in Rome.[15] Tacitus declared that the Germanic tribes had huge frames.[16] Caesar reports ruefully that the Gauls called the Romans pygmies, and that accounts of the enormous stature and military zeal of the Germans had some of his men signing and sealing their wills.[17] It says much for the discipline of the Roman army that it triumphed for so long over such fearsome foes.

The Roman army was not always composed of Romans, at least not Romans of Italic origin. Those massive barbarians made useful soldiers for Rome. In the archaeological park at Xanten in Germany stands a tombstone with a tale to tell. It depicts the cavalryman Reburrus, son of Friatto, in a classic Roman pose of victory. He is trampling the German enemy. [92] Yet he was no Roman. The inscription identifies his unit as the *Ala Frontoniana*. This auxiliary unit was stationed first on the Roman frontier with Germania, hence its name. In AD 73 it was moved to Italy, followed by a posting in Pannonia. What gives away its origin is its later name of *I Tungrorum*. It was recruited from the Germanic Tungri.[18] So the Romans had Germans fighting Germans. Probably they were nothing loath. There was no sense of national unity among either Celtic or German tribes, which was an asset to Romans intent on conquest.

From 30 BC to AD 212 Roman legionaries had to be Roman citizens, which restricted recruitment largely to Italy and the Roman colonies (*coloniae*), formed originally of legionary veterans. Intermarriage with locals gradually gave the *coloniae* a variety of genetic blends, while at the same time recruitment from them rose. Former soldiers were breeding more soldiers. We

92 *Gravestone of Reburrus, son of Friatto,* horseman of the Ala Frontoniana, *from the Archaeological Park, Xanten, Germany.*

would expect their Y-DNA to be typical of Italy, but they might never have set foot in the country. By the time of the emperor Hadrian only about 8 per cent of the legionaries were Italian-born.[19] This was only half the story. The legions were bolstered by a roughly equal number of auxiliaries, recruited primarily from non-citizens within the empire. Evidence for recruitment outside the empire is more oblique until the 3rd century AD, when a few auxiliary units with barbarian names start to appear in the record. The *Ala I Sarmatarum* in Britain was evidently manned by fierce Sarmatians.[20] By this time Sarmatians had followed the route up the Danube from the steppe into the Carpathian Basin. Two Sarmatian burials in Hungary have yielded the East Asian mtDNA N9a.[21]

From AD 212 all the inhabitants of the Roman empire were granted citizenship. Henceforth many legionaries had no claim at all to Italian blood. This makes for many an interesting speculation. Men who find themselves carrying an unexpected Y-DNA signature may wonder if it arrived in their homeland (or the homeland of their ancestors) with a Roman soldier. That is perfectly possible, but not the only option. Sometimes it is not clear just how a man crossed the empire from one extreme to the other. Palmyra was a wealthy caravan city in the Roman province of Syria. Yet we find Barates the Palmyrene burying his beloved British wife Regina on the most northerly border of the empire – at the fort of Arbeia, on Hadrian's Wall in Britain. She had been his slave, whom he freed and married. Her death aged only 30 so distressed him that he set up a fine tombstone portraying her. Since there can have been few Palmyrenes on that frontier, no doubt an inscription to '---rathes Morenus the Palmyrene' at Coria (Corbridge) is that of Barates himself. He is described as a *vexillarius*, usually meaning 'standard-bearer'. Yet at 68 he was too old to be a regular soldier. Nor were the usual details given of his service or unit. He is a man of mystery.[22] Judith Weingarten suggests that he arrived in the entourage of the emperor Septimius Severus and his Syrian wife, Julia Domna, in AD 208. Intent on the conquest of Caledonia, Severus strengthened the fortifications of Arbeia and Coria.

A less pleasant way that the Roman empire moved people around was through slavery. The ownership of one person by another was not a new concept. What was novel about the Roman use of slaves was its scale. Massive numbers were enslaved in the process of Roman conquests. Over a quarter of a million people were taken in a series of wars ending in the defeat of Carthage and Corinth in 146 BC. They included 150,000 slaves from the Greek state of Epirus, 20,000 Sardinians and 50,000 Carthaginians.[23] Julius Caesar sold entire tribes from Gaul into slavery.[24] His human haul from the Gallic Wars was one source of the wealth that paved his way to power.

One estimate of the total number of Roman slaves over the thousand years of the rise and fall of the empire is over 100 million people. The majority were born into slavery. The children of enslaved mothers became slaves. That limits the use of isotope analysis to identify the origins of Roman slaves, for it can only tell us whether an individual had travelled to the place where they were buried. An isotope study of the cemetery at the imperial estate of Vagnari in Italy did tease out a few foreigners. Their mtDNA haplogroups were not particularly informative though. Roman slaves came generally from within the conquered territories in Europe, Western Asia and North Africa. The mtDNA haplogroup mix is fairly similar over this region. However, the sample did contain at least one far-travelled individual from East Asia.[25]

One might assume that slaves were simply worked until they dropped and would scarcely have had the opportunity to leave descendants. That was certainly true of those chained in Roman galleys or condemned to work in mines. Yet at the other end of the spectrum were those freed at the end of their term of service in their master's business or as a household steward. Literate and trained in the ways of commerce, such freemen could become

Slavery

Slavery has a long and brutal history.[26] It probably began among the first civilizations of the Near East. Their earliest surviving law codes refer to slaves.[27] Slaves were often human booty: captured foreigners or prisoners of war. Many a slave was born in captivity though. The child of a slave was a slave. The Roman and Greek empires ran on slavery. [93] Massive numbers of Europeans and western Asians were enslaved in the process of the imperial conquests. Such was the demand for captive labour that it was imported from outside the Roman empire too. Slaves were obtained from Britain in the 1st century BC, before its conquest by Rome.[28] At around the same time the massive slave market on the Greek island of Delos had the capacity to process 10,000 slaves a day. This was an inducement to piracy in the surrounding seas. The capture of hapless travellers was temptingly profitable.[29]

The barbarians who swept over Europe as the Roman empire crumbled also took captives into slavery and sometimes transported them far from their homes. The Irish raided post-Roman Britain, famously taking St Patrick among their thousands of captives.[30]

The Vikings were the greatest slave-traders of their day. They supplied Iceland with captured Irish, and the Islamic empire with Slavs.[31] Arab slave markets remained active long afterwards. Between 1500 and 1800 some 1 million Christians were taken into captivity in North Africa and the Near East. The feared Barbary pirates would seize ships and raid the coasts of the Mediterranean and Atlantic, in search of men, women and children to sell.[32] Constantinople (now Istanbul) had been taken by the Turks in 1453. Most of southeastern Europe lay within the Ottoman empire for centuries. Christian boys from these territories were kidnapped and trained for the Sultan's Janissary corps. The institution of slavery continued among the Ottomans after its abolition in the United States of America in 1865.[33]

Given the pervasive nature of slavery throughout antiquity, and the habit of taking slave concubines, it seems likely that most of us have a slave or two among our countless ancestors.

93 *Chained captives are depicted on this marble relief from Smyrna (Izmir, Turkey) from the 3rd century* AD, *when Smyrna lay within the Roman empire.*

94 *Reconstruction of the atrium of the House of the Vetti at Pompeii in the Boboli Gardens in Florence.*

successful traders themselves. One of the most impressive houses in Pompeii was built by Aulus Vettius Conviva and Aulus Vettius Restitutus, thought to be wealthy freedmen, perhaps wine merchants.[34] [94]

Other foreigners flocked willingly to the hub of the empire. Rome drew traders and artisans, envoys and refugees, teachers and students. Their epitaphs give us glimpses into their lives. The tomb of Numitorius Nicanor, a Theban eye-doctor, also contained other members of his household, which included individuals from Phrygia, Smyrna and Carthage. Rome was a melting-pot. Some Roman authors railed against the level of immigration, which they felt was diluting the Roman character of the city. This seems rather short-sighted. The Italian-born probably made up about 95 per cent of its inhabitants.[35] The state consolidated its hold on the provinces by allowing high-ranking provincials to sit in the Senate. Rome was exporting its culture by allowing access to its heart. Foreigners were sucked into Rome to be Romanized, and funnelled out again to spread Latin ways.

CHAPTER FOURTEEN

The Great Wandering

To the northeast of the Roman empire barbarians pressed against its borders, but were held at bay everywhere except Dacia (present-day Romania). This province north of the Danube was the last won by Rome and first lost. Dacia was relinquished to the Goths and their allies in about AD 271. The Goths were just one of the Germanic, Slavic and other peoples looking for room to spread themselves in Late Antiquity. As the Roman empire gradually crumbled in the West from AD 376, barbarians burst across its former borders. When the complex criss-crossing of their movements consolidated around AD 700, a new Europe had emerged. While some parts of it had changed relatively little from Roman times, with their peoples still speaking a language derived from Latin, other regions had been radically altered. The balance of power had shifted. The empires of the 1st millennium BC all sprang from the advanced cultures of the Mediterranean. By the end of the 1st millennium AD, Europe was a patchwork of Christian states. This era of change is known as the Migration Period or *Völkerwanderung* (wandering of the peoples). [95]

Who were these wandering peoples? Civilization is defined by, among other things, its literacy. The barbarians were illiterate. This means that they left us no descriptions of themselves, no histories, no bureaucratic records. To learn about them, we are dependent on archaeology and the writings of the civilized. Archaeology before the era of isotope studies was not able to detect migration with certainty. Objects may move through trade. Peoples may adopt new fashions from their neighbours.

The evidence from Classical sources is no easier to fathom. The earliest authors knew little of the homelands of the barbarians. While the Mediterranean fringe of Europe was dotted with cities founded by the ancient Greeks, few Greeks penetrated lands to their north. 'I have no reliable information to pass on about the western margins of Europe', wrote Herodotus honestly in 440 BC. 'Despite my efforts, I have been unable to find anyone who has personally seen a sea on the other side of Europe.'[1]

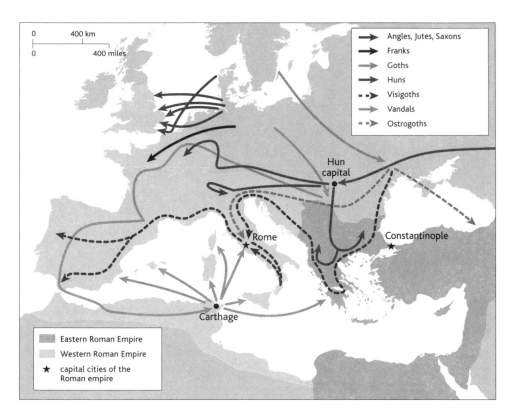

95 *Barbarian invasions as the Western Roman Empire began to crumble. Some of these movements were swift, others slow. The northern origins of the Goths and Vandals lay long in the past by the time they crossed the imperial border.*

No wonder, then, that aspects of this turmoil have been hotly debated. The idea of past migration was so unpopular after the Second World War that it became commonplace among academics to minimize the central feature of this period. Where there was incontrovertible documentary evidence of movement, archaeological fashion favoured a vision of small elites only on the move. Cultural change was explained as emulation by locals of the incoming elite. Some of the mobility of this period did indeed merely replace one elite with another. The Visigoths in Spain were vastly outnumbered by their subjects and had no impact on the latter's language or culture. Yet distaste for mass movement imposed an intellectual straitjacket. In this new century academics have been shrugging off their stays.[2]

Engines of change

What were the engines of change? The population of Europe as a whole *c.* AD 200 is estimated at 36 million, 28 million of them within the Roman empire.[3] No such figures can be accurate, but undoubtedly the bulk of Europe lay within the empire. Why and how did those outside it contrive to break into a populous zone guarded by the Roman legions?

After centuries of expansion, Rome had locked within its borders the most productive part of Europe. That was deliberate. Romans were interested in good agricultural land, mineral resources and trading opportunities. After expanding over the whole of Italy their first target was the rest of Mediterranean Europe, which had the highest levels of agricultural productivity in Europe and a sophisticated material culture. Julius Caesar and his great-great-grandnephew Claudius added the richest of the Celtic-speaking lands to the north: Gaul and Britain. Although there were attempts to conquer the Germani for the glory of it, the Romans surely knew that the Germanic economy was too poor at the time to repay the effort of conquest in either booty or taxes.[4] They settled for the Rhine as their border. By so doing the Romans established a firm frontier between the haves and have-nots. The normal human urge to seek better fortune elsewhere, if times are hard at home, was thwarted. Waves of have-nots threw themselves against the barriers, or sought a way to gain a share of imperial wealth by trade or alliance.

The Germani had been expanding out of Jutland for centuries before the Romans halted them at the Rhine. [96] The pressures behind their onward march included climate shift and environmental crises. Yet the empire itself shuddered under natural disasters, which played their part in weakening its economy, reducing its population levels and creating the opportunity for barbarians to advance. The difficulty of manning so lengthy a border, and fighting off attacks on several fronts, was another factor in the imperial collapse, along with periodic civil wars.[5]

The Slavs began their migrations after the fall of the Western Roman Empire, in part drawn by opportunities outside their homeland, and in part driven by invaders from the steppe. Good land to their west had been almost denuded of population by strife, plague and the migration of other peoples. To their east the sparsely populated forest zone offered new trapping and trading opportunities centuries later with the founding of Kievan Rus (see Chapter 17).[6]

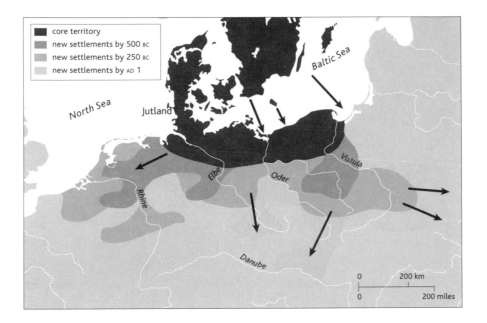

96 *The gradual expansion of the Germani eventually brought them up against the Roman frontier.*

It has long been argued that the chief trigger of the Migration Period was pressure from Asia. Attacks from the steppe pushed successive waves of Germani and Slavs across the border into the Roman empire. This was just one chapter in a long story of instability in Eastern Europe due to nomadic incursions. As one culture was laid waste, another could move into its former land.

The Danube provided the route into Central Europe from the steppe. We have already seen it in use by early waves of Indo-Europeans in the Copper Age and Cimmerians in the Iron Age. Around 500 BC the Scythians too established enclaves in the Carpathian Basin, from which they raided the Lusatian culture, the variety of Urnfield culture which extended over what is now Poland and parts of neighbouring countries [see 80]. Lusatian strongholds were burned to the ground.[7] The collapse of the Lusatian culture opened the way for the further expansion of Germani into Lusatian territory, which had begun in the north some two centuries earlier.

For the Goths and Vandals (see pp. 213–17) the route westwards was blocked by other expanding Germanic tribes, while the forest zone to the east was less appealing to them as farmers. Gradually they moved southwards to the Black Sea. Sweeping in across the steppe, the nomadic Huns displaced the Goths from their Black Sea homeland in AD 375, driving them across the Roman border.[8]

The pattern was repeated as the Avars moved in from the steppe in the mid-6th century AD, treating conquered peoples like chattels. The desire to escape the Avars explains not only the Slavic push across the Byzantine frontier into the Balkans, but their spread from Bohemia towards the Saale and Elbe after the mid-6th century and northwards into what is now Poland.[9]

Yet nomadic movements are only one aspect of the picture. The workings of nature played as great a part in shifting the balance of power from south to north, and from empire to a patchwork of kingdoms. The Germanic tribes who threatened Rome in 113 BC had been driven to look for a new homeland by the flooding of their own lands. They travelled with their women and children.[10] It was an act of desperation, driven by a catastrophe that was far from unique.

Britain was once joined to the Continent by Doggerland (see p. 60), which was submerged by the rising sea levels as glaciers melted in the early Holocene. One dramatic event speeded up the process – a tsunami around 6200 BC.[11] Since then the North Sea coast of what is now the Netherlands and Germany has been gradually subsiding.[12] Much of the Netherlands is now below sea level and has been reclaimed from the sea since around AD 1000. What made that possible is a broken strip of higher ground jutting out of the sea. It forms a natural protective barrier, within which is an alluvial plain. As the rise in sea level decelerated after 4000 BC, the plain silted up.[13]

Today the remnant of that natural embankment is the Frisian Islands, off the shore of the northern Netherlands and Germany. After a gap, the Wadden Sea Islands then lie along the west coast of Denmark. Between these island chains and the coast lies an intertidal zone called the Wadden Sea, a shallow body of water with tidal clay flats and wetlands. Some intrepid souls settled there in the Iron Age. Their settlement sites began to rise, partly by natural accumulation of debris and partly by deliberate dumping of clay and turf, to form artificial mounds known as terps (*terpen* in Dutch, *wurten* in German). These provided some degree of safety from flooding. Thousands of terps are spread along the coastal districts of the Netherlands, Germany and southern Denmark. The earliest date to around 600 BC, but terp-building expanded greatly from *c.* 200 BC.[14] Pliny the Elder was the first to leave us a description of the Wadden Sea: 'a vast tract of land, invaded twice each day and night by the overflowing waves of the ocean'. He witnessed the way of life of those 'inhabiting either the more elevated spots of land, or else eminences artificially constructed, and of a height to which they know by experience that the highest tides will never reach'.[15]

Experience was misleading. The subsidence continued. Flooding of the Belgian coastal plain and the Zeeland area started shortly after AD 200 and transformed the peatlands into wide estuaries, mud flats and salt marshes. A large area of the northern Netherlands was flooded and the Wadden Sea became connected to a large lake in the centre of the country.[16] This rise in sea level was so dramatic that many terps were deserted. Thousands of people would have been looking for new homes.

Switches of climate from around AD 250 to 550 coincided with the demise of the Western Roman Empire and the turmoil of the Migration Period. Tree-felling dates mirror the rise and fall of the empire in the west. The increase in tree-felling from 300 BC to AD 200 tells a tale of building boom and defor-estation for farming, which reached a peak around AD 250. From then on tree harvesting was in decline. During the 3rd century a drying climate was the problem. Parched land would mean dying crops, particularly in the south. Then rainfall increased during the 300s, while temperatures fell.[17]

Crop failures would have led to food shortages, weakening resistance to disease. Plagues are recorded at intervals between AD 251 and 270. In regions where there have been systematic archaeological surveys (France, Italy and the Rhineland) they reveal a drastic fall in the number of occupied rural sites in the 3rd century, suggesting a shrinking population. In Iberia there was a dramatic fall in mining. By contrast Rome's African provinces were thriving. Egypt was the breadbasket of Rome, while Tunisia supplied its pottery. There is scattered evidence that the population was actually rising in some of Rome's eastern provinces – Greece and Syria.[18] Was this a factor in Diocletian's decision to rule the Roman empire from Nicomedia in Anatolia? He divided the empire into East and West, putting a lieutenant in charge of the West. It was the start of a process that culminated with the loss of the Western Empire. Constantine the Great continued Diocletian's eastern leaning, making Constantinople (renamed Byzantium) the capital of the Roman empire in AD 330. It has been argued that the increasing popu-lation of Asia Minor and the Balkans in AD 395–476 helped save the eastern half of the empire as the West crumbled. In the Balkans, the city of Stobi was prosperous and growing, while the province of Istria was exporting grain to Ravenna.[19]

It turned even wetter in the 5th century as the Western Empire tottered and fell. Then rainfall fell sharply in the first half of the 6th century, just as other disasters struck.[20] In 536 a volcanic eruption in the tropics threw enough dust into the atmosphere to cool the northern hemisphere for over a decade.[21] Cassiodorus observed the dust veil from Ravenna. It turned the sun blue and dimmed the moon. The customary vigour of the sun's heat was wasted into feebleness, leaving no hope of harvest.[22] Then came the Plague of Justinian. The first pandemic recorded in the Western world broke out in Egypt in 541 and reached Jerusalem in the same year. All trade routes led to Constantinople. The disease reached the heart of the Byzantine empire the following spring, with devastating ferocity.[23] As Procopius wrote:

> Now the disease in Byzantium ran a course of four months, and its greatest virulence lasted about three. And at first the deaths were a little more than the normal, then the mortality rose still higher, and afterwards the tale of dead reached five thousand each day, and again it even came to ten thousand and still more than that ... many houses became completely destitute of human inhabitants.[24]

Raging on from Constantinople, the plague wiped out entire urban populations. It sped around the Mediterranean to Illyria, Greece, Italy, Gaul, Iberia and North Africa. It even reached the British Isles. It remained virulent in all these lands for just over two centuries, coming and going in an unpredictable and terrifying way.[25] Plague probably killed about half the population of Constantinople and a third of that of Europe in its first wave, while later waves killed so many more that the Byzantine empire had lost half its population to plague by AD 700.[26] The initial and gravest blow to the empire came just as Justinian was intent on restoring it to its former extent. He had recovered Italy from the Ostrogoths and Africa from the Vandals. His advances slowed after the plague. The empire was too weakened by natural disasters and fighting on other fronts to be able to achieve his dream. So the barbarian hold on the West was consolidated.

Those towns and kingdoms trading with the empire were doubtless worse affected by plague than more isolated barbarians initially. In Britain, the Anglo-Saxons pressed westwards once more in the 550s after a long lull in their advance (see p. 222).[27] Were they taking advantage of losses among the post-Roman British?

Plague mortality within Illyria from 542 may partly explain the comparative ease with which Slavs came to overwhelm Illyricum by the mid-7th century,[28] although the distraction of the Byzantine empire by war with Persia was the key military factor. The Slavs were not simply a governing elite in the Balkans. Slavic languages are spoken today over much of the former Roman province of Illyricum, which suggests that the incomers were not hugely outnumbered by the locals.

The Germani

The Germani entered Roman consciousness as unknown enemies, suddenly looming from the misty distance. Not that the Romans had a collective ethnic name for the tribes who swooped upon them in 113 BC, driven by the flooding of their own lands to look for a new homeland. Only as the frontiers of the Roman empire expanded up to the North Sea in the next century were the Cimbri securely located by Roman geographers in Jutland and the Teutones within Germania.[29]

The Germani were not a unified people. But they did have a language in common. Linguists have reconstructed that language – Proto-Germanic, the parent of a family of languages that includes Danish, Dutch, English, German, Icelandic, Norwegian and Swedish. Modern linguists named the branch after the most common Roman name for these peoples – the Germani, first mentioned by Julius Caesar.[30] When Tacitus (AD 56–117) enquired of the Germani the origin of their name, he was informed that it just happened to be the name of the tribe who first crossed the Rhine and pushed into Gaul. While the tribe had since renamed themselves the Tungri, the terror-inducing name Germani had stuck in the minds of their enemies, and had also been recently adopted by the Germani themselves as the collective name for all their tribes.[31] The geographer Ptolemy described Germania as bordered by the Rhine, the Vistula and the Danube rivers, but in Greater Germania he included Jutland (as the Cimbrian peninsula). Also included was the Scandinavian peninsula, described as a very large island called Scandia.[32] The ancient Greeks and Romans did not penetrate deep enough into the Gulf of Bothnia to realize that Scandia was actually linked to Finland.

The Germanic genetic mix

The Germani apparently sprang from a mixture of peoples, so it is no surprise that they did not have just one predominant genetic marker, to judge by their descendants. If and when scientists find ancient Y-DNA from men whom we can guess spoke Proto-Germanic, it is most likely to be a mixture of I1, R1a1a, R1b-P312 and R1b-U106, to name only the most common haplogroups found in speakers of Germanic languages today. All of these are far older than the Germanic languages and some are common among speakers of other languages too.

I1 may have appeared in the region among hunter-gatherers (see p. 66). R1a1a is shared by Germanic, Baltic, Slavic, Iranian and Indic speakers, but its subclade R1a1a1b1a3 (S221/Z284) seems notably Nordic in distribution.[33] R1b-P312 peaks in western Europe and correlates best with the former Celtic- and Italic-speaking zone. [97] Its subclade R1b-L21 is strongly concentrated in the more northerly former Celtic-speaking region [see 75]. So the presence of R1b-P312* and R1b-L21 in present-day Germanic speakers no doubt largely reflects the fact that Germani spread out over parts of the former Celtic area, such as the Alps, the Netherlands and lowland Britain, absorbing existing

97 Y-DNA R1b-P312/S116 is a large and widespread haplogroup, with many subclades predominating in former Celtic-speaking regions, yet a few smaller subclades seem Scandinavian in origin.

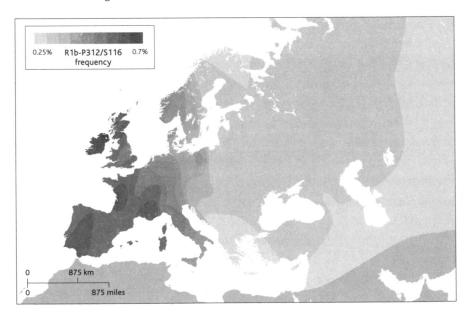

0.25%   R1b-P312/S116   0.7%
frequency

0   875 km

0   875 miles

98 *Y-DNA haplogroup R1b-U106/S21 is densest in areas that are Germanic speaking today, and found at lower levels in places that had a Germanic elite in the post-Roman period: France, Galicia and northern Italy.*

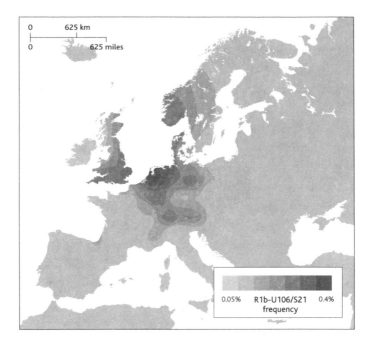

populations as they went. There has also been migration from former Celtic areas into Scandinavia over the centuries – for example Scottish communities in 16th- and 17th-century Bergen and Gothenburg.[34] Some of the L21 in Norway falls into subclades rarely seen outside the British Isles and can be presumed to have arrived from there. Yet most of the L21 in Scandinavia does not. So it is reasonable to assume that some R1b-P312* and L21 arrived in Scandinavia with Bell Beaker folk, or in Bronze Age trade. We should not imagine an impassable genetic divide between overlapping and interacting cultures. Some subclades of R1b-P312 have a distinctly Nordic distribution. Those defined by L165/S68 and L238/S182 are found in Scandinavia and the Northern and Western Isles of Scotland, which suggests that they are Norse markers which arrived in the Isles with Vikings.[35]

R1b-U106 has its peak in northern Europe and a distribution which correlates fairly well with Germanic speakers, past and present. [98] Countries with a linguistic division are particularly interesting. The level of U106 in German-speaking northeastern Switzerland is much higher (18.8 per cent) than in French-speaking northwestern Switzerland (3.7 per cent).[36] In Britain U106 levels are higher in eastern England (25 per cent) than in Wales, where a Celtic language survives. The lowest level is in northwest Wales (9 per cent), which has the highest percentage of Welsh speakers.[37] The influx of French speakers into Dutch-speaking Flanders at the end of the 16th century is recent enough to be traced through surnames. U106 was found in 26 per cent of a sample of men with authentic Flemish surnames, but only 12 per cent of the sample with a surname of French origin, which is not much higher than the level in adjoining regions of France.[38] As with other correlations between a Y-DNA haplogroup and language, it is not a one-to-one relationship with no possibility of cross-over. Such a divide would be astonishing in the real world. There was plenty of human movement in Europe before the fall of Rome. The fact remains that U106 seems to be a helpful clue to the movements of the Germani.

A sprinkling of men within that distribution carry the parent clade R1b-L11*, opening up the possibility that R1b-U106 arose from R1b-L11* in northern Europe. On the other hand, its density of distribution there suggests that it arose at the head of a wave of advance into the region.

Proto-Germanic

Linguists calculate that Proto-Germanic was spoken around 500 BC.[39] A language develops within a communicating group. In the days before modern transport and the nation state, a communicating group could not cover a vast territory. The area in which Proto-Germanic evolved was far smaller than the spread of its daughter languages today. We would expect a linguistic boundary also to be a cultural boundary. So the finger points at the Nordic Bronze Age (1730–760 BC) as the cradle of Proto-Germanic. It was a comfortable cradle for many a year. The Nordic Bronze Age began in a welcoming warmth. An earlier climate shift made southern Scandinavia as warm as present-day central Germany. Groups of people from the widespread Corded Ware and Bell Beaker cultures had moved north into Jutland and the coasts of what are now Norway and Sweden. There they melded with descendants of the Funnel Beaker and Ertebølle people into a rich Bronze Age culture.[40] The wealth and technical excellence of its bronze objects is impressive. Trade was important to this society. So was seafaring. Voyages linked Jutland and Scandia into one communicating web.[41]

However, the climate gradually deteriorated, bringing increasingly wetter and colder times to Jutland, culminating in so steep a decline in the decades around 700 BC that much agricultural land was abandoned and bog built up.[42] Pollen history reveals a similar picture in southern Sweden. Around 500 BC forest encroached on areas that had long been farmland.[43] Meanwhile an influence from eastern Sweden reached the southern Baltic shores in the Late Bronze Age, providing a clue to where some of the Scandinavian farmers were going.[44]

Scandinavia was not utterly deserted in this period. Hunters and fishermen could survive where farming failed. The Saami even expanded. The original homeland of Proto-Saami is deduced to be southern Finland. Around 650 BC Kjelmøy ceramics spread west into Scandinavia, probably marking the arrival of the Saami speakers.[45] Between AD 400 and 1300 they lived over a larger area of Sweden than they do now.[46]

Farming continued on some dry ridges, but it seems that many farmers shifted southward.[47] If pre-Proto-Germanic speakers began spilling south out of Jutland, they would soon encounter the iron-working Celts expanding northwards. The Jastorf and Pomeranian cultures seem to be the result. These were Iron Age cultures in what is now northern Germany and Poland. [99] Though clearly evolving out of the Nordic Bronze Age, elements of the (Celtic) Hallstatt culture are detectable. This was probably the time in which Proto-Germanic borrowed the Celtic words for 'iron' and 'king'.[48]

So Proto-Germanic in the end was crafted out of crisis. It seems that its final development was in the compact region of the Jastorf and Pomeranian cultures. But by the time Tacitus was writing, Germania covered a far larger area. The border between the Roman empire and Germania was the River Rhine.[49] An expanding language tends to split into dialects as the spread becomes too wide for constant communication. Eventually these dialects develop into separate languages.

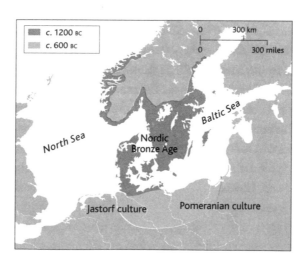

99 Nordic Bronze Age influences blended with elements of the Hallstatt culture to create the Iron Age Jastorf and Pomeranian cultures.

Branches of the Germanic tree

The first language to split away was East Germanic.[50] The Goths, Gepids, Vandals and Burgundians all seem to have spoken forms of East Germanic, though the only written record is of Gothic. No language survives from this group.

From 200 BC to AD 200 a warm, dry climate favoured cereal cultivation once more in Scandinavia.[51] As farmers were enticed northwards, the dialect that developed into Old Norse broke away from the core. It was recorded in runes from around AD 200 onwards. This was not a society with any great need for writing, but contacts with the Romans had familiarized some Germani with the Latin alphabet, which was converted c. AD 150 into a runic alphabet suited to the Germanic language.[52] By around AD 1000 Old Norse was dividing into eastern and western dialects that later evolved into the modern Scandinavian languages.[53]

100 *The Germanic languages are divided into three groups, North, East and West, but no East Germanic language survives today.*

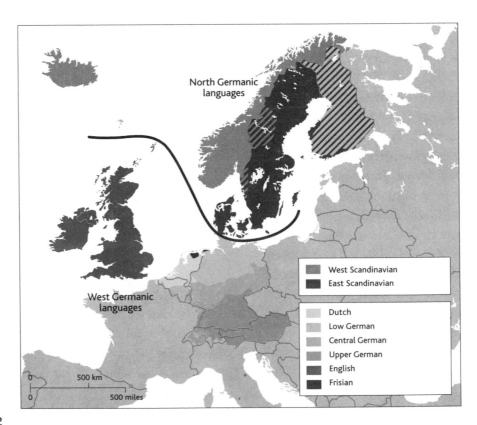

North Germanic languages

West Germanic languages

West Scandinavian
East Scandinavian

Dutch
Low German
Central German
Upper German
English
Frisian

500 km

500 miles

Western Germanic evolved from the rump of Proto-Germanic, and began to split into separate strands with the migrations westwards. The earliest split came around AD 400 as groups of Angles, Saxons and Jutes left for England, where Old English developed. German, Dutch and Frisian are among the other living languages on this branch. Upper German is spoken in southern Germany, Austria and large parts of Switzerland; this whole region was once Celtic-speaking. Thus some of the most famous Celtic Iron Age sites, including Hallstatt and La Tène, are now within the Upper German-speaking zone. [100]

Goths and Vandals

With the Goths and Vandals the Germani enter history. The trail they blazed across Europe scorched the edges of civilization, which duly took note. The very earliest records we have of these peoples are mere jottings in comparison with the pages written on their wars with Rome. In the days of Roman security, Pliny the Elder described the *Vandili* as a grouping of Germanic people, which included the *Burgodiones, Varinnae, Charini* and *Gutones*.⁵⁴ We can recognize two of these peoples, the Burgundians and Goths, among those Germanic tribes who later took over parts of the former Western Roman Empire. We should not expect much, if any, genetic distinction between these peoples. They were of the same stock, Scandinavian in origin. None was clannish to the point of exclusivity. A successful Germanic warlord could attract fighters from neighbouring groups, or even former enemies, to swell his war band. Any substantial army was polyethnic.⁵⁵

Once the Goths took possession of chunks of civilization, they could have both their past and present recorded for posterity in flattering terms. Cassiodorus, a Roman in the service of Theodoric the Great, king of the Ostrogoths (reigned 471–526), wrote a 12-volume history of this people. It does not survive, but we have a summary of it written by Jordanes, a 6th-century Roman bureaucrat of Gothic extraction. Jordanes knew little of the early history of his people. There is a tone of uncertainty about his statement that the Goths are said to have come forth long ago from the island of *Scandza* (Scandinavia) to mainland Europe (specifically an island in the River Vistula, in the case of the Gepids, who were of Gothic origin), moving from there to the coast of the Black Sea.⁵⁶

Yet there is no reason to doubt that there was a movement of Goths from Sweden to the mouth of the Vistula. By the time Classical sources first note this people, they appear in both places, though under variant names. Ptolemy places the Gutae (*Gautae*) in southern Scandia *c.* AD 150.[57] Southern Sweden historically formed Gautland (Götland), the land of the Gautar in Old Norse, whose name is retained in the present region of Götaland, Sweden. Ptolemy also mentions the *Gythones* living on the east bank of the Vistula, while Tacitus renders the name as *Gotones*.[58] The suffix *-one* may mean young or small, indicating an offspring group of the Scandinavian parent. It was dropped as the Goths emerged as an independent force further south.[59]

Pliny the Elder quotes Pytheas (who wrote *c.* 320 BC):

> Pytheas says that the Gutones, a people of Germany, inhabit the shores of an estuary of the ocean … at one day's sail from this territory is the Isle of Abalus, upon the shores of which, amber is thrown up by the waves in spring … the inhabitants … sell it to their neighbours, the Teutones.[60]

Amber explains the attraction of this region to the Goths. Initially the chief source of amber was eastern Jutland. By the 1st century AD, amber from the southern and eastern Baltic was feeding the demand from Rome.[61]

Around the mouth of the Vistula in modern Pomerelia (Poland), the Nordic-influenced Wielbark culture (*c.* AD 30 to 400) was once thought to reflect the arrival of the Goths. Yet Pytheas tells us that the *Gutones* were living there centuries earlier. Archaeologists have pointed to the continuity of the Wielbark culture from earlier cultures in the same area. The influence from eastern Sweden dates back into the Late Bronze Age.[62] That is just the time when we would expect a southern exodus from Sweden as the climate deteriorated.

The amber trade may have introduced Goths to faraway places. The main amber routes ran up the Vistula and Oder rivers to the Danube. Another amber route travelled overland from the Baltic as far as the head of the Dnieper, then downriver to the Black Sea.[63] The pull of the south drew the Goths up the Vistula during the 2nd and 3rd centuries AD, or so it seems from the spread of Wielbark culture elements. Then the predominantly Germanic Chernyakhov (or Cernjachov) culture emerged north of the Black Sea in the later 3rd and 4th centuries AD, while the number of settlements in the original Gothic heartland around the Vistula gradually decreased.[64] Alternative views of the Goths have argued against the traditional migration story.[65]

Yet without migration it is difficult to account for the development of the Gothic language.

The Goths lived for some time on the fringes of the Roman world. It was the Huns who finally drove them across the border into the empire. Hustling in from the east across the steppe, the Huns first overran the Alans east of the River Don and forced the survivors into confederacy. The Alans were Iranian-speaking descendants of the Scythians. Then the Huns displaced the Goths from their Black Sea homeland in AD 375. One group of Goths sought asylum in Thrace from Emperor Valens. His advisers greeted the news as a windfall of new troops for the emperor, who accordingly gave permission for the refugees to cross the Danube. Similar pleas from another group of Goths were refused, but they crossed the Danube anyway, swelling the influx to uncontrollable levels. Roman ill-treatment of some of the Goths led to a revolt and defeat of Roman units in Thrace. Joining forces with other Goths and even some Huns and Alans, they created a combined barbarian group that marauded over Thrace. On 9 August 378 Valens marched on the Goths from Adrianople. The Romans suffered a crushing defeat in which Valens lost his life. When the battle was over, two-thirds of the eastern army lay dead.[66] This failure to stem the barbarian advance was a token of things to come.

Emperor Gracian appointed Theodosius to deal with the problem of the Goths, who had spread from Thrace into Macedonia. Theodosius was proclaimed as Eastern Emperor on 19 January 379. He seems to have pursued a policy of divide and rule, recruiting some barbarians into his army to fight against those who still opposed him. Having finally succeeded in driving the Goths back into Thrace during 381, he reached a settlement with them on 3 October 382. The Goths were granted the right to settle along the Danube frontier, and many were to serve in the Roman army.[67]

The advance of the Huns did not halt on the steppe. In 395 they pushed south into the Eastern Roman Empire. They pillaged at will until halted by imperial troops, including Goths, at the end of 398. It seems that the thwarted Huns then rode northwestwards, driving other Germanic tribes across the Rhine into Gaul in 406. Among them were the Vandals.[68]

Who were the Vandals? Pliny (writing c. AD 77) and Tacitus (AD 98) tell us that the *Vandili* were a tribe in *Germania*.[69] Then we hear nothing more of them until they became a nuisance to the Romans. Or so it might appear, if we did not realize that the Vandals were split into at least two subgroups, the Hasding and Siling, quite apart from the Burgundians, who, as we have seen, were considered part of their confederacy by Pliny. Ptolemy places the *Silingae* roughly southwest of the Burgundians, who lived inland between the Oder and Vistula.[70] The name of the Siling is preserved in Silesia, a region now largely in southwest Poland where some Germanic river-names also survive. Most archaeologists today see the Przeworsk culture as the material manifestation of the Vandals. Beginning in the 2nd century BC, it spread southeastwards between the Vistula and Oder, then in the 2nd century AD crossed the Carpathian Mountains to the Upper Tisza River.[71]

As a result of pressure from the Huns, the Vandals were joined by a mixed horde of peoples also settled in Pannonia and nearby, notably elements of the Suebi and a group of Alans. As the confederation advanced towards the Rhine, their way was blocked by a Frankish army dispatched by the Romans. Thousands of Vandals died in the ensuing engagement, yet the barbarian horde crossed the frozen Rhine in mid-winter 406/7 and plundered their way across Gaul. In 409 they crossed the Pyrenees into Iberia. There a peace treaty was negotiated with the Romans in 411. The Alans did well out of it, receiving Lusitania (present-day Portugal) and the Mediterranean region around Carthago Nova (Cartagena). The Siling gained the rich southern province of Hispania Baetica, while the Hasding and Suebi had to be content with Galicia.[72]

Ostrogoths and Visigoths

The famous division between the Ostrogoths (eastern Goths) and Visigoths (western Goths) was actually an invention of Cassiodorus, faithfully repeated by Jordanes.[73] While the name *Ostrogothi* (Goths of the rising sun) does appear in contemporary accounts from AD 392, the other branch of the Goths was simply named the *Vesi* (the noble people). Since they are known to posterity as the Visigoths, that is the name used here. On the death of Emperor Theodosius in AD 395, the empire was divided between his sons. The Visigoths, led by Alaric, sensed the weakness of Rome and rose in rebellion. What they wanted was a homeland of their own. Alaric invaded Italy, while the timid Emperor Honorius fled to Ravenna. The story of Alaric's sack of Rome in 410 was recounted in horror by Procopius of Caesarea. Civilization shuddered. Britannia was lost to the empire in the political turmoil that followed. Yet the wheel of fortune kept Italy imperial, as Alaric died of disease in Calabria, and the army of the Visigoths left for Gaul.[74]

The Visigoths made peace with Honorius and were granted Aquitaine in 417. Then they turned their attention to Iberia, intent on seizing the lands so recently settled on the Vandals and their allies. In this they were largely successful, though the Hasding and Suebi managed to hold out in the west. Subsequent gains by the Visigoths established a Visigothic kingdom stretching from Aquitaine to the Atlantic coast of Iberia. Though the Visigoths lost most of their Gaulish territory to the Franks in 507, they kept a firm hand on Spain until the coming of the Moors. The incoming Goths must have been greatly outnumbered by their Romanized subjects. They succeeded by taking over the apparatus of government from Rome. The Goths had themselves become Romanized during their decades of alliance with the empire. One proof of this was their Christian faith. Yet their particular brand of Christianity, Arianism, caused conflict with their Catholic subjects until King Reccared I converted to Catholicism in 589. Henceforth the Goths would worship in Latin. This seems to mark the point at which the Gothic language began to drop out of use in Spain, along with Gothic fashions in dress and burial. Reccared styled himself as the successor to the Roman emperors.[75]

Under Theodoric and his father Theodemir, the Ostrogoths pushed into the Balkans. Theodoric settled in lower Moesia from 476 to 488. Then came his battle for Italy. The Western Roman Empire had sunk beneath the tide of barbarian invasions. The barbarian Odovacar (also spelled Odoacer) was placed on the throne of Italy in 476 by the imperial federate army. Theodoric negotiated a treaty with the Byzantine emperor Zeno that would grant Italy to Theodoric, if he could unseat Odovacar. Theodoric proceeded to do this, establishing the Ostrogothic Kingdom of Italy.[76] Like Reccared in Spain, Theodoric the Great modelled his rule on that of the Roman emperors. Romanized himself, he slipped all the more easily into that role. It was almost inevitable that his army would proclaim him king of the Western Empire in 493. His Italian kingdom was rich and stable. Again like the Visigoths in Spain, the Ostrogoths were greatly outnumbered by their subjects. Theodoric posted his Gothic troops in endangered border regions, or as mobile units wherever needed. Essentially the Goths ruled by consent. After Theodoric's death in 526, in-fighting weakened the royal house. The assassination of his daughter, Queen Amalasuintha, in 535 provided Emperor Justinian in Constantinople with a *casus belli*.[77] Procopius provides a detailed account of the long Gothic War (535–54) that brought an ignominious end to the Ostrogothic kingdom.[78]

Franks and Anglo-Saxons

The Franks were the Germanic people who gave France its name, while its language remained Romance, inherited from the Roman empire. This makes an interesting contrast to England, which takes both its name (Angle-land) and its language (Angle-ish) from one of the main groups of its Germanic invaders. Why are these patterns so different?

The Franks conquered most of Roman Gaul without drastically disrupting its social structure. [101] They inserted themselves as a new ruling class into the vacuum left by the collapse of Roman rule, making use of the apparatus of Roman government. Christianity, established in the late Roman period, continued to flourish. South of the Loire, descendants of the old Roman elites continued to run the estates acquired by their ancestors, in contrast to the collapse of the villa economy in England. Whereas in England urban life decayed, the Roman towns of Gaul retained at least a half-life under the Franks as the centres of bishoprics or secular government. This continuity helps to explain both the greater preservation of Roman monuments in France and the preservation of the Romance language. By contrast, the Anglo-Saxons created their own social structure. Their first settlements were scattered farmsteads. There is little sign of hierarchy until the 7th century, and then only a distinction between royal sites and others, though there was not a sole ruler of England until centuries later. The early kings were local tribal leaders, just as likely to fight each other as to fight the Britons.[79]

The Frankish approach was similar to that of the Goths, who entered the Roman empire in its time of strength. The Goths were familiar with the Roman system of government long before the opportunity came to snatch part of the crumbling empire. They became Romanized. To what degree is this true of the Franks? The Franks do not appear in the record under that name until the late Roman period. Several tribes close to the Roman frontier were considered Franks by the Romans: the *Ampsivarii, Bructerii, Chattuarii, Chamavi* and *Salii*.[80] The *Salii* were bold enough to cross the border and settle in Toxiandria (a region between the Meuse and the Scheldt rivers in present-day Netherlands and Belgium). Emperor Julian regularized the position by taking their surrender in 358.[81] As with the Goths, some Franks served in the Roman army. A few rose to top commands.[82]

By contrast, the Germani entering Britain had no use for Roman ways. They initially ignored Roman towns and villas. They created new

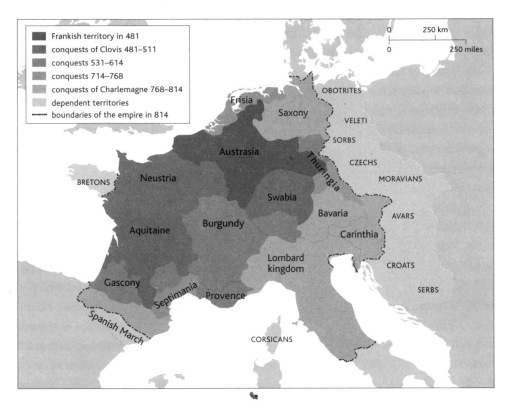

101 *The rise of the Frankish empire.*

settlements with Germanic names.[83] Roman building methods ceased; those had been based on an imperial economy, generating a huge surplus income that could be poured into specialist labour. The homeland of the Anglo-Saxons was on the fringes of farming, where agricultural surplus was low. They were accustomed to building in timber.

From the Bronze Age to the 7th century AD, the timber longhouse was the standard dwelling from southern Scandinavia to what is now northern Germany. A Bronze Age settlement at Flögeln, Lower Saxony, includes a typical longhouse, which sheltered both cattle and people in separate sections. Houses at Flögeln gradually increased in average length from the 1st to the 5th centuries. It is a similar picture in Denmark. Germanic farmers were flourishing in an improving climate it seems. Yet between the 5th and 6th centuries there was a sudden reverse trend, with longhouses becoming shorter, and cattle being moved to a separate byre. This was just the time of the migrations. That partly explains why the traditional longhouse did not arrive in Britain with the Saxons, though other types of Germanic building did. A more pressing reason would be simple lack of labour. Pioneers in a new land might find themselves short-handed.[84] An early Anglo-Saxon village occupied 420–650 has been reconstructed at West Stow, Suffolk. [102]

The Anglo-Saxon pattern suggests that migrants were bringing their families with them, and settling down to farm the land. Indeed an isotope study of the Anglian cemetery at West Heslerton, North Yorkshire, shows that both men and women were among the early settlers there.[85] The very earliest arrivals in England may have been mercenaries invited by British leaders, as the 6th-century British author Gildas tells us, but by his day the weakness of post-Roman Britain had attracted a major thrust of Germani into eastern England. He wails that those Britons who were not slain or enslaved were pushed westwards into the mountains, or even overseas.[86] (The influx of Britons into Armorica changed its name to Brittany.) Bede famously said in the 8th century that so many Angles had moved to Britain that their original homeland remained deserted even to his own day.[87] He

102 *The reconstructed early Anglo-Saxon village at West Stow, Suffolk.*

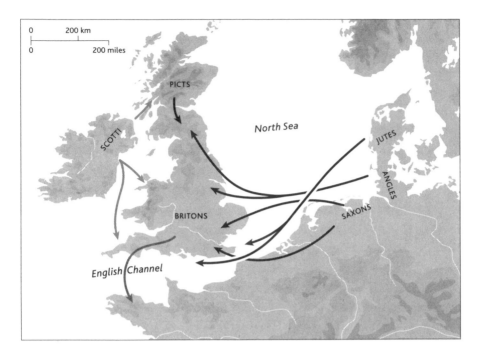

103 *Migration routes and raids,* AD 400–600.

was reporting hearsay, but archaeological evidence does indicate a post-Roman fall in population in northwest Germany, along the Frisian coast and particularly in Schleswig-Holstein, the heartland of the Angles. People along the coast were flooded out by rising sea levels, but even inland the number of settlements decreased drastically.[88] [103]

So mass migration is indicated. Scepticism has been expressed that Germanic immigrants could possibly have overwhelmed a Romano-British population in lowland Britain estimated at around 1 million even after post-Roman decline. Even fierce determination among the incoming Germani would need to be backed by numbers – perhaps a quarter of a million immigrants. One common argument has been that there simply would not have been enough ships to transport such a number. However, this assumes that the migration was a single event. Calculating up to 200,000 migrants over a migration period of about 100 years, the transport issue dwindles to a feasible 2,000 per year.[89]

The contrast between the modus operandi of the Anglo-Saxons and the Franks masks regional variation in both cases. The first areas to be taken over bear the hallmarks of a folk movement. Some later territorial acquisitions were governed more than settled. Across what is now northern France (*c.* AD 500) and East Anglia, Lincolnshire and Yorkshire (*c.* AD 450) we see the sudden appearance of a new type of burial. In these areas there are Germanic place-names. Such names extended over most of England by the time of the Domesday survey in 1068, though the degree of Anglo-Saxon settlement diminished towards the west, and Cornwall retained a Celtic language. The Anglo-Saxons had taken their conquest of England in stages. Their advance halted for a generation after the Battle of Badon, as Gildas tells us. In his day much of the west and north of the former Roman province remained British. In time, the Anglo-Saxons gained reinforcements from a continuing influx of Germanic settlers, as well as their own expanding population. When they pressed westwards once more in the 550s, they may have been taking advantage of a British population depleted by plague.

In France, the different state of affairs can be credited to Clovis, King of the Franks (*c.* 482–511). This mighty leader was so successful in battle that he gained far more land than his people could settle. As noted, south of the Loire a late Roman society continued to flourish. In northern France there was more social disruption. Yet it was Austrasia, the region of Gaul first won from the Romans by the Franks, decades before Clovis, that became German-speaking, or at least a large part of that territory between the Rhine and the Somme.[90]

We should not exaggerate the differences between the early Frankish domain and early Anglo-Saxon England. The Roman habit of erecting monumental stone buildings could not be sustained anywhere in the West in the new economic climate. It was not until Charlemagne forged an empire that the Franks could revive Roman building methods in the style known as Romanesque. By the end of the reign of Charlemagne in 814, more German-speaking regions had been added to that German-speaking core in Austrasia. As the Franks forged across Gaul, other Germanic tribes had spread south as far as present-day Austria, Switzerland and northern Italy. The Franks were initially content to be acknowledged as overlords of these regions, but Charlemagne drew them into the Frankish empire, along with Saxony [see 101]. Thus he united more of Europe than anyone had done since the fall of the Roman empire. The Franks had welded together a Romance-speaking west to a Germanic-speaking east, but it was not to last. The Eastern Frankish kingdom broke away in 911. Within present-day France, only Alsace is traditionally German speaking.

Both France and Britain gained another influx of Germanic blood from the Vikings, which complicates the genetic picture (Chapter 17). Thus far, genetic studies have been able to identify the input of Norwegian Vikings to Orkney and Shetland. It is more difficult to distinguish between Anglo-Saxons and Danish Vikings, since both came from Jutland. Yet the genetic impact of the Anglo-Saxons in England cannot be denied. Even today, after centuries of moving and mixing, that impact remains highest in East Anglia.[91] Preliminary analysis from the large People of the British Isles study suggests a very substantial contribution to the English population spreading in from the east, putatively the Anglo-Saxons.[92]

Little difference has been found in the Y-DNA signatures of a selection of regions of France, with two exceptions: Brittany and Alsace. Subclades of haplogroup R1b dominate all the tested regions, as with the rest of western Europe. R1b-M269 is the most common, except in formerly German-speaking Alsace, where R1b-U152 is just a shade ahead in the sample. As we might expect, Alsace also surpasses other French regions in its level of U106, which tends to cluster within Germanic-language countries. Brittany, on the other hand, has a level of R1b-M269 twice as high as the other regions, but also has a higher level of haplogroup I1 (12 per cent) than any of the other regions tested.[93] Brittany was only briefly subjugated by the Franks and provided a refuge for Britons fleeing the Anglo-Saxon advance. However, Brittany was conquered by Vikings in 919. The level of haplogroup I1 found in Lower Normandy (11.9 per cent) is effectively the same as that in Brittany.[94] Thus I1 is more likely to be a Viking rather than Frankish signature in Brittany, though a spread along the coast from Jutland any time from the Mesolithic cannot be ruled out on present knowledge. In Britain, the Western Isles, where Vikings settled, has almost as much I1 (18 per cent) as Germany and Denmark (19 per cent), though Norfolk – settled by Angles – is not far behind at 17 per cent.[95]

Just as R1b-U152/S28 and R1b-U106/S21 cluster together in Alsace, so they do in eastern Scotland and East Anglia. This may reflect succeeding waves of incomers from the Continent, the earliest in the Iron Age, but also the later ones of Angle and Norse, all preferring the best arable land.[96]

CHAPTER FIFTEEN
Enter the Slavs

Slavs today number nearly 270 million. Yet the Slavs were even more obscure than the Germani before Christian Slavic states emerged. There is no mention of Slavs in any surviving source before the 6th century AD. The first written Slavic language is Old Church Slavonic, which appears from AD 865.[1] This obscurity has fuelled fierce controversy over the early Slavs. There is a strong political element to this. Some Slavic countries have vied for the status of Slavic homeland.[2] To please them all, one would have to imagine a far larger homeland than linguists would accept. One would also have to ignore the evidence from Classical sources that present-day Slavic Europe was almost entirely non-Slavic in the Roman period. The logical deduction is that the Slavs expanded in the early Middle Ages from a comparatively small heartland on the fringe of the world known to the Romans. [104]

There is strong support for this picture in the striking genetic similarity of Slavic speakers. Judging from shared lengths of DNA, Slavic populations are more similar across national boundaries than non-Slavic nations. The number of DNA blocks shared between Slavic speakers is constant regardless of the geographic distance separating the two. This is consistent with these individuals having a comparatively large proportion of shared ancestry drawn from a relatively small population that expanded over a wide geographic area. This ancestry can be dated to between 1,000 and 2,000 years ago.[3]

From a silent start, the Slavs entered history with a clamour. They achieved notoriety by raiding across the Danube into the Byzantine empire. Procopius recorded the attacks of *Antae* and *Sclaveni*, starting some time before AD 531, when Justinian appointed a General of Thrace to ward them off. The Slavic ethnonym that appears in Old Church Slavonic is *Slověne*, recognizably related to *Sclaveni*, and Procopius tells us that the *Antae* spoke the same language.[4] His contemporary Jordanes explains where these tribes lived. The *Antae* dwelt in the curve of the Black Sea, between the Dniester and Dnieper. The abode of the *Sclaveni* extended from the city of

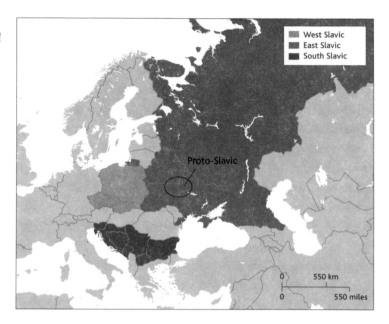

104 *Slavic languages today and the deduced homeland of the parent language.*

Noviodunum (modern Isaccea, Romania) to the Dniester, and northwards as far as the Vistula.[5] So Slavs had taken over territory earlier dominated by the Goths, until the latter were ejected by the Huns. The collapse of the Hunnic empire after AD 454 left a power vacuum on the western steppe, which some groups of Slavs exploited. It seems that the main draw was the wealth of Byzantium. From the steppe one could trade across the Black Sea. The more warlike served as soldiers in Roman employ, or raided across the border into the Balkans.[6]

Archaeologists have discovered an archaeological assemblage dotted across what is now Wallachia and southern Moldavia, and dating to the post-Hunnic period. [105, 106] It is much simpler than earlier cultures there. The pottery is hand-made rather than wheel-thrown. Settlements are small clusters of huts partly sunk into the ground, with a hearth (later an oven) in one corner. Imported luxuries are almost non-existent.[7] This matches the description Procopius gives of the hard life of the *Antae* and *Sclaveni*: they paid no heed to bodily comforts and lived in what seemed pitiful hovels from a Byzantine perspective. *Maurice's Strategikon*, a Byzantine guide to warfare, describes these peoples as independent, populous and hardy, absolutely refusing to be enslaved or governed.[8] This self-reliant culture could survive on the margins of the farming world. The river basins in the forest-steppe zone were as far northeast as arable agriculture was feasible in Europe. The early

Slavs kept cattle as well as cultivating cereals.[9] Their diet was clearly healthy, for Procopius mentions that they were exceptionally tall and stalwart men. They struck him as neither very blond nor entirely dark in colouring.[10]

This simple culture of the 5th–7th centuries has also been found in other regions – Poland, Ukraine, Bohemia, Slovakia and Moravia. As is often the way when archaeologists of different countries and languages publish separately, it has acquired a range of names including Prague, Korchak and Penkovka. For the sake of simplicity, I will use Korchak. This is the name of the type-site in Ukraine, near Zhitomir, west of Kiev. For linguistic reasons the search for the Slavic homeland has focused on the modern region of Polesia. Proto-Slavic had its own name for the hornbeam, while the words for beech, larch and yew are all Germanic loans. The hornbeam predominates in this marshy zone around the Pripet River in southern Belarus and northern Ukraine.[11]

In this area, Baltic and Slavic river-names overlap. The most archaic Slavic hydronyms encircle an area between the Middle Dnieper, Bug and Dniester rivers.[12] A Slavic homeland there could maintain a dialect continuum with Baltic on the north and Iranian on the steppe, explaining the influences of these emerging language families on the development of Proto-Slavic [see 59]. As East Germanic spread southwards to the Black Sea in the 2nd and 3rd centuries BC, it skirted the proposed Proto-Slavic homeland, explaining the borrowings from Gothic into Proto-Slavic.[13]

Jordanes tells us that the *Sclaveni* had swamps and forests for their cities.[14] This should not be taken too literally. His meaning is that Slavic

105, 106 *Pot (left) and fibula (right) of Korchak type, from the settlement of Crucea lui Ferentz near Iasi, Moldavia, second half of the 6th century.*

settlements were protected by the terrain. The culture was not urbanized. *Maurice's Strategikon* describes the Slavs living among nearly impenetrable forests, rivers, lakes and marshes, and explains how they made use of the cover in ambushes. They were particularly adept at hiding underwater, breathing through hollow reeds.[15] The Pripet marshes would be ideal for such tactics, as well as yielding fish, wildfowl and reeds for roofing, but there is no reason to suppose that the early Slavs spent all their time in marshland. The earliest datable Korchak material comes from Podolia, the west-central and southwest portions of present-day Ukraine.[16]

For a predecessor we can look to the similar Kiev culture of the Upper Dnieper Basin.[17] Herodotus describes Scythian cultivators in that area.[18] The term 'Scythian' here should not be taken as a precise and accurate ethnic designation. The early Slavs lived on the very edge of the world known to the ancient Greeks. While Herodotus could see some Scythians in close-up, thanks to Greek colonies along the north coast of the Black Sea, he had a much sketchier idea of the peoples north of them. Greek communication with the early Slavs could well have been via Iranian speakers living closer to the Greek colonists. This corresponds to the picture from Iron Age archaeological finds of farmers beside the Upper Dnieper in contact with Scythian nomads.[19] Looking for a yet earlier cultural ancestor we reach the Bronze Age Middle Dnieper group of sites in the Kiev region [see 59], with their semi-subterranean dwellings.[20]

Jordanes famously declared that the *Sclaveni* and the *Antae* were both sprung from the *Wenedarum*. The Wends or *Veneti* turn up in a rich array of other sources, but do these names refer exclusively to the Slavs? It seems not. Even if we focus only on those *Veneti* between the Baltic and the Black Sea, there appear to be two separate groups of them. Jordanes places the *Veneti* in a great expanse of land, starting near the source of the Vistula.[21] Tacitus (writing AD 98) locates the *Veneti* among the peoples on the eastern fringe of Germania, beyond whom was the stuff of fables, *terra incognita* to the Romans. The settled *Veneti* lived in the woods between the *Peucini* (Germanic speakers north of Dacia) and the *Fenni* (Finno-Ugric hunter-gatherers of Finland and the eastern Baltic).[22]

Just as earlier Greeks tended to see the whole of eastern Europe as Scythia, so later ones named it Sarmatia, after the steppe-dwellers familiar to them. Describing European Sarmatia, Ptolemy (c. AD 150) tells us that the Greater *Venedae* lived along the entire Venedicus Bay. He names tribes south of the *Venedae* both along the eastern bank of the Vistula and further east.[23] So it seems that his Venedicus Bay was the Bay of Danzig, inhabited by Baltic speakers in the Middle Ages. Pliny also places the *Veneti* along the Baltic coast,[24] as does the Late Roman *Tabula Peutingeriana*. So the *Veneti* of Ptolemy and Pliny seem to be the Western Balts. They could scarcely be Slavs, since Proto-Slavic lacks maritime terminology and had no word for amber, the chief Baltic export in Roman times.[25] Yet the use of the term 'Greater' by Ptolemy hints that another tribe was once seen as the 'Lesser *Venedae*'. The Slavs, a closely related people inhabiting a smaller territory, would fit the bill. That would explain why the *Tabula Peutingeriana* mentions, separately from the *Venadisarmatae* (Balts), the *Venedi* on the northern bank of the Danube, somewhat upstream of its mouth, where some Slavs had arrived by *c.* AD 500.

The Germanic term *Winden* or *Wenden* (Wends) was applied to neighbouring Slavic speakers by Fredegar in his 7th-century chronicle, and this usage long continued.[26] Yet Henry of Livonia in his Latin chronicle of *c.* 1200 described the clearly Baltic tribe of the *Vindi* (*Winden*) living in Courland and Livonia (in what is now Latvia). Their name lives on in the River Windau (Latvian *Venta*), with the town of Windau (Latvian *Ventspils*) at its mouth, and in Wenden, the old name of the town of Cesis in Livonia.[27] So both Balts and Slavs could be termed Wends.

The Slavic expansion

If the Slavs, obscure and landlocked, were regarded in Roman times as the country cousins of the Balts, the positions of greater and lesser were about to be reversed. The Slavs leapt from obscurity in spectacular fashion. During two centuries they spread over areas previously populated by Baltic, Germanic and Illyrian speakers. [107] No doubt they absorbed many local people, but where language change spread with them, it is testimony to mass movement. From a single Slavic language spoken around AD 500 sprang over a dozen languages spoken today over a huge part of eastern Europe. These fall into three branches: East, West and South Slavic.[28] [see 104]

Their earliest expansion was southwards to the Danube and Black Sea, to judge by the dating of the Korchak material. A position on the steppe made these migrants vulnerable to the next wave of nomads from the east, the Avars. The rise of the Avars in the latter part of the 6th century drove

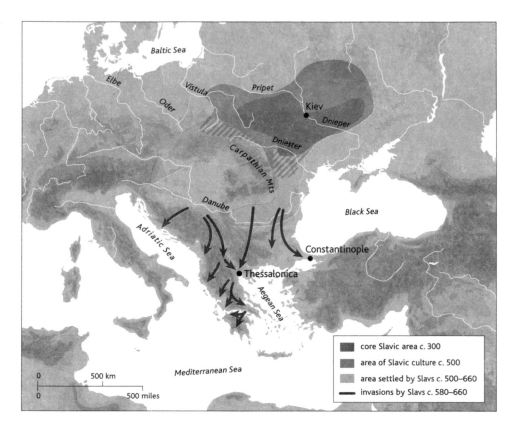

107 *The spread of Slavic culture* AD *300–660 can be traced in archaeology.*

Slavic groups over the Danube into Byzantine territory, just as the Huns had pushed the Goths across the Danube centuries earlier. This time the remains of the Roman empire, weakened by predatory powers on other fronts, could not defend the frontier. The way to the Balkans lay open to the Slavs.

While their invasions of Greece did not permanently change its linguistic landscape, further north Slavs had settled across most of the Balkans by the mid-7th century.[29] The depopulation of Illyria by the Justinian Plague in AD 542 helps to explain the comparative ease with which Slavs came to overwhelm Illyrians. In 547/8 the Slavs raided Illyria and took strongholds which were empty of defenders. After 582 the Slavs began to settle where they had previously plundered: Moesia, Thrace and Illyria, forcing the previous population to flee or be assimilated.[30]

Before the Serbs appear as a Slavic people of the Balkans, the *Serbi* were a tribe of steppe-dwellers between the Sea of Azov and the Volga.[31] They were presumably Iranian-speaking Alans. It is not impossible that some took refuge with the Slavs as the Huns raced across the steppe. If so, little sign of them beyond their name survived into the Slavic migration period.

Improvements in recent years in dating Korchak-type finds enable us to track Slavic progress around the north of the Carpathians into Central Europe, starting around AD 500 and reaching Bohemia around 550. Previous power struggles had tugged the Lombards south from Bohemia into the Middle Danube region, easing Slavic takeover of Moravia and Bohemia.[32] A century later Slavs reached the Elbe-Saale region. Here the migrants were safe from the Avars, but were deep into Germanic territory and came under Frankish hegemony. There was a flash of Slavic resistance. Dervan is mentioned in the *Chronicle of Fredegar* as the ruler of the *Surbii* (Serbs or Sorbs) from the nation of the *Sclavi* (Slavs), who briefly threw off Frankish domination in 632/3 to join forces with fellow Slavs in Moravia and Bohemia.[33] The Sorbs remain a Slavic-speaking minority in parts of Germany: Lusatia (on the border with Poland) and the Hannoversches Wendland (in a bend of the Elbe in Lower Saxony). Genetically and linguistically the Sorbs are part of the West Slavic group.[34]

Southern Poland has similar sites to Korchak from about AD 500, overlaying the abandoned sites of the Przeworsk and Wielbark cultures, which have been linked to the Vandals and Goths respectively. The area had become progressively depopulated in the previous two centuries. Within what is now Poland, only Pomerania in the north remained well populated. The losses elsewhere can be explained by the invasion of the Huns and movement south of the Goths and Vandals (see Chapter 14). The settlement void was filled by the Slavs. Here too the pioneering migrants had escaped the Avars, it seems, since there is little sign of the latter on Polish soil.[35]

A culture with both similarities to and differences from Korchak, Sukow-Dziedzice, appears in the region around the Oder, and reached the Elbe *c.* 700. This too appears Slavic, for a Bavarian geographer in the 9th century recorded Slavic names for the peoples between the Elbe and Oder. There has been a tendency to see Sukow-Dziedzice as the product of a separate group of Slavs, yet it may simply have evolved from the earlier culture of southern Poland. From about 950 a tribal society was welded by the Piast dynasty into the medieval state of Poland, which took its name from the Polans tribe.[36]

The Korchak culture also spread eastwards over more of Ukraine. Successor cultures spread northwards into what is now Russia. Slavic movement east and north of the Dnieper took them into a forest zone thinly populated by Balts. It is difficult nowadays to visualize just how thinly people were spread beyond the terrain suitable for agriculture. It would not require huge numbers of Slavic speakers to tip the balance in favour of the East Slavic tongue. What was the attraction of these wild forests? The magnet might have been the fur and slave trades of Kievan Rus (Chapter 17). By about 900, Slavs were occupying a vast area of eastern Europe, according to *The Russian Primary Chronicle*, which was not composed until the 12th century.[37]

Slavic genetic mix

The Y-DNA haplogroups R1a1a1b1a1 (M458) and I2a1b3a (L147) shadow the modern distribution of Slavic languages so closely that we must suspect that both are Slavic signatures. Yet the discoverers of M458 failed even to discuss the possibility, since they used the evolutionary effective mutation rate (see p. 30), which generally overestimates ages dramatically.[38] By contrast another study went in search of a Slavic marker. It uncovered a pattern among Western Slavs that turned out to correspond to M458. The authors point out that the pedigree mutation rate is more consistent with the archaeological record.[39] [108]

For R1a-M458 to be present so widely across the region settled by the Slavs, must mean it was found in the Slavic homeland well before the Migration Period. It would need time to spread among the people developing Proto-Slavic. The heaviest density of R1a-M458 falls around the Oder, with another peak around the Upper Vistula. That could represent a serial founder effect. Migrants intending to settle often travel in family or clan groups. A group including a number of men carrying R1a-M458 could have settled first in the Upper Vistula area. Then, half a century later, some of their descendants could have moved west to the Oder, in the migration that created the Sukow-Dziedzice culture. The subclade R1a1a1b1a1a (L260) appears to have been carried within the group settling in present-day Poland. It is a close match to a previously discovered haplotype labelled P for Polish, since it is almost exclusive to those of Polish descent.[40] The sheer numbers of R1a-M458 men moving into what is now Poland seems to have preserved a high level of variance, conveying a deceptive impression of great age there. R1a-M458 is rarer in the Balkans, peaking at 12.2 per cent on the Croatian Krk Island, with 9 per cent in Split (Croatia),

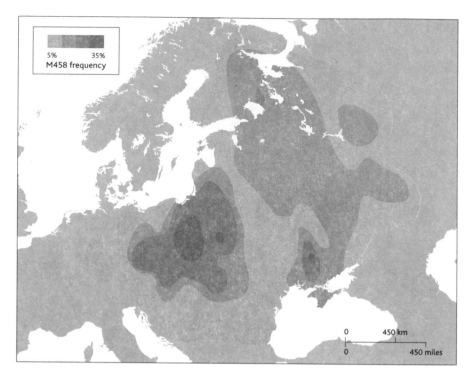

5%   35%
M458 frequency

0   450 km

0   450 miles

108 *The distribution of Y-DNA R1a-M458 is similar to that of the Slavic languages.*

8.8 per cent in the Republic of Macedonia, 8.6 per cent in Bosnia and lower frequencies elsewhere.[41]

However, I2a1b3a (L147) peaks in Bosnia and Herzegovina.[42] Although spread over most Slavic countries to some degree, this haplogroup looks particularly connected to the Slavic expansion southwards and then across the Danube. There is a striking correlation with the distribution of the Serbian language. [109, 110]

South Slavic languages replaced all the Illyrian ones spoken in antiquity, with one exception. The living language Albanian probably descends from Illyrian.[43] There is a lower level of I2a1b3a today in Greece and Albania, which retain their pre-Slavic languages, than in present-day majority Slavic-speaking nations. The level of I2a1b3a was probably lower still in Albania in the medieval period. The Arbereshe are an Albanian-speaking ethno-linguistic minority who settled in Calabria (southern Italy) about five centuries ago. Using Arbereshe surnames to identify a sample of present-day Italians with ancestors among medieval Albanians, one study established

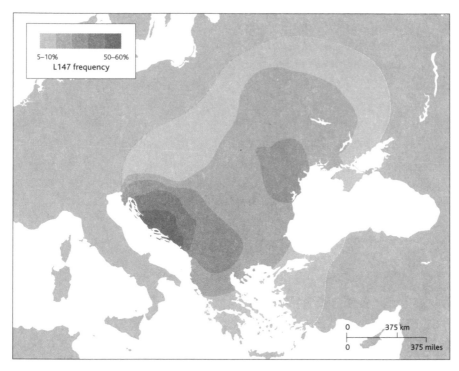

109 (above) Distribution of Y-DNA haplogroup I2a1b3a (L147).

110 (below) Countries in which Serbian is the official or a recognized minority language.

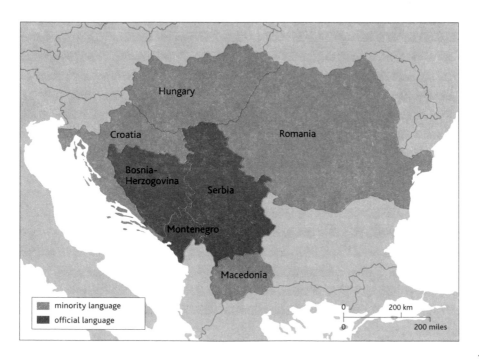

that the Y-DNA of this group has more in common with the people of the southern Balkans than with Italians. Yet the group had a lower frequency of haplogroups I2a and J2 than the present-day southern Balkans, suggesting a marked increase in the frequency of haplogroups I2a and J2 in the latter region over the last five centuries.[44]

The appearance of I2a1b3a in Turkey is of interest. Some Slavs served as auxiliaries in the Byzantine army in the 6th century, so a few may have elected to settle in Byzantium. More importantly, some 30,000 Slavs were transferred to Asia Minor by the Byzantine emperor Justinian II in the late 680s, after his offensive in Macedonia that temporarily restored imperial control.[45] In the Middle Ages the Byzantine empire fell to the Ottoman Turks, who gradually acquired control of much of the Balkans. This was another period of probable movement of I2a1b3a into Turkey. Slavery was a key part of life in the Ottoman empire (see p. 198). Christian boys from conquered countries were taken away from their families, converted to Islam and enlisted into a special branch of the Ottoman army – the Janissary corps – until its abolition in 1826.[46]

Not all men of Slavic descent will carry R1a-M458 or I2a1b3a. About half of those Sorbs, Poles, Russians and Ukrainians who have been tested have Y-DNA within the R1a1a haplogroup. Not all of that is R1a-M458. R1a1a* also appears in the Balkans, for example at about 30 per cent in Slovenia and Croatia. Also, since the Slavs absorbed local populations as they spread, it is no surprise to find among Western Slavs some of the haplogroups mentioned above as Germanic, among Southern Slavs the J and E that probably arrived with early farmers, and in Russia the N1c associated with Finno-Ugric tribes.[47]

Slavic speakers carry a wide range of mtDNA haplogroups typical of Western Eurasians. Almost half carry H, as is usual in Europe, with J at around 10 per cent and U5a the next most common at about 6 per cent. The subclade H1a is both densest and most diverse in eastern Europe.[48] U5a is ancient in Europe. It has been found in the DNA of hunter-gatherers in Germany, Poland, Russia and Sweden.[49] Since the distribution of U5a is weighted towards eastern Europe, it may have evolved in an Ice Age refuge in southeastern Europe.[50] The rarer haplogroups U4a1 and U4a2 are found at less than 2 per cent among Slavs, which is still higher than in western Europeans (0.5 per cent). U4a1 is at its densest in the Volga-Ural region, while U4a2 leans slightly towards central eastern Europe.[51]

CHAPTER SIXTEEN

Bulgars and Magyars

N omads play by their own rules. Mobility is built into their lifestyle.[1] Horse-riding stock-breeders can move themselves and their herds thousands of kilometres, and turn into instant cavalry. The grasslands of the steppe created a trans-continental highway for these horsemen. From the steppe there were natural corridors into the farmlands of Europe and China. At the west end the point of entry was the Danube Basin. To the east the Hexi or Gansu Corridor led from the Tarim Basin into northern China. Settled farmers of both Europe and China felt the mighty fist of Genghis Khan and his Mongol horde in the Middle Ages. Centuries earlier, chronicles wailed of the depredations of the Xiongnu and the Huns, who appear to be the same people. These herders of Central Asia could travel the vast steppe from Mongolia to Ukraine looking for greener pastures. A tribal territory could change in days. When bands united under a strong leader they rapidly covered large areas, creating huge empires.[2]

With new peoples came new languages. The steppe was a linguistic spread zone, which repeatedly experienced complete language replacement.[3] It was also a trade route. The famed Silk Road was in fact several routes, the northernmost of which crossed the steppe. Far more than silk travelled these ways, but the precious yarn extracted from silkworms in China was such a coveted textile in the West that the romantic name 'Silk Road' was coined by a European explorer in 1877 and has been taken up with enthusiasm. Individual traders would not usually travel the whole route from western China to Constantinople or Rome. Instead, goods would generally pass through many hands in stages along the way. At the eastern end of the route steppe nomads could supply the Chinese with horses in exchange for silk or silk floss, a padding with which to create quilted clothes against the icy steppe winters.[4]

The first people to domesticate the horse had the initial advantage. Horsemen carried Indo-European languages east across the Urals into Asia, along with their horses, as well as wheat, bronze, sheep and chariots. They

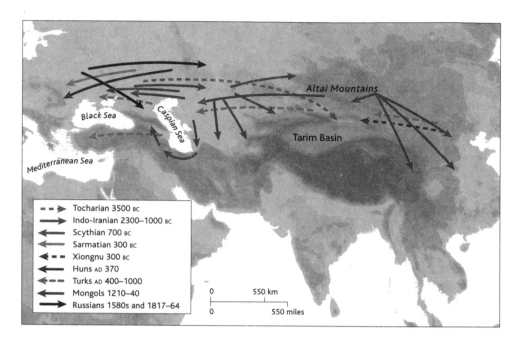

111 *Migrations east and west along the steppe corridor.*

introduced the pastoral life to the indigenous peoples of Central Asia and Mongolia. As the Asian nomads grew strong in numbers, they reversed the flow across the steppe. The Huns and Mongols reached deep into Europe and the Turks took over Anatolia. The tide turned again as the Russians rose in power and pushed eastwards into Siberia. This shuttling between East and West wove a complex cultural and genetic tapestry. [111]

Here we compare and contrast two mobile peoples. The Bulgars gave their name to Bulgaria, but not their Turkic language, while the Magyars introduced their Ugric language to Hungary. For the settled peoples of Europe, the Bulgars and Magyars were yet more mysterious marauders from the east. Yet their origins lay far apart.

The Asian nomads were speakers of Turkic and Mongolian languages, both spreading from the Asian steppe. The rise of Turkic began with the expansion of the Huns. Steppe people began to shift from Iranian to Turkic speech.[5] The peoples of Central Asia today can be distinguished genetically along linguistic lines. In general, Turkic-speaking populations are closely related to East Asian populations, while Indo-Iranian speakers cluster closer to Western Eurasians. The interesting exceptions are some Turkic-speaking populations who cluster genetically with Indo-Iranian speakers, indicating a linguistic shift.[6]

The Huns appeared northeast of the Sea of Azov, in the European-Asian borderland, around the year AD 200 and burst into Europe around 370. A unified Hun nation only developed in the next century and reached its greatest extent under the famed Attila. The Huns swept up some peoples in their path and took suzerainty over many more, creating a vast multilingual empire.[7] So little is known of the language of the Huns themselves that it can only tentatively be assigned to the Oghur branch of Turkic, the same as the language of the Bulgars.[8]

The Bulgars, also known as Bolgars and Bulghars, emerged eventually from the wreckage of the Hun empire after the death of Attila in 453. The Byzantine historian John of Nikiu refers to 'Kubratos, chief of the Huns', who was baptized in Constantinople, having grown up in the imperial palace during the reign of Heraclius (610–641).[9] By 635 Kubrat had united the Bulgar tribes to found what later became known as Great Bulgaria, between the Danube and the Volga. On his death the polity broke up. Kubrat's eldest son threw in his lot with a rising power – the Turkic Khazars, who dominated the region north of the Caucasus Mountains. The other four sons went their own ways. Asparukh led one tribe to settle near the Danube delta. A Byzantine attempt to keep the Bulgars under control in 680 resulted in a rout of Byzantine troops, who were chased as far as Varna. There the Bulgars subjugated the local Slavs, creating a buffer for themselves against the Byzantines in a new Bulgaria that extended over territories now within Romania and Bulgaria. The Bulgars here were an elite.[10] The Slavic language of their subjects is still spoken in Bulgaria today. The Thracians, who once dominated the region, had been submerged by Slavs before the Bulgars arrived.

Genetically the Bulgarians are similar to other South Slavic speakers. The Y-DNA haplogroups R1a-M458 and I2a1b3a (L147), associated with the Slavs (see pp. 232–33), are well represented. So are haplogroups E1b-V13, J2-M241 and R1b1a2a (L23), perhaps representing the Thracians. Haplogroups C, N and Q, distinctive for Central Asian Turkic speakers, occur in only 1.5 per cent of Bulgarians.[11]

Another group of Bulgars moved away from the Khazars to settle around the confluence of the Volga and Kama rivers, a region long inhabited by Finno-Ugric hunters and trappers. The area seems to have attracted a stream of nomadic incomers, both Turkic- and Iranian-speaking, who squabbled among themselves, but united under the Bulgar banner to face a common enemy.[12] One of their main trading centres was Bulgar or Bolghar, beside the Volga, well placed to speed arctic furs downriver to the Caspian. The Volga Bulgars were conquered by Genghis Khan in the 13th century. Their descendants, the Chuvash, speak the only surviving member of the Oghur branch of Turkic. The Chuvash today carry overwhelmingly Western Eurasian mtDNA haplogroups such as H (31 per cent), U (22 per cent) and K (11 per cent). Their maternal markers most closely resemble Finno-Ugric speakers rather than fellow Turkic speakers.[13]

The Magyars are extraordinary. We can seek their origins among those Uralic speakers who remained in their ancient hunting grounds near the Urals and developed the Ugric language branch, as Proto-Finnic split away (see pp. 68–70). Proto-Ugric speakers came in contact with Iranian-speaking nomads some time before 500 BC and borrowed from them the words for 'horse', 'saddle' and 'stirrup'. Evidently the Ugric hunters had taken to horse-riding. This did not turn them immediately into steppe herders. It just made them more efficient hunters.[14] Linguistically, the closest relative of Magyar is Mansi [see 23, 24]; indeed the two names spring from the same root. Their history has been dramatically different. While Mansi is an endangered language, swamped by Russian, Hungarian is the official language of a state with a population of 10 million.

What set the Magyars on a different track? We can find clues in the Hungarian language. Turkic vocabulary was acquired, as we might expect if the Magyars were trading with the Volga Bulgars. Magyar trappers could have supplied furs to the thriving Bulgar market. They seem to have lived close by, on the left bank of the Volga, in what was later called *Magna Hungaria*. What induced a section of the Magyars to take to a semi-nomadic life on the Pontic steppe c. AD 800 is unclear, but it preserved their distinct ethnic and linguistic identity, even within the expanded Khazar Khaganate. Those Magyar tribes who did not move south were subsequently absorbed by the Bashkirs to their east.[15]

That amalgamation helps to explain the curious mixture of Y-DNA haplogroups in the Bashkirs today. [112] Although they are Turkic speaking, around 17 per cent of sampled Bashkir males carry N1c (M46/Page70/ Tat), found commonly in Uralic-language speakers. That average conceals massive differences by district, ranging from 65 per cent to 3 per cent.

112 *Two Bashkir horsemen in 1814, drawn by Aleksandr Orlovsky (1777–1832).*

When populations were small, a few incomers could tip the genetic balance dramatically. The predominant haplogroups among the Bashkirs are R1b-M269 (34 per cent) and R1a1 (26 per cent), characteristic of Indo-European speakers, together with R1b-M73 (13 per cent). Of the remaining 10 per cent, some do carry typically East Asian Y-DNA haplogroups C or O, but this is a much lower percentage than we find in some Turkic speakers of Central Asia,[16] such as the Kazakhs.[17] Turkic nomads moving westwards could have absorbed so many steppe Iranian speakers that they were already a genetic mixture by the time they reached the borders of Europe.

On the steppe, the Magyars were cattle-herders and slave-raiders. They were a formidable force, by contemporary accounts. Yet attacks from the fierce Turkic Pechenegs led them to look for pastures new. In the years around AD 900, the Magyars moved up the Danube and conquered the Carpathian Basin, founding the Principality of Hungary. Hungarian tribal names included some that were Turkic and Iranian. Some renegade Khazars joined the movement.[18] Slavs were already living in the Carpathian Basin. The Principality was an ethnic mixture from the start. How were the Hungarians able to retain the Magyar language? The Magyars certainly migrated in numbers that enabled them to terrify Europe.[19] As the historian Peter Heather writes:

An orgy of equine-powered aggression saw Magyar raiding parties sweep through northern Italy and southern France with a ferocity not seen since the time of Attila.[20]

Why then do the modern Hungarians appear genetically much like their Slavic neighbours?[21] They show little of the Y-DNA haplogroup N1c found in other Uralic-speaking populations – only around 0.5 per cent.[22] Is this the result of the many population changes since the arrival of the Magyars?[23] Or did the Magyars not carry this marker? One study set out to answer this question. The team looked at 10th-century Hungarian bone samples from rich graves typical of the conquerors. Two out of four carried the marker for N1c.[24] This is a striking result, though statistically it is too small a sample to rely upon. In other words, we should not assume that exactly half of the incomers were N1c bearers. What it does prove is that N1c was among the haplogroups that arrived with the Magyars.

Another Magyar burial with a horse yielded the East Asian mtDNA N9a, also found in two earlier Sarmatian burials in Hungary.[25] This was exceptional, though. Most other mtDNA haplogroups from that period in Hungary fall into Western Eurasian lineages.[26] Overall the picture is of the Magyars imposing their rule upon a Slavic population. Subsequent immigration from neighbouring countries would further dilute the Magyar input.

CHAPTER SEVENTEEN

Vikings

The word Viking spread terror far and wide. Peaceful monks and farmers learned to fear the sail on the horizon that presaged a lightning attack by massive, axe-wielding pirates of the north. Though there was much more to the Viking Age than piracy, it will be forever defined by wanderlust and warriors. Viking in Old Norse meant sea-warriors, as far as we can tell.[1] Young Scandinavian men went 'a-viking' in the invitingly warm summers around AD 800, in search of plunder and adventure. Raiding gradually gave way to settlement and trade. The Vikings at home were farmers, fishers and hunters, and had long traded amber for metals. As they spread they created new trade routes. Captured human booty generated a slave trade, which was a major source of Viking wealth.

At the start of the Viking Age, Scandinavians lived in scattered farms. There were few villages or trade centres and no apparatus of the nation state. The same was true of the more thinly populated lands that the Vikings entered: Ireland, Scotland, Russia and Ukraine. The Scandinavian diaspora changed the dynamics of Viking life and contributed to state formation and urbanism at home and abroad.[2] One constant was the paganism of the Vikings, which set them apart from the rest of the Germanic-speaking world, by then absorbed into Christendom. Gradually the fierce followers of Thor and Odin too were Christianized. With the fall of the last temple to the Norse gods at Uppsala in 1090, a way of life was at an end.[3] So Viking is a period as much as a people.

Those participating could come from anywhere that Old Norse was spoken: the Scandinavian peninsula, Jutland and associated islands. Those on the receiving end of the Viking longsword generally lumped together all these Scandinavian marauders as Vikings, Northmen, Norsemen, Normands or Danes, according to local custom. In the east, Scandinavian traders appear as *Væringar* or Rus.[4] The Vikings distinguished between various peoples among themselves, but we should not picture these distinctions as neatly fitting the modern borders of the Scandinavian nations. The Danes lived in the lowlands of southern Scandinavia, suitable for stock-breeding – not just modern Denmark, but southern Sweden too. They were regarded by the Franks as the most powerful people among the Northmen. The Danes had merged into a kingdom by the Viking period; its influence spread as far as the Viken region around the Skagerrak, now part of Norway, though local chiefs there resisted Danish rule. The western seaboard of the Scandinavian peninsula offered shelter to other groups. A chain of offshore islands protects the coastline, forming the 'North Way', which was to give Norway its name. The scattered souls of the Norwegian fjords were separated by a huge chain of mountains from the nascent Swedes of Svealand on the eastern coast around Old Uppsala. The *Svear* were blessed with fertile lowland, and they too were ruled by a king. His writ barely ran, if at all, in the sparsely populated and heavily forested regions to the north and west of Svealand.[5]

Geographical position encouraged what we would now call Norwegians to explore westwards to Scotland, Ireland and further west, while the Danes favoured movement along the coast to Frisia, France and England, and the Swedes ventured across the Baltic to Finland, upriver into eastern Europe and across the Black Sea to Byzantium. [113] That is the picture painted in broad brushstrokes. Focus on the detail and you find the unexpected. A successful Viking leader could attract warriors from many places, hoping for a share of the spoils. Thanks to strontium isotopes, we now have an idea of who was in the army of Harald Bluetooth Gormsson, 10th-century king of Denmark. He clearly recruited far and wide. A sample of 48 burials from his fortress at Trelleborg displayed the variety of origins. The young men in its cemetery came largely from outside Denmark, perhaps from Norway or the Slavic regions. The three females in the sample were all from overseas. Some rune stones of this period in south Scandinavia refer to foreigners coming from Norway, the Slavonic areas or elsewhere on the Continent.[6]

The speakers of Old Norse were of necessity hardy sailors. The sea was the easiest way to travel from fjord to fjord around the mountain spine of the Scandinavian peninsula. Moreover, the poor soils over much of that peninsula, together with the limited northern sun, made crops meagre and created a greater dependence upon fish. Norway's long coastline was its chief asset – a source of abundant seafood. The flatter land of Jutland and southern Sweden was more suited to agriculture, but seamanship was still needed to reach the islands between these two mainlands. The Norse had developed clinker-built boats, constructed of overlapping planks. The

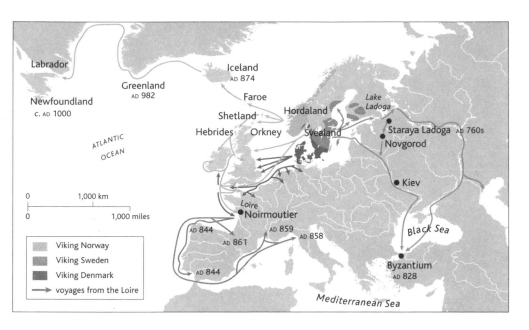

Labrador

Greenland
AD 982

Newfoundland
c. AD 1000

Iceland
AD 874

Faroe

Shetland

Hebrides   Orkney

Hordaland

Lake
Ladoga

Svealand

Staraya Ladoga AD 760s

Novgorod

ATLANTIC
OCEAN

0   1,000 km
0   1,000 miles

Viking Norway
Viking Sweden
Viking Denmark
voyages from the Loire

Loire
Noirmoutier

AD 844

AD 861

AD 859

AD 858

AD 844

Kiev

Black Sea

Byzantium
AD 828

Mediterranean Sea

113 *Viking voyages of exploration, raiding, trading and settlement.*

feared Viking longships were built in this way. The Oseberg Ship [114] now housed in the Viking Ship Museum, Oslo, is almost complete. Not all Viking ships would be as magnificent as this royal vessel, with its beautifully carved prow. It is a good example, though, of the elegant form of these shallow vessels, which could nose

114 *Oseberg Ship, c. 800, displayed in the Viking Ship Museum, Oslo, Norway.*

their way deep inland up the rivers of Europe and yet also make long sea crossings.[7]

What enticed the Vikings to venture further from home? The period c. 800 to 1200 was one of unusually mild and stable weather in northern Europe. The heyday of Norse adventuring fell in these balmy centuries. When the pack ice retreated, the way was open to Iceland, Greenland and as far as Labrador.[8] At home the clement weather no doubt made for better crops. That could lead to population growth. Excess sons might be keen to look for land elsewhere. However, the first Vikings were looking not for land but loot. Perhaps the lure was treasure, which young men could use to gain a bride or a farm, or slaves, to be exchanged for Islamic silver, which in turn would buy wine and weapons in North Sea emporia.[9] The early targets for attack were often specifically Christian. In 793 the monastery

Prehistoric transport 7: Scandinavian sea power

Viking longships are famous. Where did that sailing skill come from? The first signs of seagoing vessels in Scandinavia appear c. 2500 BC. Previously, cultural influences fed into the Scandinavian peninsula by land from the east. Suddenly that changed. Daggers from the flint-rich Limfjord region of north Jutland appear in south Norway. Though little Bell Beaker pottery seems to have made the crossing from Jutland to Norway, other elements of that culture did. Seagoing boats would be needed to make the crossing from Jutland to the Scandinavian peninsula. It was the start of Scandinavian seafaring. Log dugouts have been

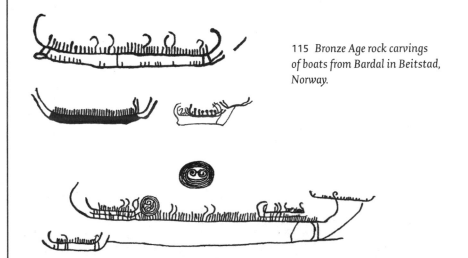

115 Bronze Age rock carvings of boats from Bardal in Beitstad, Norway.

117 *Gravestone from the island of Lindisfarne depicting men bearing swords and axes.*

founded by St Aidan on the tiny island of Lindisfarne was sacked. [117] It made a tempting target. Lying off the coast of Northumbria, the monastery

found that could have been used on rivers or even coastal waters, but our knowledge of the first seagoing Scandinavian vessels comes from the thousands of Bronze Age rock carvings of ships. [115]

Clearly part of the same tradition is the Hjortspring boat dating from 300–400 BC, with two timber horn-like extensions at prow and stern. It was a sewn, plank-built canoe intended to be paddled by ranks of oarsmen.[10] [116]

In the first centuries AD the technique of sewing planks together was replaced by overlapping planks fastened together with nails, known as clinker-building, or 'lap-strake'. Remains of such vessels were preserved in the Nydam bog in Jutland. Several later ships have survived thanks to the practice of ship burials. From about AD 400 onwards the Angles arrived in England from Jutland in clinker-built ships. A royal example was buried at Sutton Hoo in East Anglia in the 7th century. Though its timber rotted in the soil, an impression was left of its clinker-built form. This construction places it in a Nordic tradition that would last through the Viking period and well into the Middle Ages.[11]

116 *Model of the Hjortspring boat at the National Museum of Denmark in Copenhagen. It was excavated at Als in south Denmark.*

had been favoured by kings, but not protected by them. In the anguished words of the learned Alcuin of York, adviser to Charlemagne:

> The church of St Cuthbert is spattered with the blood of the priests of God, stripped of all its furnishings, exposed to the plundering of pagans – a place more sacred than any in Britain.[12]

Some of the brothers were carried away in fetters.[13] Subsequent Viking attacks were seen by churchmen as part of a religious war. If so, it had been started by Christians. From 772 Charlemagne imposed Christianity on the continental Saxons by violence, provoking revenge attacks on churches. The Saxon leader Widukind fled to his brother-in-law Sigfrid, King of Denmark, no doubt taking tales of horror with him.[14]

Genetics

Buried with grandeur in the Oseberg Ship were two women who must have been of high status. The elder may have been Queen Åsa, grandmother of Harald Fairhair. The younger carried mtDNA U7. This haplogroup is rare in Europe and is mainly found in western and southern Asia, which led to speculation that this woman or her ancestors came from the Black Sea region, as told in the legend of Odin.[15] U7 probably originated in Asia some 18,000 years ago.[16] One route into Europe could indeed be north of the Black Sea, for U7 has been found among Sarmatians on the Russian steppe c. 500 BC.[17] Its importance lies in its rarity, which might make it possible to trace lineages. A male buried in one of Denmark's earliest Christian cemeteries at Kongemarken carried U7.[18] U7 is found at low levels in parts of Sweden today.[19]

It is no easy task to identify Viking descendants outside Scandinavia purely by haplogroup. The common Y-DNA haplogroups in Scandinavia today are shared with the rest of the Germani. We have already seen how widely the Germani spread. So how can we tell the difference between the descendants of Franks and Normans in France, Anglo-Saxons and Vikings in Britain, or Vandals, Goths and Normans in Sicily? Genetic differences today between the Scandinavian peninsula and Jutland tend to be a matter of degree. We can, however, match genetic patterns with historical sources. I1a2 (L22) or R1a1a-L448 may be a clue to a Viking ancestor. I1a2 is most common in Fenno-Scandia. R1a1a-L448 appears in Fenno-Scandia and the

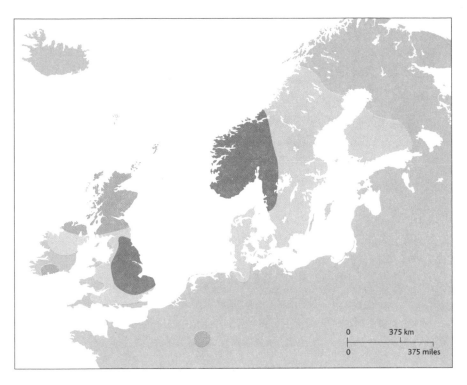

118 *These early indications of the distribution of R1a1a-L448 cannot be as accurate as scientific sampling, but do suggest that the haplogroup is Scandinavian in origin.*

British Isles, most densely in Norway. The marker L448 is too newly discovered to be included in academic papers to date, but it appears from private testing that most of the R1a1a in the British Isles falls into R1a1a-L448. [118] In Britain R1a1a appears most strongly in areas settled by Vikings, particularly those from Norway. There are strong concentrations in Caithness and on the islands of Man, Orkney and Shetland. The level in Ireland is low.[20]

Highlands and Islands

In the same decade as the attack on Lindisfarne came the first raids on monasteries in Ireland and the Western Isles of Scotland. Whence came these Vikings? The *Anglo-Saxon Chronicle* records that the very first ships of the Northmen to arrive in England had landed at Portland, Dorset. This may not have been a raid in intention, though it ended in violence. There was enough talk before this outcome for the arrivals to identify their home as

Hordaland, the district around Hardanger Fjord in western Norway.[21] With a fair wind, Shetland was only 24 hours' sail from Norway. In springtime the prevailing easterly winds would aid the voyage. In autumn the prevailing westerly winds would carry Vikings back home in time for the harvest. Bases may have been established in Orkney and Shetland at an early stage, from which they could more easily raid into Ireland, the Western Isles and the western coasts of England and France.[22] [119] Offa of Mercia (d. 796), ruler of large tracts of England, was aware of the threat. He created defended bridges on Mercian rivers to block access upriver to enemy warships.[23]

These Vikings had no loyalty to Norway. They raided there as well. In the next century those based in the Northern and Western Isles became such a nuisance to King Harald Fairhair, who had managed to weld together chiefs and petty kings into the Kingdom of Norway, that he conquered Shetland, Orkney and the Hebrides in 875. Sigurd, one of the men on Harald's expedition, became Jarl (earl) of the islands.[24] Orkney and Shetland were held for the Norwegian (and later Danish) crown until they passed to Scotland in 1468.

The Norse takeover of these northern islands was thorough. By the time that Scotland took control of them, the place-names of Orkney and Shetland were almost entirely Norse in origin.[25] The inhabitants spoke Norrœna or Norn, derived from Old West Norse. The strongest evidence, though, comes from the genes of the present inhabitants. One study found an overall Scandinavian ancestry of about 44 per cent for Shetland and 30 per cent for Orkney, with approximately equal contributions from Scandinavian

119 *Scandinavian settlement in the British Isles.*

males and females. This contrasts with the Western Isles, where the overall Scandinavian ancestry is only around 15 per cent, and where there was a disproportionately high contribution from Scandinavian males. This suggests that areas closer to Scandinavia, such as Orkney and Shetland, were settled primarily by Scandinavian family groups, while lone Vikings settling with local women was the more typical pattern further from their homeland.[26]

A team from three English universities used a novel approach to tracking down Viking DNA in the Wirral peninsula and west Lancashire. Realizing that there was a large influx of people into this area during the Industrial Revolution, they compared two different samples of men. The first sample could prove two generations of residence. The other sample was much more stringently selected: these men not only had known ancestry in the region, but a surname recorded there in medieval times. The result was enlightening. The sample with local surnames had markedly greater Scandinavian ancestry, to judge by the higher proportions of Y-DNA haplogroups R1a1a and I, which were similar to those today in the Isle of Man.[27] From archaeological evidence we know that the Isle of Man was seized from Christians by a Viking warrior elite in the early decades of the 10th century. This can be fitted into the history of Gwynedd in north Wales, which probably controlled Man as well as the closer island of Anglesey at this time. The submission of Idwal, King of Gwynedd, to English kings after 918 made him an enemy to the Viking kings of Dublin, who had assaulted Anglesey in 918. Man was probably another target.[28]

Ireland

From the Western Isles, Ireland was within striking distance. The early raids on Ireland hit island monasteries – Rechru (Rathlin or Lambay) was burnt in 795 and St Patrick's Island attacked in 798. In the next century there are increasing reports of people carried off into slavery, and from the 830s the Vikings pressed deep inland. At the time Ireland was a patchwork of petty chiefdoms, often in conflict with each other, but usually acknowledging the authority of regional kings. There was no state and power was diffuse. Ireland was ill prepared for organized resistance to Viking incursions, which in any case came without warning in the early decades. Nor were the early attacks co-ordinated by an overall authority. These were freebooters under one leader or another. In the 840s these Viking raiding parties began to set up winter camps along the coast of Ireland, which would eventually develop into Ireland's first towns.[29]

During the first 50 years of Viking raids on Ireland, the attackers came mainly from southwest Norway. Viking Age graves in northern Jaeran (the region around Stavanger) contain the densest concentration of Irish metalwork found outside Ireland.[30] In Ireland itself, typical Norwegian swords of the period AD 775–900 were found at Kilmainham and Islandbridge, Dublin.[31] [120] The loan words in Irish Gaelic from Old Norse mainly give no inkling of a particular dialect, but in about 40 cases they point to southwest Norway.[32] Another clue is locked in the genes of the common house mouse. Since it cohabits with humans, it can also travel with them. It did not spread widely into Europe until the Iron Age, so its modern distribution may tell us something about early historic human migrations. A particular mouse mtDNA lineage, christened 'the Orkney type' from its dominance there, fits well with the sphere of influence of the Norwegian Vikings. It clusters together the Orkney mice with most of those from the Western Isles, and some from Norway, Ireland and the Isle of Man. The origin point was probably Orkney.[33]

In 851 a new enemy appeared on the horizon – the *Dubh-gaill* (dark foreigners), who arrived in force and ousted their rivals the *Finn-gaill* (fair foreigners) from *Duiblinn* (Dublin.) There is a long tradition of interpreting the dark foreigners as Danes and the fair ones as Norwegians. Significantly, the term *Dubhgaill* in the annals is consistently linked to the dynasty of Ívarr (the Uí Ímhair).[34] Is it coincidence that this dynasty flew the raven banner?[35] Or could 'dark' refer to the raven?

In later centuries colourful tales clustered around the leaders of the Uí Ímhair, Óláfr and Ívarr. There were unconvincing attempts to weave them into the royal line of Norway. They also appear in the saga of Ragnarr Loðbrók, legendary king of Denmark, as his sons Óláfr the white and Ívarr the boneless. Historian

120 *Viking swords in the National Museum of Ireland from the cemeteries at Kilmainham and Islandbridge. Watercolour by James Plunket, c. 1847.*

Clare Downham has painstakingly picked fact from fiction to piece together what is really known about them. Ívarr (Ímar in Irish) and his brothers Óláfr, Ásl and Halfdan campaigned fiercely on both sides of the Irish Sea. Their impact was so great that when Ívarr died in 873, the Annals of Ulster described him as king of all the Northmen in Ireland and Britain. Where had they come from? Óláfr (Amlaíb in Irish) was described on his arrival in Ireland in 853 as the son of the king of Laithlinde. That links him to a previous entry in the annals. In 848 a Viking leader was slain in battle in Leinster. He was acting as a deputy for the self-same mysterious king of Laithlinde. Much ink has been spilt arguing the whereabouts of this kingdom. In later sources Lochland meant Norway,[36] but Norway had no king at this time. Nor would people from Norway be different from previous Norse arrivals. Much the same objections can be made to the argument that Laithlinde refers to Norse settlers in the Northern Isles.[37]

The dynasty of Ívarr introduced a new Viking modus operandi to the British Isles. Instead of the hit-and-run raid, they exacted tribute. Furthermore, the attacks were orchestrated by a royal leadership. This points indeed to the Danes. Horic, king of Denmark (d. 854), used exactly those tactics, as did his father Godfrid. Ívarr and his kin could muster great numbers of ships and fighting men, which again suggests the relatively populous southern Scandinavia as the source. However, Horic was not accused of involvement in the campaigns of Ívarr and his brothers and is unlikely to be their progenitor. The throne of Denmark was repeatedly disputed after the death of Godfrid in 810, so there was another royal line at large and able to recruit from Denmark. It starts with Harald Klak, seemingly the son of a Halfdan who was an envoy from the Danish court to Charlemagne. Harald and his brothers seized the throne in 812, only to be expelled in 814. Harald returned as a co-regent with the sons of Godfrid in 818, but fled to the Frankish court in 823, seeking support to bolster his claim to the throne. Harald's base from 826 was Rüstringen in northeast Frisia, granted to him by the Franks. The History of St Cuthbert specifically associates Ubba, Duke of the Frisians, with the Great Army of Danes which entered East Anglia in 865, led by the dynasty of Ívarr. Elsewhere Ubba is given as another brother of Ívarr.[38] The saga elements embedded in the fragmentary Annals of Ireland record that Ívarr's father was a Gofraid of royal descent.[39] Although this late material is unreliable, the name Godfrid does appear repeatedly in the dynasty of Ívarr. Also, Óláfr had a son named Carlus, and the Sword of

Carlus was part of the royal insignia in Dublin. This suggests a connection with one of the Frankish kings named Charles.[40] Harald Klak's son Godfrid continued the long association with the Frankish court which had begun with his grandfather Halfdan.[41] So Ívarr and his brothers were probably the sons of Godfrid, son of Harald Klak.

Dublin grew into a major Viking centre, the largest in Ireland and an international trade hub. Although the Irish succeeded in expelling the dynasty of Ívarr from Dublin in 902, it was retaken by the dynasty in 917 and expanded into a great port. The idea of the planned town seems to have been brought by the returning dynasty of Ívarr from their travels. Dublin grew rich on the slave trade. The English were not averse to contributing captives to the Dublin slave market, selling them to Norse-Irish traders in Bristol.[42]

How many early Dubliners were of Scandinavian origin? The artifacts they left behind suggest a blend of colonial and native groups. Culturally, the Vikings were integrated into native Irish society by the 10th century, the process aided by significant intermarriage.[43] An isotope study of Dubliners from the 9th to the 12th centuries found no clear immigrants. So it is unlikely that newcomers were continually arriving from Scandinavia or the Scottish islands. Dublin developed its own population.[44]

There is a low level of Y-DNA R1a1a in Ireland today, even in those with surnames thought to be Norse. This is not the only haplogroup that Danish Vikings could have carried, but a sample of Irishmen with supposedly Norse surnames could not be distinguished from the general Irish population.[45] It seems that the Viking contribution to the present Irish gene pool was low.

The rich lowlands

To the south, the Danes menaced the powerful Frankish empire at its height. Charlemagne's battle for Saxony was well underway and he conquered Brittany in 799. So the coast of western Europe from the River Eider to the Pyrenees was in the hands of the Franks in 799, when the first Viking raid on it was recorded. Charlemagne's final conquest of Saxony in 804 brought the Franks and Danes face to face. Charlemagne aimed to create a buffer zone by evacuating Saxons from an area beyond the Elbe and giving their former territory to the Slavic Obodrites. This was a sound move commercially, for it would have created an overland route through allied territory from Francia to the Baltic port of Reric (near present-day Wismar). Godfrid of Denmark responded in 808 by attacking the Obodrites, destroying Reric and transferring its traders to his own port at Hedeby.

Hedeby was shrewdly placed to control trade across the narrowest part of Jutland, the Schleswig isthmus, which provided a short-cut for transport from the North Sea to the Baltic. Ships could cross by river most of the way; the gap between the Treen and Schlei rivers could be covered by portage. North–south trade also passed near Hedeby, along the ancient track running along the ridge between the rivers. Godfrid protected this asset by reinforcing the massive earthwork known as the Danevirke. Hedeby proved to be a source of wealth from tolls, as Godfrid had foreseen. That made the town all too covetable. It was taken by the Franks in 974, though retaken by the Danes in 983. It was burnt by Harald Hardrada of Norway in 1050 and raided by the Slavs in 1066, after which its inhabitants retreated to Schleswig, on the other bank of the Schlei.[46]

The coast of the Low Countries, so invitingly close to Jutland, was constantly harried by Danes. The Frankish grant in 826 to Harald Klak, exiled king of Denmark, of Rüstringen in northeast Frisia, between the Weser and the Ems, may have been an early example of the policy of using Vikings as protection from other Vikings.[47] If so, it failed. The rich and important port of Dorestad, with its mint, was attacked in three successive years from 835 to 837. In 841 Charlemagne's grandson Lothar I felt compelled to accept the presence of a Harold junior (probably the nephew of Harald Klak) who, along with other Danish pirates, had for some years been terrorizing Frisia. This Harold was granted the island of Walcheren in the Scheldt estuary and neighbouring regions.[48]

Lothar continued to be troubled by members of this family. Harald Klak's son Godfrid had remained in Lothar's service since Lothar stood sponsor to him at his baptism in 826. But at some point Godfrid turned against him and returned to his own people. In 850 Godfrid teamed up with his cousin Rorik to ravage Frisia with 'a vast number of ships'. Lothar accepted the inevitable, took Rorik's allegiance and granted him Dorestad and some counties. If he hoped for peace to ensue, he was disappointed. In 852 Godfrid raided Frisia and sailed up the Scheldt and the Seine. Rorik and Godfrid felt it politic to leave for Denmark in 855. Lothar I had given Frisia to his son Lothar II. Perhaps more crucially, the death of Horic of Denmark opened up possibilities there. However, the lineage of Harald Klak failed to seize the throne. Rorik and Godfrid returned to take control of most of Frisia from their base at Dorestad.[49]

Further south, the island of Noirmoutier off the west coast of France was a repeated Viking target. It offered more than quick pickings; it was a useful base from which to raid deep along the Loire, gaining access to some of the richest monasteries and estates in the Frankish empire. According to an Aquitainian source these raiders were *Westfaldingi*, meaning that they came from the Norwegian Vestfold, west of the Oslofjord.[50]

After decades of intermittent Viking raiding, interspersed with Viking-Breton alliances, a massive fleet of Loire Vikings invaded Brittany in 919 under the command of a Norwegian named Rognvaldr. The scale of the action was unparalleled in this region. Rognvaldr eliminated all opposition, and many Bretons fled. A Breton rebellion in 931 failed. The heir to the Breton duchy, Alain Barbetorte, grew up at Athelstan's court in England. With the help of a fleet supplied by the English king, Alain landed at Dol with an army of Bretons in 936. By the following year he had fought his way to Nantes, where he expelled the Vikings in a final battle.[51]

Viking raiders made incursions up the Seine from 820 onwards, periodically settling when it proved impossible to evict them. A Norwegian, Sigtrygg, who had spent time in Ireland, joined forces with another leader, named Bjørn, to attack Paris in 857. Bjørn was joined by Hasting in 858. Hasting and Bjørn raided again and again in the Cotentin and Avranchin, turning them into deserted wastelands. In the reign of Charles the Simple (898–929), a band of Vikings under Rollo settled in the Lower Seine area. In 911 the Franks managed to prevent Rollo taking Paris and Chartres. They took the opportunity to make a treaty ceding territory around the Seine to Rollo, in return for Rollo's acknowledgment of Charles as his feudal lord. Thus Rollo became Duke of Normandy. In 924 Rollo received a further grant of Maine and the Bessin in Normandy. By 933 the Duchy of Normandy had enlarged to include the Cotentin peninsula. So the Duchy by then covered roughly the area of modern Normandy.[52]

To gain acceptance into the Kingdom of the Franks, Rollo agreed to convert to Christianity. He had already taken a concubine captured from the Frankish aristocracy, and in 911 he contracted a marriage with the daughter of Charles the Simple. His successors, William Longsword and Richard I, also made political unions.[53] No doubt a good deal of mixing went on among their followers and local women, though some Scandinavian women appear to have settled in Normandy. If the children of Vikings were raised by French-speaking mothers, it is not surprising that Old Norse vanished

121 *Normans arriving at Pevensey, southern England in 1066, depicted in the Bayeux Tapestry.*

in Normandy over just the few generations between Rollo and William the Conqueror. The Normans who arrived in England in 1066 spoke Norman French and were culturally homogeneous, whether or not they had a Viking among their ancestors. [121]

Rollo's origin is much disputed. Rollo's grandson, Richard I of Normandy, commissioned the cleric Dudo in 994 to write Rollo's biography. Dudo therefore had access to family recollections within living memory of Rollo. He makes a distinction between the Scandinavian peninsula and Denmark and tells us that Rollo was Danish. He recounts that Rollo negotiated with a Christian king of the Angles called Alstem to over-winter in his lands before raiding the Franks.[54] This may refer to the Viking Guthrum, king of East Anglia (d. 890), who took the baptismal name Athelstan. The only earlier source for Rollo's origins is a French chronicler who refers to Rollo as the son of Ketill, presumably the same Ketill whom he names as the chief of the Viking raiders against Gaul between the Seine and the Loire in 888.[55] Later Norwegian authors with every motive to claim the Norman dynasty as their own preferred to identify Rollo as *Hrolfr*, the son of a Norwegian earl whose kin figure in the sagas of the conquest of Orkney.[56] This Norwegian wealth of detail has appealed to historians ever since, but Rollo is more likely to be a Latin version of *Hrollaugr* than *Hrolfr*, and the source closest in time and place to the event is generally more reliable.

The most revealing evidence comes from place-names. Scandinavian place-names in Normandy cluster around the coast, and particularly the north of the Cotentin peninsula. They are often compounds such as Bramatot ('the plot of Brami'), incorporating the name of its Viking founder.

Most of such personal names are Norse, specifically Old Danish in some cases, but some seem to be Anglo-Danish, such as Auberville (anciently *Osberni villa*, 'Osbern's vil'), or Anglo-Saxon, such as Louvetot ('the plot of Lufa'). By contrast, a few names in the Cotentin are compounds of Gaelic names such as Muirdac, which suggests Scandinavian settlers from Ireland or the Hebrides, probably ultimately Norwegian in origin. Certain other toponyms on the northern coast of the Cotentin have parallels not in Denmark but in Norway and Norwegian settlements. For example the rocks of Dranguet, from Old Norse *drangr*, can be compared to the Drongs in Shetland and Dronga in Fair Isle.[57] The Cotentin was not included in the initial grant to Rollo. The coast there was probably settled first by other bands of Vikings. From this place-name evidence, these first settlers were from Norway or its colonies, while Rollo's own band would appear to be Danish, bolstered by recruits from East Anglia. Once the Cotentin was included in the Duchy of Normandy, Rollo's men could spread a Danish or Anglo-Danish overlay on to the area, and further west. Brittany continued to be subject to a degree of Scandinavian influence via the Duchy of Normandy well into the 11th century.[58]

The Great Army

In 865, says the *Anglo-Saxon Chronicle*, 'a great raiding army came to the land of the English and took winter quarters in East Anglia'. Æthelward's Latin translation names its leader as Ívarr. From its East Anglian base, the army took York the following year. This was the turn of the tide, when raiding gave way to settlement in England.[59] Ívarr we have already met in Ireland. His dynasty became kings of York as well as Dublin.[60] In Britain too his army was identified as the 'black heathens'.[61] The battles between the English and the invading Danes do not need to be recapitulated here. The outcome was the division of the land into a Danish north and east, known as the Danelaw, and an English and British south and west, defended by the Welsh princes and King Alfred of Wessex. Alfred's son, Edward (r. 899–924), conquered the Danelaw to create a kingdom of England, but Scandinavian settlement there is remembered in many place-names today which end in *-by* and *-thorpe*.[62]

The Vikings who came to settle brought their families too. A study of distinctly Norse burials showed that female migration may have been as significant as male, and that Norse women were in England from the start of the campaign in 865.[63] It is impossible to distinguish genetically between Angles and Danish Vikings, since both came from Jutland.[64] Yet some of the settlers in East Anglia had links further north than Jutland. Burials found in Castle Mall, Norwich, included four which stood out as Viking in the DNA analysis, with links to Orkney, Norway and the Western Isles.[65] We may picture a sprinkling of Norwegians among the Danes.

It was in the reign of Æthelred the Unready (978–1016) that the Vikings returned, more organized, more disciplined, more formidable than before. At first they raided. For example in 980 Southampton was ravaged and most of its population killed or taken prisoner. It was a repeat of the horrors of the early Viking Age. But by 994 the intruders were led by King Sweyn of Denmark himself. His determination grew to conquer Britain outright. Æthelred, in fear of Danish plots on his life and his kingdom, was persuaded to order a massacre of 'all the Danes who had sprung up in this island, sprouting like weeds amongst the wheat', on St Brice's Day (13 November) 1002.[66] This shocking act achieved nothing. Sweyn finally succeeded in his long campaign of conquest in 1013, but had little time to enjoy victory. He died on 2 February 1014. So England had its first crowned Scandinavian monarch in 1016: Sweyn's son, Cnut (d. 1035), King of Denmark, England and Norway.[67]

The far northwest

The Medieval Warm Period starting around AD 800 encouraged settlement in lands so far north that few humans had yet ventured there. Vikings began setting up homes in Iceland *c.* 874 and within 60 winters it was fully settled. So Ari Thorgilsson tells us in the earliest history of Iceland, *Íslendingabók* (*The Book of the Icelanders*). Though written in the early 12th century, long after these events, his dating is supported by the archaeological evidence.[68] Most of the Scandinavian settlers in Iceland came from southwest Norway. Some may have chosen to leave for the freedom of a new land after Harald Fairhair imposed his rule over all Norway. If we read only Ari's account, we might imagine that an outpouring from Norway was the whole story. Among the early settlers he lists Auðr, daughter of the Norwegian chieftain Ketil Flatnose, without mentioning that Auðr had spent much of her adult life in Dublin and Caithness and set sail for Iceland from the Hebrides.

He names Helgi the Lean, a Norwegian, the son of Eyvindr the Easterner, without explaining that Helgi's maternal grandfather was an Irish king, Helgi having been raised in the Hebrides and Ireland.[69] Another account, the *Landnámabók* (*Book of the Settlements*), is therefore invaluable in giving a much more detailed account of the settlers, their ancestry and descendants. Among the many from Norway was the occasional Irishman. Irish slaves are also mentioned.[70]

Several genetic studies of the Icelandic population have shown a high level of overall Scandinavian ancestry (55 per cent), but Scandinavian patrilineal ancestry is two times greater than Scandinavian matrilineal ancestry. In other words the Y-DNA is more typical of Scandinavia, while the mtDNA is more typical of the Insular Celts. This suggests that in Iceland, like the Western Isles, many male settlers took wives from Ireland or Scotland, though there were also Scandinavian families among them.[71]

Iceland yielded a particular treasure for sailors. Transparent Iceland spar could be used as a navigational aid. This crystal can depolarize light, allowing the navigator to deduce the direction of the sun even under cloudy skies. The sun stone (*solstenen*) is mentioned in Viking sagas.[72] We may guess that such sun stones aided the daring voyages westwards from Iceland undertaken by Eric the Red and his son Leif. These would fall outside the scope of this book, were it not for an intriguing discovery. Finding mtDNA haplogroup C1e in four families in Iceland caused excitement. C1 is normally only found in Native Americans or East Asians. Genealogy revealed that the four families were descended from ancestors who lived between 1710 and 1740 in the same region of southern Iceland. The island was so isolated at the time, and had been from the end of the Medieval Warm Period, that researchers are fairly confident that the C1e (a new subclade) came from a Native American woman brought from America by Vikings.[73] It certainly seems unlikely that the C1e was acquired by mixture with the Inuit in Greenland. Modern-day Greenland Inuit mainly carry mtDNA A2 and D3,[74] while a Paleo-Eskimo who lived in Greenland about 4,000 years ago fell within mtDNA haplogroup D2a1.[75]

122 *This wooden half-disc found in Uunartoq Fjord in Greenland may be the remains of a sun compass.*

Eric the Red tempted ten chieftains to leave Iceland in the 980s for the delights of the land to the west that he encouragingly named Greenland. [122] At the time, midway through the Medieval Warm Period, Greenland was certainly a lot greener than today. However, the two settlements there could not long survive the return of the icy cold. The last evidence of life in them is the testimony of a wedding in 1408.[76] Across the Davis Strait from Greenland was North America. Icelandic sagas describe voyages to the vast, thickly forested Markland and Leif's camp in Vinland. The aim was not colonization, but to bring back the timber so much needed in treeless Greenland. The discovery of a Norse settlement at the now famous site of L'Anse aux Meadows at the northern tip of Newfoundland proved the sagas were based on fact.[77]

Kievan Rus

Russia is not alone in being named after an incoming elite too small to impose its language on the country. Within Europe it shares that oddity with Bulgaria and France. Yet its national origin is even more complex. The Kingdom of the Rus was founded by Swedish merchant-adventurers. Its capital for centuries was Kiev, now the capital of Ukraine. Historians distinguish this early polity from successor states also called Rus by terming it Kievan Rus. The obscurity of its beginnings has led to both myth-making and modern scepticism of the traditional tale. *The Russian Primary Chronicle* tells us that Slavs went overseas to the Varangian Rus to seek a leader. According to the story, they selected three brothers, the eldest of whom was Rurik, who founded a royal dynasty.[78] Living descendants of the Rurikid dynasty of Russia have been found consistently to carry Y-DNA N1c1.[79] Among Europeans this haplogroup is most common among peoples speaking Uralic languages, such as Finnish, suggesting that Rurik was indeed not Slavic, and probably from a family with both Scandinavian and Finnish ancestry.

Enough mystery surrounds the first appearance of the Rus in written sources that we cannot be certain of the origin of the name, but most historians favour the notion that it comes from *ruotsi* ('men who row'), the Finnish name for the Swedes.[80] Scandinavians had crossed the Baltic to settle in what is now Finland long before. The Rus first appear in the written record when a group of them arrived in May 839 at the court of Louis the

Pious, son of Charlemagne. Their long-distance travel is apparent from this reference. They were ambassadors to Constantinople who were returning home to 'their people of the Swedes',[81] perhaps in Finland.

Amber had long been traded from the Baltic southwards to Italy, but with the collapse of the Western Roman Empire, the hub of imperial power was now Constantinople (Byzantium). To get there, Rus traders exploited the river network from the Gulf of Finland to the Black Sea, using portages to span the gaps between the rivers and bypass rapids. Their seagoing ships had to be left at Staraya Ladoga, some 13 km (8 miles) up the Volkhov River from Lake Ladoga. Smaller vessels built at Staraya Ladoga then took them further upriver.[82] A settlement grew up at this staging post in the 760s.[83] [123] The terrain through which these bold traders had to pass was wild most of the way: densely wooded and marshy. They might have encountered the occasional Finnic- or Baltic-speaking hunter before they reached Lake Ilmen. South of this lake were Slavs who had been gradually working their way northwards into Baltic territory from their heartland around the Middle Dnieper. So the trading posts at Novgorod and Kiev were important for Slavs as well as Norse. The last stretch of the traders' river journey was the most dangerous, for fierce Asian nomads, the Pecheneg, controlled the steppe zone north of the Black Sea. Arriving at last in Byzantium, the traders from the north could offer amber, wax, honey, falcons, weapons and above all slaves and arctic furs. By 885 the Rus had secured the Dnieper route by wresting from the Khazars control of the Slavic tribes along the river. So Kiev became the hub of the developing polity of the Rus.[84]

The attraction of Constantinople for barbarians was nothing new. It was a factor in the Migration Period. The wealth of the imperial capital invited both trading and raiding. There were also opportunities for mercenaries in the imperial armies. A new magnet was contact with the Eastern Caliphate via Bulgar on the Volga. Luxuriously thick northern pelts could be traded there for Arabic silver. Ibn Fadlan described the wares of the *Rusiyyah* as sables and slaves. He visited the king of the Bulgars of the Volga in 921 and witnessed the flaming ship funeral of a chief of the *Rusiyyah*. He had never seen men of such perfect physique, tall and fair, though the fastidious Arab was revolted by their uncleanliness. He does admit that the Rus washed their faces and combed their hair each morning.[85] Contact with the Caliphate may explain the unexpected presence in medieval Sweden of an Asian type of leprosy, along with the type typical in Europe. The curse of

123 *Viking finds from Staraya Ladoga, Russia, include beads, ornamented combs and a rune stick.*

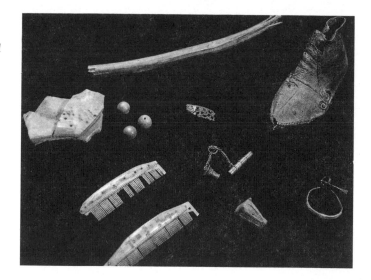

leprosy clung on in Scandinavia long after medieval leper hospitals had become redundant in most of Europe.[86]

The Scandinavian component of the Kingdom of the Rus was never more than an elite. *The Russian Primary Chronicle* records in detail a treaty of 907 between the Rus and the Byzantine emperors Leo and Alexander. All the names of the leaders of the Rus delegation were Scandinavian, though the fleet with which they apparently cowed Byzantium was manned by Slavs as well as Varangians.[87] So we should not expect a high level of Scandinavian DNA to be present in modern Russia. Nor do we find it. The Russians cluster most closely with Ukrainians and Belorussians, forming a genetic block corresponding to the linguistic one of East Slavic, with the West Slavic Poles the next closest. The relationship to Swedes is more distant. There is a significant level of Y-DNA I1 in places. The highest levels (11–12 per cent) are in northern Russia.[88] It is by no means clear that this I1 is the result of the ingressions of the Rus. There have been German settlers in Russia since the 16th century, and particularly in the reign of Catherine the Great (1729–1786). Born a German, she encouraged migration of Western Europeans to the Russian empire by offering land, transportation to Russia, and religious and political autonomy in her proclamation of 1763. Though this open-door policy was repealed in 1871, many Germans had taken advantage of it in the intervening years.[89] As so often, migration follows migration, making it difficult to disentangle the threads.

CHAPTER EIGHTEEN
Epilogue

The wanderings of Europeans did not stop with the Vikings. Indeed the most massive movement of people on Earth has taken place in the last few centuries. Europeans have spread around the globe. This book is concerned with those entering Europe, rather than leaving it. Even so there are many migrations not covered here, mainly those that fall into the fully historic period. Where human movements are well documented, there is less need for the multi-disciplinary approach advocated here.

That approach has contributed to a seismic shift in the way we view prehistory. From visions of continuity we are swinging to visions of change. The decades of anti-migrationist thinking were partly fostered by language barriers across Europe, and national research agendas. The same culture could be given different names in adjoining countries by archaeologists speaking different languages. In each case the assumption would come naturally that the culture sprang up where it was found. Recognition of the wider picture has sometimes been slow and painful. Yet the national boundaries that now loom so large in self-perceptions meant nothing at all to our distant ancestors. Recent research projects that leap those boundaries as well as disciplinary demarcation lines have boldly tackled big issues in the European past.

For the general public the new views may not fit treasured national myths. Is this a culture clash? Once upon a time narrative served a national or tribal purpose. Picture our ancestors whiling away the dark days of winter, singing or telling stories around the fire. They would glorify their ancestors, and so pass on to the next generation role models of heroism or wisdom. That strain of human culture gave birth to literature. History we can see as a non-identical twin. Though it springs from the same urge to narrative, it is driven by curiosity. What actually did happen?

There is no easy answer to that. The truth is a moving target. Academic projects on migration have sprung up in profusion over the last few years.

From these should gradually emerge a more detailed picture of the many strands woven into the European tapestry.

Certain conclusions do suggest themselves. Mobility is constant. There are people setting out on a journey every day. Many will return home that same day. Some have distant prospects in mind. There is no reason to think that people were immobile in prehistory. Though it still makes sense to look first at local level for a precursor for particular innovations, we should bear in mind that people can take new ideas, languages, technology, seed and stock as far as their impetus and ingenuity can carry them. Readers of this book may be most startled by the suggestions of long-distance travel in the late Neolithic and Copper Age. Is it really possible that dairy farming had its own pulse across Europe after the first waves of farmers? Can it really be that the Basque language had an ancestor in the Balkans? Did the Stelae People really trek all the way from the Pontic steppe to Iberia? These models are presented for future testing, in particular by ancient DNA.

Re-colonization of a deserted territory appears far more common than was once thought. The re-colonization of northern Europe after the glaciers retreated has long been understood. Radiocarbon databases now reveal local episodes of re-colonization in later periods. There are unexpected gaps in places between hunter-gatherer occupation and the first farmers. Equally unexpected is the evidence of population collapse in places after farming arrived. The traditional assumption has been that once agriculture was established in a region, it would simply continue in an unbroken sequence to modern times. We need to take into account the vagaries of climate. As any farmer will tell you, farming depends for its success on the weather. Regions could also be depopulated by other calamities, such as disease or warfare, leaving vacant lands for the next wave of immigrants.

So the arrival of newcomers in a region need not imply that they had driven away the previous occupants. Population replacement is comparatively rare. It is most likely to occur where incomers have a marked economic advantage. Those bringing farming into a hunter-gatherer economy achieve population dominance in territory that is suitable for agriculture or stock-rearing. Those bringing technological advantages which improve agricultural yields, such as animal traction, may do the same. Such episodes are few. In Europe we can pick out the takeover of the territory of Neanderthals by anatomically modern humans, the arrival of farming and the Secondary Products Revolution. All had a continent-wide impact. There were variations by region in the degree of takeover by incoming farmers or those bringing the plough. These are dwarfed, though, by the variety we see in the post-Roman movements of the Migration Period. In some areas replacement appears near total. In others the genetic impact was so negligible that we would not talk of replacement at all.

This book has telescoped movements over millennia into such a rapidly moving parade that the reader could be forgiven for thinking that Europeans are afflicted with a collective form of Saint Vitus's dance, always restless, never still for a moment. That is far from the case. The past is a weave of continuity and change.

A final word of advice may be helpful for those of you thinking of probing into your own DNA for clues to ancestry. The uniparental lines are the easiest to trace, but they are only two of the multitude of your ancestral lineages. Y-DNA haplogroups are particularly fascinating to genetic genealogists since they can be linked to surnames. Yet it might chance that your Y-DNA comes from an unexpected wanderer, unrepresentative of the majority of your ancestors. So those tests which include enough genome-wide DNA to compare yours overall to worldwide population samples (see p. 33) will give a more rounded picture of the ancestral journeys that created you.

Notes

Chapter 1: Who Are the Europeans?

1. Klein 2008; Dennell and Petraglia 2012.
2. Javed 2012; Melé 2012; Shi 2010; Xing 2010; Laval 2010; Chiaroni, Underhill and Cavalli-Sforza 2009; Gutenkunst 2009; DeGiorgio, Jakobsson and Rosenberg 2009; Deshpande, Batzoglou, Feldman and Cavalli-Sforza 2009; Ionita-Laza, Lange and Laird 2009; Li 2008; Hellenthal, Auton and Falush 2008; Jakobsson 2008; Ayub 2003.
3. Watson and Crick 1953.
4. ENCODE Project Consortium 2012.
5. Jobling, Hurles and Tyler-Smith 2004, chapter 2.
6. Jobling, Hurles and Tyler-Smith 2004, 39–40, 60–61, 252–53; van Oven and Kayser 2009.
7. Higuchi 1984.
8. Cooper and Poinar 2000; Poinar 2003, 575–79.
9. Sampietro 2006. Other criteria for the authenticity of ancient DNA include repeated amplification from the same extracts and replication in a second laboratory: Pääbo 2004.
10. The use of primers in polymerase chain reaction (PCR). Deguilloux 2011b.
11. Knapp and Hofreiter 2010.
12. Keller 2012.
13. Ricaut 2012; Pinhasi 2012.
14. Wilson and van der Dussen 1995, 2.
15. Yang 2012; Drineas, Lewis and Paschou 2010; Tian 2009; Novembre 2008; Tian 2008.
16. Ralph and Coop 2012. The technique used for these calculations is Identity by Descent (IBD).
17. Di Gaetano 2012.

Chapter 2: Migration: Principles and Problems

1. Kaiser, Burger and Schier 2012; Peregrine, Peiros and Feldman 2009; Heather 2009; Lightfoot 2008; Chapman and Hamerow 1997.
2. Green 1981.
3. Childe 1929, v–vi.
4. Clark 1966.
5. Clark 1971.
6. Anthony 1990; Anthony 1992; Härke 2006.
7. Cunliffe 2008, 21.
8. Prescott and Glørstad 2012, 3.
9. Renfrew and Bahn 2012; Greene and Moore 2010.
10. Kristiansen 2011.
11. McCormick 2011.
12. Anthony 1990.
13. Shennan 1997, 341.
14. Menk 1979; Cox and Mays 2000, 281–83; Nicolis 2001, 2, 403. People buried with Bell Beaker pottery in northern, central and eastern Europe were generally brachycephalic (short-headed front to back) in contrast to their dolichocephalic (long-headed) Neolithic predecessors and/ or Corded Ware neighbours. By contrast people associated with the early Bell Beaker pottery of Portugal and Italy were dolichocephalic. Because the position in which an infant is placed to sleep can affect skull shape, DNA is a better guide to the degree of relationship between individuals or populations.
15. Müller and van Willigen 2001.
16. Melheim 2012.
17. Harrison and Heyd 2007.
18. Cunliffe 1997, 31–36, 63–67.
19. Kohl 2006, 5.
20. Roberts and Vander Linden 2011.
21. Bayliss 2009.
22. e.g. Weninger 2009.
23. Reide 2009.
24. Shennan 2009.
25. Stevens and Fuller 2012.
26. Collard, Edinborough, Shennan and Thomas 2010.
27. Pitts 2010; Hills and Hurst 1989.
28. Leach 2010.
29. Jobling, Hurles and Tyler-Smith 2004, chapter 2.
30. van Oven and Kayser 2009. Back-mutation does occasionally occur, returning a variant to the ancestral position.
31. Soares 2009.
32. Soares 2010.
33. Cruciani, Trombetta, Massaia 2011.
34. Smith 2009; Bramanti 2009; Malmström 2009; Sánchez-Quinto 2012.
35. Fernández 2008.
36. Larson 2007.
37. Richards 2000; Semino 2000.
38. Balaresque 2010; Busby 2012.
39. Herrera 2012.
40. Chiaroni, Underhill and Cavalli-Sforza 2009; Currat 2012.
41. Moreau 2011.
42. Soares 2009.
43. Achilli 2004; Pereira 2005.
44. García 2011; Ennafaa 2009; Özbal 2004.
45. Behar 2012, supplement.
46. Jobling, Hurles and Tyler-Smith 2004, section 6.6.
47. Burgarella and Navascués 2011.
48. Jobling, Hurles and Tyler-Smith 2004, section 6.6.2.
49. Zhivotovsky 2004; Zhivotovsky 2006.
50. Shi 2010.
51. Balanovsky 2011.
52. Arredi, Poloni and Tyler-Smith 2007; Balaresque 2010; 1000 Genomes Project Consortium 2010, 1064–65; Myres 2011; Wei 2013.
53. Sjödin and François 2011. R1b1b2 = M269 in this paper, written before a name change.
54. Adler 2011.
55. Sloane 2011.
56. Haensch 2010; Schuenemann 2011; Bos 2011.
57. Vernesi 2001; Bandelt 2005.
58. e.g. Loogväli 2004.
59. Rizzi 2012; Shapiro and Hofreiter 2012.
60. Anderson 1981. Some errors were later detected in the reading of this sequence, which led to the publication of a revised version: Andrews 1999.
61. Sykes 2000; Caramelli 2008; Hervella 2012.
62. Behar 2012, supplement.
63. Behar 2012.

64. Henn 2012.
65. Patterson 2012. The method models the decay of admixture linkage disequilibrium in the target population.
66. Moorjani 2011.
67. Balloux 2010.
68. Baudouin 2005.
69. Sezgin 2009.
70. Sykes 2001, 225–28; Barham, Priestley and Targett 1999, 5–6, 48–49.
71. K. Nuthall, 'There's no place like home, says 'son of Cheddar Man', *Independent*, 9 March 1997; S. Lyall, Tracing your family tree to Cheddar Man's mum, *New York Times*, 24 March 1997.
72. Lee 2012.
73. Mallory 1989.
74. Nichols 1990.
75. Renfrew 1987.
76. Diamond and Bellwood 2003.
77. Mallory and Adams 2006, 101–03, 166, 241, 260–62.
78. Mallory 1989. Mallory discusses the numerous other proposed homelands of PIE, most of which are completely untenable. Those proposed more recently are dismissed by Simon 2009.
79. Mallory and Adams 2006.
80. Militarev 2002.
81. Some linguists argue for an Afro-Asiatic substrate in Insular Celtic, e.g. Hickey 2002 and Shisha-Halevy 2003. The idea is dismissed by Mac Eoin 2007.
82. Swadesh 1952.
83. Initially he used a list of 200 lexical items that he thought were basic to any human language and therefore resistant to cultural borrowing. Later he refined this to 100 words. See Mallory and Adams 2006, table 6.3.
84. Mallory and Adams 2006, 95.
85. Dixon 1997.
86. Zengel 1962.
87. Nettle 1999.
88. Exceptions include Sergei Starostin (1953–2005), who revised the methodology.
89. Eska and Ringe 2004.
90. Mallory and Adams 2006, 101–02.
91. Thomason 2001, 66 and chapter 9.

92. Currie and Mace 2009.
93. Woolf 2007b; Heather 2009, chapter 6.
94. Mac Eoin 2007, 114.
95. Crinion 2006; Krizman 2012.
96. Sims-Williams 2006, 32, 54, 106.
97. Sims-Williams 2006.
98. Simon 2008; Nicolaisen 2001, chapter 9.
99. Vennemann 2003.
100. Trask 1996, 72.
101. Baldi and Page 2006.
102. Mallory and Adams 2006, 447.
103. Mallory and Adams 2006, 125–27.
104. Niederstatter 2012.
105. James 1999.
106. Dzino 2010.
107. Anthony 1997.
108. Coldham 1992; Hughes 1987; Bean and Melville 1989.
109. Van De Mieroop 2007, 233.

Chapter 3: The First Europeans

1. Castañeda 2009.
2. Mellars 2011.
3. Zilhão 2007; Rougier 2007.
4. Benazzi 2011.
5. Higham 2011.
6. Shea and Sisk 2010.
7. Henshilwood 2011.
8. Vanhaeren 2006.
9. Bar-Yosef 2007; McBrearty 2007.
10. d'Errico 2012.
11. Livi-Bacci 2007, 35–36.
12. Walker 2011.
13. Mellars 2006.
14. Benazzi 2011; Mellars 2011.
15. Meyer 2012.
16. Mellars 2011.
17. Hoffecker 2011 and 2012.
18. Krause 2010.
19. Fernández Domínguez 2005; Bramanti 2009.
20. Maca-Meyer 2003; Pereira 2010.
21. Tambets 2002.
22. Metspalu 2004.
23. Higham 2012; Conard, Malina and Münzel 2009.
24. Heckel 2009.
25. Pike 2012; Valladas 2005.
26. Prat 2011.
27. Alexeeva and Bader 2000, but see Ovchinnikov and Goodwin 2003 on the claimed aDNA; Hoffecker 2002, 151, 183; Formicola 2007; Gilligan 2010.
28. Taylor 2010.
29. Outram 2001.

30. Pétrequin 2006.
31. Hertell and Tallavaara 2011; Zvelebil 2006.
32. Burov 1989.
33. Bischoff 2007; Hublin 2009.
34. Pinhasi 2012.
35. Joris and Street 2008; Zilhão 2010; Martínez-Moreno, Mora and de la Torre 2010; Wood 2013.
36. Slimak 2011.
37. Ghirotto 2011.
38. Dalton 2010.
39. Lachance 2012; Hammer 2011; Plagnol and Wall 2006.
40. Blum and Jakobsson 2011.
41. Green 2010.
42. Meyer 2012.
43. Hodson, Bergey and Diostell 2010.
44. Xing 2010; DeGiorgio, Jakobsson and Rosenberg 2009; Deshpande, Batzoglou, Feldman and Cavalli-Sforza, 2009.
45. Skoglund and Jakobsson 2011.
46. Eriksson and Manica 2012.
47. Krause 2010.
48. Meyer 2012; Reich 2011; Skoglund and Jakobsson 2011; Reich 2010.
49. Bocquet-Appel, Demars, Noiret and Dobrowsky 2005.
50. Wright 2009; Tarkhnishvili 2012; Tarasov 2000.
51. Dolukhanov 2003.
52. Brauer 2008.

Chapter 4: Mesolithic Hunters and Fishermen

1. Cunliffe 2008, chapter 3; Bailey and Spikins 2008; Bonsall, Boroneant and Radovanovic 2008.
2. Weninger 2009b.
3. Jussila 2007.
4. Reide 2009.
5. Haaland 2009.
6. Jordan and Zvelebil 2009; Haaland 2009; Huysecom 2009.
7. Wu 2012.
8. O'Connor, Ono and Clarkson 2011.
9. McGrail 2001, 172–73, 279–81; Lanting 2000.
10. Breunig 1996. A boat nearly as old at *c.* 5700 BC has been found at a Neolithic site at Bibong-ri, Korea: Park 2010. A second Neolithic boat has been found

at Uljin, Korea: *Korea Times*, 27 August 2012.
11. Anati 2001; Farajova 2011.
12. Usai and Salvatori 2007.
13. Kuzmin 2006; Adachi 2011.
14. Jordan 2010; McKenzie 2009; Vasilieva 2011.
15. Soares 2009; Tambets 2002, 451.
16. Sykes 2001, 225–26, 263 simply reveals the haplogroup to be U. ISOGG reports the mutations to be C16192T and C16270T, which define U5.
17. Malyarchuk 2010; Pala 2009.
18. Bramanti 2009 includes samples from the Narva culture, with which pointed-based pottery is connected; Malmström 2009.
19. Delsate 2009. The authors report the haplogroup as U5a but the mutations to be C16192T and C16270T, which simply define U5.
20. Hervella 2012.
21. Sánchez-Quinto 2012.
22. Molodin 2012.
23. Derenko 2010.
24. Mooder 2006.
25. Sukernik 2012.
26. Nikitin 2012.
27. Malyarchuk 2010; Ingman and Gyllensten 2007.
28. Grugni 2012.
29. Lacan 2011b.
30. Rootsi 2004; Peričić 2005; Underhill 2007 (using evolutionary effective mutation rates); Battaglia 2009. Dating from Kenneth Nordtvedt.
31. Strontium isotope evidence shows that women from the earliest farming communities in the Danube Gorges were buried at Lepenski Vir, suggesting a reciprocal mating network between the sedentary foragers at Lepenski Vir and incoming farmers. See Borić and Price 2013.
32. Underhill 2007.
33. Jordan and Zvelebil 2009; Gronenborn 2007, 87; Dolukhanov 2005.
34. Tambets 2004; Achilli 2005.
35. Soares 2010.
36. Chiaroni, Underhill and Cavalli-Sforza 2009.
37. Derenko 2007; Karlsson 2006.

(Note that N3 is the old name for N1c); Rootsi 2007.
38. Lappalainen 2008.
39. Lappalainen 2006; Carpelan, Parpola and Koskikalio 2001; Aikio 2006.
40. Huyghe 2011.
41. Ingman and Gyllensten 2007.
42. Kerr 1811–24, 1, 10. Ottar is also spelled Ohthere. Ottar used the Norse word 'Finnar' for Saami.
43. Andersen 2011.
44. Røed 2008 and 2011.
45. Abondolo 1998.
46. The classic view places the homeland in the Middle Volga-Kama region. An alternative view places it between the Ob and the Urals. Janhunen 2009 argued for a Uralic homeland somewhere closer to the Altai Mountains than the Urals. In that case the Finno-Ugric branch would have broken away first, to roam the forest around the Upper Volga, in contact with the speakers of PIE, from whom words were borrowed. He proposed that the language of the Tagar culture in the Minusinsk Basin was Proto-Samoyedic. Yet archaeological and genetic evidence show the Tagar to be descendants of the Andronovo culture of the steppe and ancestors of the Iranian-speaking Scythians. See Keyser 2009; Legrand and Bokovenko 2006.
47. Häkkinen 2012.
48. Carpelan 2001; Jordan and Zvelebil 2009, 76. But see Mallory and Adams 1997, 429–30 for a summary of various counter-arguments.
49. Tacitus, *Germania*, chapter 46.
50. Balode and Bušs 2007.
51. Fornander, Eriksson and Lidén 2008.
52. Zvelebil 2004.
53. Larsson, M. 2009.
54. Larsson, A. M. 2008.
55. Malmström 2009.
56. Skoglund 2012.
57. Villems 2002; Tambets 2002.
58. Skoglund 2012.
59. Malyarchuk 2008 and 2010b.

Chapter 5: The First Farmers

1. Bellwood 2005, 12–20.
2. Barker 2006, chapter 1.
3. Zeder 2008 and 2011; Conolly 2011.
4. Conolly 2011.
5. Powell 2009; Richerson, Boyd and Bettinger 2009; Shennan 2001.
6. Weiss and Zohary 2011.
7. Bar-Yosef 1998; Bellwood 2005, 63.
8. Watkins 2010.
9. Zeder 2008; Savard, Nesbitt and Jones 2006; Weiss and Zohary 2011.
10. Belfer-Cohen and Goring-Morris 2011.
11. Wolfe, Dunavan and Diamond 2007.
12. Faerman 2007. And see Grauer 2012, 142 for the as yet unpublished discovery of brucellosis at Atlit Yam by the same team.
13. Solecki, Solecki and Agelarakis 2004.
14. Matthews 2010.
15. Scham 2008; Schmidt 2012.
16. Croucher 2012, 133–53.
17. Schloen and Fink 2009; Pardee 2009; Struble and Herrmann 2009.
18. Vigne 2012; Manning 2010; Peltenburg and Wasse 2004.
19. Vigne, Carrère, Briois and Guilaine 2011. There were pygmy wild boar on Cyprus in the pre-Neolithic, presumed to have been introduced in the Holocene.
20. Knapp 2010.
21. Laskaris 2011.
22. Liritzis 2010.
23. Goring-Morris and Belfer-Cohen 2011.
24. Fuller 2011; Babar 2012.
25. Coward 2008.
26. Patterson 2010.
27. Hodder 2006; Braidwood 1974; Byrd 1994.
28. Jordan and Zvelebil 2009, 71.
29. Nieuwenhuyse 2010; van As, Jacobs and Nieuwenhuyse 2004.
30. Hodder 2011.
31. Haaland 2007.
32. Vandiver 1987. Without subjecting a pot to X-ray, this construction can be mistaken for coil – see Berg 2008.

33. Hodder 2011.
34. Nieuwenhuyse 2010.
35. Vandiver 1987.
36. Özdoğan 2010 and 2011.
37. Yerkes, Khalaily and Barkai 2012.
38. Berger and Guilaine 2009; Barber 1999.
39. Weninger 2006.
40. Bar-Yosef 2009.
41. Cunliffe 2008, 93–94.
42. Clare 2008. For a contrary interpretation of Tell Sabi Abyad see Akkermans 2010.
43. Roodenberg 2011.
44. Militarev 2002 and 2005.
45. Fernández 2008.
46. Arredi 2004. There is a strong correlation in Africa overall between genetics and language family: Tishkoff 2009.
47. Cruciani 2010.
48. Ottoni 2011.
49. El-Sibai 2009.
50. Tofanelli 2009.
51. Chiaroni 2010.
52. Balanovsky 2011.
53. Hammer 2009. Other haplogroups carried by Cohanim include J2a (M410), J2b (M12), J2a3h2a1c (M318), R1b1a2 (M269) and E1b1b1b2a (M123), all found in the Near East.
54. Chiaroni 2010. Note that this paper uses Zhivotovsky evolutionary rate for calculation of dates. This gives estimates roughly three times too old. J1e was the initial name given to P58/Page8.
55. Kitchen 2009 estimates a date of 3750 BC; Militarev 2005 estimates a date of 4510 BC. Such estimates cannot be as precise as these dates might suggest. (See the section on language-dating in Chapter 2 of the present work.) However, the Proto-Semitic lexicon includes words for mining and smelting: Huehnergard 2011.
56. Tofanelli 2009, supplementary table S1.
57. King 2009.
58. Rubio 1999; Vanséveren 2008.
59. Blažek 1999, 51.
60. King 2009. Using the evolutionary effective mutation rate, he theorizes an expansion of J2 between 25,000

and 19,000 BC. A germline rate would place the expansion of J2 with the growing Neolithic population.
61. Yunusbayev 2012.
62. Balanovsky 2011.
63. Rootsi 2012; Grugni 2012.
64. Coward 2008; Decker 2009.
65. Zeder 2008.
66. Güldoğan 2010; Özdoğan 2011.
67. Forenbaher and Miracle 2005.
68. Zilhão 2000 and 2001.
69. Guilaine and Manen 2007.
70. Shirai 2010, chapter 2.
71. Cortés Sánchez 2012.
72. Beja-Pereira 2006; Bonfiglio 2012.
73. Perlès 2003.
74. Bellwood 2005, 68–84 and figure 4.1.
75. Bentley 2013.
76. Gallagher, Gunther and Bruchhaus 2009.
77. Vanmontfort 2008.
78. Larson 2007; Bollongino 2008 and 2012; Coward 2008.
79. Rowley-Conwy 2004 and 2011.
80. Ammerman and Cavalli-Sforza 1971 and 1984.
81. Pinhasi, Fort and Ammerman 2005.
82. Coward 2008.
83. Bocquet-Appel, Naji, Vander Linden and Kozlowski 2009; Rowley-Conwy 2011.
84. Bocquet-Appel, Naji, Vander Linden and Kozlowski 2012.
85. Gkiasta, Russell, Shennan and Steele 2003.
86. Collard, Edinborough, Shennan and Thomas 2010; Rowley-Conwy 2011; Bayliss, Healy and Whittle 2011.
87. Pinhasi and von Cramon-Taubadel 2009.
88. von Cramon-Taubadel and Pinhasi 2011; Pinhasi and von Cramon-Taubadel 2012.
89. Haak 2005; Bramanti 2008 and 2009; Fernández 2008.
90. Serk 2004.
91. Gignoux, Henn and Mountain 2011.
92. Haak 2010.
93. Brotherton 2013.
94. Gamba 2012.
95. Lacan 2011b.
96. Gamba 2012.
97. Haak 2010.
98. Lacan 2011b.
99. Cruciani 2007.

100. Lacan 2011. Two more Late Neolithic males buried by the Dolmen of La Pierre Fritte in central France were predicted to be I2a1 from the pattern of Short Tandem Repeats (STRs): M. Lacan 2011a.
101. Chiaroni, Underhill and Cavalli-Sforza 2009; Martínez-Cruz 2012.
102. Pluciennik 1997.
103. Semino 2004.

Chapter 6: Dairy Farming

1. Evershed 2008.
2. Özdoğan 2010.
3. Conolly 2011.
4. Evershed 2008, 531.
5. Bailey 2000, 182.
6. Szostek 2005.
7. Hodder 1992, 50–62.
8. Isaksson and Hallgren 2012.
9. Spangenberg, Matuschik, Jacomet and Schibler 2008.
10. Spangenberg, Jacomet and Schibler 2006.
11. Anthony 2007, chapters 8–9.
12. von Cramon-Taubadel and Pinhasi 2011.
13. Nikitin 2012.
14. Anthony 2007, 156.
15. Craig 2005.
16. Nica 1997.
17. Bălăşescu 2008; Haimovici and Bălăşescu 2006.
18. Lazarovici 2010.
19. Kohl 2007, 45; Manzura 2005, 327.
20. Mallory and Adams 2006, 260–63.
21. Edwards 2011; Pérez-Pardal 2010.
22. Isern and Fort 2012.
23. Crombé 2010; Louwe Kooijmans 2009; Louwe Kooijmans 2007.
24. Haas 1998; O'Brien 1995.
25. Bonsall 2002.
26. Müller, Brozio 2010; Hinz 2012. TRB dates around 4400 BC have been published for Sarnow and Lącko in central Poland, but these anomalies are probably the result of confusions that can occur in dates from charcoal: Milisauskas and Kruk 2011, 237; Whittle 1996, 195. Other Funnel Beaker dates from the Kujawy region around Sarnow fit the general pattern.

27. Isaksson and Hallgren 2012.
28. Mischka 2011; Milisauskas and Kruk 2011, 236–37.
29. Malmström 2009.
30. Skoglund 2012.
31. Bramanti 2009.
32. Zvelebil 2005.
33. von Cramon-Taubadel and Pinhasi 2011.
34. Czekaj-Zastawny 2011.
35. Parkinson 2010; Roberts, Sofaer and Kiss 2008; Verschoor 2011.
36. For the clear case of spindle whorls, see Chmielewski and Gardyński 2010.
37. Zvelebil 2004; Fornander, Eriksson and Lidén 2008.
38. Craig 2011.
39. Whittle, Healy and Bayliss 2011; Collard, Edinborough, Shennan and Thomas 2010; Rowley-Conwy 2004 and 2011.
40. Copley 2003.
41. Meniel 1984.
42. Balasse and Tresset 2002.
43. Edwards 2004.
44. Bollongino 2006, supplement.
45. Raetzel-Fabian 2002; Vander Linden 2011.
46. Zimmermann, Hilpert and Wendt 2009.
47. Whittle, Healy and Bayliss 2011, fig. 15.13; Raetzel-Fabian 2002.
48. Vander Linden 2011; Milisauskas and Kruk 2011; Vanmontfort 2007; Kienlin and Valde-Nowak 2004.
49. Whittle, Healey and Bayliss 2011, 757–59, 840, 853–61.
50. Allen, Barclay and Lamdin-Whymark 2004.
51. Šoberl and Evershed 2009.
52. Vanmontfort 2001; Vanmontfort, Casseyas and Vermeersch 1997.
53. Louwe Kooijmans 2009.
54. Sheridan 2000.
55. Bocquet-Appel 2011.
56. Fu, Rudan, Pääbo and Krause 2012. See also Gignoux, Henn and Mountain 2011.
57. Shennan 2009; Shennan and Edinborough 2007; Tallavaara, Pesonen and Oinonen 2010.
58. Maniatis 2011.
59. Stevens and Fuller 2012.
60. Caulfield, O'Donnell and Mitchell 1998; Verrill and Tipping 2010.
61. Keyser 2009.

Chapter 7: The Copper Age

1. Radivojević 2010 argues for a separate origin in Serbia, but see Roberts, Thornton and Pigott 2009.
2. Childe 1930, 4–10.
3. Roberts, Thornton and Pigott 2009; Roberts 2008 and 2008b.
4. Oates 2007.
5. Ur 2010.
6. Hoffman 1986.
7. Potts 1999.
8. Roux and Courty 2005.
9. Anthony 2007, 49–50, 263–66, 282–98; Kohl 2007, 54, 58–59, 72–83; Kazarnitsky 2010.
10. Manzura 2005, 329.
11. Begemann 2010.
12. Dreyer 1998.
13. Roberts, Thornton and Pigott 2009.
14. Beja-Pereira 2004; Kimura 2011.
15. McGovern 2003; McGovern 2009; Barnard 2011.
16. Shishlina, Orfinskaya and Golikov 2003; Greenfield 2010.
17. Van de Mieroop 2007 34, 63–66. Dates for Sargon are uncertain. Van de Mieroop uses those of the Middle Chronology, which is the most popular among scholars.
18. Sherratt 1981; Greenfield 2010; Marciniak 2011; Bogucki 1993.
19. Greenfield 2010.
20. Keith 1998; Chmielewski and Gardyński 2010.
21. Shishlina, Orfinskaya and Golikov 2003.
22. Chessa 2009.
23. Greenfield 2010; Charvát 2002, 71. Greenfield gives the date of plough-marks at Susa in Iran as 5000 BC, but they were at Susa foundation level, now dated to between c. 4000 BC and c. 3500 BC – see Potts 1999, 46.
24. Anthony and Chi 2009; Bailey 2000.
25. Anthony 2007, 164–65; Lazarovici 2010.
26. Ivanov and Avramova 2000; Slavchev 2009. Excavations further north along the Black Sea coast at Durankulak found more rich graves of the same period: Kohl 2007, 46–47.
27. Haas 1998; O'Brien 1995.
28. Anthony 2007, 258–64, 290; Chernykh 2008.
29. Kohl 2007, 45–46; Korvin-Piotrovskiy 2012. It has been suggested that cattle phalanges with marked splaying found at Vădastra in Romania represent the first evidence of animal traction in Europe, but inherited deformation is an alternative possibility. So the ards made of elk antlers, traces of yoking and harnessing on steer bones and a clay model of two yoked bulls or oxen drawing a sledge, all found at Cucuteni-Tripolye sites, provide more convincing evidence of animal traction.
30. Chmielewski and Gardyński 2010.
31. Dyson and Rowland 2007, 35–44.
32. Roberts 2009.
33. Dyson and Rowland 2007, 35–44; Lilliu 1999.
34. Lilliu 1999.
35. Blasco Ferrer 2011.
36. Itan 2010.
37. Enattah 2007.
38. Höppner 2005.
39. Maggi and Pearce 2005.
40. Mallory and Adams 1997, 217–18, 317–18, 482–83, 485–86.
41. Müller 2003; Ermini 2008; Endicott 2009; phylotree.org.
42. Keller 2012. Note that his Y-DNA haplogroup, defined by marker L21, was formerly named G2a4, which nomenclature is used in this paper.
43. Sikora 2012.
44. Carozza and Mille 2007; Roberts 2009.
45. Nocete 2011; Hanning, Gauß and Goldenberg 2010. An earlier date for Iberian metallurgy was once argued, but on insecure evidence: Roberts 2008.
46. Kunst 2007.
47. García Sanjuán 2006, 154.
48. Lillios 2008.
49. García Sanjuán 2006. The ivory was probably traded from Morocco: Schuhmacher, Cardoso and Banerjee 2009.
50. Díaz-del-Río 2011; Thomas 2009.
51. Hanning, Gauß and Goldenberg 2010.
52. Roberts 2008.

53. Comrie, Matthews and Polinsky 2003; Trask 1997, chapter 6.
54. Strabo, 3.4.10.
55. Ptolemy, 2.5: Tarraconensis Hispania.
56. Talbert 2000; Santos Yanguas 1988; Ramirez Sádaba 2006.
57. Strabo, 4.2.1.
58. Trask 1996; Trask 1997, section 6.9.
59. Villar and Prósper 2005, 513.
60. Bengtson 2011.
61. Trask 1996, 67.
62. Young 2011.
63. Balanovsky 2011.
64. Martínez-Cruz 2012.
65. Aguirre 1991; Iriondo, Barbero and Manzano 2001; Santin 2006.
66. Alonso 2005.
67. Martínez-Cruz 2012; Alonso 2005; Adams 2008.
68. Rocca 2012. It represents nearly half the Iberian sample in the 1000 Genomes Project.
69. Martínez-Cruz 2012.
70. Cruciani 2007.
71. Martínez-Cruz 2012; Alfonso-Sánchez 2008; Richard 2007.
72. Ennafaa 2009.
73. García 2011.
74. Enattah 2007.
75. Laayouni, Calafell and Bertranpetit 2010.
76. Rodríguez-Ezpeleta 2010.
77. Martínez-Cruz 2012.
78. Shi 2010, using a modified form of the evolutionary effective mutation rate.
79. Gómez-Carballa 2012. The authors presume HV4 actually arose in eastern Europe, from a scattering of HV4 results from Europe. However, current haplogroup databases tend to include far more Europeans than persons from the Near East and may not therefore be fully representative.
80. Trask 2008, 102, 110, 137, 142, 148, 212, 360.
81. Pushkariova 1998. Thanks to Dr Ignacio Arrizabalaga for pointing out this paper and other linguistic comments.
82. Blasco Ferrer 2011.
83. Trask 1996, 74–75.
84. Plantinga 2012.

Chapter 8: The Indo-European Family

1. Mallory 1989.
2. Anthony 2007, 93–94 summarizes. For a more detailed discussion see Carpelan, Parpola and Koskikalio 2001. For structural similarities between Indo-European and Uralic see Dediu and Levison 2012.
3. Nichols 1997, 125–28; Mallory and Adams 2006, 82–83. The direction of borrowing is not always agreed among linguists. The words for 'bull' in PIE (*tawro-s) and Proto-Semitic (*tawr) are clearly related. It is often assumed that this represents a borrowing from the latter to the former. Huehnergard 2011 takes the opposite view and also thinks a word for 'horn' was borrowed from PIE by Proto-Semitic. The number of other words that are similar in PIE and Proto-Semitic is a matter of dispute between linguists. These similarities have formed the crux of arguments in favour of a homeland for PIE in Neolithic Anatolia. Linguistically this cannot be supported, since the lexicon of Proto-Semitic places its origin in the Copper Age Levant: Huehnergard 2011; Militarev 2005.
4. McGovern 2003 and 2009; Barnard 2011.
5. Mallory and Adams 2006, 461.
6. Kristiansen 2008.
7. Anthony 2007 draws on Ringe, Warnow and Taylor 2002 and Nakhleh, Ringe and Warnow 2005 for the IE tree.
8. Anthony 2007, 182–86, 239–47.
9. Bakker, Kruk, Lanting and Milisauskas 1999.
10. Manzura 2005, 327.
11. Parpola 2008.
12. Kirtcho 2009.
13. Milisauskas and Kruk 1991.
14. Anthony 2007, 65–72; Parpola 2008.
15. Čufar, Kromer, Tolar and Velušček 2010.
16. Anthony 2007, 69–72.
17. Anthony 2007, 258–59.
18. The Suvorovo group in the Danube Delta 4200–3900 BC appear identical culturally to the contemporary Novodanilovka group northwest of the Sea of Azov, within the broader Sredni (or Sredny) Stog culture. David Anthony considers the Suvorovo-Novodanilovka complex to represent the elite of Sredni Stog: Anthony 2007, 43–48, 75, 249–51, 260–62, fig. 13.11; Mallory 1989, 24–30, 72–73; Anthony 2013.
19. Latacz 2004, 49–71.
20. Drews 2004, 9. The one clear exception is Iberia. MtDNA from Iberian horse skeletons of the Neolithic and later showed that Lusitano group C modern horses were descended from wild mares of Iberia: Lira 2010.
21. Levine 2003.
22. Outram 2009. And see Kalieva and Logvin 2011.
23. Drews 2004, 17–22.
24. Outram 2009.
25. Warmuth 2012 supported this thesis by Bayesian analysis of mtDNA of modern horses; .
26. Anthony 2007, 64–65, 307–11; Anthony 2013.
27. The name Tokhâristân was given to Bactria after it was conquered by a confederation including Tokharians/ Tocharians, which has caused confusion, since its inhabitants wrote in an Iranian language now called Bactrian. However, the ethnonym Tokharian/Tocharian can be identified with the people who appear in Chinese sources as Yüeh-chih or Yuezhi who lived in the Tarim Basin prior to this conquest and left writings there in Tocharian. See Mallory and Mair 2000, appendix 1; Beckwith 2009, appendix B, 380–81.
28. Dirksen 2007.
29. Anthony 2007, 310–11.
30. Dodson 2009; Romgard 2008.
31. Anthony 2007, 311; Romgard 2008.
32. Jing and Campbell 2009.
33. Cai 2011.
34. Meadows 2007.
35. Tapio 2006.
36. Kuzmina 2007, ed. Mair, 95;

Romgard 2008; Thornton and Schurr 2004.

37. The language had been in the Tarim Basin long enough to develop into two versions by the time it is recorded in writing about AD 500: Carling, Pinault and Winter 2009, 48–49.
38. Mallory and Mair 2000.
39. Li 2010.
40. Anthony 2007, chapters 4 and 13.
41. Shishlina, Orfinskaya and Golikov 2003.
42. Jones-Bley 2000.
43. Chernykh and Orlovskaya 2004; Kohl 2007, 58–59.
44. Anthony 2007, 328–39.
45. Harrison and Heyd 2007; Kristiansen 2005.
46. Homer, *Iliad*, 17.51–52. Translations from the Greek vary according to the image in the mind of the translator.
47. Harrison and Heyd 2007; Kristiansen 2005.
48. Kremenetski, Chichagova and Shishlina 1999; Kremenetski 2003.
49. Anthony 2007, chapter 14; Anthony 2008. For the revised dates of Corded Ware see Wlodarczak 2009.
50. Ringe 2006, 67.
51. Mallory and Adams 2006, 78–79.
52. Bramanti 2009; Malmström 2009.
53. Müller 2010; Hinz 2012. Note that the population fall 3350 BC and rise 2900 BC represents an overall picture. The Danish Isles are an exception, showing neither the increase nor decrease. This fits with the observation of a delayed appearance of Single-Grave customs as well as an intensive development of the Funnel Beaker customs. The northeastern stylistic group of Funnel Beaker ceramics is also an exception, showing intense population growth and continuous population development.
54. Malmström 2009.
55. Haak 2008.
56. Skoglund 2012.
57. Wick 2012.
58. Anthony 2007, 361–67; Giblin 2009 looks at evidence for

the shift to a more pastoral economy.
59. Mallory 1989, 73–76; Wilkes 1992, 33–35.
60. Hincak 2007.
61. della Casa 1995; Heyd 2007.
62. Ringe, Warnow and Taylor 2002; Nakhleh, Ringe and Warnow 2005.
63. Possibly meaning 'highlanders' from PIE *bhergh* = 'high; hill, mountain'.
64. Herodotus, 7.73.
65. Wilhelm 2008.
66. Anthony 2007, 343–48; Blažek 2005.
67. Andersen 2003.
68. Kuznetsov 2006; Anthony 2007, chapter 15; Littauer and Crouwel 2002; Drews 2004.
69. Anthony 2007, 49; Van de Mieroop 2007, 131, 149–55.
70. Kristiansen and Larsson 2005, fig. 79.
71. Cunliffe 2008, 223–25; Harrison 2004; Johannsen 2010.
72. Anthony 2007, 371–82, 389–411, 452–57; Kuzmina 2007, ed. Mallory, 233.
73. Lubotsky 2001; Blench 2008; Witzel 2005.
74. Kohl 2007, chapter 5; Anthony 2007, 452–56.
75. Hancock 2002; Hancock 2010; Pamjav 2011.
76. Holland 2005, chapter 1; Kuzmina 2007 ed. Mallory, 371–73; Van De Mieroop 2007, 267.
77. Van De Mieroop 2007, chapter 15.
78. *Behistun Inscription*.
79. Panyushkina 2010.
80. Rogozhinskiy 2011, 10–22.
81. Romgard 2008, 14–15, 24–29.
82. Velasco 2010.
83. Mallory and Adams 2006, 157–58.
84. Farrokhi 2011.
85. Gharghani 2009.
86. Legrand and Bokovenko 2006; Kuzmina 2007, ed. Mair; Beckwith 2009, chapter 2.
87. Lalueza-Fox 2004.
88. Herodotus, 1.201, 4.11, 7.64. Herodotus renders the Old Persian 'Saka' as 'Sacae'. The Saka or Sak also appear in Chinese sources. From the same root comes Sugda, the name of Sogdiana and

the Sogdians. The various ethnonyms recorded for the Scythians appear to derive from the Proto-Indo-Iranian *Skuda, meaning 'shooter or archer': Beckwith 2009, 377–80. The PIE root is *(s)keud – 'to throw': Mallory and Adams 2006, 388–89.
89. Herodotus, 1.214.
90. Pseudo-Skylax, 68.5, 70 uses both ethnonyms in the forms Syrmatai and Sauromatai.
91. Guliaev 2003.
92. Herodotus, 4.22, 4. 100–17.
93. *Prometheus Bound*, formerly attributed to Aeschylus, 5th century BC, but now more usually attributed to an unknown playwright.
94. Herodotus, 4.117.
95. Thomason 2001, 6–7.
96. Guliaev 2003.
97. Berseneva 2010.
98. Anthony 2007, 329.
99. Mallory and Adams 2006, 32, 266; Mallory and Adams 1997, 213.
100. Vander Linden 2012.
101. Earle and Kristiansen 2010, chapter 1.
102. Mallory and Adams 2006.
103. Anthony 2007, 43–48; Van De Mieroop 2007, 122.

Chapter 9: Indo-Europeans and Genetics

1. Moorjani 2012.
2. The correlation with the combination of R1a1a and R1b1a2 was first pointed out by Richard Stevens in September and October 2006 in online forums for discussion of genetic genealogy, including Family Tree DNA Forums and the Rootsweb mailing list Genealogy-DNA.
3. Wells 2001; the connection between Y-DNA R-M17 and the spread of Indo-European languages was first proposed by Zerjal 1999 and supported by Quintana-Murci 2001.
4. Bouakaze 2007; Bouakaze 2009; Keyser 2009.
5. Li 2010.
6. Haak 2008.
7. Lee 2012.

8. Pamjav, Fehér, Németh and Pádár 2012; Family Tree DNA R1a1a and subclades Y-DNA Project. Estimated dates vary between these sources, according to the mutation rate used. Pamjav et al. discuss Z280, which is a subclade of Z283.

9. Arredi, Poloni and Tyler-Smith 2007, 394 gives 5,000–8,000 years old, updated by Wei 2013.

10. Cruciani, Trombetta and Antonelli 2011.

11. Myres 2011; Balaresque 2010; Arredi, Poloni and Tyler-Smith 2007; Wei 2013.

12. Estimated date of 4,600–5,200 years ago provided by Vincent Vizachero.

13. Mielnik-Sikorska 2012; R1b1a2 (2.59%), R1b1-P25 (5.19%), E1b1b1-M35 (7.79%).

14. Sengupta 2006; Myres 2011; Lobov 2007; Lobov 2009.

15. Grugni 2012.

16. Matyushin 1986, 135, 145–46 and fig. 4. The characteristic flint tools are geometric microliths.

17. Tarkhnishvili 2012.

18. Anati 2001; Farajova 2011. Geometric microliths appear at Gobustan, as in the Yangelskaya culture.

19. Schilz 2006 tested only STRs (short tandem repeats). Y-DNA haplogroups were deduced from the STRs by Dirk Schweitzer.

20. De Beule 2011.

21. Research on dates and locations by Kenneth Nordtvedt, who is not responsible for my conclusions.

22. Mallory and Adams 2006, 34.

23. Härke and Belinskij 2011.

24. Korobov 2011.

25. Josephus, *The Wars of the Jews*, 7.244.

26. Ammianus Marcellinus, 31.2.12; Cassius Dio, 69.15.

27. Keyser 2009.

28. Balanovsky 2011.

29. Herrera 2012; Grugni 2012.

30. King 2008; Underhill 2010. Note that both of these papers use the evolutionary effective mutation rate, which may give inappropriately old dates.

See the section of the present work covering genetic dating problems, pp. 28–30.

31. Grugni 2012.

32. Thangaraj 2010.

33. Sengupta 2006; Indo-European-speaking upper castes: 45.35% R1a1a-M17, 9.30% J2a-M410; Dravidian-speaking upper castes: 28.81% R1a1a-M17, 13.56% J2a-M410.

34. Nikitin 2010; Keyser 2009.

35. Haak 2008.

36. Adler 2012.

37. H5 (not tested for T4336C, which defines H5a) appears at a Bell Beaker site in Germany (Aldler 2012) and a Tagar site in Russia (Keyser 2009).

38. Baudouin 2005.

39. Behar 2012, supplement.

40. Molodin 2012.

41. Lee 2012; Keyser 2009.

42. Zhang 2010.

43. Melchior 2008.

44. Quintana-Murci 2004; Yao 2004.

45. Enattah 2008; Ingram 2009.

46. Järvelä 2009; Piepoli 2007.

47. Gerbault 2011; Gallego Romero 2012.

48. Heyer 2011.

49. Enattah 2002; Ingram 2009; Bersaglieri 2004; Xu 2010.

50. Bersaglieri 2004.

51. Vuorisalo 2012.

52. Evershed 2008, 531.

53. Burger 2007.

54. Lacan 2011.

55. Plantinga 2012.

56. Linderholm 2008.

57. Anthony 2007, 213–19; Kruts 2012.

58. The haplogroup was T4 prior to nomenclature change in 2012. Nikitin 2011; Keyser 2009.

59. Fortunato and Jordan 2010.

60. Malmström 2010.

61. Cochran and Harpending 2009, 174, 181–86.

62. Koepke and Baten 2008.

Chapter 10: Beaker Folk to Celts and Italics

1. The Celtic and Italic language families are so closely related that some linguists argue for a common ancestor – Proto-Italo-Celtic. The case in favour is made by Kortlandt 2007. It is supported by the cladistic approach of Ringe, Warnow and Taylor 2002, and Nakhleh, Ringe and Warnow 2005. Mallory and Adams 2006, 78–79 present the more sceptical case.

2. Czebreszuk and Szmyt 2003.

3. Shepherd 2012.

4. Sarauw 2007 and 2008.

5. Østmo 2012; Prescott 2012.

6. Heyd 2012.

7. Burgess and Shennan 1976.

8. Price, Knipper, Grupe and Smrcka 2004; Grupe 1997; Cox and Mays 2000, 281–83; Desideri and Besse 2010.

9. Lee 2012. Of the Y-DNA results, deeper resolution was not possible for one, except that it was negative for S21/U106. The other was positive for M269 and negative for S21/U106, but not tested for any other subclade of R1b1a2 (M269).

10. Brun 2006; Gibson and Wodtko 2011; Almagro-Gorbea 2001.

11. Lorrio and Zapatero 2005; Cunliffe 1997, 151–55; Cunliffe and Koch 2010, 2.

12. Müller and van Willigen 2001; Kunst 2001.

13. Roberts 2008.

14. Ferreira 2003; Kunst 2001.

15. Anthony 2007, figs 11.4, 12.6, 12.9.

16. Odriozola and Hurtado Pérez 2007; Parkinson 2010; Roberts, Sofaer and Kiss 2008; Verschoor 2011.

17. Carbon-14 has dated the earliest Bell Beaker pottery sites to c. 2700 BC and the earliest dates for Corded Ware to c. 2750 BC: Müller and van Willigen 2001; Wlodarczak 2009.

18. Desideri and Besse 2010; Harrison and Heyd 2007.

19. Mallory 1989, 219–20 and figs 119–21; Mallory and Adams 1997, 327; Telehin and Mallory 1994; Anthony 2007, 336–39 and fig. 13.11; Harrison and Heyd 2007; Robb 2009; Manzura 2005b; Horváth 2009; Díaz-Guardamino 2011; Scarre 2010; Ciugudean 2011.

20. The Copper Age stelae of Iberia should not be confused with the later warrior stelae of southwest Iberia. For examples of the Copper Age type see

Díaz-Guardamino 2011 and Robb 2009.
21. Wodtko 2010. Lusitanian retains the initial 'p' which is dropped in Celtic. For example Proto-Indo-European *porko-s (meaning 'young pig') becomes porcus in Latin, orcos in Gaulish and porcom in Lusitanian.
22. Quiles and López-Menchero 2011, 106.
23. Maggi and Pearce 2005.
24. Heyd 2007; Maran 2007.
25. Lemercier 2012; Harrison and Heyd 2007.
26. Müller and van Willigen 2001.
27. Desideri and Besse 2010.
28. Heyd 2007b; Heyd 2001.
29. Vander Linden 2007.
30. Busby 2012; Myres 2011.
31. Rocca 2012.
32. Fokkens, Achterkamp and Kuijpers 2008; Woodward and Hunter 2011.
33. Harrison and Heyd 2007, 185–87, 192.
34. Chiaradia, Gallay and Todt 2003; Menk 1979.
35. Lemercier 2012.
36. Garrido Pena 1997.
37. Koch 2006, 364–65, 374.
38. Mozota 2007.
39. Avienus, lines 130–35. The 19th-century Ligurian hypothesis, which posited Ligurians living over a broad swathe of Europe until penned into Liguria by the Celts, leaving a Ligurian substrate in various languages, has been discredited: Mees 2003, 16–18, 21–22.
40. Talbert 2000, map 26 seems a more credible identification than Braun 2004, 307.
41. Strabo, 2.1.40.
42. Pseudo-Skylax, 3 and 4.
43. Herodotus, book 5; Koch 2006, 898; Justinus, 43.3.
44. Strabo, 4.6.3.
45. Pliny, 4.30; Harley and Woodward 1987, 192; Roller 2006, 28. For Britain Pytheas via Strabo uses Bretannike as a feminine noun, although its form is that of an adjective. Pliny uses Britannia, with Britanniae meaning all the islands, the Britains. Diodorus, writing in Greek, has Brettanikenesos, the British

Island, and Brettanoi, the British. Ptolemy, also writing in Greek, has Bretania and Bretanikai nesoi. However, manuscript variants offer an intial 'P-' alternating with 'B-'. The name learned by Pytheas was probably Pretania or Pritannia, corresponding to the Welsh Ynys Prydein, the island of Britain, and the Irish Q-Celtic Cruithen.
46. Herodotus, 2.33 and note 619.
47. Strabo, 4.4.6.
48. Caesar, 1.1.1.
49. Diodorus Siculus, 5.32.
50. Strabo, 2.5.28.
51. O'Brien 2005.
52. Northover, O'Brien and Stos 2001.
53. Warner 2009.
54. Stevens and Fuller 2012; Collard, Edinborough, Shennan and Thomas 2010.
55. Pare 2000.
56. E.g. Dillon and Chadwick 1967.
57. James 1999. Cunliffe 2003, chapter 1 gives an account of changing attitudes towards the Celts.
58. Fitzpatrick 2011.
59. Prieto-Martínez 2012.
60. Fitzpatrick 2009; Fitzpatrick 2011; Evans, Chenery and Fitzpatrick 2006.
61. O'Brien 2012.
62. Sheridan 2008.
63. Gaelic falls into the category labelled Q-Celtic, since the 'kw' sound in PIE had been retained as 'q', whereas it had been replaced by 'p' in the P-Celtic form found in Gaulish and Brittonic.
64. Matasović 2007. For a fuller discussion and contrary view that Celtic was introduced to Ireland c. 1000 BC, see Mallory 2013, chapter 9.
65. Kristiansen 1998, 144; Cunliffe 2008, 254–58.
66. Field 1998.
67. McKinley, Schuster and Millard 2013.
68. Melheim 2012.

Chapter 11: Minoans and Mycenaeans

1. McEnroe 2002.
2. Ferrara 2010.

3. Bintliff 2012, chapter 5.
4. Berg 2009.
5. Renfrew 1972.
6. Meier 2011, 21–26.
7. Marinatos 2010.
8. Ferrara 2010.
9. Hawkins 2010, 216.
10. Herodotus, 1.56–57.
11. Homer, Odyssey, 19, 172 ff.
12. Strabo, 10.4.6.
13. Nowicki 2008.
14. Herrero 2009.
15. Palmer 1996.
16. Nelson 2005.
17. McGovern 2003 and 2009.
18. Barnard 2011.
19. Myles 2011.
20. Mallory and Adams 1997, 243–44; Mallory 2007.
21. King 2008. This study used the evolutionary mutation rate, which has been criticized as yielding dates inappropriately old.
22. Cruciani 2007.
23. Chilvers 2008.
24. Bouwman 2008.
25. Rutter 1993. In relative chronology this represents the transition between the Early Helladic II and Early Helladic III periods. The date here is taken from Voutsaki 2009.
26. Coleman 2000.
27. Maniatis 2011.
28. Broodbank 2000.
29. Stos-Gale, Gale and Gilmore 1984.
30. Kassianidou and Knapp 2005.
31. Şahoğlu 2005.
32. McGrail 2001, 112.
33. Friedrich 2006.
34. Bintliff 2012, 124.
35. Hawkins 2010.
36. Drake 2012.
37. Martin 1996, 38–43, 51–57.
38. Semino 2004; Di Gaetano 2009; King 2011.
39. Lomas 1993, 8–9.
40. Meier 2011, 21–26.
41. Herodotus; Holland 2005.

Chapter 12: Iron Age Traders and Warriors

1. Kristiansen 2002 and 2005.
2. Jantzen 2011.
3. Kristiansen 1998, chapter 4. Lusatian was once considered an independent culture and Proto-Slavic within Poland.

The political background to this is explained by Piotrowska 1998.

4. Sørensen and Rebay-Salisbury 2008.
5. Bogucki 2004.
6. Cruciani, Trombetta, Antonelli 2011.
7. Chiaroni, Underhill and Cavalli-Sforza 2009.
8. Markoe 2000, 10–11, 108. A tradition stemming from Herodotus, 1.1 that the Phoenicians came from the Red Sea probably sprang from a mistaken colour association.
9. El-Sibai 2009.
10. Zalloua 2008 argues that higher J2 together with higher levels of three Y-STR haplotypes (in men of any haplogroup) could be identified as a Phoenician signature. However, a Y-DNA haplotype cannot be inherited independently of haplogroup, so the methodology is flawed.
11. Aubet 2001 and 2008; Mata 2002.
12. The arguments of Koch 2010 for the language as Celtic did not entirely convince Zeidler 2011, who points out inconsistencies, such as a strange combination of archaic and unexpectedly young traits. As a non-linguist, I can only surmise that this might be the result of treating all inscriptions in the southwestern script as one language, rather than the older Tartessian and a later Gaulish-influenced Celtic around the Guadiana.
13. Garcia i Rubert and Gracia Alonso 2011.
14. Grau Mira 2003; Sanmarti 2009.
15. Braun 2004, 304, 309–13; *Pseudo-Skylax*, 3; Sanmarti 2009.
16. Untermann 1961.
17. Trask 1996, section 6.5.
18. Rodríguez Ramos 2003.
19. Velaza 2006 argues that Catalonia cannot be ruled out as the homeland.
20. Curchin 2009.
21. Universitat Autonoma de Barcelona, press release 27 September 2012.
22. Sanmarti 2009; Rouillard 2009.
23. Braun 2004.

24. Buxó 2008 and 2009; Terral 2004.
25. Sampietro 2005; Gamba 2008.
26. Lacan, Keyser, Crubézy and Ludes 2012.
27. Anthony 2007, 334, 336.
28. Alekseev 2002; Bouzek 2001.
29. Homer, *Odyssey*, 11.1.
30. Hellmuth 2008; Bouzek 2001, 33; Erlij 1993.
31. Herodotus, 4.1, 11–12.
32. Cunliffe 2008, 264–67.
33. The syncretism of plain-voiced and 'voice aspirated' stops.
34. Isaac 2010 outlines the linguistic evidence, but does not connect it with the Cimmerians.
35. Mikhailova 2007.
36. Cunliffe 1997, 2–4, 46–48, 51–90, 221–22, 237–38 and maps 5, 13, 14, 16, 17, 19 and 29; Cunliffe 2008, 266, 413–19 and fig. 8.25; Koch 2006, 245, 285–87.
37. Koch 2006, 788–91.
38. Pliny, 4.34.
39. Strabo, 3.1.6, 3.3.5; Talbert 2000, map 26.
40. Wodtko 2010.
41. Koch 2006, 363–65.
42. Curchin 1997.
43. Cunliffe 1997, 140–43.
44. Koch 2006, 788–91.
45. Armit, Swindles and Becker 2013; Raftery 1997 and 2005; Koch 2007.
46. Koch 2006, 505–06.
47. Fraser 2009, 89.
48. McEvoy and Bradley 2010, 117. They identify this haplogroup simply as a subclade of I1c (the name of I2a2a-M223 in about 2005); Byrne 2001, table 7.
49. Busby 2012.
50. Moore 2006. An independent study found M222 running in several additional families of Donegal and Ulster in Ireland and Galloway in Scotland: Howard and McLaughlin 2011.
51. Lacey 2006.
52. Busby 2012.
53. Koch 2006, 87–88.
54. Ptolemy, 2.2.
55. Morley 2005.
56. Boyle 2004; Boyle 2007.
57. Carter and Hunter 2003.
58. Cunliffe 1997, chapter 4.
59. Caesar, 1.1, 5, 31, 2.4, 5.12; Tacitus, *Germania*, 28.

Chapter 13: Etruscans and Romans

1. Rix 1998.
2. Ghirotto 2013. The aDNA results of an earlier paper (Vernesi 2004) have been criticized by Malyarchuk and Rogozin 2004; Bandelt 2005.
3. Pellecchia 2007.
4. Herodotus, 1.94. The Greek name for the Etruscans was *Tyrrhenoi*.
5. Bonfante and Bonfante 2002.
6. Beekes 2002; reviewed by Mahoney 2008.
7. Herodotus, 1.94.
8. Briquel 1973. Thanks to Richard Rocca for pointing out this paper and discussion of the evidence. Bradley 2000, 20–21 gives a briefer account in English.
9. Plutarch, *Marius*, 19.4.
10. Counihan 2009, and see Koch 2006, 372–73 for the same suggestion on the location of the sound change, but not considering Etruscan as the influence.
11. Koch 2006, 1142–44.
12. Montgomery 2010.
13. Koepke and Baten 2008.
14. Diodorus Siculus, 5.28, 5.32.
15. Strabo, 4.2. Strabo says that, although well supplied with milk, they did not make cheese. Pliny, 96.41 also comments that the barbarous nations which subsist on milk do not make cheese.
16. Tacitus, *Germania*, chapter 4.
17. Caesar, 1.39, 2.30 and see 4.1 for his comments on the diet and height of the Suebi.
18. Blagg and Millett 1990, 99.
19. Garnsey, Rathbone and Bowman 2000, 814.
20. Goldsworthy 2003, 74; Mattingly 2006, 223.
21. Guba 2011. These results were initially assumed to be Neolithic. The correct dating is supplied by Banffy 2012.
22. Collingwood and Wright 1965, RIB 1065, RIB 1171. It has been suggested (Burnham and Wacher 1990, 62) that he was a merchant or manufacturer of standards. However, such a trade would be too specialized to thrive in this location and

no example survives of such a usage of the word *vexillarius*. A known usage is 're-enlisted veteran', but again that falters on the lack of military details.

23. Yavetz 1988, 1–2.
24. Caesar, 2.33, 3.16.
25. Webster 2010; Prowse 2010.
26. Rodriguez 1997.
27. Roth 1997.
28. Strabo, 4.5.2.
29. Strabo, 14.5.2.
30. *Confession of St Patrick*.
31. Ferguson 2009, 98–99; Brink 2008b.
32. Davis 2004 and 2009.
33. Erdem 1996.
34. Beard 2008, 21, 117.
35. Noy 2000.

Chapter 14: The Great Wandering

1. Herodotus, 3.115.
2. Heather 2009, chapter 1.
3. McEvedy and Jones 1978.
4. Heather 2009, 4–5.
5. Duncan-Jones 2004.
6. Heather 2009, 439–45.
7. Urbanczyk 2004; Cunliffe 2008, fig. 9.1.
8. Heather 2009, 439.
9. Heather 2009, 443–45.
10. Florus, 1.38; Plutarch, *Marius*, 11.
11. Weninger 2008.
12. Vink 2007.
13. Beets and van der Spek 2000.
14. Todd 2004, 63–64.
15. Pliny, 16.1.
16. Beets and van der Spek 2000.
17. Büntgen 2011.
18. Duncan-Jones 2004.
19. Russell 1968.
20. Büntgen 2011.
21. Gräslund and Price 2012; Ferris, Cole-Dai, Reyes and Budner 2011; Larsen 2008.
22. Cassiodorus, *Letters*, 25.
23. Stathakopoulos 2006.
24. Procopius, *The History of the Wars*, 2.23.
25. Little 2006.
26. Caldwell 2006, 390.
27. ASC.
28. Soltysiak 2006.
29. Plutarch, *Marius*, 11; Florus, 1.38; Strabo, 7.2.1–2; Ptolemy, 2.10; *Res Gestae Divi Augusti*, 26; Tacitus, *Germania*, 37; Pliny, 4.28.
30. Caesar, book 4; an alternative Roman name was *Alamanni*.

31. Tacitus, *Germania*, chapter 2.
32. Ptolemy, 2.10.
33. On the basis of volunteer testees in the Family Tree DNA R1a1a and Subclades Y-DNA Project. The marker is too newly discovered to have been included in academic studies to date.
34. Murdoch and Grosjean 2005.
35. Moffat and Wilson 2011, 181–83.
36. Myres 2011.
37. Busby 2012, supplement 2.
38. Larmuseau 2012.
39. Ringe 2006, 67.
40. Vandkilde 2005; Kristiansen 2009.
41. Cunliffe 2008, 213–21.
42. Barber 2004.
43. Hannon 2008.
44. Kaliff 2001.
45. Aikio 2006.
46. Broadbent 2006.
47. Perdikaris 2004.
48. Mallory and Adams 1997, 321–22.
49. Tacitus, *Germania*, chapter 1.
50. Ringe 2006, 213.
51. Perdikaris 2004.
52. Spurkland 2010; Robertson 2012.
53. Mallory and Adams 1997, 22.
54. Pliny, 4.28.
55. Tacitus, *Germania*, 14; Wolfram 1988, 5–8.
56. Jordanes, chapters 4 and 17. Jordanes gives no date for the move to mainland Europe, but his claim (chapter 60) that the race of the Ostrogoths in AD 540 was overcome in almost its 2,030th year produced the commonly quoted calculation of 1490 BC, which has no historical value.
57. Ptolemy, 2.10.
58. Ptolemy, 3.5; Tacitus, *Germania*, 44.
59. Wolfram 1988, 20–21.
60. Pliny, 37.11.35.
61. Cunliffe 2001, 142.
62. Kaliff 2001.
63. Jovaisa 2001.
64. Heather and Matthews 1991, chapter 3.
65. Christensen 2002.
66. Ammianus, 31.3–8, 12–13; Wolfram 1988, 25.
67. Heather 1991, 149–59.
68. Thompson 1996; Phol 2004, 35.

69. Pliny, 4.28; Tacitus, *Germania*, section 2.
70. Ptolemy, 2.10. Ptolemy names the Lugi 'below' (i.e. south or southeast of) the Siling. The Lugi vanish from the record in the 3rd century, probably overrun by the expanding Vandals.
71. Phol 2004, 33, 34–35.
72. Phol 2004, 35–37.
73. Jordanes, chapter 14.
74. Procopius, 3.2.
75. Wolfram 1988; Thompson 1969.
76. Wolfram 1988, 268–84.
77. Wolfram 1988, 284–339.
78. Procopius, book 5.
79. Woolf 2007b; Heather 2009, chapter 6.
80. Heather 2009, 306.
81. Ammianus, 17. 8.3; Talbert 2000, map 11.
82. Heather 2009, 306.
83. The distribution of certain Germanic place-names suggests that some of the movement into Britain came from Saxony via the Low Countries and the Pas de Calais, with settlers opting to cross to Britain rather than press further westwards into Neustria. See Udolph 1994; Hilsberg 2009.
84. Hamerow 2002, chapter 2.
85. Montgomery 2005.
86. Gildas, chapters 23–25.
87. Bede, 1.15.
88. Hamerow 2002, 108–10.
89. Härke 2011.
90. Woolf 2007b; Heather 2009, chapter 6, maps 11–12.
91. Weale 2002; Capelli 2003; Goodacre 2005.
92. Winney 2012.
93. Ramos-Luis 2009, together with unpublished data from this study supplied by its authors to Richard Rocca.
94. Rootsi 2004.
95. Capelli 2003.
96. Moffat and Wilson 2011, 88, 90–91, 145–46.

Chapter 15: Enter the Slavs

1. Mallory and Adams 2006, 25–26.
2. Curta 2001 and 2002.
3. Ralph and Coop 2012.

4. Procopius, 7.14, 1–2, 22–30; 8.40, 5.
5. Jordanes, 5.33.
6. Heather 2009, 439.
7. Heather 2009, 388–89, 92–3; Šalkovský 2000.
8. Procopius, 7.14.22–30; *Maurice's Strategikon*, 120.
9. Parczewski 2004.
10. Procopius, 7.14.22–30.
11. Heather 2009, 389–96.
12. Andersen 1996, 49–50.
13. Andersen 2003.
14. Jordanes, 5.35.
15. *Maurice's Strategikon*, 120–21.
16. Heather 2009, 396.
17. Parczewski 2004.
18. Herodotus, 4.17–18, 52–54.
19. Mallory and Adams 1997, 104, 657–58.
20. Kruts 2012.
21. Jordanes, 5.34. Two other peoples of the Roman period had the name Veneti, one in Brittany and the other in northeastern Italy. There is no known connection between them and the Veneti of eastern Europe.
22. Tacitus, *Germania*, 46.
23. Ptolemy, 3.5.
24. Pliny, 4.97.
25. Schenker 1995, 1.4.
26. Fredegar, 57; Heather 2009, 397.
27. Schenker 1995, 1.4.
28. Blažek 2005, fig. 12.3.
29. Heather 2009, 399–405.
30. Soltysiak 2006.
31. Pliny, 6.7; Ptolemy, 5.8.13.
32. Heather 2009, 442–43.
33. Fredegar, 57.
34. Veeramah 2011; Gross 2011.
35. Buko 2008, 61–62, 86; Barford 2001.
36. Heather 2009, 406–14; Brather 2004; Buko 2005.
37. Heather 2009, 8, 414–18, 445.
38. Underhill 2010.
39. Woźniak 2010.
40. Gwozdz 2009 and 2010.
41. Underhill 2010, supplement.
42. Peričić 2005, table 1.
43. Mallory and Adams 1997, 8–11.
44. Boattini 2011.
45. Heather 2009, 403, 439.
46. Kinross 1977, 48–52, 456–57.
47. Balanovsky 2008. Note that this paper uses older names for haplogroups.
48. Loogväli 2004; Malyarchuk 2006.

49. Bramanti 2009; Malmström 2009.
50. Malyarchuk 2010.
51. Malyarchuk 2008.

Chapter 16: Bulgars and Magyars

1. Barnard and Wendrich 2008.
2. Chernykh 2008; Beckwith 2009.
3. Nichols 1997 and 1998.
4. Wood 2002, 9, 50, 53–55; Liu 2010, 3–4.
5. Nichols 2011.
6. Martínez-Cruz 2011.
7. Beckwith 2009, chapter 4; Heather 2009, chapter 5.
8. Johanson 1998.
9. John, Bishop of Nikiu, 120.47. The term 'Hun' may be generic here for steppe barbarian, though a group of Huns under Attila's son Ernac settled in the western steppe, where they remained for several generations before they disappeared as a people under that name. See Beckwith 2009, 99.
10. Fielder 2008.
11. Karachanak 2009, 2013. Note that these papers did not test for SNPs downstream of I-M423. However, private testing suggests that most if not all of the I-M423 in Bulgaria falls into the subclade I-L147. My own interpretations of the origins of these haplogroups differ from those of the authors.
12. Golden 1990.
13. Graf 2010.
14. Golden 1990; Abondolo 1998.
15. Golden 1990; Nichols 2011.
16. Lobov 2007; Lobov 2009. Those few Bashkirs so far tested by Family Tree DNA for the SNPs distinguishing eastern and western R1a1a fall into the eastern subclade defined by L342.
17. Nasidze 2005.
18. Golden 1990.
19. Nichols 2011.
20. Heather 2009, 577.
21. Ralph and Coop 2012.
22. Csányi 2008; Völgyi, Zalán, Szvetnik and Pamjav 2009.
23. Csepeli and Orkeny 1996.
24. Csányi 2008.
25. Guba 2011. All three results

were initially assumed to be Neolithic. See Banffy 2012 for the revised dating.
26. Tömöry 2007.

Chapter 17: Vikings

1. Brink 2008.
2. Skre 2008; Clark and Ambrosiani 1995.
3. Ferguson 2009, 377.
4. Brink 2008.
5. Ferguson 2009, 84; Graham-Campbell 2001, 10–16.
6. Price 2011.
7. Bill 2008; Hall 2007, 50–55.
8. Fagan 2000, chapter 1.
9. Barrett 2008.
10. Østmo 2012.
11. Bill 2008.
12. *EHD* 1, no. 193.
13. Simeon of Durham, 457.
14. Ferguson 2009, chapter 3.
15. Holck 2006.
16. Behar 2012, supplement.
17. Der Sarkissian 2011.
18. Rudbeck 2005.
19. Lappalainen 2009.
20. Moffat and Wilson 2011, 182 map.
21. ASC under year 787, rectified to 789; Woolf 2007, 46–47 argues that this incident has been wrongly dated and belongs to 798.
22. Heather 2009, 453–6; Ó Corráin 1998.
23. Haslam 1987.
24. *Orkneyinga Saga*, 26–27.
25. Fellows-Jensen 2008.
26. Goodacre 2005.
27. Bowden 2007; Harding, Jobling and King 2010.
28. Downham 2008, 180–82.
29. Byrne 2005; Ó Corráin 2008. Note that Ó Corráin tendentiously translates the entry in the Irish annals relating to the death of Ívarr (*Ímar*), 873, making him 'king of the Norwegian Vikings of the whole of Ireland and Britain'. The more accurate translation is 'king of all the Northmen of the whole of Ireland and Britain'. See Downham 2008, 259.
30. Børsheim 1997 and 2000.
31. Peirce 2002, 3–4.
32. Byrne 2005, Appendix: Old Norse borrowings into Irish.

33. Searle 2009; Jones 2012.
34. Downham 2008, xvi–xvii, 14–15.
35. One such banner was captured in Devon in 878 from a brother of Ívarr, see ASC.
36. Downham 2008, 12–16.
37. Ó Corráin 1998. For archaeological criticism of the idea of early settlement in Atlantic Scotland see Barrett 2008.
38. Woolf 2007, 71–73; Coupland 1998.
39. *Fragmentary Annals of Ireland*, 401: 'Imar son of Gothfraid son of Ragnall son of Gothfraid Conung son of Gofraid.' *Conung* is from the Old Norse *konungr*, meaning 'king'.
40. Downham 2008, 3, 7–8, 253–54.
41. Coupland 1998.
42. Hall 2007, 122–26; Wallace 2005; Downham 2009; Pelteret 1985.
43. O'Donnabhain and Hallgrímsson 2001.
44. Knudson, O'Donnabhain 2012.
45. McEvoy 2006.
46. Hall 2007, 60–63; Graham-Campbell 2001, 92–95; Von Carnap-Bornheim and Hilberg 2007; Hilberg 2008.
47. Coupland 1998.
48. *Annals of St-Bertin*, 30, 33, 35, 51; Coupland 1998.
49. Coupland 1998; *Annals of St-Bertin*, 69, 75, 81.
50. Sawyer 1997, 25–26; *Annals of St-Bertin*, 55–56.
51. Price 1989.
52. Neveux 2008, chapter 4; Ferguson 2009, chapter 9.
53. Neveux 2008, 89.
54. Dudo, chapter 5. Dudo's terminology is confused. He uses Scandia for the Scandinavian peninsula and Dacia for Denmark, apparently under the impression that the Danes hailed from Dacia originally.
55. Richer, book 1, chapters 4 and 28.
56. *Hist. Norway*, 9; Snorri Sturluson, chapter 24.
57. Renaud 2003.
58. Price 1989.
59. ASC.
60. Downham 2008.
61. *Ann. Camb.*, sub ann 866.
62. Campbell 1982, chapters 6 and 7.
63. McLeod 2011.
64. Weale 2002; Capelli 2003.
65. Ayers 2011.
66. ASC.
67. Campbell 1982, chapter 8.
68. Sigurdsson 2008.
69. Ferguson 2009, chapter 8.
70. *Landnamabok*.
71. Goodacre 2005.
72. Ropars 2012; Le Floch 2013.
73. Ebenesersdóttir 2011.
74. Helgason 2006.
75. Gilbert 2008.
76. Ferguson 2009, chapter 14; Arneborg 2008.
77. Wallace 2008.
78. *The Russian Primary Chronicle, Laurentian Text*.
79. Family Tree DNA Rurikid project.
80. Heather 2009, 466–68. The Rus appear as *Rhos* in Byzantine Greek and *Ar-Rus* in Islamic sources. The subclade carried by Rurikids is defined by the marker L1025.
81. *Annals of St-Bertin*, 44.
82. Ahola 2008.
83. Androshchuk 2008.
84. Ferguson 2009, 111–18; Heather 2009, 470–71.
85. Montgomery 2000.
86. Economou, Kjellström, Lidén and Panagopoulos 2013.
87. Riha 1969, 2.
88. Balanovsky 2008.
89. Pohl 2009.

Bibliography

Abbreviations

ASC: *The Anglo-Saxon Chronicle*, trans. and ed. Michael Swanton. London: Dent, 1996.

BAR: British Archaeological Reports.

EHD: *English Historical Documents*. London: Routledge.

PNAS: *Proceedings of the National Academy of Sciences of the United States of America.*

PRS B: *Proceedings of the Royal Society B: Biological Sciences.*

1000 Genomes Project Consortium 2010. A map of human genome variation from population-scale sequencing, *Nature*, 467, 1061–73.

Abondolo, D. 1998. *The Uralic Languages* (Routledge Language Family Series). London and New York: Routledge.

Achilli, A. et al. 2004. The molecular dissection of mtDNA Haplogroup H confirms that the Franco-Cantabrian glacial refuge was a major source for the European gene pool, *American Journal of Human Genetics*, 75 (5), 910–18.

Achilli, A. et al. 2005. Saami and Berbers: an unexpected mitochondrial DNA link, *American Journal of Human Genetics*, 76 (5), 883–86.

Achilli, A. et al. 2007. Mitochondrial DNA variation of modern Tuscans supports the Near Eastern origin of Etruscans, *American Journal of Human Genetics*, 80 (4), 759–68.

Adachi, N. et al. 2011. Mitochondrial DNA analysis of Hokkaido Jomon skeletons: remnants of archaic maternal lineages at the southwestern edge of former Beringia, *American Journal of Physical Anthropology*, 146 (3), 346–60.

Adams, S. M. et al. 2008. The genetic legacy of religious diversity and intolerance: paternal lineages of Christians, Jews, and Muslims in the Iberian peninsula, *American Journal of Human Genetics*, 83 (6), 725–36.

Adler, C. J. et al. 2011. Survival and recovery of DNA from ancient teeth and bones, *Journal of Archaeological Science*, 38 (5), 956–64.

Adler, C. J. 2012. Ancient DNA studies of human evolution. PhD thesis, Australian Centre for Ancient DNA, University of Adelaide, January 2012.

Afonso, C. A. P. 2010. Contribuição do ADN antigo para o estudo das populações do Neolítico final/Calcolítico portuguesas. Thesis, Universidade de Coimbra.

Aguirre, A. et al. 1991. Are the Basques a single and a unique population?, *Science Genetics*, 49 (2), 450–58.

Ahola, J. 2008. Vikings in the East: a report on a workshop held in Veliky Novgorod, Russia in May 10–13 2006, in *The Borderless North: The Fourth Northern Research Forum*, L. Heininen and K. Laine (eds), 68–72. Oulu: The Thule Institute, University of Oulu and Northern Research Forum.

Aikio, A. 2006. On Germanic-Saami contacts and Saami prehistory, *Journal de la Société Finno-Ougrienne (Suomalais-Ugrilaisen Seuran Aikakauskirja)*, 91, 9–55.

Akkermans, P. M. M. G. et al. 2010. Weathering climate change in the Near East: dating and Neolithic adaptations 8200 years ago, *Antiquity*, 84 (325), project gallery (online ed. only).

Alekseev, A. Y. et al. 2002. Some problems in the study of the chronology of the ancient nomadic cultures in Eurasia (9th-3rd centuries BC), *Geochronometria*, 21, 143–50.

Alexeeva, T. I. and Bader, N. O. (eds). 2000. *Homo Sungirensis, Upper Palaeolithic Man: Ecological and Evolutionary Aspects of the Investigation*. Moscow: Scientific World.

Alfonso-Sánchez, M. A. et al. 2008. Mitochondrial DNA haplogroup diversity in Basques: a reassessment based on HVI and HVII polymorphisms, *American Journal of Human Biology*, 20 (2), 154–64.

Allen, M. J., Gardiner, J. and Sheridan, A. (eds). 2012. *Is There a British Chalcolithic?*. Oxford and Oakville, CT: The Prehistoric Society/Oxbow Books.

Allen, T., Barclay, A. and Lamdin-Whymark, H. 2004. Opening the wood, making the land: the study of a Neolithic landscape in the Dorney area of the Middle Thames Valley, in *Towards a New Stone Age: Aspects of the Neolithic in South-east England* (CBA Research Report series 137), J. Cotton and D. Field (eds), 82–98. York: Council for British Archaeology.

Almagro-Gorbea, M. 2001. Los Celtas en la Península Ibérica, in *Celtas y Vettones: Catálogo de la exposición Internacional*, Excma. M. Almagro-Gorbea, M. Mariné and J. R. Álvarez-Sanchís (eds), 182–99. Ávila: Diputación Provincial de Ávila.

Alonso, S. et al. 2005. The place of the Basques in the European Y-chromosome diversity landscape, *European Journal of Human Genetics*, 13 (12), 1293–302.

Ammerman, A. J. and Cavalli-Sforza, L. L. 1971. Measuring the rate of spread of early farming in Europe, *Man*, new series 6 (4), 674–88.

Ammerman, A. J. and Cavalli-Sforza, L. L. 1984. *Neolithic Transition and the Genetics of Populations in Europe*. Princeton: Princeton University Press.

Ammianus Marcellinus, *Roman History*. London: Bohn. 1862.

Anati, E. 2001. *Gobustan Azerbaijan*. Capo di Ponte (Brescia): Edizioni del Centro; [S.l.]: WARA Archives.

Andersen, H. 1996. *Reconstructing Prehistorical Dialects: Initial Vowels in Slavic and Baltic* (Trends in Linguistics: Studies and Monographs 91). Berlin and New York: Mouton de Gruyter.

Andersen, H. 2003. Slavic and the Indo-European Migrations, in *Language Contacts in Prehistory: Studies in Stratigraphy. Papers from the Workshop on Linguistic Stratigraphy and Prehistory at the Fifteenth International Conference on Historical Linguistics, Melbourne, 17 August 2001* (Amsterdam Studies in the Theory and History of Linguistic Science, Series IV: Current Issues in Linguistic Theory, 239), H. Andersen (ed.), 45–76. Amsterdam and Philadelphia: John Benjamins Publishing Company.

Andersen, O. 2011. Reindeer-herding cultures in northern Nordland, Norway: methods for documenting traces of reindeer herders in the landscape and for dating reindeer-herding activities, *Quaternary International*, 238, 63–75.

Anderson, S. et al. 1981. Sequence and organization of the human mitochondrial genome, *Nature*, 290 (5806), 457–65.

Andrews, R. M. et al. 1999. Reanalysis and revision of the Cambridge reference sequence for human mitochondrial DNA, *Nature Genetics*, 23 (2), 147.

Androshchuk, F. 2008. The Vikings in the East, in Brink and Price 2008, 517–42.

Ann. Camb. Annales Cambriae, A.D. 682–954: Texts A–C in Parallel, ed. and trans. D. N. Dumville. 2002. Cambridge: Department of Anglo-Saxon, Norse and Celtic, University of Cambridge.

Annals of St-Bertin. The Annals of St-Bertin, ed. J. L. Nelson. 1991. Manchester: Manchester University Press.

Anthony, D. W. 1990. Migration in archaeology: the baby and the bathwater, *American Anthropologist*, 92 (4), 23–42.

Anthony, D. W. 1992. The bath refilled: migration in archeology, *American Anthropologist*, 94 (1), 174–76.

Anthony, D. W. 1997. Prehistoric migration as social process, in Chapman and Hamerow 1997, 21–32.

Anthony, D. W. 2007. *The Horse, the Wheel and Language: How Bronze Age Riders from the Eurasian Steppes Shaped the Modern World*. Princeton and Oxford: Princeton University Press.

Anthony, D. W. 2008. A new approach to language and archaeology: the Usatovo Culture and the separation of Pre-Germanic, *Journal of Indo-European Studies*, 36 (1–2), 1–51.

Anthony, D. W. 2013. Two IE phylogenies, three PIE migrations, and four kinds of steppe pastoralism, *Journal of Language Relationship*, 9 (2013), 1–22.

Anthony, D. W. and Chi, J. Y. (eds) 2009. *The Lost World of Old Europe: The Danube Valley, 5000–3500 BC*. New York/ Princeton: Institute for the Study of the Ancient World/Princeton University Press.

Armit, I., Swindles, G. T. and Becker, K. 2013. From dates to demography in later prehistoric Ireland? Experimental approaches to the meta-analysis of large 14C data-sets, *Journal of Archaeological Science*, 40 (1), 433–38.

Arneborg, J. 2008. The Norse settlements in Greenland, chapter 43 in Brink and Price 2008, 588–97.

Arredi, B. et al. 2004. A predominantly neolithic origin for Y-chromosomal DNA variation in north Africa, *American Journal of Human Genetics*, 75 (2), 338–45.

Arredi, B., Poloni, E. S. and Tyler-Smith, C. 2007. The peopling of Europe, chapter 13 in *Anthropological Genetics: Theory, Method and Applications*, M. Crawford (ed.), 380–408. Cambridge: Cambridge University Press.

Aubet, M. E. 2001. *The Phoenicians and the West: Politics, Colonies and Trade* (2nd ed.). Cambridge: Cambridge University Press.

Aubet, M. E. 2008. Political and economic implications of the new Phoenician chronologies, in *Beyond the Homeland: Markers in Phoenician Chronology* (Ancient Near Eastern Studies, Supplement 28), C. Sagona (ed.), 247–59.

Avienus, Rufus Festus, *Ora Maritima: A Description of the Seacoast from Brittany to Marseilles [Massilia]*, trans. J. P. Murphy. 1977. Chicago: Ares Publishing.

Ayers, B. 2011. The growth of an urban landscape: recent research in early medieval Norwich, *Early Medieval Europe*, 19 (1), 62–90.

Ayub, Q. et al. 2003. Reconstruction of human evolutionary tree using polymorphic autosomal microsatellites, *American Journal of Physical Anthropology*, 122, 259–68.

Babar, M. E. et al. 2012. Mitochondrial DNA diversity patterns in Pakistani buffalo, *Animal Genetics*, 43 (3), 315–17.

Bailey, D. W. 2000. *Balkan Prehistory: Exclusion, Incorporation and Identity*. London and New York: Routledge.

Bailey, G. and Spikins, P. (eds). 2008. *Mesolithic Europe*. Cambridge; New York: Cambridge University Press.

Bakker, E. J. (ed.) 2010. *A Companion to the Ancient Greek Language* (Blackwell Companions to the Ancient World). Malden, MA, Chichester and Oxford: Wiley-Blackwell.

Bakker, J. A., Kruk, J., Lanting, A. E. and Milisauskas, S. 1999. The earliest evidence of wheeled vehicles, *Antiquity*, 73 (282), 778–90.

Balanovsky, O. et al. 2008. Two sources of the Russian patrilineal heritage in their Eurasian context, *American Journal of Human Genetics*, 82, 236–50.

Balanovsky, O. et al. 2011. Parallel evolution of genes and languages in the Caucasus region, *Molecular Biology and Evolution*, 28 (10), 2905–20.

Balaresque, P. et al. 2010. A predominantly neolithic origin for European paternal lineages, *PLoS Biology*, 8 (1), e1000285.

Bălășescu, A. 2008. Considerații cu privire la exploatarea mamiferelor în așezarea Hamangia III de la Cheia = Considerations on the Mammals Management at Cheia (Hamangia culture), *Revista Pontica*, 41, 49–56.

Balasse, M. and Tresset, A. 2002. Early weaning of Neolithic domestic cattle revealed by intra-tooth variation in nitrogen isotope ratios (Bercy, France), *Journal of Archaeological Science*, 29, 853–59.

Baldi, P. and Page, B. R. 2006. Review: Europa Vasconica-Europa Semitica: Theo Vennemann, Gen. Nierfeld, in Patrizia Noel Aziz Hanna (ed.), Trends in Linguistics: Studies and Monographs 138, Mouton de Gruyter, Berlin, 2003. *Lingua*, 116 (12), 2183–220.

Balloux, F. 2010. Mitochondrial phylogeography: the worm in the fruit of the mitochondrial DNA tree, *Heredity*, 104, 419–20.

Balode, L. and Bušs, O. 2007. On Latvian toponyms of Finno-Ugrian origin, in *Borrowing of Place Names in the Uralian Languages* (Onomastica Uralica 4), R. L. Pitkänen and J. Saarikivi (eds), 27–43.

Bandelt, H.-J. 2005. Mosaics of ancient mitochondrial DNA: positive indicators of nonauthenticity, *European Journal of Human Genetics*, 13, 1106–12.

Banffy, E. et al. 2012. 'Early Neolithic' graves are in fact 6000 years younger – appeal for real interdisciplinarity between archaeology and ancient DNA research, *Journal of Human Genetics*, advance online publication, 7 June 2012.

Barber, D. C. et al. 1999. Forcing of the cold event of 8,200 years ago by catastrophic drainage of Laurentide lakes, *Nature*, 400, 344–48.

Barber, K. E. et al. 2004. Late Holocene climatic history of northern Germany and Denmark: peat macrofossil investigations at Dosenmoor, Schleswig-Holstein, and Svanemose, Jutland, *Boreas*, 33 (2), 132–44.

Barford, P. M. 2001. *The Early Slavs: Culture and Society in Early Medieval Eastern Europe*. London: British Museum Press; Ithaca: Cornell University Press.

Barham, L., Priestley, P. and Targett, A. 1999. *In Search of Cheddar Man*. Stroud: Tempus Publishing.

Barker, G. 2006. *The Agricultural Revolution in Prehistory: Why Did Foragers Become Farmers?* Oxford and New York: Oxford University Press.

Barnard, H. et al. 2011. Chemical evidence for wine production around 4000 BCE in the Late Chalcolithic Near Eastern highlands, *Journal of Archaeological Science*, 38 (5), 977–84.

Barnard, H. and Wendrich, W. (eds). 2008. *Archaeology of Mobility: Old World and New World Nomadism* (Cotsen Advanced Seminars 4). Los Angeles: Cotsen Institute of Archaeology Press, University of California.

Barrett, J. H. 2008. What caused the Viking Age?, *Antiquity*, 82 (317), 671–85.

Bar-Yosef, O. 1998. The Natufian culture in the Levant, threshold to the origins of agriculture, *Evolutionary Anthropology*, 6 (5), 159–77.

Bar-Yosef, O. 2007. The dispersal of modern humans in Eurasia: a cultural interpretation, chapter 18 in Mellars, Boyle, Bar-Yosef and Stringer 2007, 207–17.

Bar-Yosef, O. 2009. Social changes triggered by the Younger Dryas and the Early Holocene climate fluctuations in the Near East, chapter 9 in *The Archaeology of Environmental Change: Socionatural Legacies of Degradation and Resilience*, C. T. Fisher, J. B. Hill and G. M. Feinman (eds), 193–208. Tucson: University of Arizona Press.

Battaglia, V. et al. 2009. Y-chromosomal evidence of the cultural diffusion of agriculture in southeast Europe, *European Journal of Human Genetics*, 17 (6), 820–30.

Baudouin, S. V. et al. 2005. Mitochondrial DNA and survival after sepsis: a prospective study, *The Lancet*, 366, 2118–21.

Bayliss, A. 2009. Rolling out the revolution: using radiocarbon dating in archaeology, *Radiocarbon*, 51 (1), 123–47.

Bayliss, A., Healy, F. and Whittle, A. 2011. *Gathering Time: Dating the Early Neolithic Enclosures of Southern Britain and Ireland*. Oxford: Oxbow Books.

Bean, P. and Melville, J. 1989. *Lost Children of the Empire*. London: Unwin Hyman.

Beard, M. 2008. *Pompeii: The Life of a Roman Town*. London: Profile Books.

Beckwith, C. L. 2009. *Empires of the Silk Road: A History of Central Eurasia from the Bronze Age to the Present*. Princeton and Oxford: Princeton University Press.

Bede, *The Ecclesiastical History of the English People*. J. McClure and R. Collins (eds). 1994. Oxford and New York: Oxford University Press.

Beekes, R. S. P. 2002. The origin of the Etruscans, *Biblioteca Orientalis*, 59, 206–42.

Beets, D. J. and van der Spek, A. J. F. 2000. The Holocene evolution of the barrier and the back-barrier basins of Belgium and the Netherlands as a function of late Weichselian morphology, relative sea-level rise and sediment supply, *Netherlands Journal of Geosciences = Geologie en Mijnbouw*, 27, 3–16.

Begemann, F. et al. 2010. Lead isotope and chemical signature of copper from Oman and its occurrence in Mesopotamia and sites on the Arabian Gulf coast, *Arabian Archaeology and Epigraphy*, 21 (2), 135–69.

Behar, D. M. et al. 2012. A 'Copernican' reassessment of the human mitochondrial DNA tree from its root, *American Journal of Human Genetics*, 90 (4), 675–84.

Behistun Inscription, The, trans. H. C. Tolman. 1908. Nashville: Vanderbilt University Press.

Beja-Pereira, A. et al. 2004. African origins of the domestic donkey, *Science*, 304 (5678), 1781.

Beja-Pereira, A. et al. 2006. The origin of European cattle: evidence from modern and ancient DNA, *PNAS*, 103 (21), 8113–18.

Belfer-Cohen, A. and Goring-Morris, A. N. 2011. Becoming farmers: the inside story, *Current Anthropology*, 52, supplement 4, S209–20.

Bellwood, P. 2005. *First Farmers: The Origin of Agricultural Societies*. Malden, MA, Oxford and Carlton, Victoria: Blackwell.

Bellwood, P. and Renfrew, C. (eds). 2002. *Examining the Farming/Language Dispersal Hypothesis* (McDonald Institute Monographs). Cambridge: McDonald Institute for Archaeological Research.

Benazzi, S. et al. 2011. Early dispersal of modern humans in Europe and implications for Neanderthal behaviour, *Nature*, 479, 525–28.

Bengtson, J. D. 2011. The Basque language: history and origin, *International Journal of Modern Anthropology*, 4, 43–59.

Bentley, R. A. 2013. Mobility and the diversity of early Neolithic lives: isotopic evidence from skeletons, *Journal of Anthropological Archaeology*, 32.

Berg, I. 2008. Looking through pots: recent advances in ceramics X-radiography, *Journal of Archaeological Science*, 35, 1177–88.

Berg, I. 2009. X-radiography of Knossian Bronze Age vessels: assessing our knowledge of primary forming techniques, *Annual of the British School at Athens*, 104, 137–73.

Berger, J.-F. and Guilaine, J. 2009. The 8200 cal BP abrupt environmental change and the Neolithic transition: a Mediterranean perspective, *Quaternary International*, 200 (1–2), 31–49.

Bersaglieri, T. et al. 2004. Genetic signatures of strong recent positive selection at the lactase gene, *American Journal of Human Genetics*, 74 (6), 1111–20.

Berseneva, N. A. 2010. Sargat burial sites in the Middle Irtysh area: a gender analysis, *Archaeology, Ethnology and Anthropology of Eurasia*, 38 (3), 72–81.

Bill, J. 2008. Viking ships and the sea, chapter 11 in Brink and Price 2008, 170–80.

Bintliff, J. 2012. *The Complete Archaeology of Greece from Hunter-Gatherers to the 20th Century AD*. Malden, MA, Chichester and Oxford: Wiley-Blackwell.

Bischoff, J. L. et al. 2007. High-resolution u-series dates from the Sima de los Huesos hominids yields 600+/-66 kyrs: implications for the evolution of the early Neanderthal lineage, *Journal of Archaeological Science*, 34 (5), 763–70.

Blagg, T. F. C. and Millett, M. 1990. *The Early Roman Empire in the West*. Oxford: Oxbow Books.

Blasco Ferrer, E. 2011. A new approach to the Mediterranean substratum, with an appendix of Paleo-Sardinian microtoponyms, *Romance Philology*, 65 (1), 43–85.

Blažek, V. 1999. Elam: a bridge between Ancient Near East and Dravidian India?, chapter 2 in *Archaeology and Language IV: Language Change and Cultural Transformation*, R. Blench and M. Spriggs (eds), 48–78. London and New York: Routledge.

Blažek, V. 2005. On the internal classification of Indo-European languages: survey, *Linguistica online*.

Blench, R. 2008. Re-evaluating the linguistic prehistory of South Asia, in *Occasional Paper 3: Linguistics, Archaeology and the Human Past*, T. Osada and A. Uesugi (eds), 159–78. Kyoto: Indus Project, Research Institute for Humanity and Nature.

Blum, M. G. B. and Jakobsson, M. 2011. Deep divergences of human gene trees and models of human origins, *Molecular Biology and Evolution*, 28 (2), 889–98.

Boattini, A. et al. 2011. Linking Italy and the Balkans: a Y-chromosome perspective from the Arbereshe of Calabria, *Annals of Human Biology*, 38 (1), 59–68.

Bocquet-Appel, J.-P. 2011. When the world's population took off: the springboard of the Neolithic demographic transition, *Science*, 333 (6042), 560–61.

Bocquet-Appel, J.-P., Demars, P.-Y., Noiret, L. and Dobrowsky, D. 2005. Estimates of Upper Palaeolithic meta-population size in Europe from archaeological data, *Journal of Archaeological Science*, 32 (11), 1656–68.

Bocquet-Appel, J.-P., Naji, S., Vander Linden, M. and Kozlowski, J. K. 2009. Detection of diffusion and contact zones of early farming in Europe from the space-time distribution of 14C dates, *Journal of Archaeological Science*, 36, 807–20.

Bocquet-Appel, J.-P., Naji, S., Vander Linden, M., Kozlowski, J. K. 2012. Understanding the rates of expansion of the farming system in Europe, *Journal of Archaeological Science*, 39 (2), 531–46.

Bogucki, P. 1993. Animal traction and household economies in Neolithic Europe, *Antiquity*, 67 (256), 492–503.

Bogucki, P. 2004. Late Bronze Age Urnfields of Central Europe, in Bogucki and Crabtree 2004, vol. 2, 86–91.

Bogucki, P. and Crabtree, P. J. (eds). 2004. *Ancient Europe 8000 BC–AD 1000: Encyclopedia of the Barbarian World*, 2 vols. Farmington, MI: Charles Scribner's & Sons.

Bollongino, R. et al. 2006. Early history of European domestic cattle as revealed by ancient DNA, *Biology Letters*, 2 (1), 155–59.

Bollongino, R. et al. 2008. Y-SNPs do not indicate hybridisation between European aurochs and domestic cattle, *PLoS ONE*, 3 (10), e3418.

Bollongino, R. et al. 2012. Modern Taurine cattle descended from small number of Near-Eastern founders, *Molecular Biology and Evolution*, 29 (9), 2101–04.

Bonfante, G. and Bonfante, L. 2002. *The Etruscan Language* (2nd ed.). Manchester: Manchester University Press.

Bonfiglio, S. et al. 2012. Origin and spread of *Bos taurus*: new clues from mitochondrial genomes belonging to haplogroup T1, *PLoS ONE*, 7 (6), e38601.

Bonsall, C. et al. 2002. Climate change and the adoption of agriculture in North-West Europe, *European Journal of Archaeology*, 5 (1), 9–23.

Bonsall, C., Boroneant, V. and Radovanovic, I. (eds). 2008. *The Iron Gates in Prehistory: New Perspectives* (BAR International Series 1893). Oxford: Archaeopress.

Borić, D. and Price, T. D. 2013. Strontium isotopes document greater human mobility at the start of the Balkan Neolithic, *PNAS*, 110 (9), 3298–303.

Børsheim, R. L. 1997. Nye undersøkelser av Gauseldronningens grav, *Fra haug ok heidni*, 4.

Børsheim, R. L. 2000. Short notice of a recent Viking find in Norway, *Viking Heritage*, 1, 22.

Bos, K. I. et al. 2011. A draft genome of *Yersinia pestis* from victims of the Black Death, *Nature*, 478 (7370), 506–10.

Bouakaze, C. et al. 2007. First successful assay of Y-SNP typing by SNaPshot minisequencing on ancient DNA, *International Journal of Legal Medicine*, 121, 493–99.

Bouakaze, C. et al. 2009. Pigment phenotype and biogeographical ancestry from ancient skeletal remains: inferences from multiplexed autosomal SNP analysis, *International Journal of Legal Medicine*, 123, 315–25.

Bouwman, A. S. et al. 2008. Kinship between burials from Grave Circle B at Mycenae revealed by ancient DNA typing, *Journal of Archaeological Science*, 35 (9), 2580–84.

Bouzek, J. 2001. Cimmerians and early Scythians: the transition from geometric to orientalising style in the Pontic area, in *North Pontic Archaeology: Recent Discoveries and Studies* (Colloquia Pontica 6), G. R. Tsetskhladze (ed.), 33–44. Leiden, Boston and Köln: Brill.

Bowden, G. R. et al. 2007. Excavating past population structures by surname-based sampling: the genetic legacy of the Vikings in Northwest England, *Molecular Biology and Evolution*, 25 (2), 301–09.

Boyle, A. 2004. Riding into history, *British Archaeology*, 76, 22–27.

Boyle, A. et al. 2007, Site D (Ferry Fryston) in the Iron Age and Romano-British periods, in *The Archaeology of the A1 (M) Darrington to Dishforth Road Scheme*. F. Brown et al., 43–159. Lancaster: Oxford Archaeology North.

Bradley, G. 2000. *Ancient Umbria: State, Culture, and Identity in Central Italy from the Iron Age to the Augustan Era*. Oxford: Oxford University Press.

Braidwood, R. J. et al. 1974. Beginnings of village-farming communities in southeastern Turkey, *PNAS*, 71 (2), 568–72.

Bramanti, B. 2008. Ancient DNA: genetic analysis of aDNA from sixteen skeletons of the Vedrovice, *Anthropologie*, 46 (2–3), 153–60.

Bramanti, B. et al. 2009. Genetic discontinuity between local hunter-gatherers and Central Europe's first farmers, *Science*, 326 (5949), 137–40.

Brather, S. 2004. The beginnings of Slavic settlement east of the river Elbe, *Antiquity*, 78 (300), 314–29.

Brauer, A. et al. 2008. An abrupt wind shift in western Europe at the onset of the Younger Dryas cold period, *Nature Geoscience*, 1, 520–23.

Braun, T. 2004. Hecataeus' knowledge of the western Mediterranean, in *Greek Identity in the Western Mediterranean*. K. Lomas (ed.), 285–347. Leiden: Brill.

Breunig, P. 1996. The 8000-year-old dugout canoe from Dufuna (NE Nigeria), in *Aspects of African Archaeology: Papers from the 10th Congress of the PanAfrican Association for Prehistory and Related Studies*. G. Pwiti and R. Soper (eds), 461–68. Harare: University of Zimbabwe Publications.

Brink, S. 2008. Who were the Vikings? in Brink and Price 2008, 4–7.

Brink, S. 2008b. Slavery in the Viking Age, chapter 5 in Brink and Price 2008, 49–56.

Brink, S. and Price, N. (eds). 2008. *The Viking World*. London and New York: Routledge.

Briquel, D. 1973. À propos du nom des Ombriens, Mélanges de l'École française de Rome. *Antiquité*, 85 (2), 357–93.

Broadbent, N. D. 2006. The search for a past: the prehistory of the indigenous Saami in northern coastal Sweden, in *People, Material Culture and Environment in the North: Proceedings of the 22nd Nordic Archaeological Conference, University of Oulu, 18–23 August 2004*. V.-P. Herva (ed.), 13–25. Oulu: University of Oulu.

Broodbank, C. 2000. *An Island Archaeology of the Early Cyclades*. Cambridge: Cambridge University Press.

Brotherton, P. et al 2013. Neolithic mitochondrial haplogroup H genomes and the genetic origins of Europeans, *Nature Communications*, 4, no. 1764.

Brun, P. 2006. L'origine des Celtes: Communautés linguistiques et réseaux sociaux, in *Celtes et Gaulois, l'archéologie face à l'histoire: 2: la Préhistoire des Celtes, Actes de la table ronde de Bologne-Monterenzio, 28–29 mai 2005*. D. Vitali (ed.), 29–44. Glux-en-Glenne: Bibracte.

Buko, A. 2005. Unknown revolution: archaeology and the beginnings of the Polish state, in *East Central & Eastern Europe in the Early Middle Ages*, F. Curta (ed.), 162–78. Ann Arbor: University of Michigan Press.

Buko, A. 2008. *The Archaeology of Early Medieval Poland: Discoveries – Hypotheses – Interpretations* (East Central and Eastern Europe in the Middle Ages, 450–1450, vol. 1). Leiden: Brill.

Büntgen, U. et al. 2011. 2500 years of European climate variability and human susceptibility, *Science*, 331 (6017), 578–82.

Burgarella, C. and Navascués, M. 2011. Mutation rate estimates for 110 Y-chromosome STRs combining population and father–son pair data, *European Journal of Human Genetics*, 19, 70–75.

Burger, J. et al. 2007. Absence of the lactase-persistence-associated allele in early Neolithic Europeans, *PNAS*, 104 (10), 3736–41.

Burgess, C. and Shennan, S. 1976. The Beaker Phenomenon: some suggestions, in *Settlement and Economy in the Third and Second Millennia BC: Papers Delivered at a Conference Organised by the Department of Adult Education, University of Newcastle upon Tyne* (BAR 33), C. Burgess and R. Miket (eds), 309–31.

Burnham, B. C. and Wacher, J. 1990. *The Small Towns of Roman Britain*. Berkeley and Los Angeles: University of California Press.

Burov, G. M. 1989. Some Mesolithic wooden artifacts from the site of Vis I in the European North East of the U.S.S.R, in *The Mesolithic in Europe*. C. Bonsall (ed.), 391–401. Edinburgh: John Donald.

Busby, G. B. J. et al. 2012. The peopling of Europe and the cautionary tale of Y chromosome lineage R-M269, *PRS B*, 279 (1730), 884–92.

Buxó, R. 2008. The agricultural consequences of colonial contacts on the Iberian Peninsula in the first millennium B.C., *Vegetation History and Archaeobotany*, 17 (1), 145–54.

Buxó, R. 2009. Botanical and archaeological dimensions of the colonial encounter, chapter 6 in Dietler and López-Ruiz 2009, 153–66.

Byrd, B. F. 1994. Public and private, domestic and corporate: the emergence of the southwest Asian village, *American Antiquity*, 59 (4), 639–66.

Byrne, F. J. 2001. *Irish Kings and High-Kings* (2nd ed.). Dublin: Four Courts Press.

Byrne, F. J. 2005. The Viking age, chapter 16 in Ó Cróinín 2005, 609–29.

Caesar. *The Conquest of Gaul*, trans. S. A. Handford, rev. J. F. Gardner. 1982. London and New York: Penguin Books.

Cai, D. et al. 2011. Early history of Chinese domestic sheep indicated by ancient DNA analysis of Bronze Age individuals, *Journal of Archaeological Science*, 38 (4), 896–902.

Caldwell, J. C. 2006. *Demographic Transition Theory*. Dordrecht: Springer.

Campbell, J. (ed.) 1982. *The Anglo-Saxons*. London and New York: Penguin Books.

Capelli, C. et al. 2003. A Y chromosome census of the British Isles, *Current Biology*, 13, 979–84.

Caramelli, D. et al. 2008. A 28,000 years old Cro-Magnon mtDNA sequence differs from all potentially contaminating modern sequences, *PloS ONE*, 3 (3), e2700.

Carling, G., Pinault, G.-J. and Winter, W. 2009. *Dictionary and Thesaurus of Tocharian A, Volume 1: A–J*. Wiesbaden: Harrassowitz Verlag.

Carozza, L. and Mille, B. 2007. Chalcolithique et complexification sociale: quelle place pour le métal dans la définition du processus de mutation des sociétés de la fin du Néolithique en France? in *Le Chalcolithique et la construction des inégalités, 1, Le continent européen*, J. Guilaine (ed.), 195–232. Paris: Editions Errance.

Carpelan, C. 2001. Late Palaeolithic and Mesolithic settlement of the European north – possible linguistic implications, chapter 2 in Carpelan, Parpola and Koskikalio 2001, 37–53.

Carpelan, C., Parpola, A. and Koskikalio, P. (eds). 2001. *Early Contacts between Uralic and Indo-European: Linguistic and Archaeological Considerations. Papers Presented at an International Symposium Held at the Tvärminne Research Station of the University of Helsinki, 8–10 January 1999* (Mémoires de la Société Finno-Ougrienne 242). Helsinki: Finno-Ugrian Society.

Carter, S. and Hunter, F. 2003. An Iron Age chariot burial from Scotland, *Antiquity*, 77 (297), 531–35.

Cassiodorus. *The Letters of Cassiodorus being a Condensed Translation of the Variae Epistolae of Magnus Aurelius Cassiodorus Senator*, trans. T. Hodgkin. 1886. London: Henry Frowde.

Cassius Dio. *Roman History*, trans. E. Cary. 1914–27. 9 vols (Loeb Classical Library). Cambridge, MA: Harvard University Press.

Castañeda, I. S. et al. 2009. Wet phases in the Sahara/ Sahel region and human migration patterns in north Africa, *PNAS*, 106 (48), 20159–63.

Caulfield, S., O'Donnell, R. G. and Mitchell, P. I. 1998. 14C dating of a neolithic field system at Céide fields, County Mayo, Ireland, *Radiocarbon*, 40 (2), 629–40.

Chapman, J. and Hamerow, H. (eds). 1997. *Migrations and Invasions in Archaeological Explanation* (BAR International Series 664). Oxford: Archaeopress.

Charvát, P. 2002. *Mesopotamia Before History*. London and New York: Routledge.

Chernykh, E. 2008. The 'steppe belt' of stock-breeding cultures in Eurasia during the Early Metal Age, *Trabajos de Prehistoria*, 65 (2), 73–93.

Chernykh, E. N. and Orlovskaya, L. B. 2004. The radiocarbon chronology of the Pit-Grave (Yamnaya) community and the emergence of the Kurgan Cultures, *Rossijskaâ arheologiâ*, 1, 84–99.

Chessa, B. et al. 2009. Revealing the history of sheep domestication using retrovirus integrations, *Science*, 324, 532–36.

Chiaradia, M., Gallay, A. and Todt, W. 2003. Different contamination styles of prehistoric human teeth at a Swiss necropolis (Sion, Valais) inferred from lead and strontium isotopes, *Applied Geochemistry*, 18, 353–70.

Chiaroni, J. et al. 2010. The emergence of Y-chromosome haplogroup J1e among Arabic-speaking populations, *European Journal of Human Genetics*, 18, 348–53.

Chiaroni, J., Underhill, P. and Cavalli-Sforza, L. L. 2009. Y chromosome diversity, human expansion, drift and cultural evolution, *PNAS*, 106 (48), 20174–79.

Childe, V. G. 1929. *The Danube in Prehistory*. Oxford: Clarendon Press.

Childe, V. G. 1930. *The Bronze Age*. London and New York: Cambridge University Press.

Chilvers, E. R. 2008. Ancient DNA in human bones from Neolithic and Bronze Age sites in Greece and Crete, *Journal of Archaeological Science*, 35 (10), 2707–14.

Chmielewski, T. and Gardyńsk, L. 2010. New frames of archaeometrical description of spindle whorls: a case study of the late Eneolithic spindle whorls from the 1C site in Gródek, district of Hrubieszów, Poland, *Archaeometry*, 52 (5), 869–81.

Christensen, A. S. 2002. *Cassiodorus, Jordanes and the History of the Goths: Studies in a Migration Myth*.

Copenhagen: Museum Tusculanum Press, University of Copenhagen.

Ciugudean, H. 2011. Mounds and mountains: burial rituals in Early Bronze Age Transylvania, in *Bronze Age Rites and Rituals in the Carpathian Basin: Proceedings of the International Colloquium from Târgu Mureş 8–10 October 2010*. S. Berecki, R. E. Németh and B. Rezi (eds), 21–57. Târgu Mureş: Editora Mega.

Clare, L. et al. 2008. Warfare in Late Neolithic/Early Chalcolithic Pisidia, southwestern Turkey: climate induced social unrest in the late 7th millennium cal BC, *Documenta Praehistorica*, 35, 65–92.

Clark, G. 1971. *World Prehistory in New Perspective*. Cambridge: Cambridge University Press.

Clark, H. and Ambrosiani, B. 1995. *Towns in the Viking Age* (2nd ed.). Leicester: Leicester University Press.

Clark, J. G. D. 1966. Invasion hypothesis in British Archaeology, *Antiquity*, 40 (159), 172–89.

Cochran, G. and Harpending, H. 2009. *The 10,000 Year Explosion: How Civilization Accelerated Human Evolution*. New York: Basic Books.

Coldham, P. W. 1992. *Emigrants in Chains: A social history of forced emigration to the Americas of felons, destitute children, political and religious non-conformists, vagabonds, beggars and other undesirables 1607–1776*. Baltimore: Genealogical Publishing Company.

Coleman, J. E. 2000. An archaeological scenario for the coming of the Greeks ca. 3200 B.C., *The Journal of Indo-European Studies*, 28, 101–53.

Collard, M., Edinborough, K., Shennan, S. and Thomas, M. G. 2010. Radiocarbon evidence indicates that migrants introduced farming to Britain, *Journal of Archaeological Science*, 37 (4), 866–70.

Collingwood, R. G. and Wright, R. P. 1965. *The Roman Inscriptions of Britain*. Oxford: Clarendon Press.

Comrie, B., Matthews, S. and Polinsky, M. 2003. *The Atlas of Languages: The Origin and Development of Languages Throughout the World* (Facts on File Library of Language and Literature) (rev. ed.). New York: Facts on File.

Conard, N. J., Malina, M. and Münzel, S. C. 2009. New flutes document the earliest musical tradition in southwestern Germany, *Nature*, 460, 737–40.

Confession of St. Patrick, The, trans. J. Skinner. 1998. New York: Doubleday Religious Publishing Group.

Conolly, J. et al. 2011. Meta-analysis of zooarchaeological data from SW Asia and SE Europe provides insight into the origins and spread of animal husbandry, *Journal of Archaeological Science*, 38 (3), 485–754.

Cooper, A. and Poinar, H. N. 2000. Ancient DNA: do it right or not at all, *Science*, 289, 1139.

Copley, M. S. et al. 2003. Direct chemical evidence for widespread dairying in prehistoric Britain, *PNAS*, 100 (4), 1524–29.

Cortés Sánchez, M. et al. 2012. The Mesolithic–Neolithic transition in southern Iberia, *Quaternary Research*, 77 (2), 221–34.

Counihan, M. 2009. An Etruscan solution to a Celtic problem, paper read at 'Edward Lhuyd' International Conference on Language, Literature, Antiquities and Science, Aberystwyth, UK, 30 June–03 July 2009.

Coupland, S. 1998. From poachers to gamekeepers:

Scandinavian warlords and Carolingian kings, *Early Medieval Europe*, 7 (1), 85–114.

Coward, F. et al. 2008. The spread of Neolithic plant economies from the Near East to Northwest Europe: a phylogenetic analysis, *Journal of Archaeological Science*, 35 (1), 42–56.

Cox, M. and Mays, S. 2000. *Human Osteology in Archaeology and Forensic Science*. London: Greenwich Medical Media.

Craig, O. E. et al. 2005. Did the first farmers of central and eastern Europe produce dairy foods? *Antiquity*, 79, 882–94.

Craig, O. E. et al. 2011. Ancient lipids reveal continuity in culinary practices across the transition to agriculture in Northern Europe, *PNAS*, 108 (44), 17910–15.

Crinion, J. et al. 2006. Language control in the bilingual brain, *Science*, 312 (5779), 1537–40.

Crombé, P. 2010. Contact and interaction between early farmers and late hunter-gatherers in Belgium during the 6th and 5th millennium cal BC, in *Die Neolithisierung Mitteleuropas: The Spread of the Neolithic to Central Europe: International Symposium, Mainz 24 June–26 June 2005* (RGZM – Tagungen Band 4), D. Gronenborn and J. Petrasch (eds), 551–65. Mainz: RGZM.

Croucher, K. 2012. *Death and Dying in the Neolithic Near East*. Oxford: Oxford University Press.

Cruciani, F. et al. 2007. Tracing past human male movements in Northern/Eastern Africa and Western Eurasia: new clues from Y-chromosomal haplogroups E-M78 and J-M12, *Molecular Biology and Evolution*, 24 (6), 1300–11.

Cruciani, F. et al. 2010. Human Y chromosome haplogroup R-V88: a paternal genetic record of early mid-Holocene trans-Saharan connections and the spread of Chadic languages, *European Journal of Human Genetics*, 18, 800–07.

Cruciani, F., Trombetta, B., Antonelli, C. et al. 2011. Strong intra- and inter-continental differentiation revealed by Y chromosome SNPs M269, U106 and U152, *Forensic Science International: Genetics*, 5 (3), e49–52.

Cruciani, F. Trombetta, B., Massaia, A. et al. 2011. A revised root for the human Y chromosomal phylogenetic tree: the origin of patrilineal diversity in Africa, *American Journal of Human Genetics*, 88 (6), 814–18.

Csányi, B. et al. 2008. Y-chromosome analysis of ancient Hungarian and two modern Hungarian-speaking populations from the Carpathian Basin, *Annals of Human Genetics*, 72 (4), 519–34.

Csepeli, G. and Orkeny, A. 1996. The changing facets of Hungarian nationalism - nationalism reexamined, *Social Research*, 63, 247–86.

Čufar, K., Kromer, B., Tolar, T. and Velušček, A. 2010. Dating of 4th millennium BC pile-dwellings on Ljubljansko barje, Slovenia, *Journal of Archaeological Science*, 37, 2031–39.

Cunliffe, B. 1997. *The Ancient Celts*. Oxford: Oxford University Press.

Cunliffe, B. 2001. *The Extraordinary Voyage of Pytheas the Greek*. London: Allen Lane/Penguin Press.

Cunliffe, B. 2003. *The Celts: A Very Short Introduction*. Oxford: Oxford University Press.

Cunliffe, B. 2008. *Europe Between the Oceans: Themes and Variations: 9000 BC–AD 1000*. New Haven and London: Yale University Press.

Cunliffe, B. and Koch, J. T. (eds). 2010. *Celtic from the West: Alternative Perspectives from Archaeology, Genetics, Languages and Literature* (Celtic Studies Publications 15). Oxford: Oxbow Books.

Curchin, L. 1997. Celticization and Romanization of toponymy in Central Spain, *Emerita*, 65, 257–79.

Curchin, L. 2009. Toponimia antigua de Contestania y Edetania, *Lucentum*, 28, 69–74.

Currat, M. 2012. Consequences of population expansions on European genetic diversity, in Kaiser, Burger and Schier 2012, 3-15.

Currie, T. E. and Mace, R. 2009. Political complexity predicts the spread of ethnolinguistic groups, *PNAS*, 106 (18), 7339–44.

Curta, F. 2001. Pots, Slavs and imagined communities: Slavic archaeologies and the history of the Early Slavs, *European Journal of Archaeology*, 4 (3), 367–84.

Curta, F. 2002. From Kossina to Bromley: ethnogenesis in Slavic archaeology, in *On Barbarian Identity: Critical Approaches to Ethnicity in the Early Middle Ages* (Studies in the Early Middle Ages 4), A. Gillett (ed.), 201–18. Turnhout, Belgium: Brepols.

Czebreszuk, J. and Szmyt, M. (eds). 2003. *The Northeast Frontier of Bell Beakers: Proceedings of the Symposium held at the Adam Mickiewicz University, Poznań (Poland), May 26–29 2002* (Oxford: BAR International Series 1155).

Czekaj-Zastawny, A. et. al. 2011. Long-distance exchange in the Central European Neolithic: Hungary to the Baltic, *Antiquity*, 85 (327), 43–58.

Dalton, R. 2010. Neanderthals may have interbred with humans, *Nature News*, online 20 April 2010.

Davis, R. C. 2004. *Christian Slaves, Muslim Masters: White Slavery in the Mediterranean, the Barbary Coast and Italy, 1500–1800* (Early Modern History: Society and Culture). Basingstoke and New York: Palgrave Macmillan.

Davis, R. C. 2009. *Holy War and Human Bondage: Tales of Christian-Muslim slavery in the Early-Modern Mediterranean*. (Praeger Series on the Early Modern World). Santa Barbara, Denver, Oxford: Praeger Publishers.

De Beule, H. 2011. Origin, migrations and expansion of haplogroup I-L38 in relation to haplogroup R1b, *The Russian Journal of Genetic Genealogy*, 2 (1), 10–30.

Decker, J. E. et al. 2009. Resolving the evolution of extant and extinct ruminants with high-throughput phylogenomics, *PNAS*, 106 (44), 18644–49.

Dediu, D. and Levison, S. C. 2012. Abstract profiles of structural stability point to universal tendencies, family-specific factors, and ancient connections between languages, *PLoS ONE*, 7 (9), e45198.

DeGiorgio, M., Jakobsson, M. and Rosenberg, N. A. 2009. Explaining worldwide patterns of human genetic variation using a coalescent-based serial founder model of migration outward from Africa, *PNAS*, 106 (38), 16057–62.

Deguilloux, M.-F. et al. 2011. News from the west: ancient DNA from a French megalithic burial chamber, *American Journal of Physical Anthropology*, 144 (1), 108–18.

Deguilloux, M.-F. et al. 2011b. Analysis of ancient human DNA and primer contamination: one step backward one step forward, *Forensic Science International*, 210 (1–3), 102–09.

della Casa, P. 1995. The Cetina group and the transition from Copper to Bronze Age in Dalmatia, *Antiquity*, 69 (264), 565–76.

Delsate, D. et al. 2009. De l'ocre sur le crâne mésolithique (haplogroupe U5a) de Reuland-Loschbour (Grand-Duché de Luxembourg), *Bulletin de la Société Préhistorique Luxembourgeoise*, 31, 7–30.

Dennell, R. and Petraglia, M. D. 2012. The dispersal of *Homo sapiens* across southern Asia: how early, how often, how complex?, *Quaternary Science Reviews*, 47, 15–22.

Derenko, M. et al. 2007. Y-chromosome haplogroup N dispersals from south Siberia to Europe, *Journal of Human Genetics*, 52 (9), 763–70.

Derenko, M. et al. 2010. Origin and post-glacial dispersal of mitochondrial DNA haplogroups C and D in Northern Asia, *PLoS ONE*, 5 (12), e15214.

d'Errico, F. et al. 2012. Early evidence of San material culture represented by organic artifacts from Border Cave, South Africa, *PNAS*, 109 (33), 13214–19.

Der Sarkissian, C. A. I. 2011. Mitochondrial DNA in ancient human populations of Europe. PhD, thesis, University of Adelaide.

Der Sarkissian, C. et al. 2013. Ancient DNA reveals prehistoric gene-flow from Siberia in the complex human population history of north-east Europe, *PloS Genetics*, 9 (2), e1003296.

Deshpande, O., Batzoglou, S., Feldman, M. W. and Cavalli-Sforza, L. L. 2009. A serial founder effect model for human settlement out of Africa, *PRS B*, 276, 291–300.

Desideri, J. and Besse, M. 2010. Swiss Bell Beaker population dynamics: eastern or southern influences?, *Archaeological and Anthropological Sciences*, 2 (3), 157–73.

Diamond, J. and Bellwood, P. 2003. Farmers and their languages: the first expansions, *Science*, 300 (5619), 597–603.

Díaz-del-Río, P. 2011. Labor in the making of Iberian Copper Age lineages, chapter 4 in *Comparative Archaeologies: The American Southwest (AD 900–1600) and the Iberian Peninsula (3000–1500 BC)*, K. T. Lillios (ed.), 37–56. Oxford and Oakville, CT: Oxbow.

Díaz-Guardamino, M. 2011. Iconografía, lugares y relaciones sociales: Reflexiones en torno a las estelas y estátuas-menhir atribuidas a la Edad del Bronce en la Península Ibérica, in *Estelas e Estátuas-menir: da Pré à Proto-história, Actas IV Jornadas Raianas, Museu do Sabugal, 23–24 de Octubre de 2009*, R. Vilaça (ed.), 63–88.

Di Benedetto, G. et al. 2000. Mitochondrial DNA sequences in prehistoric human remains from the Alps, *European Journal of Human Genetics*, 8, 669–77.

Dietler, M. and López-Ruiz, C. (eds). 2009. *Colonial Encounters in Ancient Iberia: Phoenician, Greek, and Indigenous Relations*. Chicago: University of Chicago Press.

Di Gaetano, C. et al. 2009. Differential Greek and northern African migrations to Sicily are supported by genetic evidence from the Y chromosome, *European Journal of Human Genetics*, 17, 91–99.

Di Gaetano, C. et al. 2012. An overview of the genetic structure within the Italian population from genome-wide data, *PLoS ONE*, 7 (9), e43759.

Dillon, M. and Chadwick, N. 1967. *The Celtic Realms*. London: Weidenfeld and Nicolson

Diodorus Siculus. *The Library of History*. 1933–67. 12 vols (Loeb Classical Library). Cambridge, MA: Harvard University Press.

Dirksen, V. G. et al. 2007. Chronology of Holocene climate and vegetation changes and their connection to cultural dynamics in Southern Siberia, *Radiocarbon*, 49 (2), 1103–21.

Dixon, R. M. W. 1997. *The Rise and Fall of Languages*. Cambridge: Cambridge University Press.

Dodson, J. et al. 2009. Early bronze in two Holocene archaeological sites in Gansu, NW China, *Quaternary Research*, 72 (3), 309–14.

Dolukhanov, P. M. 2003. Hunter-gatherers of the Last Ice Age in northern Eurasia: recent research and old problems, *Before Farming: the archaeology and anthropology of hunter-gatherers* (online journal), 2003 (2), 2.

Dolukhanov, P. et al. 2005. The chronology of Neolithic dispersal in Central and Eastern Europe, *Journal of Archaeological Science*, 32 (10), 1441–58.

Downham, C. 2008. *Viking Kings of Britain and Ireland: The Dynasty of Ívarr to A.D. 1014*. Edinburgh: Dunedin Academic Press.

Downham, C. 2009. The Viking slave trade, *History Ireland*, 17 (3), 15–17.

Drake, B. L. 2012. The influence of climatic change on the Late Bronze Age collapse and the Greek Dark Ages, *Journal of Archaeological Science*, 29 (6), 1862–70.

Drews, R. 2004. *Early Riders: The Beginnings of Mounted Warfare in Asia and Europe*. London and New York: Routledge.

Dreyer, G. 1998. *Umm El-Quaab I – Das pradynastische Konigsgrab U-j und seine fruhen Schriftzeugnisse* (Deutsches Archäologisches Institute Abteilung Kairo: Archäologische Veröffentlichungen 86). Mainz: Philipp von Zabern.

Drineas, P., Lewis, J. and Paschou, P. 2010. Inferring geographic coordinates of origin for Europeans using small panels of ancestry informative markers, *PLoS ONE*, 5 (8), e11892.

Dudo. Dudo of St Quentin, *Gesta Normannorum*, trans. Felice Lifshitz. 1996. ORB Online Library.

Duncan-Jones, R. P. 2004. Economic change and the transition to Late Antiquity, chapter 2 in *Approaching Late Antiquity: The Transformation from Early to Late Empire*, S. Swain and M. Edwards (eds), 20–52. Oxford and New York: Oxford University Press.

Dyson, S. L. and Rowland, R. J. 2007. *Archaeology and History in Sardinia from the Stone Age to the Middle Ages: Shepherds, Sailors, and Conquerors*. Philadelphia: University of Pennsylvania Museum of Archaeology.

Dzino, D. 2010. *Becoming Slav, Becoming Croat: Identity Transformations in Post-Roman and Early Medieval Dalmatia* (East Central and Eastern Europe in the Middle Ages, 450–1450, vol. 12). Leiden: Brill.

Earle, T. and Kristiansen, K. (eds). 2010. *Organising Bronze Age Societies: The Mediterranean, Central Europe, and Scandinavia Compared.* Cambridge and New York: Cambridge University Press.

Ebenesersdóttir, S. S. et al. 2011. A new subclade of mtDNA haplogroup C1 found in Icelanders: evidence of pre-Columbian contact?, *American Journal of Physical Anthropology*, 144 (1), 92–99.

Eckardt, H. (ed.) 2010. *Roman Diasporas: Archaeological Approaches to Mobility and Diversity in the Roman Empire* (Journal of Roman Archaeology, Supplement 78). Portsmouth, RI.

Economou, C., Kjellström, A., Lidén, K. and Panagopoulos, I. 2013. Ancient-DNA reveals an Asian type of *Mycobacterium leprae* in medieval Scandinavia, *Journal of Archaeological Science*, 40 (1), 465–70.

Edwards, C. J. et al. 2004. Ancient DNA analysis of 101 cattle remains: limits and prospects, *Journal of Archaeological Science*, 31 (6), 695–710.

Edwards, C. J. et al. 2011. Dual origins of dairy cattle farming – evidence from a comprehensive survey of European Y-chromosomal variation, *PLoS ONE*, 6 (1), e15922.

EHD 1: English Historical Documents, vol. 1: c. 500–1042, D. Whitelock (ed.). 1955.

El-Sibai, M. et al. 2009. Geographical structure of the Y-chromosomal genetic landscape of the Levant: a coastal-inland contrast, *Annals of Human Genetics*, 73 (6), 568–81.

Enattah, N. S. et al. 2002. Identification of a variant associated with adult-type hypolactasia, *Nature Genetics*, 30 (2), 233–37.

Enattah, N. S. et al. 2007. Evidence of still-ongoing convergence evolution of the lactase persistence T-13910 alleles in humans, *American Journal of Human Genetics*, 81 (3), 615–25.

Enattah, N. S. et al. 2008. Independent introduction of two lactase-persistence alleles into human populations reflects different history of adaptation to milk culture, *American Journal of Human Genetics*, 82 (1), 57–72.

Endicott, P. et al. 2009. Genotyping human ancient mtDNA control and coding region polymorphisms with a multiplexed single-base-extension assay: the singular maternal history of the Tyrolean Iceman, *BMC Genetics*, 10 (29).

Ennafaa, H. et al. 2009. Mitochondrial DNA haplogroup H structure in North Africa, *BMC Genetics*, 10 (8).

Erdem, Y. H. 1996. *Slavery in the Ottoman Empire and its Demise, 1800–1909.* Basingstoke: Macmillan Press in association with St Antony's College, Oxford.

Eriksson, A. and Manica, A. et al. 2012. Effect of ancient population structure on the degree of polymorphism shared between modern human populations and ancient hominins, *PNAS*, 109 (35), 13956–60.

Erlij, V. 1993. The archaeological evidences of the early period of military contacts between the Black Sea north littoral and the ancient east and the 'Cimmerian problem', *CuPAUAM*, 20, 133–45.

Ermini, L. et al. 2008. Complete mitochondrial genome sequence of the Tyrolean Iceman, *Current Biology*, 18 (21), 1687–93.

Eska, J. F. and Ringe, D. 2004. Recent work in computational linguistic phylogeny, *Language*, 80 (3), 569–82.

Evans, J. A., Chenery, C. A. and Fitzpatrick, A. P. 2006. Bronze Age childhood migration of individuals near Stonehenge, revealed by strontium and oxygen isotope tooth enamel analysis, *Archaeometry*, 48 (2), 309–21.

Evershed, R. P. et al. 2008. Earliest date for milk use in the Near East and southeastern Europe linked to cattle herding, *Nature*, 455, 528–31.

Faerman, M. et al. 2007. Molecular archaeology: people, animals, and plants of the Holy Land, *Israel Journal of Earth Science*, 56, 217–30.

Fagan, B. 2000. *The Little Ice Age: How Climate Made History 1300–1850.* New York: Basic Books.

Farajova, M. 2011. Gobustan Rock Art Cultural Landscape, *Adoranten*, 41–66.

Farrokhi, J. et al. 2011. Evaluation of genetic diversity among Iranian apple (*Malus × domestica* Borkh.) cultivars and landraces using simple sequence repeat markers, *Australian Journal of Crop Science*, 5 (7), 815–21.

Fellows-Jensen, G. 2008. Scandinavian place-names in the British Isles, chapter 28 in Brink and Price 2008, 391–400.

Ferguson, R. 2009. *The Hammer and the Cross: A New History of the Vikings.* London: Allen Lane/Penguin Books.

Fernández, E. et al. 2008. Mitochondrial DNA genetic relationships at the ancient Neolithic site of Tell Halula, *Forensic Science International: Genetics Supplement Series*, 1 (1), 271–73.

Fernández Domínguez, E. 2005. Polimorfismos de DNA mitocondrial en poblaciones antiguas de la cuenca mediterránea. PhD thesis, Universitat de Barcelona.

Ferrara, S. 2010. Mycenaean texts: the Linear B Tablets, chapter 2 in Bakker 2010, 12–15.

Ferreira, S. D. 2003. Os copos no povoado Calcolítico de Vila Nova de São Pedro, *Revista Portuguesa de Arqueologia*, 6 (2), 181–228.

Ferris, D. G., Cole-Dai, J., Reyes, A. R. and Budner, D. M. 2011. South Pole ice core record of explosive volcanic eruptions in the first and second millennia A.D. and evidence of a large eruption in the tropics around 535 A.D., *Journal of Geophysical Research*, 116, D17308.

Field, D. 1998. Round barrows and the harmonious landscape: placing Early Bronze Age burial monuments in South-East England, *Oxford Journal of Archaeology*, 17 (3), 309–26.

Fielder, U. 2008. Bulgars in the Lower Danube region, in *The Other Europe in the Middle Ages: Avars, Bulgars, Khazars, and Cumans* (East Central and Eastern Europe in the Middle Ages, 450–1450, vol. 2), F. Curta (ed.), 151–236. Leiden: Brill.

Fitzpatrick, A. 2009. In his hands and in his head: the Amesbury Archer as a metalworker, in *Bronze Age Connections: Cultural Contact in Prehistoric Europe*, P. Clark (ed.), 176–88. Oxford: Oxbow Books.

Fitzpatrick, A. P. 2011. *The Amesbury Archer and the Boscombe Bowmen 1: Early Bell Beaker Burials at Boscombe Down, Amesbury, Wiltshire, Great Britain: Excavations at Boscombe Down.* Salisbury: Trust for Wessex Archaeology Ltd.

Florus, Lucius Annaeus. *The Epitome of Roman History*, trans. E. S. Forster. 1929 (Loeb Classical Library). Cambridge, MA: Harvard University Press.

Fokkens, H., Achterkamp, Y. and Kuijpers, M. 2008. Bracers or bracelets? About the functionality and meaning of Bell Beaker wrist-guards, *Proceedings of the Prehistoric Society*, 74, 109–40.

Forenbaher, S. and Miracle, P. 2005. The spread of farming in the Eastern Adriatic, *Antiquity*, 79 (305), 514–28.

Formicola, V. 2007. From the Sunghir children to the Romito dwarf: aspects of the Upper Paleolithic funerary landscape, *Current Anthropology*, 48 (3), 446–52.

Fornander, E., Eriksson, G. and Lidén, K. 2008. Wild at heart: approaching Pitted Ware identity, economy and cosmology through stable isotopes in skeletal material from the Neolithic site Korsnäs in Eastern Central Sweden, *Journal of Anthropological Archaeology*, 27, 281–97.

Fortunato, L. and Jordan, F. 2010. Your place or mine? A phylogenetic comparative analysis of marital residence in Indo-European and Austronesian societies, *Philosophical Transactions of the Royal Society B*, 365 (1559), 3913–22.

Fragmentary Annals of Ireland, ed. and trans. J. N. Radner. 1978. Dublin: Dublin Institute for Advanced Studies.

Fraser, J. E. 2009. *From Caledonia to Pictland: Scotland to 795* (The New Edinburgh History of Scotland 1). Edinburgh: Edinburgh University Press.

Fredegar. *The Fourth Book of the Chronicle of Fredegar with its Continuations*, trans. J. M. Wallace-Hadrill. 1960. Westport, CT: Greenwood Press.

Friedrich, W. L. et al. 2006. Santorini eruption radiocarbon dated to 1627–1600 B.C., *Science*, 312 (5773), 548.

Fu, Q., Rudan, P., Pääbo, S. and Krause, J. 2012. Complete mitochondrial genomes reveal Neolithic expansion into Europe, *PLoS ONE*, 7 (3), e32473.

Fuller, D. Q. 2011. Finding plant domestication in the Indian subcontinent, *Current Anthropology*, 52 (S4), S347–62.

Galanaki, I., Tomas, H., Galanakis, Y. and Laffineur, R. (eds). 2007. *Between the Aegean and the Baltic Seas: Prehistory across Borders. Proceedings of the International Conference, Bronze and Early Iron Age Interconnections and Contemporary Developments between the Aegean and the Regions of the Balkan Peninsula, Central and Northern Europe, University of Zagreb, 11–14 April 2005* (Aegaeum: Annales d'archéologie égéenne de l'Université de Liège et UT-PASP 27). L'Université de Liège and University of Texas at Austin.

Gallagher, A., Gunther, M. M. and Bruchhaus, H. 2009. Population continuity, demic diffusion and Neolithic origins in central-southern Germany: the evidence from body proportions, *HOMO: Journal of Comparative Human Biology*, 60, 95–126.

Gallego Romero, I. et al. 2012. Herders of Indian and European cattle share their predominant allele for lactase persistence, *Molecular Biology and Evolution*, 29 (1), 249–60.

Gamba, C. et al. 2008. Population genetics and DNA preservation in ancient human remains from Eastern Spain, *Forensic Science International: Genetics Supplement Series*, 1 (1), 462–64.

Gamba, C. et al. 2012. Ancient DNA from an early Neolithic Iberian population supports a pioneer colonization by first farmers, *Molecular Ecology*, 21 (1), 45–56.

García, O. et al. 2011. Using mitochondrial DNA to test the hypothesis of a European post-glacial human recolonization from the Franco-Cantabrian refuge, *Heredity*, 106, 37–45.

Garcia i Rubert, D. and Gracia Alonso, F. 2011. Phoenician trade in the North-East of the Iberian Peninsula: a historiographical problem, *Oxford Journal of Archaeology*, 30 (1), 33–56.

García Sanjuán, L. 2006. Funerary ideology and social inequality in the late prehistory of the Iberian South-West (*c.* 3300–850 cal BC), in *Social Inequality in Iberian Late Prehistory* (BAR International Series 1525), P. Díaz-del-Río and L. García Sanjuán (eds), 149–69. Oxford: Archaeopress.

Garnsey, P., Rathbone, D. and Bowman, A. K. (eds). 2000. *Cambridge Ancient History*, 11: *The High Empire 70–192* (2nd ed.). Cambridge, New York and Melbourne: Cambridge University Press.

Garrido Pena, R. 1997. Bell Beakers in the southern Meseta of the Iberian Peninsula: socioeconomic context and new data, *Oxford Journal of Archaeology*, 16, 187–209.

Gerbault, P. et al. 2011. Evolution of lactase persistence: an example of human niche construction, *Philosophical Transactions of the Royal Society B*, 366 (1566), 863–77.

Gharghani, A. et al. 2009. Genetic identity and relationships of Iranian apple (*Malus* × *domestica* Borkh.) cultivars and landraces, wild *Malus* species and representative old apple cultivars based on simple sequence repeat (SSR) marker analysis, *Genetic Resources and Crop Evolution*, 56 (6), 829–42.

Ghirotto, S. et al. 2011. No evidence of Neandertal admixture in the mitochondrial genomes of early European modern humans and contemporary Europeans, *American Journal of Physical Anthropology*, 146 (2), 242–52.

Ghirotto, S. et al. 2013. Origins and evolution of the Etruscans' mtDNA, *PLoS ONE*, 8 (2), e55519.

Giblin, J. I. 2009. Strontium isotope analysis of Neolithic and Copper Age populations on the Great Hungarian Plain, *Journal of Archaeological Science*, 36 (2), 491–97.

Gibson, C. and Wodtko, D. 2011. The background of the Celtic languages: theories from archaeology and linguistics, in *Die Ausbreitung des Indogermanischen. Thesen aus Sprachwissenschaft, Archäologie und Genetik, Akten der Arbeitstagung der Indogermanischen Gesellschaft Würzburg, 24.–26. September 2009*, H. Hettrich (ed.). Wiesbaden: Reichert-Verlag.

Gignoux, C. R., Henn, B. M. and Mountain, J. L. 2011. Rapid, global demographic expansions after the origins of agriculture, *PNAS*, 108 (15), 6044–49.

Gilbert, M. T. P. et al. 2008. Paleo-Eskimo mtDNA genome reveals matrilineal discontinuity in Greenland, *Science*, 320 (5884), 1787–89.

Gildas. *The Ruin of Britain &c*, trans. and ed. H. Williams (Cymmrodorion Record Series, No. 3). 1899.

Gilligan, I. 2010. The prehistoric development of clothing: archaeological implications of a thermal model, *Journal of Archaeological Method and Theory*, 17, 15–80.

Gkiasta, M., Russell, T., Shennan, S. and Steele, J. 2003. Neolithic transition in Europe: the radiocarbon record revisited, *Antiquity*, 77 (295), 45–62.

Golden, P. M. 1990. The peoples of the Russian forest belt, in *The Cambridge History of Early Inner Asia*, vol. 1. D. Sinor (ed.), 229–55. Cambridge: Cambridge University Press.

Goldsworthy, A. 2003. *The Complete Roman Army*. London and New York: Thames & Hudson.

Gómez-Carballa, A. et al. 2012. Genetic continuity in the Franco-Cantabrian region: new clues from autochthonous mitogenomes, *PLoS ONE* 7 (3), e32851.

Goodacre, S. et al. 2005. Genetic evidence for a family-based Scandinavian settlement of Shetland and Orkney during the Viking periods, *Heredity*, 95, 129–35.

Goring-Morris, N. and Belfer-Cohen, A. 2011. Neolithization processes in the Levant: the outer envelope, *Current Anthropology*, 52, supplement 4, S195–208.

Graf, O. M. et al. 2010. Chuvash origins: evidence from mtDNA markers. Abstract from a presentation at the April 14–17, 2010 meeting of the American Association of Physical Anthropologists.

Graham-Campbell, J. (ed.) 2001. *The Viking World*. London: Frances Lincoln.

Gräslund, B. and Price, N. 2012. Twilight of the gods? The 'dust veil event' of AD 536 in critical perspective, *Antiquity*, 86 (332), 428–43.

Grauer, A. L. (ed.). 2012. *A Companion to Paleopathology* (Blackwell Companions to Anthropology 1). Chichester: Wiley-Blackwell.

Grau Mira, I. 2003. Settlement dynamics and social organization in eastern Iberia during the Iron Age (eighth–second centuries BC), *Oxford Journal of Archaeology*, 22 (3), 261–79.

Green, R. E. et al. 2010. A draft sequence of the Neandertal genome, *Science*, 328 (5979), 710–22.

Green, S. 1981. *Prehistorian: A Biography of V. Gordon Childe*. Bradford-on-Avon: Moonraker Press.

Greene, K. and Moore, T. 2010. *Archaeology: An Introduction* (5th ed.). New York and Abingdon: Routledge.

Greenfield, H. J. 2010. The Secondary Products Revolution: the past, the present and the future, *World Archaeology*, 42 (1), 29–54.

Gronenborn, D. 2007. Beyond the models: Neolithisation in Central Europe, *Proceedings of the British Academy*, 144, 73–98.

Gross, A. et al. 2011. Population-genetic comparison of the Sorbian isolate population in Germany with the German KORA population using genome-wide SNP arrays, *BMC Genetics*, 12 (67).

Grugni, V. et al. 2012. Ancient migratory events in the Middle East: new clues from the Y-chromosome variation of modern Iranians, *PLoS ONE*, 7 (7), e41252.

Grupe, G. et al. 1997. Mobility of Bell Beaker people revealed by strontium isotope ratios of tooth and bone: a study of southern Bavarian skeletal remains, *Applied Geochemistry*, 12 (4), 517–25.

Guba, S. et al. 2011. HVS-I polymorphism screening of ancient human mitochondrial DNA provides evidence for N9a discontinuity and East Asian haplogroups in the Neolithic Hungary, *Journal of Human Genetics*, online 15 September 2011.

Guilaine, J. and Manen, C. 2007. From Mesolithic to Early Neolithic in the Western Mediterranean, in Whittle and Cummings 2007, 21–51.

Güldoğan, E. 2010. Mezraa-Teleilat settlement Impressed Ware and transferring Neolithic life style?, in Matthiae 2010, vol. 3, 375–80.

Guliaev, V. I. 2003. Amazons in the Scythia: new finds at the Middle Don, Southern Russia, *World Archaeology*, 35 (1), 112–25.

Gutenkunst, R. N. et al. 2009. Inferring the joint demographic history of multiple populations from multidimensional SNP frequency data, *PLoS Genetics*, 5 (10), 1–11.

Gwozdz, P. 2009. Y-STR mountains in haplospace, Part II: application to common Polish clades, *Journal of Genetic Genealogy* 5 (2), 159–85.

Gwozdz, P. S. et al. 2010. Letter to JoGG re: Y-STR mountains in haplospace, Part II: application to common Polish clades, *Journal of Genetic Genealogy*, 6 (1), 1.

Haak, W. et al. 2005. Ancient DNA from the first European farmers in 7500-year-old Neolithic sites, *Science*, 310 (5750), 1016–18.

Haak, W. et al. 2008. Ancient DNA, strontium isotopes, and osteological analyses shed light on social and kinship organization of the Later Stone Age, *PNAS*, 105 (47), 18226–31.

Haak, W. et al. 2010. Ancient DNA from European early Neolithic farmers reveals their Near Eastern affinities, *PLoS Biology*, 8 (11), e1000536.

Haaland, R. 2007. Porridge and pot, bread and oven: food ways and symbolism in Africa and the Near East from the Neolithic to the present, *Cambridge Archaeological Journal*, 17 (2), 167–83.

Haaland, R. 2009. Aquatic resource utilization and the emergence of pottery during the late Palaeolithic and Mesolithic: a global perspective from the Nile to China, chapter 9 in *Water, Culture and Identity: Comparing Past and Present Traditions in the Nile Basin Region*, T. Østigård (ed.), 213–35. Bergen: BRIC.

Haas, J. et al. 1998. Synchronous Holocene climatic oscillations recorded on the Swiss Plateau and at timberline in the Alps, *The Holocene*, 8 (3), 301–09.

Haensch, S. et al. 2010. Distinct clones of *Yersinia pestis* caused the Black Death, *PLoS Pathogens* 6 (10), e1001134.

Haimovici, S. and Bălăşescu, A. 2006. Zooarchaeological study of the faunal remains from Techirghiol (Hamangia culture, Dobrogea, Romania), *Cercetări arheologice*, 13, 371–91.

Häkkinen, J. 2012. Early contacts between Uralic and Yukaghir, in *Per Urales ad Orientem Iter polyphonicum multilingue Festskrift tillägnad Juha Janhunen på hans sextioårsdag den 12 februari 2012*. (Mémoires de la Société Finno-Ougrienne 264), T. Hyytiäinen, L. Jalava, J. Saarikivi and E. Sandman (eds), 91–101. Helsinki: Finno-Ugrian Society.

Hall, R. 2007. *Exploring the World of the Vikings*. London and New York: Thames & Hudson.

Hamerow, H. 2002. *Early Medieval Settlements: The Archaeology of Rural Communities in North-West Europe 400–900* (Medieval History and Archaeology). Oxford and New York: Oxford University Press.

Hammer, M. F. et al. 2009. Extended Y chromosome haplotypes resolve multiple and unique lineages of the Jewish priesthood, *Human Genetics*, 126, 707–17.

Hammer, M. F. et al. 2011. Genetic evidence for archaic admixture in Africa, *PNAS*, 108 (37), 15123–28.

Hancock, I. 2002. *We Are the Romani People*. Hatfield: University of Hertfordshire Press.

Hancock, I. 2010. Mind the doors! The contribution of linguistics, chapter 1 in *All Change: Romani Studies Through Romani Eyes*. D. Le Bas and T. Acton (eds), 5–26. Hatfield: University of Hertfordshire Press.

Hanning, E., Gauß, R. and Goldenberg, G. 2010. Metal for Zambujal: experimentally reconstructing a 5000-year-old technology = Metal para Zambujal: reconstrucción experimental de una tecnología de 5.000 años, *Trabajos de Prehistoria*, 67 (2), 287–304.

Hannon, G. E. et al. 2008. The Bronze Age landscape of the Bjäre peninsula, southern Sweden, and its relationship to burial mounds, *Journal of Archaeological Science*, 35 (3), 623–32.

Harding, S., Jobling, M. and King, T. 2010. *Viking DNA: The Wirral and West Lancashire Project*. Birkenhead and Nottingham: Countyvise and Nottingham University Press.

Härke, H. 2006. Archaeologists and migrations: a problem of attitude?, in *From Roman Provinces to Medieval Kingdoms: Rewriting Histories*, T. F. X. Noble (ed.), 262–76. New York and Abingdon: Routledge.

Härke, H. 2011. Anglo-Saxon immigration and ethnogenesis, *Medieval Archaeology*, 55, 1–28.

Härke, H. and Belinskij, A. B. 2011. Klin-Jar: Ritual und Gesellschaft in einem langzeitbelegten Gräberfeld im Nordkaukasus, *TÜVA-Mitteilungen: Tübinger Verein zur Förderung der ur- und frühgeschichtlichen Archäologie*, 12, 37–49.

Harley, J. B. and Woodward, D. 1987. *The History of Cartography*, vol. 1: *Cartography in Prehistoric, Ancient, and Medieval Europe and the Mediterranean*. Chicago: University of Chicago Press.

Harrison, R. 2004. *Symbols and Warriors: Images of the European Bronze Age*. Bristol: Western Academic and Specialist Press.

Harrison, R. and Heyd, V. 2007. The transformation of Europe in the third millennium BC: the example of 'Le Petit-Chasseur I + III' (Sion, Valais, Switzerland), *Praehistorische Zeitschrift*, 82 (2), 129–214.

Haslam, J. 1987. Market and fortress in England in the reign of Offa, *World Archaeology*, 19 (1), 76–93.

Hawkins, S. 2010. Greek and the languages of Asia Minor to the Classical Period, chapter 15 in Bakker 2010, 213–27.

Heather, P. J. 1991. *Goths and Romans 332–489* (Oxford Historical Monographs). Oxford: Oxford University Press.

Heather, P. 2009. *Empires and Barbarians: Migration, development and the birth of Europe*. London, Basingstoke and Oxford: Macmillan.

Heather, P. and Matthews, J. 1991. *The Goths in the Fourth Century*. Liverpool: Liverpool University Press.

Heckel, C. 2009. Physical characteristics of mammoth ivory and their implications for ivory work in the Upper Paleolithic, *Mitteilungen der Gesellschaft für Urgeschichte*, 18, 71–91.

Helgason, A. et al. 2006. MtDNA variation in Inuit populations of Greenland and Canada: migration history and population structure, *American Journal of Physical Anthropology*, 130 (1), 123–34.

Hellenthal, G., Auton, A. and Falush, D. 2008. Inferring human colonization history using a copying model, *PLoS Genetics*, 4 (5), e1000078.

Hellmuth, A. 2008. The chronological setting of the so-called Cimmerian and Early Scythian material from Anatolia, *Ancient Near Eastern Studies*, 45, 102–22.

Henn, B. M. et al. 2012. Cryptic distant relatives are common in both isolated and cosmopolitan genetic samples, *PLoS ONE*, 7 (4), e34267.

Henshilwood, C. S. et al. 2011. A 100,000-year-old ochre-processing workshop at Blombos Cave, South Africa, *Science*, 334 (6053), 219–22.

Herodotus. *The Histories*, trans. R. Waterfield. 1998. Oxford and New York: Oxford University Press.

Herrera, K. J. et al. 2012. Neolithic patrilineal signals indicate that the Armenian plateau was repopulated by agriculturalists, *European Journal of Human Genetics*, 20, 313–20.

Herrero, B. L. 2009. The Minoan fallacy: cultural diversity and mortuary behaviour on Crete at the beginning of the Bronze Age, *Oxford Journal of Archaeology*, 28 (1), 29–57.

Hertell, E. and Tallavaara, M. 2011. Hunter-gatherer mobility and the organisation of core technology in Mesolithic north-eastern Europe, in *Mesolithic Interfaces. Variability in Lithic Technologies in Eastern Fennoscandia* (Monographs of the Archaeological Society of Finland 1), T. Rankama (ed.), 94–110. Helsinki: Archaeological Society of Finland.

Hervella, M. et al. 2012. Ancient DNA from hunter-gatherer and farmer groups from Northern Spain supports a random dispersion model for the Neolithic expansion into Europe, *PLoS ONE*, 7 (4) e34417.

Heyd, V. 2001. On the earliest Bell Beakers along the Danube, in Nicolis 2001, 387–409.

Heyd, V. 2007. When the West meets the East: The eastern periphery of the Bell Beaker phenomenon and its relation to the Aegean Early Bronze Age, in Galanaki, Tomas, Galanakis and Laffineur 2007, 91–104.

Heyd, V. 2007b. Families, prestige goods, warriors and complex societies: Beaker groups of the 3rd millennium cal BC along the Upper and Middle Danube, *Proceedings of the Prehistoric Society*, 73, 327–79.

Heyd, V. 2012. Growth and expansion: social, economic and ideological structures in the European Chalcolithic, chapter 7 in Allen, Gardiner and Sheridan 2012, 98–114.

Heyer, E. et al. 2011. Lactase persistence in central Asia: phenotype, genotype, and evolution, *Human Biology*, 83 (3), 379–92.

Hickey, R. 2002. Internal and external forces again: changes in word order in Old English and Old Irish, *Language Sciences*, 24 (3–4), 261–83.

Higham, T. et al. 2011. The earliest evidence for anatomically modern humans in northwestern Europe, *Nature*, 479, 521–24.

Higham, T. et al. 2012. Testing models for the beginnings of the Aurignacian and the advent of figurative art and music: the radiocarbon chronology of Geißenklösterle, *Journal of Human Evolution*, 62 (6), 664–76.

Higuchi, R. et al. 1984. DNA sequences from the quagga, an extinct member of the horse family, *Nature*, 312, 282–84.

Hilberg, V. 2008. Hedeby: an outline of its research history, chapter 8 (2) in Brink and Price 2008, 101–11.

Hills, C. and Hurst, H. 1989. A Goth at Gloucester?, *The Antiquaries Journal*, 69 (1), 154–58.

Hilsberg, S. 2009. Place-Names and Settlement History: Aspects of Selected Topographical Elements on the Continent and in England. MA thesis, University of Leipzig.

Hincak, Z. 2007. Anthropological analysis of Neolithic and Early Bronze Age skeletons: a classical and molecular approach (East Slavonia, Croatia), *Collegium Antropologicum*, 31 (4), 1135–41.

Hinz, M. et al. 2012. Demography and the intensity of cultural activities: an evaluation of Funnel Beaker societies (4200–2800 cal BC), *Journal of Archaeological Science*, 39 (10), 3331–40.

Hist. Norway. A History of Norway and the Passion and Miracles of the Blessed Ólafr, trans. D. Kunin. 2001. London: Viking Society for Northern Research Text Series, 13.

Hodder, I. 1992. *Theory and Practice in Archaeology*. London and New York: Routledge.

Hodder, I. 2006. *Çatalhöyük: The Leopard's Tale, Revealing the Mysteries of Turkey's Ancient 'Town'*. London and New York: Thames & Hudson.

Hodder, I. 2011. Human-thing entanglement: towards an integrated archaeological perspective, *Journal of the Royal Anthropological Institute*, 17 (1), 154–77.

Hodson, J. A., Bergey, C. M. and Diostell, T. R. 2010. Neandertal genome: the ins and outs of African genetic diversity, *Current Biology*, 20 (12), R517–19.

Hoffecker, J. F. 2002. *Desolate Landscapes: Ice-Age Settlement in Eastern Europe* (Rutgers Series in Human Evolution). New Brunswick and London: Rutgers University Press.

Hoffecker, J. F. 2011. The early upper Paleolithic of eastern Europe reconsidered, *Evolutionary Anthropology: Issues, News, and Reviews*, 20 (1), 24–39.

Hoffecker, J. F. 2012. A new framework for the Upper Paleolithic of Eastern Europe, Abstracts European Society for the Study of Human Evolution, Bordeaux, September 2012, 80.

Hoffman, M. A. et al. 1986. A model of urban development for the Hierakonpolis region from Predynastic through Old Kingdom times, *Journal of the American Research Center in Egypt*, 23, 175–87.

Holck, P. 2006. The Oseberg Ship burial, Norway: new thoughts on the skeletons from the grave mound, *European Journal of Archaeology*, 9 (2–3), 185–210.

Holland, T. 2005. *Persian Fire*. London: Little, Brown; New York: Doubleday.

Homer. *Iliad*, trans. E. V. Rieu, rev. P. Jones. 2003. London: Penguin.

Homer. *Odyssey*, trans. E. V. Rieu. 1965. London: Penguin.

Höppner, B. et al. 2005. Prehistoric copper production in the Inn Valley (Austria), and the earliest copper in central Europe, *Archaeometry*, 47 (2), 293–315.

Horváth, T. 2009. The intercultural connections of the Baden culture, *ΜΩΜΟΣ*, 6, 101–14.

Howard, W. E. and McLaughlin, J. D. 2011. A dated phylogenetic tree of M222 SNP haplotypes: exploring the DNA of Irish and Scottish surnames and possible ties to Niall and the Uí Néill kindred, *Familia: Ulster Genealogical Review*, 27, 14–50.

Hublin, J. J. 2009. The origin of Neandertals, *PNAS*, 106, 16022–27.

Huehnergard, J. 2011. Proto-Semitic language and culture, in *The American Heritage Dictionary of the English Language* (5th ed.), 2066–69. Boston and New York: Houghton, Mifflin and Harcourt.

Hughes, R. 1987. *The Fatal Shore: History of the Transportation of Convicts to Australia, 1787–1868*. London: Collins Harvill.

Huyghe, J. R. 2011. A genome-wide analysis of population structure in the Finnish Saami with implications for genetic association studies, *European Journal of Human Genetics*, 19 (3), 347–52.

Huysecom, E. et al. 2009. The emergence of pottery in Africa during the tenth millennium cal BC: new evidence from Ounjougou (Mali), *Antiquity*, 83 (322), 905–17.

Ingman, M. and Gyllensten, U. 2007. A recent genetic link between Sami and the Volga-Ural region of Russia, *European Journal of Human Genetics*, 15, 115–20.

Ingram, C. J. E. et al. 2009. Lactose digestion and the evolutionary genetics of lactase persistence, *Human Genetics*, 124 (6), 579–91.

Ionita-Laza, I., Lange, C. and Laird, N. M. 2009. Estimating the number of unseen variants in the human genome, *PNAS*, 106 (13), 5008–13.

Iriondo, M., Barbero, M. C. and Manzano, C. 2001. HUMF13A01 in autochthonous Basques and in genetically related populations, *International Journal of Anthropology*, 16 (4), 225–33.

Isaac, G. R. 2010. The origins of the Celtic languages: language spread from east to west, chapter 7 in Cunliffe and Koch 2010, 162–65.

Isaksson, S. and Hallgren, F. 2012. Lipid residue analyses of Early Neolithic funnel-beaker pottery from Skogsmossen, eastern Central Sweden, and the earliest evidence of dairying in Sweden, *Journal of Archaeological Science*, 39 (12), 3600–09.

Isern, N. and Fort, J. 2012. Modelling the effect of Mesolithic populations on the slowdown of the Neolithic transition, *Journal of Archaeological Science*, 39 (12), 3671–76.

Itan, Y. et al. 2010. A worldwide correlation of lactase persistence phenotype and genotypes, *BMC Evolutionary Biology*, 10, 36.

Ivanov, I. S. and Avramova, M. 2000. *Varna Necropolis: The Dawn of European Civilization* (Treasures of Bulgaria 1). Sofia: Agató.

Jakobsson, M. et al. 2008. Genotype, haplotype and copy-number variation in worldwide human populations, *Nature*, 451, 998–1003.

James, S. 1999. *The Atlantic Celts: Ancient People or Modern Invention?* London: British Museum Press.

Janhunen, J. 2009. Proto-Uralic – what, where, and when?, *The Quasquicentennial of the Finno-Ugrian Society: Suomalais-Ugrilaisen Seuran Toimituksia = Mémoires de la Société Finno-Ougrienne*, 258, 57–78.

Jantzen, D. et al. 2011. A Bronze Age battlefield? Weapons and trauma in the Tollense Valley, north-eastern Germany, *Antiquity*, 85, 417–33.

Järvelä, I. et al. 2009. Molecular genetics of human lactase deficiencies, *Annals of Medicine*, 41 (8), 568–75.

Javed, A. et al. 2012. Recombination networks as genetic markers in a human variation study of the Old World, *Human Genetics*, 131 (4), 601–13.

Jing, Y. and Campbell, R. 2009. Recent archaeometric research on 'the origins of Chinese civilisation', *Antiquity*, 83 (319), 96–109.

Jobling, M. A., Hurles, M. E. and Tyler-Smith, C. 2004. *Human Evolutionary Genetics: Origins, People and Disease*. New York and Abingdon: Garland Publishing.

Johannsen, J. W. 2010. The wheeled vehicles of the Bronze Age on Scandinavian rock-carvings, *Acta Archaeologica*, 81, 150–250.

Johanson, L. 1998. The history of Turkic, in *The Turkic Languages* (Routledge Language Family Descriptions), L. Johanson and É. Á. Csató (eds), 81–125. London and New York: Routledge.

John, Bishop of Nikiu. *The Chronicle of John, Bishop of Nikiu Translated from Zotenberg's Ethiopic Text*, trans. R. H. Charles. 1916. London: Text and Translation Society/Williams & Norgate.

Jones, E. P. et al. 2012. Fellow travellers: a concordance of colonization patterns between mice and men in the North Atlantic region, *BMC Evolutionary Biology*, 12, 35.

Jones-Bley, K. 2000. Sintashta burials and their western European counterparts, in *Kurgans, Ritual Sites, and Settlements: Eurasian Bronze and Iron Age* (BAR International Series 890), J. Davis-Kimball, E. M. Murphy, L. Koryakova and L. T. Yablonksy (eds), 126–34. Oxford: Archaeopress.

Jordan, P. 2010. Understanding the spread of innovations in prehistoric social networks: new insights into the origins and dispersal of early pottery in Northern Eurasia, in *Transference. Interdisciplinary Communications 2008/2009*, W. Østreng (ed.). Centre for Advanced Study, Oslo (internet publication).

Jordan, P. and Zvelebil, M. (eds). 2009. *Ceramics Before Farming: The Dispersal of Pottery Among Prehistoric Eurasian Hunter-gatherers* (University College London Institute of Archaeology Publications). Walnut Creek, CA: Left Coast Press.

Jordan, P. and Zvelebil, M. 2009. *Ex oriente lux*: the prehistory of hunter-gatherer ceramic dispersals, chapter 1 in Jordan and Zvelebil 2009, 33–89.

Jordanes. *The Origins and Deeds of the Goths*, trans. C. C. Mierow. 1908. Princeton: Princeton University Press.

Joris, O. and Street, M. 2008. At the end of the 14C time scale – the Middle to Upper Paleolithic record of western Eurasia, *Journal of Human Evolution*, 55, 782–802.

Josephus. *The Works of Flavius Josephus*, trans. William Whiston. 1895. Auburn and Buffalo: John E. Beardsley.

Jovaisa, E. 2001. The Balts and the amber, in *Baltic Amber: Proceedings of the International Interdisciplinary Conference Baltic Amber in Natural Sciences Archaeology and Applied Arts, 13–18 September 2001, Vilnius, Palana, Nida*, A. Butrimas (ed.), 149–56. Vilnius: Vilnius Academy of Fine Arts Press.

Jussila, T. et al. 2007. The Mesolithic settlement in NE Savo, Finland and the earliest settlement in the eastern Baltic Sea, *Acta Archaeologica*, 78 (2), 43–162.

Justinus, Marcus Junianus. *Epitome of the Philippic Histories of Trogus Pompeius*, trans., with notes, by the Rev. J. S. Watson. 1853. London: Henry G. Bohn.

Kaiser, E., Burger, J. and Schier, W. (eds). 2012. *Population Dynamics in Prehistory and Early History*. De Gruyter ebook.

Kalieva, S. S. and Logvin, V. N. 2011. On the origins of nomadism in the Asian steppes, *Archaeology, Ethnology and Anthropology of Eurasia*, 39 (3), 85–93.

Kaliff, A. 2001. *Gothic Connections: Contacts Between Eastern Scandinavia and the Southern Baltic Coast 1000 BC–500 AD* (Occasional Papers in Archaeology 26). Uppsala: Uppsala University.

Karachanak, S. et al. 2009. Y-Chromosomal haplogroups in Bulgarians, *Comptes rendus de l'Académie bulgare des Sciences*, 62 (3), 393–400.

Karachanak, S. et al. 2013. Y-Chromosome diversity in modern Bulgarians: new clues about their ancestry, *PLoS ONE* 8 (3), e56779.

Karlsson, A. O. 2006. Y-chromosome diversity in Sweden: a long-time perspective, *European Journal of Human Genetics*, 14, 963–70.

Kassianidou, V. and Knapp, A. B. 2005. Archaeometallurgy in the Mediterranean: the social context of mining, technology, and trade, in *The Archaeology of Mediterranean Prehistory*, E. Blake and A. B. Knapp (eds), 215–51. Malden, MA, and Oxford: Blackwell.

Kazarnitsky, A. A. 2010. The Maikop crania revisited, *Archaeology, Ethnology and Anthropology of Eurasia*, 38 (1), 148–55.

Keith, K. 1998. Spindle whorls, gender, and ethnicity at Late Chalcolithic Hacinebi Tepe, *Journal of Field Archaeology*, 25 (4), 497–515.

Keller, A. et al. 2012. New insights into the Tyrolean Iceman's origin and phenotype as inferred by whole-genome sequencing, *Nature Communications*, 3, 698.

Kerr, R. (ed.). 1811–24. *A General History and Collection of Voyages and Travels*, 18 vols. Edinburgh: William Blackwood.

Keyser, C. et al. 2009. Ancient DNA provides new insights into the history of south Siberian Kurgan people, *Human Genetics*, 126 (3), 395–410.

Kienlin, T. L. and Valde-Nowak, P. 2004. Neolithic transhumance in the Black Forest Mountains, SW Germany, *Journal of Field Archaeology*, 29 (1–2), 29–44.

Kimura, B. et al. 2011. Ancient DNA from Nubian and Somali wild ass provides insights into donkey ancestry and domestication, *PRS B*, 278 (1702), 50–57.

King, R. 2009. Neolithic migrations in the Near East and the Aegean: linguistic and genetic correlates, chapter 8 in Peregrine, Peiros and Feldman 2009, 112–26.

King, R. J. et al. 2008. Differential Y-chromosome Anatolian influences on the Greek and Cretan Neolithic, *Annals of Human Genetics*, 72, 205–14.

King, R. J. et al. 2011. The coming of the Greeks to Provence and Corsica: Y-chromosome models of archaic Greek colonization of the western Mediterranean, *BMC Evolutionary Biology*, 11 (69).

Kinross, J. P. D. 1977. *The Ottoman Centuries: The Rise and Fall of the Turkish Empire*. New York: Morrow; London: Cape.

Kirtcho, L. 2009. The earliest wheeled transport in Southwestern Central Asia: new finds from Altyn-Depe, *Archaeology, Ethnology and Anthropology of Eurasia*, 37 (1), 25–33.

Kitchen, A. et al. 2009. Bayesian phylogenetic analysis of Semitic languages identifies an Early Bronze Age origin of Semitic in the Near East, *PRS B*, 276 (1668), 2703–10.

Klein, R. 2008. Out of Africa and the evolution of human behavior. *Evolutionary Anthropology: Issues, News, and Reviews*, 17 (6), 267–81.

Knapp, B. 2010. Cyprus's earliest prehistory: seafarers, foragers and settlers, *Journal of World Prehistory*, 23 (2), 79–120.

Knapp, M. and Hofreiter, M. 2010. Next generation sequencing of ancient DNA: requirements, strategies and perspectives, *Genes*, 1, 227–43.

Knudson, K. J., O'Donnabhain, B. et al. 2012. Migration and Viking Dublin: paleomobility and paleodiet through isotopic analyses, *Journal of Archaeological Science*, 39 (2), 308–20.

Koch, J. T. (ed.). 2006. *Celtic Culture: A Historical Encyclopedia*, 5 vols. Santa Barbara, CA: ABC-CLIO.

Koch, J. T. 2007. *An Atlas for Celtic Studies: Archaeology and Names in Ancient Europe and Early Medieval Ireland, Britain, and Brittany* (Celtic Studies Publications 12). Oxford: Oxbow Books and Celtic Studies Publications.

Koch, J. T. 2010. Paradigm shift? Interpreting Tartessian as Celtic, chapter 9 in Cunliffe and Koch 2010, 185–301.

Koepke, N. and Baten, J. 2008. Agricultural specialization and height in ancient and medieval Europe, *Explorations in Economic History*, 42 (2), 127–46.

Kohl, P. L. 2006. The early integration of the Eurasian steppes with the ancient Near East: movements and transformations in the Caucasus and central Asia, chapter 1 in *Beyond the Steppe and the Sown: Proceedings of the 2002 University of Chicago Conference on Eurasian Archaeology* (Colloquia Pontica 13), D. L. Peterson, L. M. Popova and A. T. Smith (eds), 3–39. Leiden and Boston: Brill.

Kohl, P. L. 2007. *The Making of Bronze Age Eurasia* (Cambridge World Archaeology). Cambridge, New York and Melbourne: Cambridge University Press.

Korobov, D. S. 2011. Settlement of Alanic tribes in various areas of the North Caucasus according to archeological data and written sources, *Anthropology and Archeology of Eurasia*, 50 (1), 51–73.

Kortlandt, F. 2007. *Italo-Celtic Origins and Prehistoric Development of the Irish Language*. Amsterdam and New York: Editions Rodopi B.V.

Korvin-Piotrovskiy, A. G. 2012. Tripolye Culture in Ukraine, chapter 1 in Menotti and Korvin-Piotrovskiy 2012, 6–18.

Krause, J. et al. 2010. The complete mitochondrial DNA genome of an unknown hominin from southern Siberia, *Nature*, 464, 894–97.

Kremenetski, C. V. 2003. Steppe and forest-steppe belt of Eurasia: Holocene environmental history, chapter 2 in Levine, Renfrew and Boyle 2003, 11–27.

Kremenetski, C. V., Chichagova, O. A. and Shishlina, N. I. 1999. Palaeoecological evidence for Holocene vegetation, climate and land-use change in the low Don basin and Kalmuk area, southern Russia, *Vegetation History and Archaeobotany*, 8 (4), 233–46.

Kristiansen, K. 1998. *Europe Before History* (New Studies in Archaeology). Cambridge and New York: Cambridge University Press.

Kristiansen, K. 2002. The tale of the sword: swords and sword-fighters in Bronze Age Europe, *Oxford Journal of Archaeology*, 21, 319–32.

Kristiansen, K. 2005. What language did Neolithic pots speak? Colin Renfrew's European farming-language-dispersal model challenged, *Antiquity*, 79 (305), 694–95.

Kristiansen, K. 2008. Eurasia in the Bronze and early Iron Ages, *Antiquity*, 82 (318), 1113–18.

Kristiansen, K. 2009. Proto-Indo-European languages and institutions – an archaeological approach, in *Departure from the Homeland: Indo-Europeans and Archaeology* (Journal of Indo-European Studies Monograph Series 56), M. Vander Linden and K. Jones-Bley (eds), 11–140. Washington, DC: Institute for the Study of Man.

Kristiansen, K. 2011 Theory does not die it changes direction, chapter 6 in *Death of Archaeological Theory*. J. Bintliff and M. Pearce (eds), 72–79. Oxford and Oakville, CT: Oxbow Books.

Kristiansen, K. and Larsson, T. 2005. *The Rise of Bronze Age Society: Travels, Transmissions and Transformations*. Cambridge and New York: Cambridge University Press.

Krizman, J. et al. 2012. Subcortical encoding of sound is enhanced in bilinguals and relates to executive function advantages, *PNAS*, published online before print 30 April, 2012.

Kruts, V. 2012. The latest stage of the development of the Tripolye culture, chapter 10 in Menotti and Korvin-Piotrovskiy 2012, 230–53.

Kunst, M. 2001. Invasions? Fashion? Social Ranks? Consideration concerning the Bell Beaker phenomenon in Copper Age fortifications of the Iberian peninsula, in Nicolis 2001, 81–90.

Kunst, M. 2007. Zambujal (Torres Vedras, Lisboa): relatório das escavações de 2001, *Revista Portuguesa de Arqueologia*, 10 (1), 95–118.

Kuzmin, Y. V. 2006. Chronology of the earliest pottery in East Asia: progress and pitfalls, *Antiquity*, 80 (308), 362–71.

Kuzmina, E. E. 2007. *The Origin of the Indo-Iranians*. J. P. Mallory (ed.). Leiden and Boston: Brill.

Kuzmina, E. E. 2007. *The Prehistory of the Silk Road*. V. H. Mair (ed.). Philadelphia: University of Pennsylvania Press.

Kuznetsov, P. F. 2006. The emergence of Bronze Age chariots in eastern Europe, *Antiquity*, 80 (309), 638–45.

Laayouni, H., Calafell, F. and Bertranpetit, J. 2010. A genome-wide survey does not show the genetic distinctiveness of Basques, *Human Genetics*, 127, 455–58.

Lacan, M. 2011a. La Néolithisation du bassin méditerranéen: Apports de l'ADN ancien. Thesis Université Toulouse III Paul Sabatier, presented 12 December 2011.

Lacan, M. 2011b. Ancient DNA suggests the leading role played by men in the Neolithic dissemination, *PNAS*, 108 (45), 18255–59.

Lacan, M. et al. 2011. Ancient DNA reveals male diffusion through the Neolithic Mediterranean route, *PNAS*, 108 (24), 9788–91.

Lacan, M., Keyser, C., Crubézy, E. and Ludes, B. 2012. Ancestry of modern Europeans: contributions of ancient DNA, *Cellular and Molecular Life Sciences*, online first 10 October 2012.

Lacey, B. 2006. *Cenél Conaill and the Donegal Kingdoms*, AD 500–800. Dublin: Four Courts Press.

Lachance, J. et al. 2012. Evolutionary history and adaptation from high-coverage whole-genome sequences of diverse African hunter-gatherers, *Cell*, 150 (3), 457–69.

Lalueza-Fox, C. et al. 2004. Unravelling migrations in the steppe: mitochondrial DNA sequences from ancient central Asians, *PRS B*, 271 (1542), 941–47.

Landnamabok. The Book of Settlements: Landnamabok, trans. H. Pálsson and P. Edwards. 1972. Winnipeg: University of Manitoba Press.

Lanting, L. N. 2000. Dates for origin and diffusion of the European logboat, *Palaeohistoria*, 39–40, 627–53.

Lappalainen, T. et al. 2006. Regional differences among the Finns: a Y-chromosomal perspective, *Gene*, 376 (2), 207–15.

Lappalainen, T. et al. 2008. Migration waves to the Baltic Sea region, *Annals of Human Genetics*, 72, 337–48.

Lappalainen, T. et al. 2009. Population structure in contemporary Sweden – a Y-chromosomal and mitochondrial DNA analysis, *Annals of Human Genetics*, 73 (1), 61–73.

Larmuseau, M. H. D. et al. 2012. In the name of the migrant father. Analysis of surname origins identifies genetic admixture events undetectable from genealogical records, *Heredity*, 109 (2), 90–95.

Larsen, L. B. et al. 2008. New ice core evidence for a volcanic cause of the A.D. 536 dust veil, *Geophysical Research Letters*, 35, L04708.

Larson, G. et al. 2007. Ancient DNA, pig domestication, and the spread of the Neolithic into Europe, *PNAS*, 104, 15276–81.

Larsson, A. M. 2008. The hand that makes the pot...: craft traditions in South Sweden in the third millennium BC, in *Breaking the Mould: Challenging the Past through Pottery* (Prehistoric Ceramics Research Group: Occasional Paper 6; BAR International Series 1861), I. Berg (ed.), 81–91. Oxford: Archaeopress.

Larsson, M. 2009. Pitted Ware culture in eastern and middle Sweden: material culture and human agency, chapter 14 in Jordan and Zvelebil 2009, 395–419.

Laskaris, N. et al. 2011. Late Pleistocene/Early Holocene seafaring in the Aegean: new obsidian hydration dates with the SIMS-SS method, *Journal of Archaeological Science*, 38 (9), 2475–79.

Latacz, J. 2004. *Troy and Homer: Towards a Solution of an Old Mystery*, trans. K. Windle and R. Ireland. Oxford and New York: Oxford University Press.

Laval, G. et al. 2010. Formulating a historical and demographic model of recent human evolution based on resequencing data from noncoding regions, *PLoS ONE*, 5 (4), e10284.

Lazarovici, C.-M. 2010. New data regarding the chronology of the Precucuteni, Cucuteni and Horodiştea-Erbiceni cultures, *PANTA RHEI: Studies on the Chronology and Cultural Development of South-Eastern and Central Europe in Earlier Prehistory Presented to Juraj Pavúk on the Occasion of his 75th Birthday. Studia Archaeologica et Mediaevalia*, 11, 71–94. Bratislava: Comenius University.

Leach, S. et al. 2010. A Lady of York: migration, ethnicity and identity in Roman Britain, *Antiquity*, 84 (323), 131–45.

Lee, E. J. et al. 2012. Emerging genetic patterns of the European neolithic: perspectives from a late neolithic bell beaker burial site in Germany, *American Journal of Physical Anthropology*, 148 (4), 571–79.

Le Floch, A. et al. 2013. The sixteenth century Alderney crystal: a calcite as an efficient reference optical compass?, *Proceedings of the Royal Society A*, 469 (2153).

Legrand, S. and Bokovenko, N. 2006. The emergence of the Scythians: Bronze Age to Iron Age in South Siberia, *Antiquity*, 80 (310), 843–79.

Lemercier, O. 2012. Interpreting the Beaker phenomenon in Mediterranean France: an Iron Age analogy, *Antiquity*, 86 (331), 131–43.

Levine, M. 2003. Focusing on Central Eurasian archaeology: East meets West, chapter 1 in Levine, Renfrew and Boyle 2003, 1–7.

Levine, M., Renfrew, C. and Boyle, K. (eds). 2003. *Prehistoric Steppe Adaptation and the Horse* (MacDonald Institute Monographs). Cambridge: University of Cambridge.

Li, C. et al. 2010. Evidence that a West-East admixed population lived in the Tarim Basin as early as the early Bronze Age, *BMC Biology*, 8 (15).

Li, J. Z. et al. 2008. Worldwide human relationships inferred from genome-wide patterns of variation, *Science*, 319, 1100–04.

Lightfoot, E. (ed.). 2008. *Movement, Mobility and Migration* (Archaeological Review from Cambridge, 23.2).

Lillios, K. T. 2008. *Heraldry for the Dead: Memory, Identity, and the Engraved Stone Plaques of Neolithic Iberia*. Austin: University of Texas Press.

Lilliu, G. 1999. *Arte e religione della Sardegna prenuragica: Idoletti, ceramiche, oggetti d'ornamento*. Sassari: Carlo Delfino editore.

Linderholm, A. 2008. Migration in prehistory: DNA and stable isotope analyses of Swedish skeletal material. PhD thesis, Stockholm.

Lira, J. et al. 2010. Ancient DNA reveals traces of Iberian Neolithic and Bronze Age lineages in modern Iberian horses, *Molecular Ecology*, 19 (1), 64–78.

Liritzis, I. 2010. Strofilas (Andros Island, Greece): new evidence for the Cycladic final Neolithic period through novel dating methods using luminescence and obsidian hydration, *Journal of Archaeological Science*, 37, 1367–77.

Littauer, M. A. and Crouwel, J. H. 2002. *Selected Writings on Chariots and other Early Vehicles, Riding and Harness* (Studies in the Culture and History of the Ancient Near East 6), P. Raulwing (ed.). Leiden, Boston and Köln: Brill.

Little, L. K. 2006. Life and afterlife of the first plague pandemic, chapter 1 in Little (ed.) 2006, 3–32.

Little, L. K. (ed.). 2006. *Plague and the End of Antiquity: The Pandemic of 541–750*. Cambridge: Cambridge University Press.

Liu, X. 2010. *The Silk Road in World History*. Oxford and New York: Oxford University Press.

Livi-Bacci, M. 2007. *A Concise History of World Population* (4th ed.). Malden, MA, Oxford and Carlton, Victoria: Blackwell.

Lobov, A. S. et al. 2007. Structure of the gene pool of Bashkir subpopulations, *European Journal of Human Genetics*, 15, supplement 1, P1135.

Lobov, A. S. 2009. Struktura genofonda subpopulyatsii bashkir. Dissertatsii na soiskanie uchenoy stepeni kandidata biologicheskix nauk. Ufa.

Lomas, K. 1993. *Rome and the Western Greeks, 350 BC–AD 200: Conquest and Acculturation in Southern Italy*. London: Routledge.

Loogväli, E.-L. et al. 2004. Disuniting uniformity: a pied cladistic canvas of mtDNA haplogroup H in Eurasia, *Molecular Biology and Evolution*, 21 (11), 2012–21.

Lorrio, A. J. and Zapatero, G. R. 2005. The Celts in Iberia: an overview, *E-Keltoi, the Journal of Interdisciplinary Celtic Studies*, 6: *The Celts in the Iberian Peninsula*.

Louwe Kooijmans, L. P. 2007. The gradual transition to farming in the Lower Rhine Basin, in Whittle and Cummings 2007, 287–309.

Louwe Kooijmans, L. P. 2009. The agency factor in the process of Neolithisation – a Dutch case study, *Journal of Archaeology in the Low Countries*, 1 (1), 27–54.

Lubotsky, A. 2001. The Indo-Iranian substratum, in Carpelan, Parpola and Koskikallio 2001, 301–17.

Maca-Meyer, N. et al. 2003. Mitochondrial DNA transit between West Asia and North Africa inferred from U6 phylogeography, *BMC Genetics*, 4, 15.

McBrearty, S. 2007. Down with the revolution, chapter 12 in Mellars, Boyle, Bar-Yosef and Stringer 2007, 133–52.

McCormick, M. 2011. History's changing climate: climate science, genomics, and the emerging consilient approach to interdisciplinary history, *Journal of Interdisciplinary History*, 42 (2), 251–73.

McEnroe, J. C. 2002. Cretan questions: politics and archaeology 1898–1913, chapter 4 in *Labyrinth Revisited: Rethinking 'Minoan' Archaeology*, Y. Hamilakis (ed.), 59–72. Oxford and Oakville, CT: Oxbow Books.

Mac Eoin, G. 2007. What language was spoken in Ireland before Irish?, in Tristram 2007, 113–25.

McEvedy, C. and Jones, R. 1978. *Atlas of World Population History*. Harmondsworth: Penguin.

McEvoy, B. et al. 2006. The scale and nature of Viking settlement in Ireland from Y-chromosome admixture analysis, *European Journal of Human Genetics*, 14, 1288–94.

McEvoy, B. P. and Bradley, D. G. 2010. Irish Genetics and Celts, chapter 5 in Cunliffe and Koch 2010, 107–20.

McGovern, P. E. 2003. *Ancient Wine: The Search for the Origins of Viniculture*. Princeton: Princeton University Press.

McGovern, P. E. 2009. *Uncorking the Past: The Quest for Wine, Beer and Other Alcoholic Beverages*. Berkeley: University of California Press.

McGrail, S. 2001. *Boats of the World from the Stone Age to Medieval Times*. Oxford and New York: Oxford University Press.

McKenzie, H. G. 2009. Review of early hunter-gatherer pottery in Eastern Siberia, in Jordan and Zvelebil 2009, 166–207.

McKinley, J. I., Schuster, J. and Millard, A. 2013. Dead-Sea connections: a Bronze Age and Iron Age ritual site on the Isle of Thanet, chapter 6 in *Celtic from the West 2: Rethinking the Bronze Age and the Arrival of Indo-European in Atlantic Europe*, B. Cunliffe and J. T. Koch (eds). Oxford: Oxbow.

McLeod, S. 2011. Warriors and women: the sex ratio of Norse migrants to eastern England up to 900 AD, *Early Medieval Europe*, 19 (3), 332–53.

Maggi, R. and Pearce, M. 2005. Mid fourth-millennium copper mining in Liguria, north-west Italy: the earliest known copper mines in Western Europe, *Antiquity*, 79 (303), 66–77.

Mahoney, A. 2008. Review of R. S. P. Beekes, The Origin of the Etruscans, *Etruscan Studies*, 11 (1), article 12.

Mallory, J. P. 1989. *In Search of the Indo-Europeans: Language, Archaeology and Myth*. London: Thames & Hudson.

Mallory, J. P. 2007. The Indo-European language family: the historical question, in *A History of Ancient Greek: From the Beginnings to Late Antiquity*, A.-F. Christidis (ed.), 170–77. Cambridge: Cambridge University Press.

Mallory, J. P. 2013. *The Origins of the Irish*. London and New York: Thames & Hudson.

Mallory, J. P. and Adams, D. Q. (eds). 1997. *Encyclopedia of Indo-European Culture*. London: Fitzroy Dearborn Publishers.

Mallory, J. P. and Adams, D. Q. 2006. *Oxford Introduction to Proto-Indo-European and the Proto-Indo-European World*. Oxford: Oxford University Press.

Mallory, J. P. and Mair, V. H. 2000. *The Tarim Mummies: The Mystery of the First Europeans in China*. London and New York: Thames & Hudson.

Malmström, H. et al. 2009. Ancient DNA reveals lack of continuity between Neolithic hunter-gatherers and contemporary Scandinavians, *Current Biology*, 19, 1–5.

Malmström, H. et al. 2010. High frequency of lactose intolerance in a prehistoric hunter-gatherer population in northern Europe, *BMC Evolutionary Biology*, 10, 89.

Malyarchuk, B. A. et al. 2006. Mitochondrial DNA variability in the Czech population, with application to the ethnic history of Slavs, *Human Biology*, 78 (6), 681–95.

Malyarchuk, B. et al. 2008. Mitochondrial DNA phylogeny in Eastern and Western Slavs, *Molecular Biology and Evolution*, 25 (8), 1651–58.

Malyarchuk, B. et al. 2010. The peopling of Europe from the mitochondrial haplogroup U5 perspective, *PLoS ONE*, 5 (4), e10285.

Malyarchuk, B. et al. 2010b. Mitogenomic diversity in Tatars from the Volga-Ural region of Russia, *Molecular Biology and Evolution*, 27 (10), 2220–26.

Malyarchuk, B. A. and Rogozin, I. B. 2004. On the Etruscan mitochondrial DNA contribution to modern humans, *American Journal of Human Genetics*, 75 (5), 920–23.

Maniatis, Y. 2011. 14C dating of a Final Neolithic–Early Bronze Age transition period settlement at Aghios Ioannis on Thassos (North Aegean), *Radiocarbon*, 53 (1), 21–37.

Manning, S. et al. 2010. The earlier Neolithic in Cyprus: recognition and dating of a Pre-Pottery Neolithic A occupation, *Antiquity*, 84 (325), 693–706.

Manzura, I. 2005. Steps to the steppe: or, how the North Pontic region was colonised, *Oxford Journal of Archaeology*, 24 (4), 313–38.

Manzura, I. 2005b. The proto-Bronze Age cemetery at Durankulak: a look from the East, in *Prehistoric Archaeology and Theoretical Anthropology and Education*, in L. Nikolova, J. Fritz and J. Higgins (eds), Reports of Prehistoric Research Projects 6–7, 51–55. Salt Lake City and Karlovo.

Maran, J. 2007. Seaborne contacts between the Aegean, the Balkans and the Central Mediterranean in the 3rd millennium BC – the unfolding of the Mediterranean world, in Galanaki, Tomas, Galanakis and Laffineur 2007, 3–21.

Marciniak, A. 2011. The Secondary Products Revolution: empirical evidence and its current zooarchaeological critique, *Journal of World Prehistory*, 24, 117–30.

Marinatos, N. 2010. *Minoan Kingship and the Solar Goddess: A Near Eastern Koine*. Chicago: University of Illinois Press.

Markoe, G. E. 2000. *The Phoenicians* (Peoples of the Past). London: British Museum Press.

Martin, T. R. 1996. *Ancient Greece from Prehistoric to Hellenistic Times*. New Haven: Yale University Press.

Martínez-Cruz, B. et al. 2011. In the heartland of Eurasia: the multilocus genetic landscape of Central Asian populations, *European Journal of Human Genetics*, 19, 216–23.

Martínez-Cruz, B. et al. 2012. Evidence of pre-Roman tribal genetic structure in Basques from uniparentally inherited markers, *Molecular Biology and Evolution*, 29 (9), 2211–22.

Martínez-Moreno, J., Mora, R. and de la Torre, I. 2010. The Middle-to-Upper Palaeolithic transition in Cova Gran (Catalunya, Spain) and the extinction of Neanderthals in the Iberian Peninsula, *Journal of Human Evolution*, 58 (3), 211–26.

Mata, D. R. 2002. The ancient Phoenicians of the 8th and 7th centuries BC in the Bay of Cadiz: state of the research, in *The Phoenicians in Spain: An Archaeological Review of the Eighth–Sixth Centuries B.C.E. A Collection of Articles Translated from Spanish*, M. R. Bierling (ed. and trans.), 155–98. Winona Lake, IN: Eisenbrauns.

Matasović, R. 2007. Insular Celtic as a language area, in Tristram 2007, 93–112.

Matthews, R. et al. 2010. Investigating the Early Neolithic of western Iran: the Central Zagros Archaeological Project (CZAP), *Antiquity*, 84 (323), project gallery (online edition only).

Matthiae, P. et al. (eds). 2010. *Proceedings of the 6th International Congress of the Archaeology of the Ancient Near East*, 3 vols. Wiesbaden: Harrassowitz Verlag.

Mattingly, D. 2006. *An Imperial Possession: Britain in the Roman Empire* (Penguin History of Britain). London: Penguin.

Matyushin, G. 1986. The Mesolithic and Neolithic in the southern Urals and central Asia, chapter 10 in *Hunters in Transition: Mesolithic Societies of Temperate Eurasia and their Transition to Farming*, M. Zvelebil (ed.), 133–50. Cambridge, New York and Melbourne: Cambridge University Press.

Maurice's Strategikon: Handbook of Byzantine Military Strategy, trans. G. T. Dennis (Middle Ages Series). 1984. Philadelphia: University of Pennsylvania Press.

Meadows, J. R. S. et al. 2007. Five ovine mitochondrial lineages identified from sheep breeds of the Near East, *Genetics*, 175 (3), 1371–79.

Mees, B. 2003. Stratum and shadow: a genealogy of stratigraphy theories from the Indo-European West, in *Language Contacts in Prehistory: Studies in Stratigraphy. Papers from the Workshop on Linguistic Stratigraphy and Prehistory at the Fifteenth International Conference on Historical Linguistics, Melbourne, 17 August 2001* (Amsterdam Studies in the Theory and History of Linguistic Science, Series IV: Current Issues in Linguistic Theory, 239), H. Andersen (ed.), 11–44. Amsterdam and Philadelphia: John Benjamins Publishing Company.

Meier, C. 2011. *The Culture of Freedom: Ancient Greece and the Origins of Europe*. Oxford and New York: Oxford University Press.

Melchior, L. et al. 2008. Rare mtDNA haplogroups and genetic differences in rich and poor Danish Iron-Age villages, *American Journal of Physical Anthropology*, 135, 206–15.

Melé, M. et al. 2012. Recombination gives a new insight in the effective population size and the history of the Old World human populations, *Molecular Biology and Evolution*, 29 (1), 25–30.

Melheim, L. 2012. Towards a new understanding of Late Neolithic Norway – the role of metal and metal working, in Prescott and Glørstad 2012, 70–81.

Mellars, P. 2006. Archeology and the dispersal of modern humans in Europe: deconstructing the Aurignacian, *Evolutionary Anthropology*, 15, 167–82.

Mellars, P. 2011. The earliest modern humans in Europe, *Nature*, 479, 283–85.

Mellars, P., Boyle, K., Bar-Yosef, O. and Stringer, C. (eds). 2007. *Rethinking the Human Revolution: New Behavioural and Biological Perspectives on the Origin and Dispersal of Modern Humans* (McDonald Institute Monographs). Cambridge: McDonald Institute for Archaeological Research.

Meniel, P. 1984. Les vestiges animaux chasséens du 'Camp de César' à Catenoy (Oise), *Revue archéologique de Picardie*, 1 (1–2), 205–11.

Menk, R. 1979. Le phenomène campaniforme: structure biologiques et intégration historique, *Archives Suisses d'anthropologie générale*, 43, 259–84.

Menotti, F. and Korvin-Piotrovskiy, A. G. (eds). 2012. *The Tripolye Culture: Giant-settlements in Ukraine: Formation, Development and Decline*. Oxford and Oakville, CT: Oxbow Books.

Metspalu, M. et al. 2004. Most of the extant mtDNA boundaries in south and southwest Asia were likely shaped during the initial settlement of Eurasia by anatomically modern humans, *BMC Genetics*, 5 (26).

Meyer, M. et al. 2012. A high-coverage genome sequence from an archaic Denisovan individual, *Science*, 338 (6104), 222–26.

Mielnik-Sikorska, M. et al. 2012. Genetic data from Y chromosome STR and SNP loci in Ukrainian population, *Forensic Science International: Genetics*, published online 6 June 2012 ahead of print.

Mikhailova, T. A. 2007. Macc, Cailín and Céile – an Altaic element in Celtic?, in Tristram 2007, 4–24.

Milisauskas, S. and Kruk, J. 1991. Utilization of cattle for traction during the later Neolithic in southeastern Poland, *Antiquity*, 65 (248), 562–66.

Milisauskas, S. and Kruk, J. 2011. Middle Neolithic/ Early Copper Age, continuity, diversity, and greater complexity, 5500/5000–3500 BC, chapter 8 in *European Prehistory: A Survey* (2nd ed.). (Interdisciplinary Contributions to Archaeology), S. Milisauskas (ed.), 223–91. New York, Dordrecht and London: Springer.

Militarev, A. 2002. The prehistory of a dispersal: the Proto-Afrasian (Afroasiatic) farming lexicon, in Bellwood and Renfrew 2002, 135–50.

Militarev, A. Y. 2005. Once more about glottochronology and the comparative method: the Omotic-Afrasian case, *Aspects of Comparative Linguistics*, 1, 339–40.

Mischka, D. 2011. The Neolithic burial sequence at Flintbek LA 3, north Germany, and its cart tracks: a precise chronology, *Antiquity*, 85 (329), 742–58.

Moffat, A. and Wilson, J. E. 2011. *The Scots: A Genetic Journey*. Edinburgh: Berlinn.

Molodin, V. I. et al. 2012. Human migrations in the southern region of the West Siberian Plain during the Bronze Age: archaeological, palaeogenetic and anthropological data, in Kaiser, Burger and Schier 2012, 93–111.

Montgomery, J. E. 2000. Ibn Fadlan and the Rusiyyah, *Journal of Arabic and Islamic Studies*, 3, 1–25.

Montgomery, J. et al. 2005. Continuity or colonization in Anglo-Saxon England? Isotope evidence for mobility, subsistence practice, and status at West Heslerton, *American Journal of Physical Anthropology*, 126, 123–38.

Montgomery, J. et al. 2010. Gleaming, white, and deadly: using lead to track human exposure and geographic origins in the Roman period in Britain, in Eckardt 2010, 199–226.

Mooder, K. P. et al. 2006. Population affinities of Neolithic Siberians: a snapshot from prehistoric Lake Baikal, *American Journal of Physical Anthropology*, 129 (3), 323–481.

Moore, L. T. et al. 2006. A Y-chromosome signature of hegemony in Gaelic Ireland, *American Journal of Human Genetics*, 78 (2), 334–38.

Moorjani, P. 2011. The history of African gene flow into southern Europeans, Levantines, and Jews, *PLoS Genetics*, 7 (4), e1001373.

Moorjani, P. et al. 2012. Estimating a date of mixture of ancestral South Asian populations. Poster presented at a conference of the Society of Molecular Biology and Evolution, Dublin, 23–26 June 2012, P-2033.

Moreau, C. et al. 2011. Deep human genealogies reveal a selective advantage to be on an expanding wave front, *Science*, 334 (6059), 1148–50.

Morley, C. 2008. Chariots and migrants in East Yorkshire: dismantling the argument, in Lightfoot (ed.), 69–91.

Mozota, F. B. 2007. Celtiberians: problems and debates, section 4.3. Celtiberian: a non-Celtic Indo-European language?, *E-Keltoi, the Journal of Interdisciplinary Celtic Studies*, 6: *The Celts in the Iberian Peninsula*.

Müller, J. 2010. Ritual cooperation and ritual collectivity: the social structure of the middle and younger Funnel Beaker North Group (3500–2800 BC), Jungsteinsite.de.

Müller, J., Brozio, J.-P. et al. 2010. Periodisierung der Trichterbecher-Gesellschaften. Ein Arbeitsentwurf, Jungsteinsite.de.

Müller, J. and van Willigen, S. 2001. New radiocarbon evidence for European Bell Beakers and the consequences for the diffusion of the Bell Beaker Phenomenon, in Nicolis 2001, 59–75.

Müller, W. et al. 2003. Origin and migration of the Alpine Iceman, *Science*, 302 (5646), 862–66.

Murdoch, S. and Grosjean, A. (eds). 2005. *Scottish Communities Abroad in the Early Modern Period*. Leiden: Brill.

Myles, S. et al. 2011. Genetic structure and domestication history of the grape, *PNAS*, published online 18 January, ahead of print.

Myres, N. M. et al. 2011. A major Y-chromosome haplogroup R1b Holocene era founder effect in Central and Western Europe, *European Journal of Human Genetics*, 19 (1), 95–101.

Nakhleh, L., Ringe, D. and Warnow, T. 2005. Perfect phylogenetic networks: a new methodology for reconstructing the evolutionary history of natural languages, *Language, Journal of the Linguistic Society of America*, 81 (2), 382–420.

Nasidze, I. et al. 2005. Genetic evidence for the Mongolian ancestry of Kalmyks, *American Journal of Physical Anthropology*, 128 (4), 846–54.

Nelson, M. 2005. *The Barbarian's Beverage: A History of Beer in Ancient Europe*. London: Routledge.

Nettle, D. 1999. Is the rate of linguistic change constant?, *Lingua*, 108 (2–3), 119–36.

Neveux, F. 2008. *A Brief History of the Normans: The Conquests That Changed the Face of Europe*, trans. H. Curtis. London: Constable and Robinson.

Nica, M. 1997. Unitate și diversitate în culturile neolitice de la dunărea de jos = Unity and diversity of Neolithic cultures on the lower Danube, *Revista Pontica*, 30, 105–16.

Nichols, J. 1990. Linguistic diversity and the first settlement of the New World, *Language*, 66, 475–521.

Nichols, J. 1997. The epicenter of the Indo-European linguistic spread, in *Archaeology and Language I: Theoretical and Methodological Orientations*, R. Blench and M. Spriggs (eds), 122–48. London: Routledge.

Nichols, J. 1998. The Eurasian spread zone and the Indo-European dispersal, in *Archaeology and Language*

II: Correlating Archaeological and Linguistic Hypotheses, R. Blench and M. Spriggs (eds), 220-66. London: Routledge.

Nichols, J. 2011. Forerunners to globalisation: the Eurasian steppe and its periphery, in Language Contact in Times of Globalization (Studies in Slavic and General Linguistics 38), C. Hasselblatt, P. Houtzagers and R. van Pareren (eds), 177-95. Amsterdam and New York: Rodopi.

Nicolaisen, W. F. H. 2001. Scottish Place-Names (2nd ed.). London: Batsford.

Nicolis, F. (ed.) 2001. Bell Beakers Today: Pottery, People, Culture, Symbols in Prehistoric Europe. Proceedings of the International Colloquium, Riva del Garda (Trento, Italy), 11-16 May 1998. Trento: Provincia Autonoma di Trento.

Niederstatter, H. et al. 2012. Pasture names with Romance and Slavic roots facilitate dissection of Y chromosome variation in an exclusively German-speaking Alpine region, PLoS ONE, 7 (7), e41885.

Nieuwenhuyse, O. P. et al. 2010. Not so coarse, nor always plain - the earliest pottery of Syria, Antiquity, 84 (323), 71-85.

Nikitin, A. et al. 2010. Comprehensive site chronology and ancient mitochondrial DNA analysis from Verteba Cave - a Trypillian Culture site of Eneolithic Ukraine, Interdisciplinaria archaeologica: Natural Sciences in Archaeology, 1 (1), 9-18.

Nikitin, A. 2011. Bioarchaeological analysis of Bronze Age human remains from the Podillya region of Ukraine, Interdisciplinaria archaeologica: Natural Sciences in Archaeology, 2 (1), 9-14.

Nikitin, A. et al. 2012. Mitochondrial haplogroup C in ancient mitochondrial DNA from Ukraine extends the presence of East Eurasian genetic lineages in Neolithic Central and Eastern Europe, Journal of Human Genetics, 57, 610-12.

Nocete, F. et al. 2011. Direct chronometry (14C AMS) of the earliest copper metallurgy in the Guadalquivir Basin (Spain) during the third millennium BC: first regional database, Journal of Archaeological Science, 38 (12), 3278-95.

Northover, J. P. N., O'Brien, W. and Stos, S. 2001. Lead isotopes and metal circulation in Beaker/Early Bronze Age Ireland, Journal of Irish Archaeology, 10, 25-47.

Novembre, J. et al. 2008. Genes mirror geography within Europe, Nature, 456 (7218), 98-101.

Nowicki, K. 2008. The Final Neolithic (Late Chalcolithic) to Early Bronze Age transition in Crete and the southeast Aegean islands: changes in settlement patterns and pottery, chapter 13 in Escaping the Labyrinth: The Cretan Neolithic in Context, V. Isaakidou and P. Tomkins (eds), 201-28. Oxford: Oxbow Books/ Sheffield Studies in Aegean Archaeology.

Noy, D. 2000. Foreigners at Rome: Citizens and Strangers. London: Duckworth with the Classical Press of Wales.

Oates, J. 2007. Early Mesopotamian urbanism: a new view from the north, Antiquity, 81 (313), 585-600.

O'Brien, S. R. et al. 1995. Complexity of Holocene climate reconstructed from a Greenland ice core, Science, 270 (5244), 1962-64.

O'Brien, W. 2005. Ross Island: Mining, Metal and Society in Early Ireland (Bronze Age Studies 6). Galway: National University of Ireland, Department of Archaeology.

O'Brien, W. 2012. The Chalcolithic in Ireland: a chronological and cultural framework, chapter 14 in Allen, Gardiner and Sheridan 2012, 211-25.

O'Connor, S., Ono, R. and Clarkson, C. 2011. Pelagic fishing at 42,000 years before the present and the maritime skills of modern humans, Science, 334 (6059), 1117-21.

Ó Corráin, D. 1998. The Vikings in Scotland and Ireland in the ninth century, Peritia, 2, 177-208.

Ó Corráin, D. 2008. The Vikings and Ireland, chapter 31 in Brink and Price 2008, 428-33.

Ó Cróinín, D. (ed.). 2005. A New History of Ireland, vol. 1: Prehistoric and Early Ireland. Oxford and New York: Oxford University Press.

O'Donnabhain, B. and Hallgrímsson, B. 2001. Dublin: the biological identity of the Hiberno-Norse town, in Medieval Dublin II: Proceedings of the Friends of Medieval Dublin Symposium 2000 (Pt. 2), S. Duffy (ed.), 65-87. Dublin: Four Courts Press.

Odriozola, C. P. and Hurtado Pérez, V. M. 2007. The manufacturing process of 3rd millennium BC bone based incrusted pottery decoration from the Middle Guadiana river basin (Badajoz, Spain), Journal of Archaeological Science, 34, 1794-803.

Olsen, S. L. 2006. Early horse domestication on the Eurasian steppe, chapter 17 in Documenting Domestication: New Genetic and Archaeological Paradigms, M. Zeder, D. G. Bradley, E. Emshwiller and B. D. Smith (eds), 245-69. Berkeley and Los Angeles: University of California Press.

Orkneyinga Saga: The Orkneyinga Saga, trans. and ed. H. Palsson and P. Edwards. 1978. London: Penguin.

Østmo, E. 2012. Late Neolithic expansion to Norway. The beginning of a 4000-year-old shipbuilding tradition, chapter 6 in Prescott and Glørstad 2012, 63-69.

Ottoni, C. et al. 2011. Deep into the roots of the Libyan Tuareg: a genetic survey of their paternal heritage, American Journal of Physical Anthropology, 145, 118-24.

Outram, A. K. 2001. Economic anatomy, element abundance and optimality: a new way of examining hunters' bone transportation choices, in Proceedings of Archaeological Sciences '97 (BAR International Series 939), A. Millard (ed.), 117-26. Oxford: BAR.

Outram, A. K. et al. 2009. The earliest horse harnessing and milking, Science, 323 (5919), 1332-35.

Ovchinnikov, I. V. and Goodwin, W. 2003. Ancient human DNA from Sungir?, Journal of Human Evolution, 44, 389-92.

Özbal, R. et al. 2004. Tell Kurdu Excavations 2001, Anatolica, 30, 72-73.

Özdoğan, M. 2010. Westward expansion of the Neolithic way of life: sorting the Neolithic package into distinct packages, in Matthiae 2010, vol. 1, 883-93.

Özdoğan, M. 2011. Archaeological evidence on the westward expansion of farming communities from eastern Anatolia to the Aegean and the Balkans, Current Anthropology, 52 (S4), S415-30.

Pääbo, S. et al. 2004. Genetic analyses from ancient DNA, Annual Review of Genetics, 38, 645-79.

Pala, M. et al. 2009. Mitochondrial haplogroup U5b3: a distant echo of the Epipaleolithic in Italy and the legacy of the early Sardinians, *American Journal of Human Genetics*, 84, 1–8.

Palmer, R. 1996. Wine and viticulture in the Linear A and B texts of the Bronze Age Aegean, chapter 17 in *Origins and Ancient History of Wine*, P. E. McGovern, S. J. Fleming and S. H. Katz (eds), 278–95. Amsterdam: Gordon and Breach.

Pamjav, H. et. al. 2011. Genetic structure of the paternal lineage of the Roma people, *American Journal of Physical Anthropology*, 145, 21–29.

Pamjav, H., Fehér, T., Németh, E. and Pádár, Z. 2012. Brief communication: new Y-chromosome binary markers improve phylogenetic resolution within haplogroup R1a1, *American Journal of Physical Anthropology*, 149 (4), 611–15.

Panyushkina, I. P. et al. 2010. First tree-ring chronology from Andronovo archaeological timbers of Bronze Age in central Asia, *Dendrochronologia*, 28 (1), 13–21.

Parczewski, M. 2004. Slavs and the early Slav culture, in Bogucki and Crabtree 2004, vol. 2, 414–16.

Pardee, D. 2009. A new Aramaic inscription from Zincirli, *Bulletin of the American Schools of Oriental Research*, 356, 51–71.

Pare, C. F. E. 2000. Bronze and the Bronze Age, in *Metals Make the World Go Round: The Supply and Circulation of Metals in Bronze Age Europe. Proceedings of a Conference Held at the University of Birmingham in June 1997*, C. F. E. Pare (ed.), 1–32. Oxford: Oxbow Books.

Park, G. et al. 2010. Dating the Bibong-ri Neolithic site in Korea: excavating the oldest ancient boat, *Nuclear Instruments and Methods in Physics Research B*, 268, 1003–07.

Parkinson, W. A. et al. 2010. Elemental analysis of ceramic incrustation indicates long-term cultural continuity in the prehistoric Carpathian Basin, *Archaeology, Ethnology and Anthropology of Eurasia*, 38 (2), 64–70.

Parpola, A. 2008. Proto-Indo-European speakers of the Late Tripolye culture as the inventors of wheeled vehicles: linguistic and archaeological considerations, in *Proceedings of the 19th Annual UCLA Indo-European Conference* (The Journal of Indo-European Studies Monograph Series 54), K. Jones-Bley, M. E. Huld, A. Della Volpe and M. Robbins Dexter (eds), 1–59. Washington, DC: Institute for the Study of Man.

Patterson, M. A. et al. 2010. Modelling the Neolithic transition in a heterogeneous environment, *Journal of Archaeological Science*, 37 (11), 2929–37.

Patterson, N. J. et al. 2012. Ancient admixture in human history, *Genetics*, Published ahead of print, 7 September, 2012.

Peirce, I. G. 2002. *Swords of the Viking Age*. Woodbridge and Rochester, NY: Boydell Press.

Pellecchia, M. et al. 2007. The mystery of Etruscan origins: novel clues from *Bos taurus* mitochondrial DNA, *PRS B*, 274, 1175–79.

Peltenburg, E. and Wasse, A. (eds). 2004. Neolithic Revolution: new perspectives on southwest Asia in light of recent discoveries on Cyprus (Levant Supplementary Studies 1). Oxford: Oxbow Books.

Pelteret, D. A. E. 1985. Slavery in Anglo-Saxon England, chapter 9 in *The Anglo-Saxons: Synthesis and Achievement*, J. D. Woods and D. A. E. Pelteret (eds), 117–33. Waterloo, Ontario: Wilfred Laurier University Press.

Perdikaris, S. 2004. Pre-Roman Iron Age Scandinavia, in Bogucki and Crabtree 2004, vol. 2, 269–75.

Peregrine, P. N., Peiros, I. and Feldman, M. (eds). 2009. *Ancient Human Migrations: A Multidisciplinary Approach*. Salt Lake City: University of Utah Press.

Pereira, L. et al. 2005. High-resolution mtDNA evidence for the late-glacial resettlement of Europe from an Iberian refugium, *Genome Research*, 15, 19–24.

Pereira, L. et al. 2010. Population expansion in the North African Late Pleistocene signalled by mitochondrial DNA haplogroup U6, *BMC Evolutionary Biology*, 10, 390.

Pérez-Pardal, L. et al. 2010. Multiple paternal origins of domestic cattle revealed by Y-specific interspersed multilocus microsatellites, *Heredity*, 105, 511–19.

Peričić, M. et al. 2005. High-resolution phylogenetic analysis of Southeastern Europe traces major episodes of paternal gene flow among Slavic populations, *Molecular Biology and Evolution*, 22 (10), 1964–75.

Perlès, C. 2003. An alternate (and old-fashioned) view of Neolithisation in Greece, *Documenta Prehistorica*, 30, 99–113.

Pétrequin, P. et al. 2006. Travois et jougs néolithiques du lac de Chalain à Fontenu (Jura, France), in *Premiers Chariots, Premiers Araires: La diffusion de la traction animale en Europe pendant les IVe et IIIe millénaires avant notre ère* (CRA Monographie 29), P. Pétrequin et al. (eds), 87–105. Paris: CNRS.

Phol, W. 2004. The Vandals: fragments of a narrative, chapter 1 in *Vandals, Romans and Berbers: New Perspectives on Late Antique North Africa*, A. H. Merrills (ed.), 31–48. Aldershot and Burlington, VT: Ashgate.

Piepoli, A. et al. 2007. Genotyping of the lactase-phlorizinhydrolase C/T-13910 polymorphism by means of a new rapid denaturing high-performance liquid chromatography-based assay in healthy subjects and colorectal cancer patients, *Journal of Biomolecular Screening*, 12 (5), 733–39.

Pike, A. W. G. et al. 2012. U-Series dating of Paleolithic art in 11 caves in Spain, *Science*, 336 (6087), 1409–13.

Pinhasi, R. et al. 2011. Revised age of late Neanderthal occupation and the end of the Middle Paleolithic in the northern Caucasus, *PNAS*, 108 (21), 8611–16.

Pinhasi, R., Fort, J. and Ammerman, A. J. 2005. Tracing the origin and spread of agriculture in Europe, *PLoS Biology*, 3 (12), e436.

Pinhasi, R. and von Cramon-Taubadel, N. 2009. Craniometric data supports demic diffusion model for the spread of agriculture into Europe, *PLoS ONE*, 4 (8), e6747.

Pinhasi, R. and von Cramon-Taubadel, N. 2012. A craniometric perspective on the transition to agriculture in Europe, *Human Biology*, 84 (1), 45–66.

Pinhasi, R. et al. 2012. The genetic history of Europeans, *Trends in Genetics*, 28 (10), 496–505.

Piotrowska, D. 1998. Biskupin 1933–1996: archaeology, politics and nationalism, *Archaeologia Polona*, 35–36, 255–85.

Pitts, M. 2010. Wealthy man in Roman Gloucester was migrant Goth, *British Archaeology*, 113, 7.

Plagnol, V. and Wall, J. D. 2006. Possible ancestral structure in human populations, *PLoS Genetics*, 2, 972–79.

Plantinga, T. S. et al. 2012. Low prevalence of lactase persistence in Neolithic Spain, *European Journal of Human Genetics*, 20 (7), 778–82.

Pliny the Elder. *The Natural History*, trans. J. Bostock and H. T. Riley. 1855. London: Taylor and Francis.

Pluciennik, M. 1997. Radiocarbon determinations and the Mesolithic–Neolithic transition in Southern Italy, *Journal of Mediterranean Archaeology*, 10, 115–50.

Plutarch. The Life of Marius, included in *Fall of the Roman Republic: Six Lives by Plutarch*, trans. R. Warner, intro. and notes R. Seager. 1972. Harmondsworth: Penguin.

Pohl, J. O. 2009. *Volk auf dem Weg*: transnational migration of the Russian-Germans from 1763 to the present day, *Studies in Ethnicity and Nationalism*, 9 (2), 267–86.

Poinar, H. N. 2003. The top 10 list: criteria of authenticity for DNA from ancient and forensic samples, *International Congress Series*, 1239, 575–79.

Potts, D. T. 1999. *The Archaeology of Elam: Formation and Transformation of an Ancient Iranian State*. Cambridge, New York and Melbourne: Cambridge University Press.

Powell, A. et al. 2009. Late Pleistocene demography and the appearance of modern human behavior, *Science*, 324 (5932), 1298–1301.

Prat, S. et al. 2011. The oldest anatomically modern humans from far Southeast Europe: direct dating, culture and behavior, *PLoS ONE*, 6 (6), e20834.

Prescott, C. 2012. Third millennium transformations in Norway: modelling an interpretive platform, chapter 10 in Prescott and Glørstad 2012, 115–27.

Prescott, C. and Glørstad, H. (eds). 2012. *Becoming European*. Oxford and Oakville, CT: Oxbow Books.

Price, N. S. 1989. *The Vikings in Brittany*. London: Viking Society for Northern Research, University College London, pub. simultaneously as *Saga-Book XXII* 6.

Price, T. D. et al. 2011. Who was in Harold Bluetooth's army? Strontium isotope investigation of the cemetery at the Viking Age fortress at Trelleborg, Denmark, *Antiquity*, 85 (328), 476–89.

Price, T. D., Knipper, C., Grupe G. and Smrcka, V. 2004. Strontium isotopes and prehistoric human migration: the Bell Beaker period in Central Europe, *European Journal of Archaeology*, 7 (1), 9–40.

Prieto-Martínez, M. P. 2012. Perceiving changes in the third millennium BC in Europe through pottery, chapter 4 in Prescott and Glørstad 2012, 30–47.

Procopius. *History of the Wars*, trans. H. B. Dewing. 1914–40. 7 vols (Loeb Classical Library). Cambridge, MA: Harvard University Press.

Prowse, T. L. et al. 2010. Stable isotope and mtDNA evidence for geographic origins at the site of Vagnari, Italy (1st–4th centuries AD), in Eckardt 2010, 175–98.

Pseudo-Skylax's Periplous – The Circumnavigation of the Inhabited World: Text, Translation and Commentary, ed., trans. and commentary G. Shipley. 2011. Exeter: Bristol Phoenix Press/University of Exeter Press.

Ptolemy, Claudius. *The Geography*. No reliable complete English translation is in print; that used is trans. E. L. Stevenson. 1932. New York: New York Public Library.

Pushkariova, S. F. 1998. Primario e secundario en los nombres vascos de los metales, *Fontes linguae vasconum: Studia et documenta*, 30 (79), 417–28.

Quiles, C. and López-Menchero, F. 2011. *A Grammar of Modern Indo-European* (3rd ed.). Badajoz, Spain: Indo-European Language Association.

Quintana-Murci, L. et al. 2001. Y-chromosome lineages trace diffusion of people and languages in Southwestern Asia, *American Journal of Human Genetics*, 68, 537–42.

Quintana-Murci, L. et al. 2004. Where West meets East: the complex mtDNA landscape of the southwest and central Asian corridor, *American Journal of Human Genetics*, 74, 827–45.

Radivojević, M. et al. 2010. On the origins of extractive metallurgy: new evidence from Europe, *Journal of Archaeological Science*, 37 (11), 2775–87.

Raetzel-Fabian, D. 2002. Monumentality and communication: Neolithic enclosures and long-distance tracks in West Central Europe. Jungsteinsite. de.

Raftery, B. 1997. *Pagan Celtic Ireland: The Enigma of the Irish Iron Age*. (2nd ed.). London: Thames & Hudson.

Raftery, B. 2005. Iron Age Ireland, chapter 6 in Ó Cróinín 2005, 134–81.

Ralph, P. and Coop, G. 2012. The geography of recent genetic ancestry across Europe, Cornell University Library eprints: arXiv:1207.3815v1 [q-bio.PE].

Ramirez Sádaba, J. L. 2006. Las ciudades Vasconas segun las fuentes literarias y su evolucion en la tardoantigüedad, *Antigüedad y Cristianismo (Murcia)*, 23, 185–99.

Ramos-Luis, E. et al. 2009. Phylogeography of French male lineages, *Forensic Science International: Genetics Supplement Series*, 2, 439–41.

Reich, D. et al. 2010. Genetic history of an archaic hominin group from Denisova Cave in Siberia, *Nature*, 468, 1053–60.

Reich, D. et al. 2011. Denisova admixture and the first modern human dispersals into southeast Asia and Oceania, *American Journal of Human Genetics*, 89 (4), 516–28.

Reide, F. 2009. Climate and demography in early prehistory: using calibrated 14C dates as population proxies, *Human Biology*, 81 (2–3), 309–37.

Renaud, J. 2003. La toponymie normanique: reflet d'une colonisation, in *La Progression des Vikings, des raids à la colonisation*, A.-M. Flambard Hericher (ed.), 189–206. Rouen: Publications de l'Université de Rouen.

Renfrew, C. 1972. *The Emergence of Civilisation: The Cyclades and the Aegean in the Third Millennium BC*. London: Methuen. Repr. 2011, Oxford: Oxbow Books; Oakville, CT: David Brown Book Co.

Renfrew, C. 1987. *Archaeology and Language: The Puzzle of Indo-European Origins*. London: Jonathan Cape.

Renfrew, C. and Bahn, P. 2012. *Archaeology: Theories, Methods and Practice* (6th ed.). London and New York: Thames & Hudson.

Res Gestae Divi Augusti: Text, Translation and Commentary, trans. A. Cooley. 2009. Cambridge: Cambridge University Press.

Ricaut, F.-X. 2012. A time series of prehistoric mitochondrial DNA reveals Western European genetic diversity was largely established by the Bronze Age, *Advances in Anthropology*, 2 (1), 14–23.

Richard, C. et al. 2007. An mtDNA perspective of French genetic variation, *Annals of Human Biology*, 34 (1), 68–79.

Richards, M. et al. 2000. Tracing European founder lineages in the Near Eastern mtDNA pool, *American Journal of Human Genetics*, 67, 1251–76.

Richer. *Richer of Saint-Rémi, Histories, I: Books 1 and 2*, ed. and trans. J. Lake (Dumbarton Oaks Medieval Library). 2011. Cambridge, MA: Harvard University Press.

Richerson, P. J., Boyd, R. and Bettinger, R. L. 2009. Cultural innovations and demographic change, *Human Biology*, 81 (2–3), 211–35.

Riha, T. (ed.). 1969. *Readings in Russian Civilization, Vol. 1: Russia Before Peter the Great* (2nd ed.). Chicago: University of Chicago Press.

Ringe, D. 2006. *From Proto-Indo-European to Proto-Germanic* (A History of English, 1). Oxford and New York: Oxford University Press.

Ringe, D., Warnow, T. and Taylor, A. 2002. Indo-European and computational cladistics, *Transactions of the Philological Society*, 100 (1), 59–129.

Rix, H. 1998. *Rätisch und Etruskisch*. Innsbruck: Institut für Sprachwissenschaft der Universität Innsbruck.

Rizzi, E. et al. 2012. Ancient DNA studies: new perspectives on old samples, *Genetics Selection Evolution*, 44 (21).

Robb, J. 2009. People of stone: stelae, personhood and society in prehistoric Europe, *Journal of Archaeological Method and Theory*, 16 (3), 162–83.

Roberts, B. 2008. Creating traditions and shaping technologies: understanding the earliest metal objects and metal production in Western Europe, *World Archaeology*, 40 (3), 354–72.

Roberts, B. 2008b. Migration, craft expertise and metallurgy: analysing the spread of metal in Western Europe, in Lightfoot (ed.), 27–45.

Roberts, B. W. 2009. Production networks and consumer choice in the earliest metal of Western Europe, *Journal of World Prehistory*, 22 (4), 461–81.

Roberts, B. W., Thornton, C. P. and Pigott, V. C. 2009. Development of metallurgy in Eurasia, *Antiquity*, 83, 1012–22.

Roberts, B. W. and Vander Linden, M. (eds). 2011. *Investigating Archaeological Cultures: Material Culture, Variability, and Transmission*. New York, Dordrecht, Heidelberg and London: Springer.

Roberts, S., Sofaer, J. and Kiss, V. 2008. Characterization and textural analysis of Middle Bronze Age Transdanubian inlaid wares of the Encrusted Pottery Culture, Hungary: a preliminary study, *Journal of Archaeological Science*, 35 (2), 322–30.

Robertson, J. S. 2012. How the Germanic Futhark came from the Roman alphabet, *Futhark: International Journal of Runic Studies* 2, 7–25.

Rocca, R. et al. 2012. Discovery of Western European R1b1a2 Y chromosome variants in 1000 Genomes Project data: an online community approach, *PLoS ONE* 7 (7), e41634.

Rodríguez, J. P. (ed.). 1997. *The Historical Encyclopedia of World Slavery*. 2 vols. Santa Barbara, CA: ABC-CLIO.

Rodríguez-Ezpeleta, N. et al. 2010. High-density SNP genotyping detects homogeneity of Spanish and French Basques, and confirms their genomic distinctiveness from other European populations, *Human Genetics*, 128 (1), 113–17.

Rodríguez Ramos, J. 2003. La cultura ibérica desde la perspectiva de la epigrafía. Un ensayo de síntesis, *Iberia*, 3, 17–38.

Røed, K. H. et al. 2008. Genetic analyses reveal independent domestication origins of Eurasian reindeer, *PRS B*, 275 (1645), 1849–55.

Røed, K. H. et al. 2011. Elucidating the ancestry of domestic reindeer from ancient DNA approaches, *Quaternary International*, 238 (1–2), 83–88.

Rogozhinskiy, A. E. 2011. Rock art sites in Kazakhstan, in *Rock Art in Central Asia: A Thematic Study*, J. Clottes (ed.), 9–42. Paris: International Council on Monuments and Sites.

Roller, D. W. 2006. *Through the Pillars of Herakles: Greco-Roman Exploration of the Atlantic*. London: Routledge.

Romgard, J. 2008. *Questions of Early Human Settlements in Xinjiang and the Early Silk Road Trade, with an Overview of the Silk Road Research Institutions and Scholars in Beijing, Gansu and Xinjiang* (Sino-Platonic Papers 185), ed. V. Mair. Philadelphia: University of Pennsylvania.

Roodenberg, M. S. A. 2011. A preliminary study of the burials from Late Neolithic–Early Chalcolithic Aktopraklık, *Anatolica*, 37, 17–43.

Rootsi, S. et al. 2004. Phylogeography of Y-chromosome haplogroup I reveals distinct domains of prehistoric gene flow in Europe, *American Journal of Human Genetics*, 75, 128–37.

Rootsi, S. et al. 2007. A counter-clockwise northern route of the Y-chromosome haplogroup N from Southeast Asia towards Europe, *European Journal of Human Genetics*, 15, 204–11.

Rootsi, S. et al. 2012. Distinguishing the co-ancestries of haplogroup G Y-chromosomes in the populations of Europe and the Caucasus, *European Journal of Human Genetics*, 20 (12), 1275–82.

Ropars, G. et al. 2012. A depolarizer as a possible precise sunstone for Viking navigation by polarized skylight, *Proceedings of the Royal Society A: Mathematical, Physical and Engineering Sciences*, 468 (2139), 671–84.

Roth, M. T. (trans.). 1997. *Law Collections from Mesopotamia and Asia Minor* (2nd ed.) Atlanta: Scholars Press.

Rougier, H. et al. 2007. Peştera cu Oase 2 and the cranial morphology of early modern Europeans, *PNAS*, 104 (4), 1165–70.

Rouillard, P. 2009. Greeks and the Iberian peninsula: forms of exchange and settlements, chapter 5 in Dietler and López-Ruiz 2009, 129–50.

Roux, V. and Courty, M.-A. 2005. Identifying social entities at a macro-regional level: Chalcolithic ceramics of south Levant as a case study, in *Pottery Manufacturing Processes: Reconstruction and Interpretation. Actes du XIVème Congrès de l'UISPP* (BAR International Series 1349), D. Bosquet, A. Livingstone-Smith and R. Martineau (eds), 201–14. Oxford: Archaeopress.

Rowley-Conwy, P. 2004. How the West was lost: a reconsideration of agricultural origins in Britain, Ireland, and southern Scandinavia, *Current Anthropology*, 45 (S4), S83–113.

Rowley-Conwy, P. 2011. Westward Ho! The spread of agriculture from Central Europe to the Atlantic, *Current Anthropology*, 52 (S4), S431–51.

Rubio, G. 1999. On the alleged 'Pre-Sumerian Substratum', *Journal of Cuneiform Studies*, 51, 1–16.

Rudbeck, L. et al. 2005. MtDNA analysis of human remains from an early Danish Christian cemetery, *American Journal of Physical Anthropology*, 128, 424–29.

Russell, J. C. 1968. That earlier plague, *Demography*, 5 (1), 174–84.

Russian Primary Chronicle, The. Laurentian Text, trans. and ed. S. H. Cross and O. P. Sherbowitz-Wetzor. 1953. Cambridge, MA: The Mediaeval Academy of America.

Rutter, J. B. 1993. Review of Aegean Prehistory II: the prepalatial Bronze Age of the southern and central Greek mainland, *American Journal of Archaeology*, 97 (4), 745–97.

Şahoğlu, V. 2005. The Anatolian trade network and the Izmir region during the Early Bronze Age, *Oxford Journal of Archaeology*, 24 (4), 339–61.

Šalkovský, P. 2000. Slavic habitat in the early Middle Ages, in *Slovaks in the Central Danubian Region in the 6th to 11th Century*, M. Kucera (ed.), 107–31. Bratislava: Slovenské národné múzeum.

Sampietro, M. L. et al. 2005. The genetics of the pre-Roman Iberian Peninsula: a mtDNA study of ancient Iberians, *Annals of Human Genetics*, 69 (5), 535–48.

Sampietro, M. L. et al. 2006. Tracking down human contamination in ancient human teeth, *Molecular Biology and Evolution*, 23 (9), 1801–07.

Sampietro, M. L. et al. 2007. Palaeogenetic evidence supports a dual model of Neolithic spreading into Europe, *PRS B*, 274, 2161–67.

Sánchez-Quinto, F. et al. 2012. Genomic affinities of two 7,000-year-old Iberian hunter-gatherers, *Current Biology*, 22 (16), 1494–99.

Sanmarti, J. 2009. Colonial relations and social change in Iberia (seventh to third centuries BC), chapter 2 in Dietler and López-Ruiz 2009, 49–90.

Santin, I. et al. 2006. Killer cell immunoglobulin-like receptor (KIR) genes in the Basque population: association study of KIR gene contents with type 1 diabetes mellitus, *Human Immunology*, 67 (1–2), 118–24.

Santos Yanguas, J. 1988. Identificación de las ciudades antiguas de Álava, Guipúzcoa y Vizcaya: Estado de la cuestión, *Studia Historica: Historia Antigua*, 6, 121–30.

Sarauw, T. 2007. Male symbols or warrior identities? The archery burials of the Danish Bell Beaker Culture, *Journal of Anthropological Archaeology*, 26 (1), 65–87.

Sarauw, T. 2008. Danish Bell Beaker pottery and flint daggers – the display of social identities?, *European Journal of Archaeology*, 11 (1), 23–47.

Savard, M., Nesbitt, M. and Jones, M. K. 2006. The role of wild grasses in subsistence and sedentism: new evidence from the northern Fertile Crescent, *World Archaeology*, 38 (2), 179–96.

Sawyer, P. (ed.). 1997. *The Oxford Illustrated History of the Vikings*. Oxford: Oxford University Press.

Scarre, C. 2010. Stone people: monuments and identities in the Channel Islands. Paper of the European Megalithic Studies Group Meeting held in 2010 at Kiel University. Jungsteinsite.de.

Scham, S. 2008. The world's first temple, *Archaeology*, 61 (6).

Schenker, A. M. 1995. *The Dawn of Slavic: An Introduction to Slavic Philology*. New Haven: Yale University Press.

Schilz, F. 2006. Molekulargenetische Verwandtschafts-analysen am prähistorischen Skelettkollektiv der Lichtensteinhöhle. Dissertation, Göttingen.

Schloen, D. and Fink, A. S. 2009. New excavations at Zincirli Höyük in Turkey (Ancient Sam'al) and the discovery of an inscribed mortuary stele, *Bulletin of the American Schools of Oriental Research*, 356, 1–13.

Schmidt, K. 2012. Göbekli Tepe and the revolution of symbols, in *A Companion to the Archaeology of the Ancient Near East* (Blackwell Companions to the Ancient World), 2 vols, D. T. Potts (ed.), vol. 1, 150–59. Oxford: Wiley-Blackwell.

Schuenemann, V. J. et al. 2011. Targeted enrichment of ancient pathogens yielding the pPCP1 plasmid of *Yersinia pestis* from victims of the Black Death, *PNAS*, 108 (38), E746–E752.

Schuhmacher, T. X., Cardoso, J. L. and Banerjee, A. 2009. Sourcing African ivory in Chalcolithic Portugal, *Antiquity*, 83 (322), 983–97.

Searle, J. B. et al. 2009. Of mice and (Viking?) men: phylogeography of British and Irish house mice, *PRS B*, 276 (1655), 201–07.

Semino, O. et al. 2000. The genetic legacy of paleolithic *Homo sapiens sapiens* in extant Europeans: a Y chromosome perspective, *Science*, 290, 1155–59.

Semino, O. et al. 2004. Origin, diffusion, and differentiation of Y-chromosome haplogroups E and J: inferences on the Neolithization of Europe and later migratory events in the Mediterranean area, *American Journal of Human Genetics*, 74, 1023–34.

Sengupta, S. et al. 2006. Polarity and temporality of high-resolution Y-chromosome distributions in India identify both indigenous and exogenous expansions and reveal minor genetic influence of central Asian pastoralists, *American Journal of Human Genetics*, 78 (2), 202–21.

Serk, P. 2004. Human Mitochondrial DNA Haplogroup J in Europe and Near East, Thesis, Tartu.

Sezgin, E. et al. 2009. Association of Y chromosome haplogroup I with HIV progression, and HAART outcome, *Human Genetics*, 125 (3), 281–94.

Shapiro, B. and Hofreiter, M. (eds). 2012. *Ancient DNA: Methods and Protocols* (Methods in Molecular Biology, 840). New York: Humana Press.

Shea, J. J. and Sisk, M. L. 2010. Complex projectile technology and *Homo sapiens* dispersal into western Eurasia, *PaleoAnthropology*, 2010, 100–22.

Shennan, S. 1997. *Quantifying Archaeology* (2nd ed.). Edinburgh: Edinburgh University Press.

Shennan, S. 2001. Demography and cultural innovation: a model and its implications for the emergence of modern human culture, *Cambridge Archaeological Journal*, 11 (1), 5–16.

Shennan, S. 2009. Evolutionary demography and the population history of the European Early Neolithic, *Human Biology*, 81 (2–3), 339–55.

Shennan, S. and Edinborough, K. 2007. Prehistoric population history: from the Late Glacial to the Late Neolithic in Central and Northern Europe, *Journal of Archaeological Science*, 34 (8), 1339–45.

Shepherd, I. 2012. Is there a Scottish Chalcolithic?, chapter 11 in Allen, Gardiner and Sheridan 2012, 164–71.

Sheridan, A. 2000. Achnacreebeag and its French connections: vive the 'Auld Alliance', in *The Prehistory and Early History of Atlantic Europe* (BAR S861), J. C. Henderson (ed.), 1–16. Goteborg: Archaeopress.

Sheridan, A. 2008. Upper Largie and Dutch–Scottish connections during the Beaker period, in *Between Foraging and Farming: An Extended Broad Spectrum of Papers Presented to Leendert Louwe Kooijmans* (Analecta Praehistorica Leidensia 40), H. Fokkens et al. (eds), 247–60. Leiden: Leiden University Press.

Sherratt, A. 1981. Plough and pastoralism: aspects of the secondary products revolution, chapter 10 in *Pattern of the Past: Studies in Honour of David Clarke*, I. Hodder, G. Isaac and N. Hammond (eds), 261–305. Cambridge: Cambridge University Press.

Shi, W. et al. 2010. A worldwide survey of human male demographic history based on Y-SNP and Y-STR data from the HGDP-CEPH populations, *Molecular Biology and Evolution*, 27 (2), 385–93.

Shirai, N. 2010. *The Archaeology of the First Farmer-Herders in Egypt: New Insights into the Fayum Epipalaeolithic and Neolithic*. Leiden: Leiden University Press.

Shisha-Halevy, A. 2003. Celtic syntax, Egyptian-Coptic syntax, *Das Alte Ägypten und seine Nachbarn: Festschrift Helmut Satzinger*, 245–302. Krems: Österreichisches Literaturforum.

Shishlina, N. I., Orfinskaya, O. V. and Golikov, V. P. 2003. Bronze Age textiles from the North Caucasus: new evidence of fourth millennium BC fibres and fabrics, *Oxford Journal of Archaeology*, 22 (4), 331–44.

Sigurdsson, J. V. 2008. Iceland, chapter 42 in Brink and Price 2008, 571–78.

Sikora, M. et al. 2012. On the Sardinian ancestry of the Tyrolean Iceman. Abstract of paper prepared for the annual meeting of the American Society for Human Genetics, San Francisco, 6–10 November 2012.

Simeon of Durham. *The Historical Works of Simeon of Durham*, trans. J. Stevenson. 1855. The Church Historians of England, vol. 3, part 2. London: Seeleys.

Simon, Z. 2008. How to find the Proto-Indo-European homeland? A methodological essay, *Acta Antiqua*, 48, 289–303.

Simon, Z. 2009. Some critical remarks on the recent PIE homeland and ethnogenesis theories, *Indogermanische Forschungen*, 114, 60–72.

Sims-Williams, P. 2006. *Ancient Celtic Place-Names in Europe and Asia Minor* (Publications of the Philological Society, 39). Oxford and Boston: Blackwell.

Sjödin, P. and François, O. 2011. Wave-of-advance models of the diffusion of the Y chromosome haplogroup R1b1b2 in Europe, *PLoS ONE*, 6 (6), e21592.

Skoglund, P. et al. 2012. Origins and genetic legacy of Neolithic farmers and hunter-gatherers in Europe, *Science*, 336 (6080), 466–69.

Skoglund, P. and Jakobsson, M. 2011. Archaic human ancestry in East Asia, *PNAS*, 108 (45), 18301–06.

Skre, D. 2008. The development of urbanism in Scandinavia, in Brink and Price 2008, 83–93.

Slavchev, V. 2009. The Varna Eneolithic cemetery in the context of the Late Copper Age in the East Balkans, chapter 9 in Anthony and Chi 2009, 192–211.

Slimak, L. et al. 2011. Late Mousterian persistence near the Arctic Circle, *Science*, 332 (6031), 841–45.

Sloane, B. 2011. *The Black Death in London*. Stroud: The History Press.

Smith, S. E. et al. 2009. Inferring population continuity versus replacement with aDNA: a cautionary tale from the Aleutian Islands, *Human Biology*, 81 (4), 407–26.

Snorri Sturluson. *Heimskringla: Harald Harfager's Saga*.

Soares, P. et al. 2009. Correcting for purifying selection: an improved human mitochondrial molecular clock, *American Journal of Human Genetics*, 84 (6), 740–59.

Soares, P. et al. 2010. The archaeogenetics of Europe, *Current Biology*, 20, R174–83.

Šoberl, L. and Evershed, R. 2009. Organic residue analysis of pottery samples from Warren Field timber hall and the Crathes Castle overflow car park site, in *A Tale of the Unknown Unknowns: A Mesolithic Pit Alignment and a Neolithic Timber Hall at Warren Field, Crathes, Aberdeenshire*, H. K. Murray, J. C. Murray and S. M. Fraser (eds), 93–97. Oxford: Oxbow Books.

Solecki, R. S., Solecki, R. L. and Agelarakis, A. P. 2004. *The Proto-Neolithic Cemetery in Shanidar Cave* (Texas A&M University Anthropology Series, 7). College Station: Texas A&M University Press.

Soltysiak, A. 2006. The plague pandemic and Slavic expansion in the 6th–8th centuries, *Archaeologia Polonia*, 44, 339–64.

Sørensen, M. L. S. and Rebay-Salisbury, K. 2008. Landscapes of the body: burials of the Middle Bronze Age in Hungary, *European Journal of Archaeology*, 11 (1), 49–74.

Spangenberg, J. E., Jacomet, S. and Schibler, J. 2006. Chemical analyses of organic residues in archaeological pottery from Arbon Bleiche 3, Switzerland – evidence for dairying in the late Neolithic, *Journal of Archaeological Science*, 33 (1), 1–13.

Spangenberg, J. E., Matuschik, I., Jacomet, S. and Schibler, J. 2008. Direct evidence for the existence of dairying farms in prehistoric Central Europe (4th millennium BC), *Isotopes in Environmental and Health Studies*, 44 (2), 189–200.

Spurkland, T. 2010. The Older Fuþark and Roman script

literacy, *Futhark: International Journal of Runic Studies*, 1, 65–84.

Stathakopoulos, D. 2006. Crime and punishment: the plague in the Byzantine Empire, chapter 5 in Little 2006, 99–118.

Stevens, C. J. and Fuller, D. Q. 2012. Did Neolithic farming fail? The case for a Bronze Age agricultural revolution in the British Isles, *Antiquity*, 86 (333), 707–22.

Stos-Gale, Z. A., Gale, N. H. and Gilmore, G. R. 1984. Early Bronze Age Trojan metal sources and Anatolians in the Cyclades, *Oxford Journal of Archaeology*, 3 (3), 23–44.

Strabo. *The Geography*, trans. H. L. Jones. 1917–32. 8 vols (Loeb Classical Library). Cambridge, MA: Harvard University Press.

Struble, E. J. and Herrmann, V. R. 2009. An eternal feast at Sam'al: the new Iron Age mortuary stele in context, *Bulletin of the American Schools of Oriental Research*, 356, 15–49.

Sukernik, R. I. et al. 2012. Mitochondrial genome diversity in the Tubalar, Even and Ulchi: contribution to prehistory of native Siberians and their affinities to Native Americans, *American Journal of Physical Anthropology*, 148 (1), 123–38.

Swadesh, M. 1952. Lexicostatistic dating of prehistoric ethnic contacts, *Proceedings of the American Philosophical Society*, 96, 452–63.

Sykes, B. C. 2000. Report on DNA recovered from the Red Lady of Paviland, in *Paviland Cave and the 'Red Lady': A Definitive Report*, S. Aldhouse-Green (ed.), 75–77. Bristol: published for the SCARAB Research Centre of the University of Wales College, Newport and the Friends of the National Museum of Wales by the Western Academic & Specialist Press.

Sykes, B. 2001. *The Seven Daughters of Eve*. London: Bantam.

Szostek, K. et al. 2005. The diet and social paleostratigraphy of Neolithic agricultural population of the Lengyel culture from Osłonki (Poland), *Przeglad Antropologiczny – Anthropological Review*, 68, 29–41.

Tacitus. *Germania*, included in Tacitus, *Agricola, Germania*, trans. H. Mattingly, rev. with intro. and notes by J. B. Rives. 2009. London and New York: Penguin Books.

Talbert, R. J. A. (ed.). 2000. *Barrington Atlas of the Greek and Roman World*. 2 vols. Princeton and Woodstock: Princeton University Press.

Tallavaara, M., Pesonen, P. and Oinonen, M. 2010. Prehistoric population history in eastern Fennoscandia, *Journal of Archaeological Science*, 37 (2), 251–60.

Tambets, K. et al. 2002. Complex signals for population expansions in Europe and beyond, in Bellwood and Renfrew 2002, 449–58.

Tambets, K. et al. 2004. The western and eastern roots of the Saami: the story of genetic outliers told by mitochondrial DNA and Y chromosomes, *American Journal of Human Genetics*, 74 (4), 661–82.

Tapio, M. et al. 2006. Sheep mitochondrial DNA variation in European, Caucasian, and Central Asian areas, *Molecular Biology and Evolution*, 23 (9), 1776–83.

Tarasov, P. E. et al. 2000. Last glacial maximum biomes reconstructed from pollen and plant macrofossil data from northern Eurasia, *Journal of Biogeography*, 27, 609–20.

Tarkhnishvili, D. et al. 2012. Palaeoclimatic models help to understand current distribution of Caucasian forest species, *Biological Journal of the Linnean Society*, 105, 231–48.

Taylor, T. 2010. *The Artificial Ape: How Technology Changed the Course of Human Evolution*. New York and Basingstoke: Palgrave Macmillan.

Telehin, D. Y. and Mallory, J. P. 1994. *The Anthropomorphic Stelae of the Ukraine: The Early Iconography of the Indo-Europeans* (Journal of Indo-European Studies Monograph 11). Washington, DC: Institute for the Study of Man.

Terral, J.-F. 2004. Historical biogeography of olive domestication (*Olea europaea* L.) as revealed by geometrical morphometry applied to biological and archaeological material, *Journal of Biogeography*, 31, 63–77.

Thangaraj, K. 2010. The influence of natural barriers in shaping the genetic structure of Maharashtra populations, *PLoS ONE* 5 (12), e15283.

Thomas, J. T. 2009. Approaching specialisation: craft production in Late Neolithic/Copper Age Iberia, *Papers from the Institute of Archaeology, University College London*, 19, 67–84.

Thomason, S. G. 2001. *Language Contact: An Introduction*. Edinburgh: Edinburgh University Press.

Thompson, E. A. 1969. *The Goths in Spain*. Oxford: Clarendon Press.

Thompson, E. A. 1996. *The Huns* (The Peoples of Europe) (rev. ed.). Oxford and Malden, MA: Blackwell.

Thornton, C. P. and Schurr, T. G. 2004. Genes, language and culture: an example from the Tarim Basin, *Oxford Journal of Archaeology*, 23 (1), 83–106.

Tian, C. et al. 2008. Analysis and application of European genetic substructure using 300 K SNP information, *PLoS Genetics*, 4 (1), e4.

Tian, C. et al. 2009. European population genetic substructure: further definition of ancestry informative markers for distinguishing among diverse European ethnic groups, *Molecular Medicine*, 15 (11–12), 371–83.

Tishkoff, S. A. et al. 2009. The genetic structure and history of Africans and African Americans, *Science*, 324 (5930), 1035–44.

Todd, M. 2004. *The Early Germans* (The Peoples of Europe) (2nd ed.). Malden, MA, Oxford and Carlton, Victoria: Wiley-Blackwell.

Tofanelli, S. et al. 2009. J1-M267 Y lineage marks climate-driven pre-historical human displacements, *European Journal of Human Genetics*, 17, 1520–24.

Tömöry, G. et al. 2007. Comparison of maternal lineage and biogeographic analyses of ancient and modern Hungarian populations, *American Journal of Physical Anthropology*, 34 (3), 354–68.

Trask, R. L. 1996. Origin and relatives of the Basque language: review of the evidence, in *Towards a History of the Basque Language* (Amsterdam Studies in the Theory and History of Linguistic Science, Series IV: Current Issues in Linguistic Theory 131), J. I. Hualde et al. (eds), 65–77. Amsterdam: John Benjamins Publishing Company.

Trask, R. L. 1997. *The History of Basque*. London and New York: Routledge.

Trask, R. L. 2008. *Etymological Dictionary of Basque*, edited for web publication by M. W. Wheeler.

Tristram, H. L. C. (ed.) 2007. *The Celtic Languages in Contact: Papers from the Workshop within the Framework of the XIII International Congress of Celtic Studies, Bonn, 26–27 July 2007*. Potsdam: Universitätsverlag Potsdam.

Udolph, J. 1994. *Namenkundliche Studien zum Germanenproblem* (Reallexikon der germanischen Altertumskunde, Ergänzungsbände 9). Berlin: De Gruyter.

Underhill, P. A. et al. 2007. New phylogenetic relationships for Y-chromosome haplogroup I: reappraising its phylogeography and prehistory, in Mellars, Boyle, Bar-Yosef and Stringer 2007, 33–44.

Underhill, P. A. et al. 2010. Separating the post-Glacial coancestry of European and Asian Y chromosomes within haplogroup R1a, *European Journal of Human Genetics*, 18 (4), 479–84.

Untermann, J. 1961. *Sprachräume und Sprachbewegungen im vorrömischen Hispanien*. Wiesbaden: Harrassowitz.

Ur, J. A. 2010. Cycles of civilization in Northern Mesopotamia, 4400–2000 BC, *Journal of Archaeological Research*, 18, 387–431.

Urbanczyk, P. 2004. Iron Age Poland, in Bogucki and Crabtree 2004, vol. 2, 414–16.

Usai, D. and Salvatori, S. 2007. The oldest representation of a Nile boat, *Antiquity*, 81 (314), project gallery (online edition only).

Valladas, H. et al. 2005. Bilan des datations carbone 14 effectuées sur des charbons de bois de la grotte Chauvet, *Bulletin de Société préhistorique française*, 102, 109–13.

van As, A., Jacobs, L. and Nieuwenhuyse, O. P. 2004. Early pottery from Late Neolithic Tell Sabi Abyad II, Syria, *Leiden Journal of Pottery Studies*, 20, 97–110.

Van De Mieroop, M. 2007. *A History of the Ancient Near East ca. 3000–323 BC*. (2nd ed.). Malden, MA, Oxford and Carlton, Victoria: Blackwell.

Vander Linden, M. 2007. What linked the Bell Beakers in third millennium BC Europe?, *Antiquity*, 81, 343–52.

Vander Linden, M. 2011. To tame a land: archaeological cultures and the spread of the Neolithic in western Europe, chapter 15 in Roberts and Vander Linden 2011, 289–307.

Vander Linden, M. 2012. Demography and mobility in North-Western Europe during the third millennium cal. BC, in Prescott and Glørstad 2012, 19–29.

Vandiver, P. B. 1987. Sequential slab construction: a conservative southwest Asiatic ceramic tradition, ca. 7000–3000 B.C., *Paléorient*, 13 (2), 9–35.

Vandkilde, H. 2005. A review of the Early Late Neolithic period in Denmark: practice, identity and connectivity. Jungsteinsite.de.

Vanhaeren. M. et al. 2006. Middle Paleolithic shell beads in Israel and Algeria, *Science*, 312 (5781), 1785–88.

Vanmontfort, B. 2001. The group of Spiere as a new stylistic entity in the Middle Neolithic Scheldt Basin, *Notae Praehistoricae*, 21, 139–43.

Vanmontfort, B. 2007. Bridging the gap: the Mesolithic-Neolithic transition in a frontier zone, *Documenta Praehistorica*, 34, 105–18.

Vanmontfort, B. 2008. Forager-farmer connections in an 'unoccupied' land: first contact on the western edge of LBK territory, *Journal of Anthropological Archaeology*, 27, 149–60.

Vanmontfort, B., Casseyas, C. and Vermeersch, P. M. 1997. Neolithic ceramics from Spiere 'De Hel' and their contribution to the understanding of the earliest Michelsbergculture, *Notae Praehistoricae*, 17, 123–34.

van Oven, M. and Kayser, M. 2009. Updated comprehensive phylogenetic tree of global human mitochondrial DNA variation, *Human Mutation*, 30 (2), E386–94. Updated online at http://www.phylotree.org.

Vanséveren, S. 2008. A 'new' ancient Indo-European language? On assumed linguistic contacts between Sumerian and Indo-European 'Euphratic', *Journal of Indo-European Studies*, 36, 371–82.

Vasilieva, I. N. 2011. The early neolithic pottery of the Volga-Ural region (based on the materials of the Elshanka culture), *Archaeology, Ethnology and Anthropology of Eurasia*, 39 (2), 70–81.

Veeramah, K. R. et al. 2011. Genetic variation in the Sorbs of eastern Germany in the context of broader European genetic diversity, *European Journal of Human Genetics*, 19 (9), 995–1001.

Velasco, R. et al. 2010. The genome of the domesticated apple (*Malus* × *domestica* Borkh.), *Nature Genetics*, 42 (10), 833–39.

Velaza, J. 2006. Lengue vs. cultura material: el (viejo) problema de la lengua indigena de Catalunya, *Actes de la III Reunió Internacional d'Arqueologia de Calafell (Calafell, 25 al 27 de novembre de 2004)* (Arqueo Mediterrània, 9), 273–80. Barcelona: Universitat de Barcelona.

Vennemann, T. 2003. *Europa Vasconica, Europa Semitica* (Trends in Linguistics Studies and Monographs 138), P. N. A. Hanna (ed.). Berlin: Mouton de Gruyter.

Vernesi, C. et al. 2001. Genetic characterization of the body attributed to the evangelist Luke, *PNAS*, 98 (23), 13460–63.

Vernesi, C. et al. 2004. The Etruscans: a population-genetic study, *American Journal of Human Genetics*, 74 (4), 694–704.

Verrill, L. and Tipping, R. 2010. Use and abandonment of a Neolithic field system at Belderrig, Co. Mayo, Ireland: evidence for economic marginality, *The Holocene*, 20 (7), 1011–21.

Verschoor, C. 2011. Bone in Funnel Beaker pottery. Bone based incrusted pottery decoration from the Dutch Funnel Beaker West Group. Bachelor thesis, Leiden University.

Vigne, J.-D. 2012. First wave of cultivators spread to Cyprus at least 10,600 y ago, *PNAS*, 109 (22), 8445–49.

Vigne, J.-D., Carrère, I., Briois, F. and Guilaine, J. 2011. The early process of mammal domestication in the Near East: new evidence from the Pre-Neolithic and Pre-Pottery Neolithic in Cyprus, *Current Anthropology*, 52 (S4), S255–71.

Villar, F. and Prósper, B. M. 2005. *Vascos, Celtas e Indoeuropeos: Genes y lenguas*. Salamanca: Ediciones Universidad de Salamanca.

Villems, R. et al. 2002. Archaeogenetics of Finno-Ugric speaking populations, in *The Roots of Peoples and Languages of Northern Eurasia IV, Oulu 18.8.–20.8. 2000*, K. Julku (ed.), 271–84. Societas Historiae Fenno-Ugricae.

Vink, A. et al. 2007. Holocene relative sea-level change, isostatic subsidence and the radial viscosity structure of the mantle of northwest Europe (Belgium, the Netherlands, Germany, southern North Sea), *Quaternary Science Reviews*, 26 (25-28), 3249-75.

Völgyi, A., Zalán, A., Szvetnik, E. and Pamjav, H. 2009. Hungarian population data for 11 Y-STR and 49 Y-SNP markers, *Forensic Science International: Genetics*, 3, e27-28.

Von Carnap-Bornheim, C. and Hilberg, V. 2007. Recent archaeological research in Haithabu, in *Post-Roman Towns, Trade and Settlement in Europe and Byzantium 1: The Heirs of the Roman West*, J. Henning (ed.), 199-218. Berlin: de Gruyter.

von Cramon-Taubadel, N. and Pinhasi, R. 2011. Craniometric data support a mosaic model of demic and cultural Neolithic diffusion to outlying regions of Europe, *PRS B*, 278 (1720), 2874-80.

Voutsaki, S. et al. 2009. Middle Helladic Lerna: relative and absolute chronologies, in *Tree-rings, Kings, and Old World Archaeology and Environment: Papers Presented in Honour of Peter Ian Kuniholm*, S. W. Manning and M. J. Bruce (eds), 151-61. Oxford: Oxbow.

Vuorisalo, T. et al. 2012. High lactose tolerance in North Europeans a result of migration, not in situ milk consumption, *Perspectives in Biology and Medicine*, 55 (2), 163-74.

Walker, R. S. et al. 2011. Evolutionary history of hunter-gatherer marriage practices, *PLoS ONE*, 6 (4), e19066.

Wallace, B. 2008. The discovery of Vinland, chapter 44 in Brink and Price 2008, 604-12.

Wallace, P. F. 2005. The archaeology of Ireland's Viking-age towns, chapter 22 in Ó Cróinín 2005, 814-41.

Warmuth, V. 2012. Reconstructing the origin and spread of horse domestication in the Eurasian steppe, *PNAS*, 109 (21), 8202-06.

Warner, R. et al. 2009. The gold source found at last?, *Archaeology Ireland*, 23 (2), 22-25.

Watkins, T. 2010. New light on Neolithic revolution in south-west Asia, *Antiquity*, 84 (325), 621-34.

Watson, J. D. and Crick, F. 1953. Molecular structure of nucleic acids: a structure for deoxyribose nucleic acid, *Nature*, 171, 737-38.

Weale, M. E. 2002. Y chromosome evidence for Anglo-Saxon mass migration, *Molecular Biology and Evolution*, 19, 1008-21.

Webster, J. 2010. Routes to slavery in the Roman world: a comparative perspective on the archaeology of forced migration, in Eckardt 2010, 45-66.

Wei, W. et al. 2013. A calibrated human Y-chromosomal phylogeny based on resequencing, *Genome Research*, 23 (2), 388-95.

Weiss, E. and Zohary, D. 2011. The Neolithic southwest Asian founder crops: their biology and archaeobotany, *Current Anthropology*, 52 (S4), S237-54.

Wells, R. S. et al. 2001. The Eurasian heartland: a continental perspective on Y-chromosome diversity, *PNAS*, 98 (18), 10244-49.

Weninger, B. et al. 2006. Climate forcing due to the 8200 cal BP event observed at Early Neolithic sites in the eastern Mediterranean, *Quaternary Research*, 66, 401-20.

Weninger, B. et al. 2008. The catastrophic final flooding of Doggerland by the Storegga Slide tsunami, *Documenta Praehistorica*, 35, 1-24.

Weninger, B. et al. 2009. The impact of rapid climate change on prehistoric societies during the Holocene in the eastern Mediterranean, *Documenta Praehistorica*, 36, 7-59.

Weninger, B. et al. 2009b. A radiocarbon database for the Mesolithic and early Neolithic in Northwest Europe, chapter 9 in *Chronology and Evolution within the Mesolithic of North-West Europe: Proceedings of an International Meeting, Brussels May 30th-June 1st 2007* (2009), P. Crombé et al. (eds), 143-76. Newcastle upon Tyne: Cambridge Scholars Publishing.

Whittle, A. W. R. 1996. *Europe in the Neolithic: The Creation of New Worlds* (Cambridge World Archaeology). Cambridge, New York and Melbourne: Cambridge University Press.

Whittle, A. and Cummings, V. (eds). 2007. *Going Over: The Mesolithic-Neolithic Transition in North-West Europe* (Proceedings of the British Academy, 144). Oxford: Oxford University Press for the British Academy.

Whittle, A., Healy, F. and Bayliss, A. 2011. *Gathering Time: Dating the Early Neolithic Enclosures of Southern Britain and Ireland*, 2 vols. Oxford: Oxbow Books.

Wick, J. et al. 2012. Injured but special? On associations between skull defects and burial treatment in the Corded Ware culture of central Germany, chapter 9 in *Sticks, Stones and Broken Bones: Neolithic Violence in a European Perspective*, R. Shulting and L. Fibiger (eds), 151-74. Oxford and New York: Oxford University Press.

Wilhelm, G. 2008. Hurrian (chapter 4) and Urartian (chapter 5), in *The Ancient Languages of Asia Minor*, R. D. Woodard (ed.), 95-137. Cambridge and New York: Cambridge University Press.

Wilkes, J. 1992. *The Illyrians* (The Peoples of Europe). Oxford and Cambridge, MA: Blackwell.

Wilson, K. and van der Dussen, J. (eds). 1995. *The History of the Idea of Europe* (rev. ed.) (*What is Europe?*, book 1). Milton Keynes: the Open University; Abingdon and New York: Routledge.

Winney, B. et al. 2012. People of the British Isles: preliminary analysis of genotypes and surnames in a UK-control population, *European Journal of Human Genetics*, 20, 203-10.

Witzel, M. 2005. Central Asian roots and acculturation in South Asia: linguistic and archaeological evidence from Western Central Asia, the Hindukush and Northwestern South Asia for early Indo-Aryan language and religion, in *Occasional Paper 1: Linguistics, Archaeology and the Human Past*, T. Osada (ed.), 87-211. Kyoto: Indus Project, Research Institute for Humanity and Nature.

Wlodarczak, P. 2009. Radiocarbon and dendrochronological dates of the Corded Ware culture, *Radiocarbon*, 51 (2), 737-49.

Wodtko, D. S. 2010. The problem of Lusitanian, chapter 11 in Cunliffe and Koch 2010, 335-67.

Wolfe, N. D., Dunavan, C. P. and Diamond, J. 2007. Origins of major human infectious diseases, *Nature*, 447, 279-83.

Wolfram, H. 1988. *History of the Goths*, trans. T. J. Dunlap.

Berkeley and Los Angeles: University of California Press.

Wood, F. 2002. *The Silk Road: Two Thousand Years in the Heart of Asia*. Berkeley and Los Angeles: University of California Press.

Wood, R. et al. 2013. Radiocarbon dating casts doubt on the late chronology of the Q:1 Middle to Upper Palaeolithic transition in southern Iberia, *PNAS*, published online 4 February 2013 before print.

Woodward, A. and Hunter, J. 2011. *An Examination of Prehistoric Stone Bracers from Britain*. Oxford: Oxbow Books.

Woolf, A. 2007. *From Pictland to Alba 789–1070* (The New Edinburgh History of Scotland, 2). Edinburgh: Edinburgh University Press.

Woolf, A. 2007b. Apartheid and economics in Anglo-Saxon England, chapter 10 in *Britons in Anglo-Saxon England*, N. Higham (ed.), 115–29. Woodbridge: Boydell Press.

Woźniak, M. et al. 2010. Similarities and distinctions in Y chromosome gene pool of Western Slavs, *American Journal of Physical Anthropology*, 142 (4), 540–48.

Wright, H. T. 2009. Humanity at the Last Glacial Maximum: a cultural crisis, chapter 6 in Peregrine, Peiros and Feldman 2009, 55–73.

Wu, X. et al. 2012. Early pottery at 20,000 years ago in Xianrendong Cave, China, *Science*, 336 (6089), 1696–700.

Xing, J. et al. 2010. Toward a more uniform sampling of human genetic diversity: a survey of worldwide populations by high-density genotyping, *Genomics*, 96 (4), 199–210.

Xu, L. et al. 2010. The -22018A allele matches the lactase persistence phenotype in northern Chinese populations, *Scandinavian Journal of Gastroenterology*, 45 (2), 168–74.

Yang, W.-Y. et al. 2012. A model-based approach for analysis of spatial structure in genetic data, *Nature Genetics*, 44, 725–31.

Yao, Y.-G. 2004. Different matrilineal contributions to genetic structure of ethnic groups in the Silk Road region in China, *Molecular Biology and Evolution*, 21 (12), 2265–80.

Yavetz, Z. 1988. *Slaves and Slavery in Ancient Rome*. Brunswick, NJ: Transaction Publishers.

Yerkes, R. W., Khalaily, H. and Barkai, R. 2012. Form and function of Early Neolithic bifacial stone tools reflects changes in land use practices during the Neolithization process in the Levant, *PLoS ONE*, 7 (8), e42442.

Young, K. L. et al. 2011. Autosomal short tandem repeat genetic variation of the Basques in Spain, *Croatian Medical Journal*, 52 (3), 372–83.

Yunusbayev, B. et al. 2012. The Caucasus as an asymmetric semipermeable barrier to ancient human migrations, *Molecular Biology and Evolution*, 29 (1), 359–65.

Zalloua, P. A. et al. 2008. Identifying genetic traces of historical expansions: Phoenician footprints in the Mediterranean, *American Journal of Human Genetics*, 83 (5), 633–42.

Zeder, M. A. 2008. Domestication and early agriculture in the Mediterranean basin: origins, diffusion, and impact, *PNAS*, 105 (33), 11597–604.

Zeder, M. A. 2011. The origins of agriculture in the Near East, *Current Anthropology*, 52, supplement 4, S221–35.

Zeidler, J. 2011. Review of Barry W. Cunliffe, John T. Koch (ed.), *Celtic from the West: Alternative Perspectives from Archaeology, Genetics, Language, and Literature*. Celtic Studies Publications 15. Oxford/Oakville, CT: Oxbow Books, 2010. *Bryn Mawr Classical Review*, 2011.09.57.

Zengel, M. S. 1962. Literacy as a factor in language change, *American Anthropologist*, 64 (1), 132–39.

Zerjal, T. et al. 1999. The use of Y-chromosomal DNA variation to investigate population history: recent male spread in Asia and Europe, in *Genomic Diversity: Applications in Human Population Genetics*, S. S. Papiha, R. Deka and R. Chakraborty (eds), 91–101. New York: Kluwer Academic/Plenum Publishers.

Zhang, F. et al. 2010. Prehistoric East–West admixture of maternal lineages in a 2,500-year-old population in Xinjiang, *American Journal of Physical Anthropology*, 142 (2), 314–20.

Zhivotovsky, L. A. et al. 2004. The effective mutation rate at Y chromosome short tandem repeats, with application to human population-divergence time, *American Journal of Human Genetics*, 74, 50–61.

Zhivotovsky, L. A. 2006. Difference between evolutionary effective and germ line mutation rate due to stochastically varying haplogroup size, *Molecular Biology and Evolution*, 23 (12), 2268–70.

Zilhão, J. 2000. From the Mesolithic to the Neolithic in the Iberian peninsula, chapter 6 in *Europe's First Farmers*, T. D. Price (ed.), 144–82. Cambridge, New York, Melbourne and Madrid: Cambridge University Press.

Zilhão, J. 2001. Radiocarbon evidence for maritime pioneer colonization at the origins of farming in west Mediterranean Europe, *PNAS* 98 (24), 14180–85.

Zilhão, J. et al. 2007. The Peştera Cu Oase people, Europe's earliest modern humans, chapter 21 in Mellars, Boyle, Bar-Yosef and Stringer 2007, 249–62.

Zilhão, J. et al. 2010. Pego do Diabo (Loures, Portugal): dating the emergence of anatomical modernity in westernmost Eurasia, *PLoS ONE*, 5 (1), e8880.

Zimmermann, A., Hilpert, J. and Wendt, K. P. 2009. Estimations of population density for selected periods between the Neolithic and AD 1800, *Human Biology*, 81 (2–3), 357–80.

Zvelebil, M. 2004. Pitted Ware and related cultures of Neolithic Northern Europe, in Bogucki and Crabtree 2004, vol. 1, 431–34.

Zvelebil, M. 2005. *Homo habitus*: agency, structure and the transformation of tradition in the constitution of the TRB foraging-farming communities in the North European plain (ca. 4500–2000 BC), *Documenta Praehistorica*, 32, 87–101 .

Zvelebil, M. 2006. Mobility, contact, and exchange in the Baltic Sea basin 6000–2000 BC, *Journal of Anthropological Archaeology*, 25 (2), 178–92.

Sources of Illustrations

Title page: National Museum, Bucharest; 1 Drazen Tomic, adapted from a map by Genome Research Limited; 2 Jacopin/Science Photo Library; 3 Drazen Tomic, after Shennan 2009; 4 Drazen Tomic, after Soares 2009; Behar 2012; 5 Drazen Tomic; 6 Drazen Tomic, adapted from Soares 2010; 7 Drazen Tomic, adapted from Herrera 2012; 8 Drazen Tomic, adapted from Achilli 2004; 9 Drazen Tomic; 10 Drazen Tomic, based on Sims-Williams 2006; 11 Drazen Tomic, adapted from Mellars 2011, with addition from Hoffecker 2012; 12 Photo Vladimir Gorodnyanskiy; 13 Chauvet-Pont-d'Arc Cave, Ardèche; 14 WARA, Centro Camuno di Studi Preistorici, Capo di Ponte; 15 Photo Carles Lalueza-Fox; 16 Drazen Tomic; 17 University of Belgrade, Serbia; 18 Gobustan National Park, Azerbaijan; 19 Rowena Alsey, after Vasilieva 2011; 20 Drazen Tomic, adapted from Chiaroni, Underhill and Cavalli-Sforza 2009; 21 Library of Congress, Washington, DC; 22 Drazen Tomic, adapted from Chiaroni, Underhill and Cavalli-Sforza 2009; 23 Drazen Tomic; 24 adapted from Languages of the World, University of Graz; 25 Drazen Tomic; 26 Photo Arpag Mekhtarian; 27 Trevor Watkins; 28 Klaus Schmidt/DAI; 29 John Hios/akg-images; 30 after Mellaart; 31 © Peter M. M. G. Akkermans, Tell Sabi Abyad Project, Leiden University; 32 Drazen Tomic, adapted from Berger and Guilaine 2009; 33 Drazen Tomic, adapted from Wikimedia Commons; 34 Drazen Tomic, adapted from Chiaroni, Underhill and Cavalli-Sforza 2009; 35 Drazen Tomic; 36 Peter Bull Art Studio; 37 Drazen Tomic, adapted from Achilli 2007; 38 Drazen Tomic, adapted from Chiaroni, Underhill and Cavalli-Sforza 2009; 39 British Museum, London; 40 Drazen Tomic; 41 State History Museum, Moscow; 42 National Historical Museum, Stockholm (Inv. nr. 12367); 43 Drazen Tomic, adapted from Whittle, Healy and Bayliss 2011, fig. 14.176; 44 National Museums of Scotland; 45 Drazen Tomic, after Fu, Rudan, Pääbo and Krause 2012; 46 Iraq Museum, Baghdad; 47 Drazen Tomic; 48 Archaeological Museum, Varna; 49 National Museum of Romanian History, Bucharest; 50 G. A. Sanna National Museum, Sassari; 51 Almería Museum, Santa Fe de Mondújar; 52 Drazen Tomic; 53 adapted from Nakhleh, Ringe and Warnow 2005; 54 Photo D. Telegin; 55 British Museum, London; 56 Drazen Tomic, adapted from a map by David Anthony; 57 Drazen Tomic, adapted from a map by Lynda D'Amico for Mallory; 58, 59 Drazen Tomic, adapted from a map by David Anthony; 60 National Archaeological Museum, Athens; 61 Photo Frances K. Fielding; 62 Rowena Alsey; 63 Electa/akg-images; 64 British Museum, London; 65 Drazen Tomic, adapted from Wikimedia; 66, 67 Drazen Tomic, adapted from Myres 2011; 68 Drazen Tomic, adapted from 23andMe; 69 Drazen Tomic, adapted from Gerbault 2011; 70 British Museum, London; 71–73 Drazen Tomic; 74 Drawing E. Brennan; 75 Drazen Tomic after Richard Rocca; 76 Faculty of Archaeology, Leiden University, drawing by M. Oberndorf; 77 Heraklion Archaeological Museum, Crete; 78 National Archaeological Museum, Athens; 79 Drazen Tomic; 80 Drazen Tomic, adapted from Cunliffe 2008; 81 Drawing José-Manuel Benito Álvarez; 82 Drazen Tomic, after Richard Rocca; 83 National Archaeological Museum of Spain, Madrid; 84, 85 Drazen Tomic, adapted from Cunliffe 2008; 86 Gelben Haus City Museum, Esslingen am Neckar; 87 National Museum of Ireland, Dublin; 88 British Museum, London; 89 National Etruscan Museum, Rome; 90, 91 Drazen Tomic; 92 LVR-Archaeological Park, Xanten; 93 Ashmolean Museum, Oxford; 94 House of the Vettii, reconstruction, Boboli Gardens, Florence; 95, 96 Drazen Tomic; 97 Drazen Tomic, adapted from Myres 2011; 98 Drazen Tomic, after Richard Rocca; 99, 100, 101 Drazen Tomic; 102 Marka/Superstock; 103, 104 Drazen Tomic; 105, 106 Archaeological Museum, Zagreb; 107 Drazen Tomic; 108 Drazen Tomic, adapted from Underhill 2010; 109–111 Drazen Tomic; 112 Drawing Aleksander Orlowski; 113 Drazen Tomic; 114 Viking Ship Museum, Oslo; 115 Drawing Christian Bickel; 116 National Museum of Denmark, Copenhagen; 117 Topham Picturepoint; 118 Drazen Tomic, adapted from Family Tree DNA: R1a1a and Subclades Y-DNA Project; 119 Drazen Tomic; 120 National Museum of Denmark, Copenhagen; 121 Bayeux Tapestry Museum; 122 National Museum of Denmark, Copenhagen; 123 Ashmolean Museum, Oxford.

Index